DAISY HAY

Daisy Hay was born in Oxford in 1981. She is the author of *Young Romantics*: *The Shelleys, Byron and Other Tangled Lives*, for which she was awarded the Rose Mary Crawshay Prize by the British Academy and highly commended by the John Llewellyn Rhys Prize. She has a BA and a PhD in English Literature from the University of Cambridge and an MA in Romantic and Sentimental Literature from the University of York. In 2009–10 she was the Alistair Horne Fellow at St Antony's College, Oxford and in 2010–12 she held a visiting scholarship at Wolfson College, Oxford. In 2012–13 she was a Fellow at the Radcliffe Institute for Advanced Study, Harvard University. She is currently a Lecturer in English Literature and Archival Studies at the University of Exeter and a BBC Radio 3 New Generation Thinker. She lives in Devon.

ALSO BY DAISY HAY

Young Romantics

DAISY HAY

Mr and Mrs Disraeli

A Strange Romance

VINTAGE

For Matthew and Freddy

1 3 5 7 9 10 8 6 4 2

Vintage
20 Vauxhall Bridge Road,
London SW1V 2SA

Vintage is part of the Penguin Random House group of companies
whose addresses can be found at global.penguinrandomhouse.com.

Penguin
Random House
UK

First published in Vintage in 2016

First published in hardback by Chatto & Windus in 2015

www.vintage-books.co.uk

A CIP catalogue record for this book
is available from the British Library

ISBN 9780099597445

Printed and bound by CPI Group (UK) Ltd, Croydon CR0 4YY

MIX
Paper from
responsible sources
FSC® C018179

Penguin Random House is committed to a sustainable future
for our business, our readers and our planet. This book is
made from Forest Stewardship Council® certified paper

Contents

Preface

'My wife is a very clever woman', Disraeli is reputed to have said, 'but she can never remember who came first, the Greeks or the Romans.' Benjamin and Mary Anne Disraeli are figures around whom anecdotes coalesce: about what they wore, what they did and what they said. Mary Anne apparently told Queen Victoria that she always slept with her arms around Disraeli's neck. Disraeli, when asked if he had read a new novel, is rumoured to have replied, 'When I want to read a novel I write one.' If one were to read something other than a novel one had written, he had views about what that work should be too. 'Read no history: nothing but biography, for that is life without theory.'

When the Disraelis were born, government was organised according to aristocratic faction; they died in the era of professional politics. In their lifetimes Britain's empire grew until it covered swathes of the globe. They witnessed the development of rail travel, photography and the telegraph, and the transformation of their country from an agricultural to an industrialised nation. Their story is history, despite Disraeli's disavowal of the subject. But it is also a fiction. Those who disliked them thought their romance artificial, its grand gestures contrived. Those who were fond of them thought there was something fantastic about their good fortune. They themselves spun stories around their partnership, but they also made the tales they spun come true.

This book is about the way in which the Disraelis conjured their romance into being in a world thick with stories. In their youth they read versions of themselves in the epistolary novels of the late eighteenth century; in the

1820s and 30s they saw their aspirations reflected in the silver-fork novels Disraeli and his literary contemporaries produced at great speed. They were middle-aged when the Victorian novel came to maturity in the 1850s, the literary form that finds drama in the everyday. Theirs was thus the great age of fiction, when the novel made a romance of reality and turned ordinary men and women, living ordinary lives, into heroes and heroines.

Both were born storytellers. As an old lady resplendent in jewels and bright fabrics, Mary Anne pretended to have worked in her youth as a milliner or, in her more creative moments, as a barefooted factory girl. Disraeli, the sober-suited statesman, invented for himself an illustrious ancestry featuring an ancient family who escaped from Spain to Venice and then to England. Both were also keepers of stories. Mary Anne was a skilled and dedicated collector of documents, and the results of her impulse to collect and curate are visible today at the Bodleian Library in Oxford, where the Disraelis' papers are held. These papers constitute an archive of unparalleled richness, numbering over 50,000 separate items. The political sections of this archive have been extensively studied by scholars of Disraeli, but the 10,000 items relating specifically to Mary Anne have historically received little attention. Yet the archive in its entirety represents Mary Anne's great creative achievement. That we can recover so much of her and Disraeli's biographies is due to her efforts to catalogue the various chapters of their lives.

～

This book traces the intertwined story of Mr and Mrs Disraeli through their papers. My sense of their archive and the story it reveals has evolved over the course of several years of immersive reading in the Special Collections Reading Room at the Bodleian Library. These years have been among the most stimulating of my professional life. They have also been the coldest, courtesy of the relocation of the Bodleian's manuscript holdings to a temporary reading room in a minimally heated and underinsulated 1950s basement. This relocation means that at the time of writing you have to be a hardy creature to work on a Bodleian manuscript in winter, or to be amongst the heroic Special Collections Reading Room staff.

The cold of the Special Collections Reading Room has opened up the

Disraelis' history for me in unexpected ways. Their letters are full of refer-
ences to being cold; to the way in which the cold confines the body and
chills the mind. At Stowe House, while waiting to meet the Queen, they
shiver in draughty halls and inadequate evening garb. At Osborne, the
Queen's house on the Isle of Wight, he wears two greatcoats and a waistcoat
as protection against the elements. Disraeli's father Isaac will not stir from
his fireside in winter, even for the fresh air the doctor has ordered; his sister
Sarah is compelled to cancel excursions to London when the east wind
whistles through her hired carriage. Mary Anne's servants run back and
forth from the House of Commons with warm clothes and boots to protect
Disraeli from the chills of the debating chamber, until snow stops carriage
wheels from turning and forces both master and mistress to stay inside.

Cold is also present in the Disraelis' papers in less physical ways. In 1792,
the year of Mary Anne's birth, the steel of the guillotine glints for the first
time in France and the French King, Louis XVI, is arrested, imprisoned and
tried for his life. By the time of Disraeli's birth in 1804, Britain and France
have been fighting for over a decade and war has become the sullen backdrop
to the affairs of the nation. In this climate, free speech is not a luxury the
government is prepared to afford its citizens, and political dissenters are spied
on, arrested, and hounded out of their homes and their country by the rough
justice of the mob. Mary Anne is the daughter of a sailor; Disraeli is of Jewish
descent. Yet for all the insecurity of their beginnings they become, over the
course of their lives, able to shelter themselves from the cold, in both its
physical and metaphorical manifestations.

∼

The Disraelis' biographies are not the only narrative to emerge from their
papers. Much of the reading I did over the course of my winters in the
Bodleian was of letters written to Mary Anne by women who have disap-
peared from history. Taken together, the cases of these women point to the
elements of the Disraelis' story that were at once universal and exceptional.
They show how unusual Mary Anne was, as they reveal the vulnerability of
those in her circle of acquaintance who were unmarried, widowed, or
compelled to remain in unhappy households by convention and circumstance.
Mary Anne understood the stories of less fortunate women as a counterpoint

to her own and in that spirit they appear throughout this book, shadowing its central romance. Disraeli too derived his sense of self and his place in the world from paper. His shadows were not people he knew but Byron and Shelley, his literary forefathers. He was one of the last Romantics, shaped by the power of his own romance and the books he read.

Disraeli has, of course, been much written about by historians and biographers. Robert Blake's 1966 biography remains definitive, and has been joined in recent decades by a host of other works, including a rich study of Disraeli's early life by Jane Ridley and a provocative account of his sexuality by William Kuhn. Those who wish to trace the thinking of this most mercurial of men can do so through his letters, magnificently edited by the scholars of the Disraeli Project at Queen's University, Canada. Mary Anne has herself been the subject of two short biographies by James Sykes and Mollie Hardwick, published in 1928 and 1972 respectively. Sykes wrote when myth still obscured Mary Anne's origins, and he concentrated his efforts on separating fact and fiction in her own retellings of her story. In *Mrs Dizzy*, Mollie Hardwick brought a novelist's eye to Mary Anne's history and collated many anecdotes relating to her conversational style, which was quite unlike that of her contemporaries.

When the Disraelis are read alongside each other, however, a different kind of story emerges. This is not a story only about politics, although its background is political; or a story only about a single unusual woman forging a place for herself alongside a prominent man. Disraeli's private papers point to the necessity of reading his life as biographers have in recent decades read those of unknown women, watching for alternative narratives, listening to things not said. In the case of both Disraelis this mode of reading charts a path through the fog of anecdote and offers the possibility of a portrait of a marriage unobscured by mythology.

That marriage was as surprising, eccentric and important as its hero and heroine. The Disraelis' story is about luck, and the path not taken, and the transformative effects of a good match for a man and woman of modest means in nineteenth-century Britain. It traces a journey from coldness to autumnal sunshine, and charts a marriage that wrote itself into happiness. It relates the history of people who remake themselves through their reading and writing, but also of people who disappear. And it is a story about what happens after the wedding, when the marriage plot is over.

Part One

At the Beginning

(1792–1839)

CHAPTER ONE

Storytelling

> But you a very fairy, must
> Have had another birth,
> For never could the cold dull clay
> Have been your native earth.
>
> It must have been some charmed spot,
> From whence your being sprung,
> A lovely & a sunny place,
> Where still the World was young.
> ('To Mrs Wyndham Lewis, with *The Book of Beauty*')

Mary Anne Disraeli was born on 11 November 1792 in the village of Brampford Speke in Devon. Brampford Speke was a small farming community four miles north of Exeter, with a church at its centre and an assortment of cottages and farmhouses scattered along the surrounding lanes. Mary Anne was the second child of John Evans, a naval seaman, and Eleanor Viney, a vicar's daughter. In later years she took pains to shroud her age and the date of her birth in mystery, prompting this poetic flight of fancy from an admirer. 'Childhood yet lingers at your head', 'To Mrs Wyndham Lewis' continued, 'so soon from most exiled. In ready kindness mirth & grace / You know you are a child.'[1]

The house in which Mary Anne grew up was the home of her Evans grandparents and was less the picturesque 'charmed spot' of her admirer's imagination than a noisy working farm. A pen-and-ink drawing of the house during the period of Mary Anne's childhood shows a white thatched building with three tall chimneys standing in one corner of a square farmyard. Barns and outbuildings surround the other sides of the yard and the house itself is small – probably no more than seven or eight rooms – with little additional space for a young family. Anyone living there would have been intimately aware of the daily events of farm life as they unfolded outside the windows.

Mary Anne was brought up in this house by her mother and grandparents and never knew her father. From her parents' courtship letters, however, which she kept all her life, she learnt something of his character, and something too of the opposition her parents faced when they announced their intention to marry. Little is known of John Evans's background, but he was evidently not considered a suitable match for a young lady of Eleanor Viney's class. The Vineys were an old family of some standing, and Eleanor was related via her mother to several branches of the landed gentry, including the Lamberts, owners of Boyton Manor in Wiltshire since the sixteenth century, and the Scropes of Castle Combe, also in Wiltshire, who could trace their name and their ownership of Castle Combe back 500 years.

John Evans, in contrast, had no ancient lineage to bolster his prospects. 'It is true I cannot boast a long chain of distinguished forefathers', he told Eleanor when the objections of her family to their marriage appeared insurmountable. 'It will not be pleasant at a future day to hear you . . . reproached for having united yourself to a man that may be held in contempt by the rest of your family.'[2] Early in their courtship he also acknowledged that Eleanor had found him 'truly in the rough', but continued, 'it is your business to bend, burnish and shape me to whatever form will make you most happy and if you are not completely so 'twill be your own fault'.[3] John Evans was not remotely abashed by the social disparity between him and his bride. If her family persisted in withholding Eleanor's dowry, then they would wait until they could support themselves on his pay, and she, meanwhile, should 'have more fortitude and a firmer reliance on her Lord & Master'.[4] Yet John was not merely a martinet. He combined firmness with passion and took a frank delight in the good things in life. Writing to Eleanor in 1786, two years before their marriage, he chided her for being a virtuously punctual early riser. 'Do you think you little Hussy I will allow you to be so regular when I am your acknowledged Master, do you imagine I will go to bed at 10 & rise by 7? – dont mistake me, I am grown quite a drone, beside it is in bed the moments fly.'[5]

Only John Evans's side of the courtship correspondence survives, so we have to infer Eleanor's responses to such statements from his letters. These suggest she was rather less sanguine about the future than he. 'Fear is the most destructive of all passions and will sooner overturn the Human powers than any other', he told her in January 1787.[6] Yet they also suggest that she had a will of her own, and that that will could be forcibly expressed. Their epistolary courtship was punctuated by quarrels prompted by a tension between her intuitive, emotional response to circumstance and his more practical stance. 'Dont believe', he told her at one point, 'that my composition is made up of Frigid materials. I certainly have as quick a sense of pain and consequently pleasure as you.'[7] By 1788, the couple had put aside their differences and won consent from the Vineys to their marriage. That consent was grudging. Eleanor received a smaller marriage settlement than her sister Bridget, who was married on the same day, and incurred the displeasure of a well-off aunt, Anne Viney, who appears in the courtship letters as one of the chief obstacles to the marriage. 'Your aunt is at present the only Barrier between us and Earthly happiness', wrote John exasperatedly at one point.[8]

Anne Viney contented herself with leaving her disobliging niece an annuity worth £1,000 less than that left to her more obedient sister, but by the time she died in 1800, John was beyond the reach of either her whims or her money. After their marriage in 1788, he and Eleanor made their home with his parents in Brampford Speke. Their son, another John, was born in 1790, and Mary Anne two years later. John Evans was frequently away with his ship, and in 1794, when Mary Anne was two, he died of a fever while serving in the West Indies. Although he was always an absent figure in the lives of his wife and children, his death nevertheless changed their lives, cutting them off from his naval world and depriving them of any prospect of a settled domestic life. It also confirmed Brampford Speke as his family's only refuge, and it was here that Mary Anne lived for her first fifteen years.

Mary Anne left no account of the years she spent in Brampford Speke, and documentary evidence for this period of her life is scarce. Only one undated letter survives to give us any indication of what her childhood was like, and that letter was written from the house of friends. Composed in a childish copperplate hand it reads, 'Our School is broke up and I am very comfortable with three pleasant companions, with whom and my Brother I shall spent the holidays very agreeable. he unite with me, in duty to you, and all friends, and in wishing they may enjoy the pleasures of the season. I am my dear Mama your dutiful Daughter Mary Anne Evans.'[9]

This missive is a little more revealing than its innocuous content might initially suggest. From its subject if not from its erratic grammar it is clear that Mary Anne received an education of sorts, although it is more likely to have been from a governess shared with another family rather than from a school as we would understand it.* Eleanor Viney was more than capable of teaching her own children to read and write, so given her straitened circumstances it is noteworthy that she sent her daughter away to obtain the accomplishments of a young lady. It is possible that the cramped farm at Brampford Speke was not quite the sanctuary for Eleanor's growing children that it was for Eleanor herself, since Mary Anne and her brother evidently remained with their friends even when 'school' broke up, rather than return home.

In 1807, Mary Anne's grandparents died and Eleanor had to leave Brampford Speke. She moved to Cathedral House in Gloucester, which had been in the Viney family for many years. In 1807 Cathedral House was in the possession of Eleanor's brother James Viney, although it is not clear whether he was actually in residence when his sister and her children lived there.

James Viney was an officer in the Royal Artillery, and in 1808 he joined Wellington's army in the Spanish peninsula. He commanded regiments at the key Napoleonic battles of Roliça, Vimiera and Corunna, and by 1834 had become Major General Sir James Viney, having been given a knighthood and made Companion of the Bath in recognition of his military service. Mary Anne was fond of her uncle and he of her, although he could be irascible and appears from his letters to have been something of a rake, who

---

* Mary Anne was an erratic speller, and some consistent mistakes ('idia' for 'idea', 'sail' for 'sale') recur throughout her letters. Like many of her correspondents she wrote fast, and not always in complete sentences. Throughout this book mistakes in spelling and grammar in manuscript letters by her and others are transcribed verbatim, and are not marked by [sic].

fathered at least two illegitimate sons and was full of hare-brained money-making schemes. His nephew John (Mary Anne's older brother) was inspired by his example to volunteer for the army, and followed him to the Peninsula. John too fought at Roliça and Vimiera, and was quickly promoted first to ensign and then to lieutenant. His promotions were obtained through purchase, as was normal practice at the time. At the Battle of Talavera in 1809, he distinguished himself by capturing a French standard, and he also took part in the Siege of Badajoz in 1812.

Mary Anne did her utmost to shield her mother from the dangers John faced, although this cannot have been easy as they followed his progress up the Spanish Peninsula in letters, newspapers and army gazettes. John's absence affected the lives of Eleanor and Mary Anne in practical ways too. Eleanor's husband, parents and parents-in-law were dead, her brother and her son were away fighting, and she and her daughter had not only to fend for themselves but also to find the money to pay for John's promotions. Perhaps motivated by these practical concerns, in 1808 she remarried. Her new husband was one Thomas Yate, a lieutenant in the Worcestershire Militia. Yate joined in 1796 as a surgeon's mate, a position that required only the most rudimentary medical training [10] In the 1790s he served with the Militia in Ireland, where Britain retained a defensive military presence right through the Napoleonic wars, but he was never engaged in battle. The Militia was based in Exeter in 1805–6, which is probably when he met Eleanor, but by the time of their marriage in 1808 it had moved to Portsmouth, and it is likely that it was there that he, Eleanor and Mary Anne made their first home.

Thomas Yate has traditionally been dismissed by biographers of the Disraelis as a shadowy, unsatisfactory figure. His letters, however, suggest that he was an attentive husband and a dutiful stepfather who immersed himself in the affairs of his adopted family and did his best to help them. Mary Anne always wrote of him kindly and conspired with him to defend her mother from unpleasantness whenever possible. He worked hard to disentangle the tortuous financial arrangements between Eleanor and her brother James, in which mortgages were transferred and loans made and recalled with dizzying frequency. The family lived on income from his naval stocks and on the slender rents deriving from property inherited by Eleanor. Attempts to increase the value of these funds seem to have taken up much of Yate's time.

Eleanor's marriage resulted in more upheavals for her daughter, as the family followed the Worcestershire Militia first to Portsmouth and then in 1814 to Bristol, where they moved between a series of rented houses. It was an uncertain, peripatetic existence, in which relocation from house to house was driven by necessity as the family's small income rose and fell. Eleanor wrote to her son that she was relieved to be out of Portsmouth and settled in Bristol since 'this Place is more reasonable than Ports which is necessary as by the Peace with France Mr Yate loses the best part of his Income':[11] a loss of income attributable to the diminution of the value of naval stocks following the Battle of Waterloo, and the accompanying reduction in the salaries of reservists like Yate. The move to Bristol suited Mary Anne. Eleanor reported that she found the society 'very preferable to Portsmouth', and that she enjoyed meeting people of her own age.[12]

It is hard to get a sense of the daily rhythms of Mary Anne's life at this stage, since in later life she richly embroidered accounts of her youth. She told Sir Stafford Northcote and others that she had been a milliner's apprentice[13] and her friend Mrs Duncan Stewart that she had worked as a factory girl and walked barefoot to work every morning before being rescued by her first husband, who in this account fell in love with her in all her ragged glory.[14] Neither story had any basis in fact. The family's resources were not so stretched as to render it necessary for Eleanor Viney's daughter to work for her living, and the documentary evidence that does survive suggests instead a life filled with social visits and some dutiful voluntary work at a local Sunday school. Her closest friends during this period were the Clutton sisters – Elizabeth, Barbara, Dolly and Frances – who lived at Pensax in Worcestershire. Their father Thomas Clutton served throughout the 1790s in the Militia with Thomas Yate, and it was probably in 1805–6, when the Militia was based in Exeter and Eleanor and the children were living in Brampford Speke, that the two families met. By 1808 Thomas Clutton had died and his widow and daughters had moved to Pensax, where both Mary Anne and Eleanor were frequent visitors. In the 1860s Dolly wrote to Mary Anne of her memories of 'our early love – and wanderings up to our knees in snow & dirt at Pensas'. The two women kept up their correspondence until Dolly's death, and her children subsequently described Mary Anne as their mother's oldest friend.[15]

Mary Anne may not have experienced the life of a factory drudge that she later recounted, but nor was her youth untouched by suffering. In 1812, when she was twenty, Thomas Yate's brother committed suicide, apparently fearing the prospect of a court martial. Richard Yate had followed his brother into the Worcestershire Militia in 1799, but he resigned his commission to join the regular army and served in the Peninsula between 1808 and 1812. By the winter of 1812 he had returned with his regiment to barracks at Kingsbridge in Devon and his suicide note suggests he believed he was about to be discovered in some regimental accounting irregularity. The note, rambling in its desperation, also reveals something of the toll the Peninsula War took on men like Richard Yate, James Viney and John Evans, who spent years away from home as the British army, under the command of the Duke of Wellington, pushed Napoleon's forces back through Portugal and Spain into France. In the military communities in which Mary Anne grew up, the absence of these men and the changes wrought in them by war were particularly evident. 'I must say', Richard Yate wrote with some understatement, 'it is truly unfortunate after having stopped for war four years . . . to suffer by my own hand at last.' 'I beg', he continued, in a note addressed to Thomas Yate, 'you will not nor any of my relations allow yourselves to be too much affected at my determination.'[16]

Given the circumstances of Richard Yate's death, it is hard to see how this wish could have been fulfilled. The local newspaper gave graphic details about how he managed to shoot himself with a musket, leaning the gun against a wall and forcing the trigger with his sword. The press reports made no mention of accusations of fraud or a looming court martial, although whether out of ignorance, respect for a serving officer, or because the accusations and court martial were figments of Yate's troubled mind is not clear. 'The deceased', ran one report, 'had lately returned with his regiment from the Peninsula, and it appearing on evidence that he had for some time past displayed symptoms of a disordered mind, the jury without hesitation returned a verdict of *Lunacy*.'[17]

Even without the rumours of dishonourable behaviour hinted at in Richard Yate's explanation for his actions, no young woman of marriageable age would have wanted to be associated with a story of suicide (still an illegal act) and insanity. The family's move in 1814 from Portsmouth to Bristol may therefore have been well timed, allowing Mary Anne, now twenty-two and beyond her girlhood, to disentangle herself from a claustrophobic network of military families and establish herself in society untainted by any whiff of scandal. Marriage offered an obvious way out of a financially precarious home life, and what Mary Anne lacked in a dowry she made up for with looks and vivacity. She was a petite beautiful flirt with a mass of kiss-curls: admirers sent paeans in praise of her tiny feet and young men wrote mournfully that she was insensible to the anxiety her teasing induced in them. Her brother John described her as 'cold' and her heart as 'particular'. She was evidently not prepared to accept a husband who made no attempt at romance.[18] Candidates for her hand were required to hymn their devotion to her in poetry, some of which Disraeli discovered and copied into her commonplace book decades later. One Henry Harrison went so far as to ask Eleanor for permission to marry her and wrote at great length on how his feelings for her transcended his desire to obey his mother, who 'has always declared it her wish to have her sons affection <u>prudently</u> settled when young'. He also referred to a quarrel with Mary Anne but noted reassuringly that 'it has frequently been the case with me, after any little difference with my sister, that we were afterwards if possible more cordial than ever' – hardly the sentiments to secure the heart of a romantically inclined young lady.[19]

By 1815, Henry Harrison and his fellow admirers were facing competition of a serious nature. Wyndham Lewis was the son of an ancient Welsh family and a major shareholder in the Dowlais Iron Works near Merthyr Tydfil in South Wales. Wyndham inherited his shares in Dowlais from one of its founders, his grandfather Thomas Lewis, and by 1815 was running the ironworks in partnership with the other major shareholder, John Guest. Wyndham never involved himself in the day-to-day management as Guest did, partly because Guest was the real genius behind the works' dramatic expansion, and partly because his business interests also encompassed banking, the development of the railways and the law. From a maternal uncle he inherited the estate of Greenmeadow outside Cardiff, and a conservative estimate of his income puts it at around £11,000 a year.

Money meant that Wyndham ranked highly on an Austenian scale of eligibility. In *Pride and Prejudice*, published in 1813, Mrs Bennet is desperate for one of her daughters to marry Mr Darcy for his £10,000 a year, and her family is much more well-to-do than was Mary Anne's. Wyndham was not, however, quite the Mr Darcy to Henry Harrison's Mr Collins that his wealth alone suggests. He was fourteen years older than Mary Anne, a distinctly unromantic thirty-six when they met. His income came from trade: it was a brilliant marriage for Mary Anne in material terms, but it did not elevate her to the aristocracy or even the 'Upper 10,000' who made up smart London society. And Wyndham had a past, in the form of an illegitimate daughter called Frances to whom he left an annuity of £60 a year and of whose existence Mary Anne was aware. His temperament was also utterly different from that of his putative bride. He was a serious, thoughtful man, not given to acting rashly, and despite his circumstances he was notoriously tight-fisted. At one stage he even went to the lengths of hiring the morning newspapers rather than buying them. But he was as captivated by Mary Anne's good looks and rapid conversational style as the earnest young men who had previously attempted to woo her. Mary Anne was looking for someone to sweep her off her feet, and Wyndham rose to the challenge. He wrote page after page of dubious poetry in which he praised her beauty, her eyes and, rather more dampeningly, her virtue and her modesty. She was his 'beauteous charmer', his 'lovely girl', his 'bright maid'. 'Where is Wyndham's joy, if Mar'ann flies?' The unknowing world might cry 'See there the maid with bosom cold! / Indifference o'er her heart presides, / And love & lovers she derides', yet he, her true love, knew of the 'grateful tumult' hidden behind her capricious exterior.[20]

The poetry suggests that Wyndham, aware of Mary Anne's reputation but entranced by her beauty, thought that he could mould her into the virtuous wife he wanted, even as she did her best to persuade him to adopt the persona of the ardent lover. It may have been an affair of the heart for him, in which concerns about lineage, money and flightiness were put to one side, but for her it was firmly an affair of the head, in which romance did not arise spontaneously but had to be invented to fill an emotional vacuum. Her brother John, camped with his regiment outside Paris after the fall of Napoleon, was beside himself with delight at the fact that his wilful sister had made such a strategic choice. Reacting to her 'kindly' description of Wyndham, he noted approvingly, 'you do not speak like a blind lover'. 'You mention', he continued, 'that Mr Lewis's family are very good on both sides.'[21]

Some sense of the courtship of this oddly matched couple can be gleaned from the letters Wyndham wrote to Mary Anne during their engagement. His bulletins were formal, full of detailed accounts of his travels and his business affairs. Mary Anne evidently required more than the muted expressions of affection he offered. 'If you co'd see into my heart you wo'd be assured that you have no cause to entertain the slightest doubt of the unshakable Love of your most affectionate Wyndham Lewis', ended one letter.[22] Another mourned a look of 'scornful anger' directed towards him. 'That I love you truly most truly I call Heavn' to witness & I never can place my affections on another.'[23] Wyndham evidently needed Mary Anne's love and missed her company when parted from her, but he was also wary of her moods and what he perceived to be a levity so excessive as to border on the hysterical. In one undated letter he tried to explain that his devotion to her was unswerving but that it was tested by her behaviour. 'You certainly have a most amiable and virtuous heart oh that you wo'd always consult its dictates when you seem overwhelm'd by an excessive flow of spirits – if you knew how bewitching you were in your softer moods you would never give way to any rhapsodies.'[24]

Like her mother, Mary Anne married a calm, phlegmatic man, who, like her father, was simultaneously entranced and disturbed by his intended's passions. Wyndham's letters evoke a bride who was highly strung and easily provoked to jealousy, but who was also full of energy and determined to find excitement in a match made for material gain. They suggest a groom devoted to his beloved in her moments of quietness, made anxious by her whims and outbursts. It was not, perhaps, the most secure foundation for a life together, but many of their contemporaries made marriages that were even less well suited. In the end, anxieties and jealousies were put aside, and Mary Anne Evans became Mary Anne Lewis on 22 December 1815.

~

Benjamin Disraeli was born on 21 December 1804, twelve years after Mary Anne. In the memoir of his father he published in 1849, he claimed to be descended from Venetian ancestors who assumed the name D'Israeli 'in order that their race might be for ever recognised'.[25] The truth was rather less romantic. Disraeli's grandfather came from Ferrara in Italy, arriving in England in 1748. The family papers suggest that all Disraeli's efforts to establish the nobility of his lineage failed to find any genealogical line beyond his great-grandfather, but it was crucial to his conception of himself to be part of an ancient Jewish aristocracy quite as grand as the English aristocracy whose traditions he assumed. His mother's family, the Basevis, were in fact more distinguished than the Disraelis and could be traced back to 1492, but Disraeli was never remotely interested in his maternal ancestry. It was his name that mattered to him, along with the sense that he was fulfilling his destiny as the son of a noble line. In adulthood he dropped the apostrophe from his name while his parents retained it. They were always 'of Israel': he was simply Disraeli.

He was the eldest son and second child of Isaac D'Israeli and his wife Maria, and was born in London at their house, 6 Kings Road, Bedford Row. Isaac greeted his birth in laconic fashion, writing to the publisher John Murray that 'I wish to speak to you concerning the Index which they are calling for – the work is finished – Mrs D'I is in the beginning of labour – so that I cant go out.'[26] A few days later he wrote again to Murray requesting some books, and reported that 'Mrs D and Child are doing well.'[27] It was typical of Isaac that he should combine news of his newborn son with requests for books and questions about work. He was an affectionate, proud father, devoted to his two elder children, Benjamin and Sarah (born in 1802), and benignly interested in the pursuits of his younger sons: Ralph, born in 1809, and James, born in 1813. (A fourth son, Naphtali, was born in 1807 but died in infancy.) Above all he was a man of letters: a scholar and literary historian and a much-admired writer. In 1791 he published the first edition of his *Curiosities of Literature*, a multi-volume work in which he combined portraits of literary figures with commentary and analysis. From its first appearance *Curiosities* was tremendously popular, tapping as it did into an eighteenth-century enthusiasm for anthologies, observation and anecdote. Writing to John Murray in 1818, Byron summed up the affection in which Isaac was held by the literary world: 'I have a great respect for *Israeli* and his talents, and have read his works over and over and over repeatedly, and have been amused by them greatly, and instructed often . . . I don't know a living man's books I take up so often, or lay down more reluctantly, as *Israeli's*.'[28]

By the time of Benjamin's birth, Isaac had settled into the mode of life that would sustain him into old age: long days reading in his library, work on new editions of *Curiosities* and other literary titles, a genial social life among the publishers and antiquarian book dealers of literary London. The arrival of his children did little to disrupt this. Disraeli claimed to have been 'born in a library', and the bookish atmosphere of 6 Kings Road was not remotely disturbed by the presence in its quiet rooms of a growing family. Isaac's wife Maria, whom he married in February 1802, hardly figures in the family correspondence, and in later life Disraeli had nothing to say about her. It is almost impossible to glean an impression of her from the surviving evidence, since she appears as a silent figure in a family of opinionated, loquacious writers. It is notable, however, that the homes she made for her husband and children were happy ones, and her daughter and younger sons appear to have been fond of her. Disraeli's biographer Jane Ridley has suggested that his silence on the subject of his mother tells us more about his disappointment at her refusal to recognise his talents than it does about her, noting that in the letters from her that do survive she appears intelligent and engaged but not easily impressed by her eldest son's achievements.[29] Disraeli was sent first to a small school in Islington and then to a Noncomformist boarding school at Blackheath. Much of his education took place under his father's eye. He had the run of the library and mixed from his earliest days with Isaac's literary friends: John Murray, the Poet Laureate Robert Southey, and Byron's friend and fellow poet Samuel Rogers.

Disraeli venerated his father's work and his opinions, worried about his health, and did his best, as his own public profile grew, to protect him from unpleasantness. As important was his sister Sarah, two years his senior. Sarah and Benjamin formed a strong pairing in the family, separated by age and temperament from their younger brothers. They looked alike (both had their mother's dark hair, pale skin and strong features, in contrast to the fairer Ralph and James) and they shared a passion for books. Sarah was intelligent and vicariously ambitious. Although she had literary plans of her own, from an early age her energy was centred on her brother, in whose abilities she had unwavering faith. Her devotion and support were vital to Disraeli, first as he sought to establish himself among his peers at school, and subsequently as he fought to claim a place in the world of politics and letters. He repaid her devotion with total loyalty. His affection sustained her all her life.

In 1816 Isaac's father Benjamin died. His death brought about two major changes in the family's circumstances. First, it left them better off and allowed them to move to a larger house at 6 Bloomsbury Square, which would remain Disraeli's home until the second half of the 1820s. Second, it paved the way for a final break with their Jewish roots. For some years Isaac had been in dispute with the authorities of the Bevis Marks synagogue, after he contravened the synagogue's rules by refusing to take the office of Warden of the Congregation or to pay the fine of £40 levied in consequence of his refusal. The death of his father meant there was no point in continuing with the outward observances of a faith in which he had no religious interest. In March 1817 he withdrew from the synagogue and, at the insistence of his friend Sharon Turner, who believed it to be crucial to the children's prospects that they should belong to a faith, had them baptised Anglicans. Ralph and James were baptised on 11 July at St Andrew's, Holborn, and Benjamin and Sarah a month later.

Disraeli was thirteen when he was baptised, and the ceremony changed the course of his life. Jews could not sit in the House of Commons, so without being baptised he could not have pursued a political career. When the bar on Jewish MPs was lifted in 1858 he was already leading the Conservative Party in the Commons, something unthinkable had he not been a practising member of the Church of England. But while Isaac's dispute with the Bevis Marks authorities opened a door for his son, it also marked an irrevocable separation between Disraeli and his Jewish heritage. From 1817 that heritage would become increasingly mysterious and romantic as Disraeli gloried in myth-making about his ancestry without suffering any of the penalties felt by practising Jews. Cut off from his lineage but still separated from his literary and political contemporaries by race, he occupied a hinterland between two traditions: one Jewish, one Christian. In both he was an outsider. Like Mary Anne, poised for marriage to Wyndham Lewis, he was moving steadily away from his origins, and shaping his own conception of those origins would become increasingly important as he grew up.

~

1815, the year of Mary Anne's wedding, was the year when Britain's war with France came to an end on the field of Waterloo. But although the long years of conflict were over, poverty was rife. On the streets of London and

Bristol, the cities where Disraeli and Mary Anne lived, returning soldiers with no homes to go to collapsed in frosty streets and died.[30] They were both remade by Anglican ritual, she by marriage and he by baptism, but Britain was still governed by aristocratic families who would not willingly open their doors to a sailor's daughter or a Jew. Disraeli and Mary Anne knew that they would have to be made to do so, compelled to stop and listen by exceptional voices and extraordinary stories.

CHAPTER TWO

Tall Tales

ETHEL BENNETT, ANNA BENNETT, LUCY BENNETT

Ethel, Anna and Lucy Bennett were the elder daughters of Mr Bennett of Pythouse, Wiltshire. Mr Bennett was a bad manager of the family's finances, and with five unmarried daughters at home (two of whom were too young to be released from the schoolroom) life at Pythouse was unhappy. Each season Ethel, Anna and Lucy came to London to hunt for husbands and each year they returned to the country without a suitor between them. In the mid 1820s Ethel found an aristocrat to marry but the marriage was wretched, and before many years had passed, rumours of her infidelities appeared in the gossip pages of the press. Anna and Lucy were determined to find more congenial spouses and turned their gaze to the army, only to be disappointed by a succession of soldiers. Their hearts alighted on raffish half-pay officers, matches their debt-ridden father refused to allow. In 1829, after they had been on the marriage market for a decade, a soldier with whom Lucy was in love walked out of a first-floor window at his mess, expecting to find a balcony. He fell sixteen feet, broke his back and died a week later, after which both sisters retired from the matrimonial lists.

~

'I would not be unmarried for all the world', wrote Mary Anne to her brother John in the middle of the 1820s. 'I have just as much nay more attention than the girls – married women being the fashion – without having the misery of looking out for an establishment.'[1] The Bennetts were her cousins and Ethel, Lucy and Anna among her closest friends, and she witnessed every twist and turn of their hunt for husbands. Their story emerges in the letters she wrote to John throughout the 1820s, and it reveals how dramatically her own prospects were altered by marriage. The Bennett sisters were from a grander family than her, due to to the marriage made by their mother, but they were dependent on her goodwill for carriage rides, cast-off dresses and introductions to the eligible young men who continued to cluster about her; and they treated her house as a refuge from their own home. Mary Anne's status as the wife of a rich man gave her independence of which Ethel, Anna and Lucy could only dream, and their presence in her drawing room, where they passed hours each day lamenting the possibility of eternal spinsterhood, served as a constant reminder of the fate she escaped on the day of her wedding.

~

After their marriage in December 1815, Wyndham took Mary Anne to Greenmeadow, his estate outside Cardiff. Greenmeadow was a medieval farmstead, settled in rolling, fertile land overlooking the River Taff, and the oldest parts of the house dated back centuries. The house no longer survives and all the accounts of it date from after Wyndham and Mary Anne made extensive alterations in the early 1820s, so we know more about Mary Anne's reaction to finding herself mistress of Greenmeadow than we do about the house itself during her first years there. She revelled in the freedom her own home gave her. She hunted with her brother-in-law's harriers, planned ambitious renovations to the house and filled its guest quarters with visitors drawn from Cardiff and local landed families, who left traces of their presence in the poetry she kept. Most of it was by unattached young men who combined praise of the house with admiration for their alluring hostess. One 'H.L.B.' noted enviously that 'the Rose of Enjoyment is Lewis's Flow'r' and another visitor not possessed of poetic prowess wrote doggerel in praise of his bedroom, expiating on its muslin curtains, pale pink sheets ('like fair Maidens Bloom') and lavender-scented pillows, before complaining of 'One thing only needful without which are few charms / But a Batchelors fate – not one in his arms.'[2]

With Wyndham frequently away on business, Mary Anne was left to plot her own course at home. Her immediate social circle was drawn from the Lewis family and had at its heart Wyndham's brother William Price

Lewis, known universally as 'The Governor', who lived a few miles away at New House in Llanishen. William Lewis was a clergyman of the old school; a robust figure with no religious interest and multiple parishes, for which he did little more than install curates and collect tithes. Scandal lurked in his past just as it did in his brother's, but while Wyndham made some provision for his illegitimate daughter, William disclaimed all interest in his offspring. After making an improvident marriage in his youth, he abandoned his wife and had to be bullied by his parents-in-law into making a contribution to the upkeep of his children after her death (they claimed that his desertion sent her into a decline from which she never recovered). He spent his days hunting and drinking, and Mary Anne enjoyed his company immensely. In Cardiff there were balls and assemblies to attend in the company of Mary and Catherine Williams, young unmarried relations of Wyndham's. Each year Wyndham took her to Cheltenham for the social season, which she attended in the company of her cousin Harriet Semper. In 1819 she went to Paris for the first time. During Wyndham's absences she made regular visits to Pensax, home of her childhood friends the Cluttons, and rejoiced as they in their turn married and found new authority as wives and mothers.

Mary Anne loved children and lavished affection and attention on those of her friends, but she had no babies of her own. In the hundreds of letters by her that survive, she makes almost no reference to her childlessness, and those references that do survive are oblique. Nevertheless they suggest that at times she felt it deeply. Writing to her brother John in the 1830s, twenty years after her wedding, she confessed that 'so far from the world hardening my heart I think it has got more affectionate at least I am sure I am fonder of my husband mama & you – had I children I suppose my affections would be more divided'.[3] Her letters to John in the 1820s contained regular updates about the number of children born to her friends, with Dolly Clutton, married to a Mr Whitmore Jones, leading the field by producing ten between 1820 and 1835. After the birth of Dolly's fifth child Mary Anne remarked that she thought five was quite enough[4] and after the arrival of the ninth she wrote, 'Dolly has now nine children I am as happy as the day is long without any',[5] a defensive assertion that rings with some relief at having escaped the physical trauma of continual childbearing.

There are indications in Wyndham's letters to Mary Anne that she did become pregnant in the years after her marriage and that the viability of her pregnancies was a source of anxiety for them both. In January 1817 he wrote from Bristol that 'I highly approve of your forbearance in not accepting the invitations you have received & keeping yourself composed & quiet' and also that the doctor, Mr Cooper, 'does not think you ought to eat many sweet things such as Jellies &c as they will injure your general appetite & prevent you from eating a sufficient quantity of food that is more wholesome'. Just over a year later, in March and April 1818, his letters again became for a brief period unusually concerned with her health, appetite and daily activities.[6] Whether or not Mary Anne was conceiving and miscarrying during this period, it seems probable that she felt her childlessness most acutely in the years immediately following her marriage, when her friends were adding to their families at a great rate and when both she and those around her would have expected her to produce a Lewis heir.

Deprived of the distraction of children, Mary Anne was compelled to shape a role for herself as a wife without a nursery. One of the problems she faced was that in the 1810s and 1820s the nature of marriage itself was in flux. By the 1830s the concept of companionate marriage – that is of marriage as the meeting of hearts and minds – had filtered through to all classes, and had become the ideal to which men and women of marriageable age aspired. Prior to this the status of marriage was complicated by differing social standards. The poor did not always legally marry, and aristocrats, forced into dynastic matches designed to secure land rather than hearts, were frequently adulterous. While it was far harder for women than men to subvert their marriage vows, powerful women such as Lady Oxford, mistress of both Byron and Sir Francis Burdett, or Lady Jersey, mistress of the Prince Regent, nevertheless managed to cuckold their husbands and emerge with their reputations and influence intact.

Mary Anne was married too early to be obliged to pretend that her rich husband was also her soulmate in order to conform to a social norm, but her class – and his – was too indeterminate to allow her to acknowledge that theirs was a marriage of convenience. Wyndham's fortune was aristocratic in its extent but not its source, and the wives of rich industrialists were permitted nothing like the freedom of their social superiors. Mary Anne's activities were constrained by a bourgeois middle-class morality that emerged in the early decades of the nineteenth century and bloomed during Queen Victoria's reign. In the 1820s this moral code was still evolving, meaning that she was caught between an aristocratic eighteenth-century view of marriage as a contract based on rational practicality and a newer cultural assumption that marriage should be the expression of perfect harmony and true love. She was also caught between an earlier assumption that a husband and wife possessed of considerable means should lead lives largely independent of each other and an increasingly powerful expectation that a wife's domain was her home; that her role was to procreate, or, failing that, to be a submissive prop and stay to her husband.

Mary Anne wanted more. As the years passed and no children came, her progress between Greenmeadow, Cheltenham, Pensax and Bristol became restless. Left alone by Wyndham in Cheltenham, she occupied herself by writing a fantasy of physical attraction, influenced by the novels she read and made safe through a bathetic concluding twist. 'I was left <u>all alone in my loveliness</u>. On the second day I pass'd an interesting looking man in the passage but it was his companion who mostly attracted my attention – he had the most beautiful black eyes I ever saw in my life.' The companion watches her closely over the next few days, following her into rooms and sitting, arrestingly enigmatic, by her side. Fevered by the attention, she retires to bed to read, only to be disturbed in the most alarming fashion:

> I was startled by a noise from behind the small stand up bed and out he rush'd – I could not breath or move for terror, he threw himself on the bed – I was ringing the bell – he was at my feet & I could not get away from him – I then screamed half panic waiters chambermaids & came to my assistance and a beautiful girl happened she threw her arms round his neck saying dearest Gustave why do I find you here – but oh the brute the horrendous brute what do you think he did say he began to bark like any other dog – and began to eat up my supper.[7]

∽

In 1820 George III died after many years of illness and insanity. The Prince Regent became King and his marriage, spectacularly disastrous even by Royal standards, exploded into its final act. The new Queen, Caroline of Brunswick, had been living abroad for many years after decades of estrangement from her husband. Their only child, Princess Charlotte, died in childbirth in 1817, prompting an outpouring of national grief. Caroline's years abroad were dogged by spies working for her husband, who was desperate to find proof of her infidelity and so divorce her. None of the spies was able to find concrete evidence of adultery, and when her husband succeeded to the throne, Caroline returned to England to claim her crown. The King, a notorious adulterer, responded by compelling the government to introduce a Bill of Pains and Penalties against her in the House of Lords, designed to prove her marital guilt and strip her of her title.

During the summer of 1820 the 'Trial of Queen Caroline' dominated public life. Caroline cut a dramatic figure as she swept into the House of Lords each day to hear the evidence against her, and her cause became a rallying point for radicals determined to bring down the King and his government. The popular support garnered by Caroline led those in power to fear that a verdict against her would result in revolution and the Bill was dropped. George IV nevertheless succeeded in barring his wife from his coronation, public support for her fell away, and less than a year later she was dead.

Mary Anne was absorbed by Caroline's story, following newspaper reports of the trial avidly and canvassing the respective popularity of the King and Queen among her friends and correspondents. She was bored and found diversion as a result of George III's death. The accession of the new King triggered an election as well as a scandal, and Mary Anne was quick to seize on the fact that the election heralded the possibility of change. The seat of Cardiff was controlled by the Marquis of Bute and held by his brother, Lord James Stuart. Standing for Parliament was an expensive business when voters had to be bribed and every vote paid for, and Lord James, realising he lacked the funds to stand again, sent in his resignation. To Mary Anne's delight, Wyndham was persuaded by her and the local Tories to stand in his place. 'They say', she told John, 'I am so popular that I must canvass tomorrow, which I shall do.' But the election offered more than the temporary thrill of the campaign trail. 'If W succeeds we shall have a house in town & fit up this beautifully.'[8]

The combination of Wyndham's bribes, Mary Anne's popularity and a dashing campaign livery of red ribbons won the day and Wyndham was duly elected the Member for Cardiff. He joined the back benches of Lord Liverpool's Tory administration, which by 1820 had been in power for eight years. In February 1821 the Lewises moved to London, where they took up residence in a series of rented Mayfair addresses while they hunted for a house of their own. Their first house was in Old Burlington Street near Berkeley Square, where the Bennetts lived during the season. It cost twenty-five guineas a week, had three drawing rooms as well as a large dining room, and offered ample scope for entertaining.

If Mary Anne imagined that once she opened her doors fashionable London would flock to her parties, she soon found out her mistake. Wyndham proved to be a singularly undistinguished MP, who, in the decade and a half he spent in Parliament, got to his feet to speak only eight times. The Lewises were not in a position to offer anyone patronage and had no influence to trade, so they had little opportunity to build a social network. Their isolation was exacerbated by the fact that they personified the new money feared by high society. In the 1820s, faced with the prospect of invasion by a new class of industrialists, the old order responded by closing ranks. Exclusive clubs such as Almacks flourished, places to which one could gain entry only if one knew the right people. Codes of dress and manners became increasingly rigid and served as physical symbols of caste. The dandy, for example, as exemplified by the understated elegance of Beau Brummell, gained his cultural power because he set a standard impossible to meet without a valet, the right tailor and impeccable taste. Popular fiction of the period reflected this anxiety, and was peopled by encroaching manufacturers threatening the purity of the aristocratic pool. 'There is nobody whose business it is to look after society, and who has a decided right to keep every one in his proper sphere', mourns a dowager marchioness in Charlotte Bury's *The Separation*, published in 1830. 'Till there is, we shall never see the end of this confusion.'[9]

As a result, Mary Anne's circle in the first part of the 1820s was predominantly restricted to members of her extended family. The husbandless Bennett girls were her most frequent companions: they whiled away mornings at her house, drove out with her in her carriage in the afternoon, and exchanged formal visits in the evening. William Lewis also took a house in London and was a frequent evening caller, as was Mary Anne's uncle James Viney, who had retired from active army service and passed his days frittering money away on eccentric business ventures, practising his singing, and leering at the young women who kept his niece company. In addition to the Bennett sisters, these included Catherine and Mary Williams, Wyndham's nieces from Wales, Mary Anne's cousin Emma Scrope and, on the rare occasions that they were able to escape their families, Dolly Whitmore Jones and her sister Bessy, the friends of Mary Anne's childhood.

Mary Anne described the pattern of her days in a letter to John written from Portman Square, where the Lewises moved after the lease on Old Burlington Street expired. 'I am seldom out of bed until eleven, and often later – and then eating breakfast answering notes seeing the tradespeople with patterns & & and talking to Wyndham fully occupies my time with morning visitors until ½ past three O clock when the carriage comes, & one of the girls and myself drive about shopping morning visits to the park until near six, dine at seven, go to sleep afterwards for an hour and then sing play work or read & talk the rest of the Even'g, we have not been to many parties yet.'[10] This somewhat sparse social schedule was enlivened by one new friendship. Rosina Wheeler was a temperamental Irish beauty in her early twenties whom Mary Anne met at John's instigation. She was rumoured to have had a liaison with an English army officer whom she pursued from England to Ireland[11] and she later taunted her husband by telling him how much she once loved Mary Anne's brother,[12] suggesting that John was the officer about whom the rumours circulated (a supposition supported by John's Irish posting and his own numerous affairs). When Rosina was in London, Mary Anne saw her almost every day, and she looked on as Uncle Viney fixed his roving eye on her friend. 'He is a great admirer of Rosina's', she reported, '& between you & me takes strange liberties with her . . . I had no idia he was so fond of kissing the girls.'

Mary Anne's drawing room, populated by Rosina, James Viney and a giggling chorus of Bennett and Williams sisters, teetered on the edge of respectability. 'We were obliged to give Rosina so many lectures to make her behave herself – she has such very high spirits . . . she cannot bear my Uncle now although at first she had certainly some thoughts of him – he told her one day before us all, he should like to suck her lips, the girls & I scream'd with laughter you never heard how he went on.'[13] Ensconced in London but excluded from its upper echelons and still surrounded only by relations, Mary Anne sought new ways of feeling and experiencing the world. Pushing at the boundaries of socially acceptable conduct was one way to test the limits of one's sphere; seeking fresh physical sensations was another. So she rode half-broken horses in Hyde Park, drank champagne and 'beautiful ale' and during summers in Wales, rolled underground through the Dowlais mine on tram wagons with Catherine and Mary Williams, 'screaming and laughing all the way'.[14]

~

We know about such escapades because throughout the 1820s Mary Anne wrote long letters to her brother John, serving with his regiment overseas. Her loyalty to John ran deeper than that to her husband and she was prepared to go to any lengths to help him. Keeping him happy and helping him gain a promotion were the two ambitions that dominated her existence, and they tested her relationship with Wyndham. John could render her deliriously joyous and intolerably miserable: she called him the 'delight and torment of my life' and he had a greater impact on her equilibrium than anyone else in her circle.[15] The delight was triggered by love, the torment by John's constant demands for money. He was a spendthrift with no interest in saving or earning his own living, preferring instead to live off the generosity of his sister and her rich husband. Wyndham was not inclined to subsidise his indolent brother-in-law and was disturbed by Mary Anne's devotion to her sibling. Mary Anne attributed this to jealousy – 'he cannot bear me to love you as I do' – and she may well have been right, but Wyndham was also angered by the way John battened on his sister, disrupting her peace for his own ends.[16]

John accumulated debts by overspending on luxuries for himself and was continually asking Mary Anne to settle his accounts with angry tradesmen. In addition his career prospects depended on his having the resources to purchase his promotions, first to captain and then to major. Buying commissions was an expensive business and officers not born into independent means frequently sought out investors who would lend them the purchase money in return for hefty interest. Whenever the opportunity for promotion arose for John (something that happened only occasionally, when a senior officer resigned), Eleanor and Thomas Yate, James Viney, and Mary Anne and Wyndham all became involved in a joint negotiation about how to raise the necessary funds. John's career was thus a family endeavour, and one in which Wyndham participated reluctantly. He was too careful with money to make loans without security, and Mary Anne expended much energy coaching her brother about how best to convince her husband of his creditworthiness. Thomas Yate worked with her to wring money out of Wyndham for John and was a witness to the strain his demands placed on both Mary Anne and her husband. 'I have seen much of Mr Lewis', he wrote to John in 1827. 'He feels vexed and displeased with you; writing letters to his wife that make her not only uneasy, but he says, at the time very unhappy; which he says no one has a right to do.'[17]

In 1826 the news that John was to be posted with his regiment to Mauritius tested Mary Anne's loyalty to both him and her husband. The one person whom she would not permit John to disturb was their mother, and the rare occasions on which she reprimanded him arose when he caused Eleanor pain and anxiety. 'Do not talk of expected battles to her, or say that you are to be sent abroad until the order is literally arrived', she told him in 1825.[18] The news that his preparations to leave for Mauritius were being hampered by debt provoked a rare spurt of anger, since it forced her to divert funds from Eleanor to him. 'The inclosed 31£ which I send you was to have been for her . . . I rose the money by the sail of my white lace vail and two rings which I got sold for me in London – You have not only taken this sum from her but the money she sent you besides. Indeed John I do not know what sort of heart you can have to repeat such conduct so repeatedly.'[19] Wyndham refused to advance money for his brother-in-law's kit, despite Mary Anne sending John the wording for a request most likely to meet with approval. Mary Anne was distressed by Wyndham's intransigence and scraped the necessary funds together by selling more trinkets and borrowing from James Viney. Simultaneously she organised a secret postal system centred on a series of poste restante addresses. Her efforts ensured that during John's absence abroad she could continue to communicate with her only true confidant without Wyndham's knowledge.

In 1820, the year in which Mary Anne moved to London, fifteen-year-old Disraeli responded to a letter from John Murray asking for his opinion on a new play. His view was uncompromising. 'I cannot conceive these acts to be as effective on the stage as you seemed to expect.'[20] The confidence of Disraeli's reply illuminates some of the particularities of his character in the period immediately following his release from school. At fifteen, he was unshakeably convinced that he had a right to be heard, and his conviction prompted others to take him more seriously than they might otherwise have done. Why one of the most powerful figures in British publishing should have solicited the views of a fifteen-year-old is unclear, and it is possible that Murray was merely humouring the son of an old friend. But there was something about Disraeli that made people listen to him. He had an intensity of outlook and a clarity of thought that added weight to his sentiments and earned him an audience. That audience might disagree with him and might find him wrong-headed, but he could not be ignored.

In July 1820 he made his first foray into print, publishing a short story in Leigh Hunt's *Indicator*. Set during the Civil War and somewhat self-consciously entitled 'A True Story', it related the unhappy tale of a beautiful young lady driven to insanity by discovering that the Cavalier soldier she loved was married. Two things stand out about 'A True Story' apart from Disraeli's youth at the time of its publication. Its presence in *The Indicator* – a short-lived journal that encapsulated Leigh Hunt's poetic and political philosophy and championed the work of Shelley, Keats and others in his circle – suggests a desire on the part of Disraeli to ally himself with the liberal, radical voices of second-generation Romanticism. And the opening of the story presented an image of the sensitive youth Disraeli perceived himself to be:

When I was a young boy, I had delicate health, and was somewhat of a pensive and contemplative turn of mind; it was my delight in the long summer evenings to slip away from my noisy and more robust companions, that I might walk in the shade of a venerable wood, my favourite haunt, and listen to the cawing of the old rooks, who seemed as fond of this retreat as I was.[21]

Disraeli subsequently wrote many more descriptions of his youthful self, but this one stands out because it dates from the period of his boyhood and gives us an insight into his adolescent conception of himself as a neophyte poet, more in sympathy with nature than with his contemporaries. His experiences at school, which he later used as material for his fiction, gave him reason to turn to solitude for relief. After his baptism opened up the possibility of an Anglican education, he was sent to Higham Hall, a private school in Epping Forest. Both his younger brothers subsequently went to Winchester, and Disraeli later resented the fact that he alone had been deprived of the public school education that would have smoothed his journey up the political ladder. The education he received at Higham Hall was patchy and he was bullied by anti-Semitic schoolfellows. Jane Ridley suggests that he may also have been bullied on account of his latent homosexuality; a suggestion supported by his depiction of passionate boyhood friendships in his early novels.[22]

Disraeli left Higham Hall at fifteen, possibly at the school's instigation; probably because Isaac and Maria were unhappy at the education and the treatment he was receiving (that they sent their younger sons elsewhere gives weight to this theory). He was too young to join the scions of grand families at Oxford or Cambridge, so for a year he read in Isaac's library before being articled to a firm of solicitors in 1821, the idea of university apparently abandoned for good. He spent his evenings in the theatre, tried his hand at writing plays, and in 1824 sent John Murray the manuscript of a novel entitled *Alymer Papillon*, which Murray declined to publish. Disraeli accepted his decision with the verbal equivalent of an insouciant head toss, telling Murray, 'I think therefore that the sooner it be put behind the fire, the better, and as you have some small experience in burning MSS., you will be perhaps so kind as to consign it to the flames': a strikingly impertinent reference to the burning of Byron's memoirs overseen by Murray earlier in the year.[23]

It is another sign of Disraeli's youthful confidence that he dared to write like this to Murray, and that in so doing he made an implicit comparison between his own work and Byron's. Byron was Disraeli's hero and the figure on whom he modelled his own persona. Byron was a genius, isolated from his countrymen by his refusal to conform to their petty morality. He was an exile, hounded out of England by a benighted establishment threatened by his brilliance. He was a style icon, his clothes and attitudes copied by legions of fans during his years of popularity. He was a sexual adventurer who followed his heart, forming relationships dictated by passion rather than convention, with young men as well as women. And he was a hero, who died fighting for Greek freedom.

Byron's example thus gave Disraeli a context for his own future. It showed how it might be possible to fashion a public image from the raw materials of alienated brilliance, and it also demonstrated the power of the connection between politics and literature. Byron's story provided some answers to the fundamental questions facing Disraeli at twenty. Who am I? What will I do? Who, or what, do I want to become? Disraeli was far from the only young man to face these questions or to embrace the cult of Byron, but he internalised his devotion to the poet so completely that it had a significant impact on his own life.

In 1824, the year of Byron's death, this devotion gave an intellectual justification to Disraeli's first foreign excursion. A month after receiving Murray's rejection, he left England in the company of his friend William Meredith, who was informally engaged to Disraeli's sister Sarah, and Isaac, who kept a benign eye on the two young men. Following the path mapped out by Byron in the third canto of *Childe Harold's Pilgrimage*, they travelled through Belgium to the Rhine valley, visiting Brussels, Antwerp, Cologne, Mainz and Heidelberg. They toured the field of the Battle of Waterloo, saw cathedrals and grand city streets, ate new food and drank large quantities. Isaac, Disraeli told Sarah, 'was most frisky on his landing and on the strength of mulled claret etc. was quite the lion of Ostend'.[24] For his part Isaac, called 'The Governor' by both Disraeli and Meredith, permitted his charges to discover the twin delights of European travel and Rhine wine for themselves. 'The governor allows us to debauch to the utmost and Hocheimer Johannisberg Rudelsheirnien Ashanhausen and a thousand other varieties are unsealed and floored with equal rapidity.'[25] Touring with Isaac and Meredith instilled in Disraeli a love of European travel that lasted all his life, and it also established a model – again pioneered by Byron – in which foreign adventure functioned as a refuge for the young man of genius unable to harness his talent.

Disraeli's Rhine adventure left him disinclined to pursue a legal calling. While working as a solicitor he met John Powles, who was connected with various Latin-American mining companies. In 1825 a mining bubble was developing in England, prompting a stock-market boom, and Disraeli, full of confidence and ignorance, believed that with Powles he could make his fortune. He borrowed considerable sums to buy shares, and convinced John Murray to follow his example. When the market began to slump, he attempted to prop it up by publishing pamphlets at his own expense on the security of mining investments.

Buoyed by apparent success and oblivious to the fact that he had bought into a mirage, Disraeli persuaded Murray and Powles that they should use their new-found – and imaginary – wealth to establish a new daily newspaper, to be called *The Representative*. He envisaged it as an antidote to *The Times*, and saw it as a way in which he could shape political opinion. (That Murray and Powles acquiesced demonstrates that older heads than Disraeli were fooled by the mining bubble, but also reveals something of Disraeli's powers of persuasion.) The three agreed that Murray would put up half the money and Powles and Disraeli a quarter each, and that Disraeli would help Murray in the search for an editor. To this end he travelled to Edinburgh to persuade Walter Scott's son-in-law, John Gibson Lockhart, to take on the role. Lockhart declined, angling instead for the editorship of another of Murray's publications, the powerful *Quarterly Review*. A cabal of *Quarterly* grandees led by John Wilson Croker moved against both Lockhart and Disraeli, and at the point that Murray's faith in the project was foundering, the mining bubble burst, leaving no funds for the paper. Murray proceeded with publication against his better judgement; *The Representative* limped on for six months with no official editor before folding, losing thousands of pounds and heaping ignominy on all those involved in its production.

The rest of the actors in the *Representative* episode were significantly older than Disraeli and had between them a wealth of experience. They nevertheless felt compelled to listen to his proposals and manoeuvre behind his back. The shadow of Scott's fame did not deter him as he travelled north, and nor did the taste-shaping power of the *Quarterly* coterie. Murray was furious and temporarily broke with him, but Disraeli's sense of his own worth was unshaken. He had already experimented with three occupations: lawyer, stock-market speculator, newspaper proprietor. At twenty-two all had failed him, so he decided instead to become a novelist.

His first novel, *Vivian Grey*, appeared in 1826 and lampooned Murray and many of London's luminaries. *Vivian Grey* was a silver-fork novel, part of a new wave of fashionable fiction that developed in the 1820s and continued to be popular into the 1830s and 40s. Silver-fork novels were genre fiction, predominantly produced by the publishing house of Henry Colburn, a shrewd businessman with his finger firmly on the pulse of mass-market literary taste. Colburn understood that a growing middle-class readership wanted stories of aristocratic celebrity; that a young lady languishing away her days in search of a husband would part with her pin money more quickly to read generic romances featuring handsome dukes than for beautifully crafted novels such as *Mansfield Park* or *Emma*. Similarly that young lady, ensconced in the private, intimate space of her bedroom, would read novel after novel about the attempts of her social superiors to find husbands in Almacks and grand country houses, because such novels spoke to her fantasy of romantic fulfilment twinned with riches and social elevation. The young lady's mother, meanwhile, would display a similar appetite for novels that claimed to reveal the habits of the rich: how they ate, dressed and talked. She would consume books about Byron with fascinated prurience and would therefore need little encouragement to read about fictional Byrons in order to experience again the delightful frisson generated by the ambiguous morality of aristocratic behaviour.

The vast majority of silver-fork novels were written by authors who stood outside the world about which they wrote. They purported to offer a window into the lives of a rich elite but their authors had their noses pressed against the glass alongside their readers. Silver-fork novelists stitched together their semblance of reality by listening to gossip, reading society newspapers and imagining themselves to be part of an aristocratic world from which they were excluded. This was how Disraeli, a twenty-two-year-old with little experience of the world and no acquaintance among the aristocracy, managed to produce a novel that anatomised them.

Vivian Grey tells the story of a young man emerging from school and navigating his way through a series of social and political intrigues. Like Disraeli's, his background is modest and his schooling undistinguished. Like Disraeli he is determined to become a powerful figure. Disraeli later disowned *Vivian Grey*, describing it in the 1870s as 'essentially a puerile work',[26] and before it was reissued in 1853 he cut its more intemperate passages. Many of these related to its fictionalisation of *The Representative* episode, refigured as a political rather than journalistic awakening. John Murray reappears in the novel as the Marquis of Carabas, a drunken shadow of a man fruitlessly scheming to harness Vivian's charm and intellect to bolster his own influence. Vivian's adventures on Carabas's behalf take him into the homes of the rich and famous, and frame an anthropological study of this milieu as relentless as it is guileless.

The first volume of *Vivian Grey* was published by Henry Colburn on 22 April 1826. Its authorship remained a secret and some of the initial reviews were favourable. The *Literary Gazette* – owned by Colburn – thought its characters were drawn with 'great spirit, vividness, and truth', although it also commented on the limits of the novel's ambition.[27] But once the news leaked out that the author was not a young man of fashion but a callow nobody, such tempered praise vanished from the critical scene. The worst attack came in the *Literary Magnet*, in an article entitled 'Nuisances of the Press'. The *Magnet* castigated *Vivian Grey* as 'trash' and Disraeli, in a phrase borrowed from the novel, as 'a swindler – a scoundrel – a liar, – a base, deluding, flattering, fawning villain'. It labelled his attempts to be fashionable 'abundantly ludicrous' and allied hero and author in order to mock Disraeli's dandified demeanour and to insinuate his effeminacy. 'Vivian Grey is quite a love of a man; wears violet-covered slippers . . . Report says, that this would-be-exquisite, – this fashionable cutpurse, is intended by the author as a picture of himself. He may possibly have delineated his own character without knowing it.'[28]

Vivian Grey was Disraeli's first attempt to weave fantasy around his identity, to use fiction to claim a significance denied him by birth, race and education. Novel-writing offered a way to escape reality just as novel-reading allowed young women to dream of improbable futures. Disraeli staked his reputation on a story, believing he could become someone other than himself and convince others of this transformation through the act of writing. The failure of *Vivian Grey* to achieve any of this therefore mattered deeply. It suggested that ambition was no match for circumstance, that you needed more than talent to break into the world of politics and letters. It was a bitter blow, compounded by the fact that the novel made the rift with Murray permanent. He was appalled by his portrayal and blamed Isaac for allowing Disraeli to publish. The decades-long friendship between the two older men came to an abrupt end and Murray never forgave Disraeli for what he perceived as a treacherous betrayal.

The storm triggered by *Vivian Grey* made Disraeli ill. He took to his bed and for the next two years, between the ages of twenty-four and twenty-six, existed in a state of nervous debility, with no direction and few occupations. He fell into lethargy and despondency with the same conviction with which he imposed his will on Murray and his vision of aristocratic London on London's aristocrats, his experience of failure as absolute as his earlier certainty of triumph. As a young man Isaac had also suffered from periods of emotional exhaustion and was seriously concerned by the sight of his son brought low. In the summer of 1826 he contrived a plan with his friends Benjamin and Sara Austen to shake Disraeli out of himself. The Austens were going to Italy via Paris and Switzerland and it was agreed that Disraeli would accompany them. Driving in a closed carriage over the Jura ridge he saw the High Alps for the first time, with Mont Blanc silhouetted against a cloudless sky. In Geneva he made the acquaintance of Byron's boatman, with whom he rowed every night on the lake, lapping up stories of his idol.

∼

Mary Anne was absorbed by *Vivian Grey*. She copied chunks of it into her commonplace book, excerpting more than from any other novel of the period. She was exactly the kind of reader to whom silver-fork novels appealed: bored, well-off, not of exclusive London society, but increasingly determined to break into it. To do so it was imperative that Wyndham remain in Parliament so that they had a defined place in the political world. Mary Anne threw herself into the election campaign of 1825–6, flattering and charming every potential ally who crossed her path. 'The people had supposed I should give myself airs', she told John from Swansea. 'So fancy how charmed they are at my <u>constant courtesy</u>.'[29]

With Wyndham in Parliament, Mary Anne reasoned, it would be easier to persuade him to lend John money to purchase his promotion to major. 'If Wyndham gains his Election all here will tell him it is thro me I shall then ask him as a friend to promise me to advance the money for your

Majority.'³⁰ So she donned outfits calculated to appeal to patriotic constituents, parading around Cardiff in a flannel gown, mob cap and a tall Welsh black hat. She hosted grand dinners and balls in the assembly rooms at Cardiff and Swansea, made public appearances and, despite her protestations of exhaustion, enjoyed the attention she received and the negotiations necessary to buy votes in an unreformed election. Ultimately corruption in the constituency proved her undoing. Midway through the campaign the Marquis of Bute decided he wanted his seat back, his brother having elected to stand for Parliament once more. Wyndham managed to get himself selected as the Tory candidate for the borough of Aldeburgh in Suffolk and was back in Parliament by the summer of 1827, but the whole affair gave Mary Anne a thorough disgust for Wales and the Welsh. Aldeburgh, moreover, was such a rotten seat that even Wyndham, the very model of an unreformed Tory, was taken aback at the amount of money necessary to secure his election. Meanwhile Greenmeadow was let to tenants and the Lewises redoubled their efforts to find a permanent London home.

With Wyndham absorbed in house-hunting, a return to Parliament and multiple business interests, Mary Anne looked elsewhere for entertainment. In May 1827 she told John that 'Wyndham is quite a reform'd character & goes with me every where', suggesting that for much of the previous year she was left to her own devices.³¹ She took a new protégée under her wing, an eight-year-old called Eliza Gregory who had a marvellous singing voice. Mary Anne petted Eliza and intended to have her trained as a singer but Wyndham intervened and sent the girl home, concerned that she was becoming spoiled and unfitted for life with her family. Deprived of this diversion, Mary Anne found new friends in the circle surrounding Henry Somerset, Marquis of Worcester, to whom she was introduced by her cousin Pierce Porter. Lord Worcester was chiefly known for his affair with the courtesan Harriette Wilson, who wrote about their relationship at length in her *Memoirs*, published in 1825. His set was composed of actresses, singers and men famous for familial scandals and serial womanising. Under his aegis Mary Anne met Augustus Berkeley and his brother, both of whom were implicated in one of the most dramatic inheritance frauds of the nineteenth century. Harriette Wilson, whose standards for male behaviour were not high, dismissed Augustus as a 'ruffian' and made public sport of his attempts to seduce her.³²

Worcester arranged for Mary Anne to look round Crockfords, London's notorious casino usually barred to women, and exchanged letters with her that portray a relationship premised on flirtatious exchanges. 'The sweet Pea drops his Head in gratitude to the Verbena & will prostrate him self before that sweet scented & graceful plant in the course of the day', ran one such note, its ornate code loitering between chivalry and dalliance.[33] Worcester's uncle, Lord Fitzroy Somerset, met Mary Anne in Brighton and took her and her maid for loose women, in an incident she reported to Worcester. 'I was walking . . . rather late in the evening, with my maid when we passed him in the street & he began to sing & was going to notice me in some way not seeing my face. Like my worthless sex I enjoy'd a little mischief so did not disappoint him by allowing him to find out that I was the treasure he thought he had discovered.'[34]

Both in public and private Mary Anne courted scandal. At a party she was importuned by a drunken colonel who kissed her shoulder and then turned his drink over her: he was bundled out by his host but the fracas was reported in the *Morning Chronicle*.[35] An anonymous correspondent, signing himself 'Veritas', wrote to inform her that a duel had been fought after two gentlemen disagreed about her reputation. Writing because of his conviction that 'the reckless traducer of female faith and honour ought to be exposed', Veritas reported that a Mr Robert Jackson, a barrister, had attacked Mary Anne in public, making such improper observations on her character as to provoke a Mr William O'Connell to challenge him to fight. 'But for the interference of the police', Veritas wrote, 'the tongue of the calumniator would have been silenced for ever or he would have been taught a lesson that he should carry with him to his tomb.'[36]

To be the subject of duels might inject some variety into a mundane existence but it threatened Mary Anne's pursuit of social acceptability. Duelling was an aristocratic activity and not something with which a woman in Mary Anne's position could afford to be associated. By the 1820s a programme of aristocratic reform was under way, with campaigners such as William Wilberforce seeking to stamp out the four aristocratic vices of duelling, suicide, gambling and adultery, which were thought to be corrupting public morals. By 1832, the year of the Great Reform Act, the moral as well as political tone was increasingly set by the middle classes, and an upper-class disregard for bourgeois standards of polite behaviour had fallen out of fashion. Among the Worcester set Mary Anne's position was doubly vulnerable because her presence there identified her with a mode of being that was no longer acceptable even for aristocrats, and that threatened to place the wife of an iron magnate beyond the social pale. In 1827, with Wyndham actively campaigning to return to Parliament, the Lewises finally made a decisive move to entrench themselves at the heart of Tory London. In February they bought a house: No. 1 Grosvenor Gate, Park Lane.

Grosvenor Gate transformed Mary Anne's existence. It provided her with a home entirely her own, a space she could create and control. Greenmeadow was Wyndham's house, part of the Lewis inheritance, but Grosvenor Gate belonged to them both. Wyndham bought the house from the developer, so the Lewises were the first people to live there, and he handed Mary Anne control of its decor and furnishings as well as a generous budget.

Grosvenor Gate still stands, on the corner of Park Lane and Upper Grosvenor Street. Today it is separated from Hyde Park by lanes of traffic, but when Mary Anne lived there, its balconies and bay windows looked directly over the park below. The remains of her decorative scheme are just visible in the house today, although it is now occupied by the offices of a property management company. Ornate cornicing and plasterwork runs through the building and grand fireplaces survive in the principal rooms. Also still present is the central staircase, the elegant sweep of which gave Mary Anne much pleasure. It trains your eye up four flights to take in the height of the house and culminates in an elegant cupola, which floods the hall with light. But the grand public spaces of the building are all show. Its corner position results in a house smaller than its exterior suggests and with space for big rooms on only two of its four sides. There is something theatrical about the contrast between its grand staircase and light-flooded dual-aspect drawing rooms and the small, dark rooms tucked into corners around the back walls in which the Lewises slept, dressed and ate.

Grosvenor Gate was a house built for entertaining and display, designed to impress rather than to house a family. Mary Anne filled it with bright materials and vivid contrasts calculated to capture the attention of her contemporaries, themselves the owners of brocade-draped homes. Crimson carpet ran through the drawing rooms, vying with gold damask curtains. Cushions and chairs were upholstered in white and rose velvet, and dark mahogany furniture jostled with marble occasional tables, gilt-trimmed chaise longues, green Dresden vases and ebony writing desks. The male spaces of the dining room and library were a more sober brown but were still decked out in gold trim. The bedrooms and boudoirs were hung with chintz, and even the servants' rooms were stuffed full of furniture, pieces bought and then discarded according to fashion and the dictates of Mary Anne's changing taste.

Grosvenor Gate established Mary Anne in the heart of Mayfair and as the near neighbour of many prominent Tories. Some old connections followed her to the house, including Wyndham's niece Catherine, who lived with the Lewises for much of 1827 and who became engaged under Mary Anne's chaperonage. Another frequent visitor was Rosina Wheeler, who reappeared in Mary Anne's life after her marriage to Edward Lytton Bulwer in 1826. Bulwer was a man-about-town who was beginning to make a name for himself as a writer. His mother fiercely objected to his marriage to Rosina and cut off his allowance, prompting him to turn to his pen in order to earn a living. His novels met with great success and he and Rosina established themselves in London society, where they lived beyond their means. Their marriage appeared happy but Mary Anne thought it 'not a good match'.[37] She and Rosina, now both ensconced in their own homes, exchanged visits almost every day. In contrast the Bennett sisters ceased to figure prominently in Mary Anne's circle after 1827. Their search for husbands had become a bore and desperation made their conduct too unpredictable to render them suitable company for Mary Anne's new acquaintances.

The most important friendship Mary Anne formed as a result of her move to Grosvenor Gate was with her neighbour Mary Dawson. Mary Dawson was the mother of five little boys, to whom Mary Anne became deeply attached. The Dawson children ran in and out of her house, stayed with her when their parents were away, begged for rides in her carriage, and looked on her as a second mother. Mary Dawson encouraged this, seeing in Mary Anne an unfulfilled maternal generosity that offered nothing but good to her own sons. Robert Dawson was nine when Mary Anne met the family. He was her particular favourite and remembered her with huge affection. Visiting her was a reward for lessons well done, and he continued to write to her and support her through his adulthood.

Mary Dawson was the sister of Robert Peel, the Tory Home Secretary. Peel was a new kind of politician: personally ambitious, politically astute and from a well-off, but provincial, manufacturing background. Two-party politics was still in its infancy in Britain in 1827 and the label 'Tory' only came into common usage towards the end of the decade.[38] Peel was among the first generation of politicians to define themselves exclusively by party allegiance and was in the vanguard of Tory leaders who had to whip their MPs into voting along party lines. He was in and out of office in 1827 since he refused to serve under his arch-rival George Canning, or to stand by Canning's support for Catholic Emancipation (the legal process, hotly debated in the second half of the 1820s, through which many restrictions on Catholics in Britain were removed). But even during his time on the back benches Peel was emerging as one of the most powerful politicians in the country. In 1829 he established the first modern police force, and when Canning died and (after a short-lived coalition) the Duke of Wellington became Prime Minister, Peel consolidated his position as the Premier's right-hand man. Together Wellington and Peel put together a distinctively Tory administration, which was required, in the final years of the decade, to deal with riots and frame-breaking in manufacturing districts, an economic downturn, a disunited Cabinet, trouble in Ireland, the Catholic question and intensifying demands from the middle classes for political emancipation and reform.

Peel connected his sister to all the most prominent figures in the political elite – both those from great houses and those whose power was more recently acquired. Mary Dawson in turn paved the way for Mary Anne and Wyndham to join this world. The result was that when Mary Anne announced her first large ball at Grosvenor Gate in July 1827, fashionable London answered her invitation. Wellington, who lived at nearby Apsley House, led the way, followed by the Duchess of Rutland and legions of hopeful debutantes. Mary Anne's old friend Lord Worcester – still useful, if dangerous – dragooned all the eligible young men of his acquaintance into attending.

Even by the lavish standards of the period, Mary Anne's party decorations were astonishing. Flowers wound through the staircase banisters, and the boudoirs were hung with white and pink muslin to give them a tented, Eastern appearance. Plants, muslin drapes, mirrors and lamps made the drawing rooms appear, according to Wellington, 'like a fairy land'. In the supper room Mary Anne contrived a show-stopping table decoration: a windmill, complete with turning sails, perched above a stream in which swam gold and silver fish. 'I was proud of this', she told John, 'because it was the only part of supper interfered with, having given the man cook the idia.' None of this was necessarily in the best of taste, but since Mary Anne made sure her guests were entertained and well fed, questions of taste were of little moment. The Duchess of Rutland planned to stay only briefly but enjoyed herself so much she sent her carriage away and waltzed with the other guests until daybreak. And the Duke of Wellington told Mary Anne that her ball was the best of the season. 'Are you not dazzled', she asked John, 'at your little Whizzy having receiv'd the noble Hero at her house.'[39] A few weeks later she was mentioned in the *Morning Post* as one of the distinguished visitors at a ball held by Lady Reith, one of only a few House of Commons wives to be so named.

~

In the summer of 1827 John wrote to Mary Anne from Mauritius to tell her that a major in his regiment intended to sell out and that his rank would therefore become available for purchase. The position cost £1,750. Wyndham refused to advance any portion of such a large sum without security. Mary Anne worked on him furiously, negotiating with her entire family in order to put the funds in place. In November 1827 she was able to write to John that she had succeeded, having secured a gift of £500 from her uncle James Viney and a loan from Wyndham for the remainder, guaranteed by written undertakings and mortgages from her uncle, her mother and Thomas Yate. John agreed to pay Wyndham regular interest and to save money from his salary to pay off the principal. Mary Anne wrote of the importance of meeting Wyndham's stipulations and was overjoyed when, in December 1827, John was gazetted major as a result of her efforts.

Mary Anne received a letter from John in the spring of 1828, telling of his gratitude for her efforts. Then he stopped communicating. He left letter after letter unanswered, made no attempt to pay Wyndham interest on his loan, and in May 1829 the Lewises learnt that he had dishonoured drafts issued through the army agents Cox and Greenwood. Wyndham was furious and Mary Anne distraught. 'I truly hope to keep the knowledge of these dishonoured bills from Mama as it would half kill her.'[40] After a year of silence she wrote again, attempting to convey her anguish. 'I cannot tell you how all this distresses me it appears so scampish & dishonourable for Gods sake my own dear Brother write & explain.'[41] In March 1830 she made a further attempt, having heard news of John's social activities in Mauritius from another source. 'Is it possible John you do not love me this idia sometimes makes my heart ready to break.'[42] When John did eventually write in the spring of 1830, he gave no explanation for either his silence or his debts.

John's ingratitude was incomprehensible to all those who knew him, but for Mary Anne the pain it caused was double-edged, since it made a mockery of the sacrifice she had made for him. Unbeknownst to anyone but James Viney and John, she had perpetrated a fraud, raising £500 for the majority herself by borrowing money and subsequently selling jewellery, clothes and lace, before funnelling the money through James Viney to make it appear a gift from him.* The Yateses and Wyndham had no idea of this, and Mary Anne lived in fear of Wyndham's anger should he discover the truth. 'Wynd would never forgive me did he ever know it.'[43] When John reneged on his promises, it implied she had risked the stability of her marriage for nothing. When he did write, it was only to tell her to stop nagging him about the debt.

Wyndham responded to John's behaviour by threatening to report him to the colonel of his regiment, sending Mary Anne into a panic and triggering yet more deceit. Writing in secret, she drafted an apologetic letter from John to Wyndham, promising faithfully to pay his debts without delay. She then put the money in place at Cox and Greenwood herself, selling more of her possessions in order to do so. Her strategy worked and Wyndham forgave John, at least temporarily. In 1831 Mary Anne learnt that her brother had

---

* Arriving at a contemporary figure for the equivalence or buying power of £500 is an inaccurate science, but the debt that Mary Anne took on for John would probably have been worth over £25,000 in today's money. Wyndham's income settled at around £10,000 and put him among the richest industrialists in the country. In *Pride and Prejudice*, Mr Bingley is able to maintain Netherfield and subsequently buy his own estate from an income of £5,000 a year, ten times the sum Mary Anne borrowed for John.

been spending his money on mistresses and possibly on an illegitimate child, which at least explained his behaviour even if it did not excuse it. And despite the lies she told Wyndham, and the debt she took on without his knowledge, John's affairs brought the Lewises closer together. Bereft of the security of her brother's love, Mary Anne took comfort from her husband. During John's long silence she described Wyndham as 'the dearest kindest of husbands', determined to show her loyalty to her spouse even as she deceived him.[44]

From a historical distance, John's hold over his sister appears mystifying, but he was the person she loved best in the world and her loyalty to him was unflinching. With no children of her own, an ageing parent who depended on her and a husband to whom she was only moderately attached, she was emotionally isolated, despite the burgeoning numbers of visitors in her drawing room. She filled her house with people and showered a succession of protégés with affection but had no one who could read her moods and for whom there was no need to perform a role. John failed to be that figure but she never gave up hope that he might one day become the idealised brother of her imagination.

∼

In the same letter in which she extolled Wyndham's virtues, Mary Anne also wrote that 'Nothing talk'd of here but the Catholic question'. In early 1829 Robert Peel reluctantly dropped his long-held opposition to Emancipation and allowed the measure to be put to the House of Commons. This was seen in some quarters as a blow to the Anglican establishment of Britain, and Mary Dawson, fearing that rioting mobs would target her house in revenge for her brother's apostasy, sent her children to stay at Grosvenor Gate. Once the law was passed, public attention turned with renewed force to the question of more wide-ranging political reform and to the need to abolish rotten parliamentary boroughs like Aldeburgh, where corruption was endemic and votes were bought rather than won. Wyndham was out of Parliament in 1829, having resigned as the MP for Aldeburgh when the collapse of pig iron hit his income and made it impossible for him to purchase enough votes to win re-election, but despite this experience he was instinctively anti-Reform. Both he and Mary Anne were exhausted by the strain placed on them by John's affairs, financial pressure and a combustible public mood. In August 1830 they left England for France on the first leg of a European tour planned to last between four and six months. Mary Anne saw Mont Blanc's glacier at Chamonix, narrowly escaped being robbed by Italian bandits, went to the opera and picture galleries, and skirted revolutions in Florence and Paris.

~

Disraeli also left England for Europe in 1830. He spent much of the period between 1828 and 1830 in a state of collapse, trapped in a depression triggered by the failure of *Vivian Grey* and the gulf he perceived to be opening between him and his more successful contemporaries. He retreated to Bradenham, a Queen Anne house near High Wycombe in Buckinghamshire on which Isaac had taken a long lease. The move to Bradenham ended the D'Israelis' long association with Bloomsbury and fostered instead a connection between the family and High Wycombe and its surrounding villages. Isaac and Maria took up permanent residence at Bradenham along with Sarah, and they offered the house as a refuge for their sons. Ralph and James immersed themselves in country pursuits and good living and Disraeli, surrounded by calm and quiet, began to write again, embarking on a second novel. *The Young Duke* was another silver-fork novel, a coming-of-age romance featuring young men and women of staggering fortune and elegance. It fulfilled the requirements of the evolving genre more successfully than had *Vivian Grey* and did so less acerbically. Scarred by his early experiences with the press and determined to make a success of his writing, Disraeli took the precaution of sending a draft of *The Young Duke* to a fellow author before circulating it for publication. Edward Lytton Bulwer and Disraeli began to correspond in the summer of 1829, exchanging books and polite compliments. Both were ambitious and literary and both had some experience of mixed critical reception, although Bulwer's press had been more extensive and positive than Disraeli's. Each modelled himself on Byron, affecting a pose of dandified disdain designed to make himself stand out from the crowd. Each found in the other an instinctively sympathetic figure.

Bulwer gave Disraeli the confidence to re-enter the literary world. He praised *Vivian Grey*, terming it a work of 'wonderful promise', but he also warned Disraeli against repeating the stylistic tricks that brought him critical opprobrium. 'You have attained in the Book more than the excellencies of Vivian Grey – but I do not think you have vigilantly enough avoided the faults.'[45] He also warned Disraeli that in getting details of clothing and fashion wrong he exposed himself to ridicule: valuable advice for a young man attempting to join a new tribe.

Disraeli finished *The Young Duke* and sold it to Colburn for £500, to be paid on publication. He then borrowed £500, adding to the mountain of debts that had accumulated in the aftermath of his mining speculations, and prepared to leave England. His chosen companion on this tour was William Meredith, Sarah D'Israeli's fiancé. Once again Isaac and Maria hoped that foreign travel would clear his head, aid his health, and allow him to fulfil his promise on his return. Once again Disraeli saw the Continent as a place to which he could escape. This time he planned to travel further afield, to the East, where he would reinvent himself as a new Byron and from where he would return refashioned, ready for a new political age. In June 1830 George IV died, the last link to the heady days of the Regency in which dandies flourished, Mary Anne married and Disraeli grew to maturity. In the same month Disraeli sailed from Falmouth to Gibraltar, and a month later Eleanor Yate wrote to John that the new King, William IV, was preparing to dissolve Parliament. 'What a bustle the different Elections will make throughout the Country.'[46]

CHAPTER THREE

Tittle-Tattle

ELEANOR PIGOTT

In 1823 Eleanor Pigott reached the end of her endurance and left her home, her child and her husband. From the moment she broke her wedding vows her brother barred her from his house and her sisters refused to be seen with her. She fled to Paris, where she took up residence with a French chevalier. For a while she was happy, surrounded by people who did not know her history. But the chevalier disappeared and she was left alone, deprived of his money and affection. She grew pale and thin, her French acquaintances fell away and the English in Paris refused to associate with her. Her former friends exchanged stories about the men she lived with and the low company she kept. After twenty years of exile, her sisters, freed by his death from the restraining influence of their brother, began to pay her occasional visits when they journeyed to France, and slowly she was readmitted to the outer reaches of her family circle. But she remained a marked woman, barred from the world into which she was born.

∾

Eleanor Pigott was Mary Anne's cousin, and Mary Anne was more sympathetic than many to her plight. 'I pity her with all my heart and soul', she told John. 'If she had had a kinder husband she would never have gone astray.'[1] On visits to France she made a point of meeting Eleanor in private and of bringing her books and other amusements, although the two women never appeared together in public. She reported news back to her family following these visits, keeping open a fragile channel of communication between Eleanor and her sisters. But she also knew that there were times

44

when it was important not to tell what one knew. 'Mrs Pigott is coming to England soon', she noted when rumours of Eleanor's infidelities filtered back from earlier European travels. 'They do not appear to know any thing of the reports about her, I took your advice & said nothing.'[2]

Mary Anne knew better than most that a careless word could prove a woman's undoing. As Wyndham grew distant, absorbed in his mines, gossip about her conduct threatened her carapace of social conformity, in which appearances at Court, grand parties and friendships with the right sort of people insulated her origins from scrutiny. Eleanor's story confirmed following one's heart to be a risky business and the pleasure to be gained from acting on passion as transient. For a woman in Mary Anne's position to keep a roof over her head she had to keep her reputation spotless and her marriage intact, no matter what the emotional costs.

~

The Lewises' European travels were cut short by the sudden death, in March 1831, of Mary Anne's stepfather Thomas Yate. They hurried home from Frankfurt to comfort her mother and to help her piece together a new life as a widow. In the same year Disraeli also returned unexpectedly to England, again as the result of a death. In January 1831 he was in Constantinople, to where he had travelled from Athens. He had temporarily parted company with his fellow traveller, Sarah's fiancé William Meredith, but had acquired two new companions: James Clay, a friend of his brother Ralph, and Clay's servant Giovanni Batista Falcieri, known as Tita. Tita was a more compelling character than his master and his story more glamorous. He was Byron's servant, originally his gondolier and then his major-domo, and had been with him at his death. He was a big, shaggy, bearded figure, whose looks and history exuded romance. Disraeli was captivated by him, by the very idea of acquaintance with a participant in Byron's story. He described him to Ralph: 'Byron died in his arms, and his mustachios touch the earth. Withal mild as a lamb, tho' he has two daggers always about his person.'[3]

From Constantinople Disraeli sailed in the company of Clay and Tita to Egypt and in Cairo was reunited with Meredith. While the two young men lingered in Cairo, planning the next stage of their adventure, Meredith fell ill with smallpox, dying on 19 July. Disraeli was left to break the news to the Merediths and his own family. 'READ THIS ALONE', he put at the top of his letter to Isaac. He knew that Meredith's death threatened to destroy Sarah, who had put off her wedding for years as Meredith established himself in the world and won the consent of his family to their marriage. Apart from the emotional blow of losing her fiancé, Sarah, now aged twenty-nine, also lost her best prospect of children and a home of her own. 'Our innocent lamb, our angel is stricken', wrote Disraeli to Isaac.[4] To Sarah herself he wrote in a different vein:

> Oh! my sister, in this hour of overwhelming affliction my thoughts are only for you. Alas! my beloved! if you are lost to me, where, where, am I to fly for refuge! I have no wife, I have no betrothed, nor since I have been better acquainted with my own mind and temper, and situation, have I sought them. Live then my heart's treasure for one, who has ever loved you with a surpassing love, and who would cheerfully have yielded his own existence to have saved you the bitterness of reading this. Yes! my beloved! be my genius, my solace, my companion, my joy! We will never part, and if I cannot be to you all of our lost friend, at least we will feel, that Life can never be a blank while illumined by the pure and perfect love of a Sister and a Brother![5]

Disraeli wrote this letter the day after Meredith's death, when his shock and grief were still raw. Its tenor is not as unusual as might first appear, dating as it does from an age when unmarried sisters frequently lived with and kept house for their bachelor brothers and when sibling love, like friendship between men, was expressed more intensely than is commonly now the case. Yet even given these caveats, Disraeli's letter is extraordinary. It proposes that he and Sarah should be as each other's spouse, albeit through a 'pure and perfect love'. It establishes Sarah as his muse ('my genius') as well as his companion and support. And it turns her tragedy into a meditation on his own emotional existence. Yet it is also calibrated to offer the most comfort and reassurance to a distraught woman. Stripped of its hyperbole, the letter's messages are simple. You are not alone. I am here. You are, and always will be, the most important person in my life.

Once Meredith was buried, Disraeli hastened to England, arriving in Falmouth in September. Just over a week later he was at Bradenham, face to face with his sister and the rest of his family. Apart from comforting Sarah he had one other important task: to convince Isaac that he should appoint Tita, who wanted work in England, as his servant and general factotum. When Tita arrived the following year, he was installed at Bradenham, where he became a figure of considerable importance. He was not always a straightforward employee, since he was given to taking holidays at short notice in order to meet fellow members of Byron's entourage, and was something of a bogeyman among the village boys at Bradenham, who on one occasion claimed to have been beaten by him and had him hauled before the magistrate. The Disraelis testified that he had never left the house and Sarah's account of the incident illustrates that he was more than a mere servant. 'You can imagine this is a very annoying affair', she told Disraeli, 'very disagreeable to Papa who hates to be bored, & we are also afraid may disgust Tita.'[6] Boring Isaac and disgusting Tita were both dangers to be taken seriously, since each could disrupt the calm of the household and Tita frequently required soothing when political developments raised his temper. But he made Bradenham a happier place and brought colour to the lives of his employers.

Despite his protestations of devotion to Sarah, Disraeli did not stay with her long. He returned from Bradenham to London, where he took lodgings in fashionable St James's and began the process of positioning himself as a person of significance, initiated into the mysteries of the East. *The Young Duke* had been published during his absence abroad and had received more favourable reviews than *Vivian Grey*. Now he turned to a third novel, *Contarini Fleming* (1832), more directly autobiographical than his previous work. Its subtitle was 'A Psychological Romance', and in the preface to the 1846 edition Disraeli described it as a portrait of 'the development and formation of the poetic character'. Contarini is a solitary figure but he also has an urge to join the public fray; to act as well as imagine. The novel asks whether one can be both poet and politician and suggests that the man of genius has a responsibility to take up both callings. Contarini wishes to pass his life 'in the study and the creation of the Beautiful' but recognises this may not be possible: 'Such is my desire; but whether it will be my career is, I feel, doubtful. My interest in the happiness of my race is too keen to permit me for a moment to be blind to the storms that lour on the horizon of society. Perchance also the political regeneration of the country to which I am devoted may not be distant, and in that great work I am resolved to participate.'[7]

In the years that followed the publication of *Contarini Fleming*, Disraeli, like Contarini, attempted to be a poetical politician, and a political poet. He published pamphlets and essays on the French Revolution of 1830 and the English constitution. He produced another novel (*Alroy*), a novella (*Iskander*) and a long poem grandly entitled *The Revolutionary Epick*, which he hoped would proclaim him to be the true inheritor of the Romantic mantle. The poem received little attention, but his voice nevertheless gradually began to be heard in the hubbub. Through force of will he made people look at him and made them listen to what he had to say. There were flirtations – with Ellen Meredith, sister of William, and Lady Charlotte Bertie, a brilliant young woman desperately unhappy at home – and an affair with Mrs Bolton, the wife of his doctor. His debts racked up and he became wary of bailiffs lurking in the shadows.

In 1834 he was able to boast to Sarah that 'I have had great success in society this year in every respect. I am as popular with the Dandies as I was hated by the second rate men. I make my way easily in the highest set, where there is no envy, malice etc., and where they like to admire and be amused.'[8] 'To admire and be amused': he was permitted to attend gatherings of 'the highest set' as a jester rather than one of the company. He was a curiosity, a social nonentity with a certain distinction that allowed him to chart a course usually reserved to those from more privileged backgrounds. He met Frances, Marchioness of Londonderry, a political hostess of reach and power who became a valued correspondent and the recipient of his most chivalrous letters, and he rekindled his friendship with Edward Lytton Bulwer, with whom he worked to personify disenchantment.

It was through Bulwer that Disraeli met Lady Blessington and Count D'Orsay, with whom he formed enduring friendships. Lady Blessington had been born Marguerite Gardiner in Ireland in 1789. Her first husband was an abusive drunk and she lived openly as the mistress of the man who rescued her from him. In 1818 she married Lord Blessington and the couple and their entourage spent much of the 1820s travelling abroad. The most important member of their caravan was Alfred, Count D'Orsay, a French exquisite. Lord Blessington married D'Orsay to his fifteen-year-old daughter Harriet in order to yoke him into his family and line of inheritance. Harriet was given no choice in the matter and D'Orsay promised not to assert his conjugal rights until she came of age. In fact he had no interest in doing so: he married Harriet in order to inherit Blessington's money and his interest was focused on Lady Blessington, not her stepdaughter. After Blessington's death in 1829, Lady Blessington and D'Orsay returned to London and settled eventually at Gore House in Kensington, with appearances maintained by D'Orsay officially having quarters next door.

Lady Blessington's past precluded the presence of respectable women in her drawing rooms. Her soirées were men-only affairs that attracted many a young writer, among them Bulwer and Charles Dickens. Her charm lay not just in the quality of her conversation but in the fact that she was herself a serious literary figure, the editor of various annuals and magazines, the author of novels and a memoir of Byron, whom she met in Genoa in 1823. A young American journalist, Nathaniel Parker Willis, attended Lady Blessington's salon in the 1830s and later published accounts of his experiences. His *Pencillings by the Way* included a portrait of Disraeli during this period. 'D'Israeli had arrived before me, and sat in the deep window, looking out upon Hyde Park, with the last rays of daylight reflected from the gorgeous gold flowers of a splendidly embroidered waistcoat', he wrote of one occasion that took place before Lady Blessington moved to Kensington. 'Patent leather pumps, a white stick, with a black cord and tassel, and a quantity of chains about his neck and pockets, served to make him, even in the dim light, rather a conspicuous object.' 'D'Israeli has one of the most remarkable faces I ever saw', he continued. 'He is lividly pale, and but for the energy of his action and the strength of his lungs, would seem a victim to consumption. His eye is black as Erebus, and has the most mocking and lying-in-wait sort of expression conceivable. His mouth is alive with a kind of working and impatient nervousness, and when he has burst forth, as he does constantly, with a particularly successful cataract of expression, it assumes a curl of triumphant scorn that would be worthy of a Mephistopheles.'[9]

~

The England to which Disraeli returned in 1831 was in the throes of the biggest upheaval since the Glorious Revolution of 1688. Eleanor Yate had predicted that the election of 1830 would produce a 'bustle' in the country, and she was right: for the first time in over a century, an election precipitated the fall of the government. Against a background of rural suffering, manufacturing riots and trouble in Ireland, the traditional Tory vote fell away. Wellington's administration was followed by a Whig coalition led by Lord Grey, a long-time proponent of political reform. For fifteen months Grey battled Parliament and the King to pass a Reform Bill, eventually succeeding in June 1832. The Reform Act did away with the most rotten parliamentary boroughs, went some way to redistributing seats according to population (thereby strengthening the representation of new industrial cities such as Liverpool and Manchester), and increased the size of the electorate by about 45 per cent.

The Reform Act did not turn Britain into a democracy. The post-Reform electorate accounted for less than 5 per cent of the population, and power still remained concentrated in the hands of a tiny minority. It did, however, represent the first step on the road towards universal suffrage and effectively enfranchised the male middle classes. For the first time shop-owners, tenant farmers and members of the professions were able to articulate their demands through the ballot box and became a constituency no political party could afford to ignore. The parliamentary battles over the Reform Act also opened up clear dividing lines between the Whigs and the Tories. The Act marked the end of aristocratic coalitions between landed grandees and hastened the evolution of two-party politics. It changed the political landscape and appeared to offer young men like Disraeli the opportunity to break through traditional party strongholds.

Both Disraeli and Bulwer stood for Parliament in the first post-Reform election in December 1832, when the new electorate responded to their enfranchisement by handing the Whigs a landslide victory. The House of Commons was the place where a young man could make a name for himself and where the disadvantages of birth, while still apparent, might be overcome through the acquisition of influence and support. In 1820 Mary Anne came to understand that politics might have a transformative social potential for those within its structures; twelve years later, Disraeli, who was twelve years younger than Mary Anne, experienced a similar awakening as he sought to make the transition from literary commentator to political actor. Bulwer was already in Parliament, having been first elected in April 1831, and he was repaid for his support for Reform with victory as an Independent in Lincoln. Disraeli stood as a Radical in High Wycombe but had little chance of success against the Whig incumbent Charles Grey, son of the Prime Minister. Despite the Byronic vision articulated in *Contarini Fleming* of the poet as a leader of men, a man with no allies had little chance of gaining a seat.

In order to join Bulwer in Parliament Disraeli needed not poetry but powerful friends. He acknowledged this in the election scenes of another novel, *A Year at Hartlebury* (1834), which he co-authored with Sarah.[10] *A Year at Hartlebury* is focused on a bruising country election, based on Disraeli's experiences at High Wycombe. On hustings day its candidates are heckled by the mob, their supporters make rash promises as they vie for votes and special constables club the heads of boys at random. Local men turn into polling pundits: there is 'nothing like an election', according to the authors, 'to make an impudent fellow of importance'.[11] On election night the singing of noisy wassailers rings round the town and the candidates' friends roam the streets 'to confirm the wavering, to re-animate the drooping, and to gain over the adverse'.[12] One side forces the others' supporters into carriages and sends them to London, so as to prevent them from exercising their vote.

Sarah and Disraeli published *A Year at Hartlebury* under pseudonyms and in a brief preface written by Sarah announced themselves as a married couple. 'Our honeymoon being over, we have amused ourselves during the autumn by writing a novel. All we hope is that the Public will deem our literary union as felicitous as we find our personal one.' Sarah was the driving force behind *A Year at Hartlebury*. Although it was originally envisaged as a joint project, she wrote most of the narrative sections and structured the plot, while Disraeli provided only the political scenes. At the end she killed off the character based on Disraeli, having already undermined his morals and character, so that the novel models him as husband, politician and, eventually, dead villain. Sarah watched the 1832 election from the sidelines, but in *A Year at Hartlebury* she had a small measure of revenge.

Wyndham Lewis also stood for election in 1832, this time for the Tories in the urban constituency of Maidstone. Mary Anne was confident of victory but Wyndham was more sceptical, noting the extent of anti-Tory sentiment among the electorate. In the event he was defeated by only ten votes, a respectable result for a known anti-Reformer, and he secured his position as the presumptive Tory candidate for the seat. 'Not one of our Tory friends have been successful at their Elections', Mary Anne told John. 'There are only about 100 Tories returned out of 600 Members & those only by money or the most overpowering family influence some people think that all this will end in our having a Republic.'[13]

After the diversion of electioneering, the rhythm of Mary Anne's days continued as before. She appeared at Court and at balls, held lavish parties at Grosvenor Gate, gossiped with Rosina Lytton Bulwer and flirted with men who paid her more attention than her husband. She dabbled in match-making, introducing Wyndham's business partner John Guest to Lady Charlotte Bertie. Lady Charlotte had briefly been the focus of Disraeli's romantic attention, one of a number of women to figure in his story in the 1830s as putative brides. John Guest was twenty-seven years older than Lady Charlotte and, as a dissenter with a background in trade, emphatically not of her world. But the match turned out to be an excellent one and Mary Anne, writing amidst expanses of empty days and long evenings, boasted of her matchmaking triumph to John. 'My friends here appear diverted at my making Mr Guest marry whom I pleased and congratulate me on the success of my theatrics.'[14]

~

Disraeli and Mary Anne met for the first time on 1 April 1832, at a party held by Bulwer and Rosina. They did so at Mary Anne's instigation. 'I was introduced "by particular desire" to Mrs Wyndham Lewis', Disraeli told Sarah. 'A pretty little woman, a flirt and a rattle; indeed gifted with a volubility I should think unequalled, and of which I can convey no idea. She told me that she liked silent, melancholy men. I answered that I had no doubt of it.'[15] Sarah, who knew Mary Anne only by repute, retorted, 'for silent read stupid'.[16]

That year, separate friendships with Bulwer and Rosina brought Disraeli and Mary Anne into adjoining circles. After their first meeting in April, he began to figure occasionally on her guest lists and she in his correspondence. Two days after the Bulwers' party, Disraeli wrote Mary Anne a polite note, expressing the wish that '*la belle du monde* is quite well this morn!' signed as Walter Scott's courtly knight, 'Raymond de Toulouse'. Mary Anne later annotated the note as 'the first . . . I ever received from dear Dizzy'.[17]

In January 1833 Disraeli and Mary Anne joined the Bulwers in a private box at Covent Garden. In March that year he attended 'a large and agreeable dinner party at the Wyndham Lewe's'.[18] Between April and June he was present at three more of Mary Anne's parties, one a breakfast 'when magnificent plate is to be presented from Maidstone to our host the defeated Conservative', one a 'large soireé' and one 'a most sumptuous dejeuner, which was attended by the very best set'.[19] In August 1833 Sarah wrote to Disraeli to ask him to send her some invitations so she could relive his social life at second hand. Influenza had recently swept through London, prompting him to the following reply: 'I send you all the invitations I co[ul]d scrape up, but I fear there are few anterior to the Influenza when Mrs Lewis made a great burning.'[20] By this point Mary Anne was taking a proprietorial interest in Disraeli, confiscating his letters in order to protect him from contaminating germs. Sarah, immured in the country with her parents, had to be content with the scraps that escaped Mary Anne's fire.

On 16 October 1834 the Palace of Westminster went up in flames. Its medieval buildings burnt quickly and crowds gathered to witness the most spectacular inferno in living memory, the painter J.M.W. Turner among them. Mary Anne was briefly absent from London at the time, to her disappointment. 'It must have been a terrifying <u>beautiful</u> sight.'[21] As plans were laid for the Houses of Parliament to rise again in neo-Gothic splendour, the political balance shifted once more, this time back to the Tories. After months of infighting in the Whig Cabinet following the resignation of Grey as Prime Minister, William IV sent for Wellington and asked him to form a government. Wellington declined, saying that Peel was now the de facto Tory leader, and Peel rushed back from holiday in Italy to take up the Premiership.

Disraeli redoubled his fight for a place in the structures of power. Between

1832 and 1835 he made repeated attempts to get into Parliament, battling vested interests and prejudice along the way. He tried to gain a footing in London clubland, but was blackballed by the Travellers and the Athenaeum before being admitted to the newly formed Tory Carlton Club. He published pamphlets and letters that articulated his political shift from Radical to Tory and embroiled himself in a vicious spat with the Irish leader Daniel O'Connell. O'Connell heard a garbled version of a story in which Disraeli appeared to attack him and responded in a diatribe subsequently published in the newspapers. In conclusion he gave voice to the anti-Semitism threaded through Disraeli's story. 'His name shows that he is of Jewish origin . . . He has just the qualities of the impenitent thief on the Cross, and I verily believe, if Mr Disraeli's family herald were to be examined, and his genealogy traced, the same personage would be discovered to be the heir at law of the exalted individual to whom I allude.'[22]

Disraeli challenged O'Connell to a duel when he read this attack, and then, on learning O'Connell had sworn never to fight another duel after killing a previous opponent, reissued the challenge to his son. Both men were arrested by the police before the duel could take place and bound over to keep the peace, but the affair still confirmed Disraeli as a man not afraid to confront his opponents. By the time of O'Connell's attack he had also acquired one powerful supporter who helped limit the consequences of the affair. His new ally was Lord Lyndhurst, the former Tory Lord Chancellor. Lyndhurst recognised the quality of Disraeli's intellect and made use of him, sending him to conduct party business on his behalf. Disraeli took no formal payment for the work he did for Lyndhurst but received instead an education in the workings of the Tory Party as well as connections to its most influential figures. In the election of 1835, thanks to Lyndhurst, he stood for the first time as a Tory. Again he was defeated but he nevertheless joined the list of men thought suitable for selection as Tory candidates in winnable seats.

The 1835 election promised a further recovery for the Tory Party, now regrouping under Peel's leadership after the bloodbath of the Reform Act. 'You have no idia John how excited a contested Election is', wrote Mary Anne after Wyndham had agreed to stand again at Maidstone. 'The Whigs are in complete disgrace – you must be a tory or radical the change in political feeling in our favour is quite extraordinary, the people find out they get nothing by reform.'²³ Mary Anne had always been an enthusiastic canvasser but in 1835 she consolidated her role as campaign impresario. She understood instinctively that elections were about generating excitement and emotion and that in a post-Reform environment spirit and style mattered as much as who one knew. She worked tirelessly to make herself and Wyndham popular in the town so that by election day there was a groundswell of public support. Wyndham was escorted to the hustings by over a hundred townsmen and Mary Anne, appearing at the balcony of her hotel to wave him off, was also cheered by the crowd. When victory was announced, Wyndham was taken in procession to the town hall, where he was met by Mary Anne, fetched by another group of jubilant supporters. Purple was Wyndham's campaign colour and Mary Anne adorned herself with a purple cap, shawl and bows. At the evening celebrations she and Wyndham danced in the New Year, and were, she told John, 'the hero & heroine of the even'g'. As they left Maidstone the next day, guns saluted them and the townsfolk unhitched their horses so local men could pull their carriage past streets of crowd-filled windows from which people shouted and waved purple flags.

One person made a serious attempt to thwart Wyndham's victory. In Dublin a man called Westerman May published a poem entitled 'Lewisiana', which excoriated Wyndham and Mary Anne as well as other members of the Lewis family. Westerman May was Wyndham's son-in-law, the husband of his illegitimate daughter Frances. The gist of his attack was that Wyndham had an illegitimate son as well as a daughter, and that in order to hide his son from his avaricious wife he forced him to toil as a carpenter. He accused Wyndham of making a secret Roman Catholic marriage (like the Prince Regent) and so of committing bigamy with Mary Anne. He presented him as a pathetic shadow of a man, corrupt, weak and immoral. But in his poem, dedicated to the electors of Maidstone, he reserved most of his vitriol for Mary Anne, caricaturing her as a harridan who fornicated with a relative before her marriage and with a succession of men after it. He accused her of 'acts replete with foul disgrace' and described her having sex with a passing stranger in an anteroom at a ball. The poem, written in mock-heroic stanzas, culminated in a discussion of Mary Anne's childlessness:

In fact, 'twas easy to discover,
His wife could never be a mother!
The *real* cause I cannot state,
Because 'twould be indelicate,
It is not altogether right
To call her an HEMAPHRODITE –
Although to truth I'm nearer coming,
In stating 'that she's *not a woman:*'
To sex she is a mere pretender,
A monster of the neuter gender![24]

It would be easy to dismiss such outlandish cruelty as the ravings of an unstable individual and it is doubtful whether the pamphlet circulated widely in Maidstone. Yet Westerman May's animus towards Mary Anne merits some attention. He held her responsible for Wyndham's lack of interest in his daughter, claiming she separated father and child and then banned all communication between them. He was sufficiently familiar with the Lewis family to know that Catherine and Mary Williams appeared in society under Mary Anne's aegis and to castigate them for so doing. He despised Wyndham and hated Mary Anne enough to publish gynaecological slanders about her and to insinuate elsewhere that she carried venereal diseases. May's pamphlet survives among Mary Anne's papers so it seems likely he sent it to her and that she must have read it and decided to keep it. No mention of the poem appeared in the Maidstone press and Wyndham's victory in 1835 was commanding, so May did not have the political impact for which he hoped. Mary Anne never referred in any of her letters to May or his poem so we have to deduce its emotional impact from the uncharacteristic silence of a woman whose correspondence touched on almost every other aspect of her life.

One evening in February 1836 Rosina Lytton Bulwer burst into her husband's chambers in Albany to find dinner for two laid on the table, a shawl on the sofa and the figure of a strange woman flitting into the bedroom. She threw the woman out and raged at Bulwer, attracting the attention of the neighbours, before fleeing to Mary Anne for comfort. She stayed at Grosvenor

Gate as her marriage ended, and in public Mary Anne was loud in her support. To John she described Rosina as 'a perfect wife . . . (<u>except in temper</u>)'. Rosina asked Wyndham to act as her trustee but he refused, according to Mary Anne because 'he does not like any thing but peace & quietness'.[25]

For two years after their wedding in 1827 Rosina and Bulwer appeared happy in each other's company, mounting lavish entertainments and living beyond their means. They had two children and when apart exchanged letters written in their own brand of baby talk. But from 1829 Bulwer frequently made excuses to be absent from his family and Rosina dined almost daily with Mary Anne rather than sit at home alone. When they were together the Bulwers quarrelled, and by 1834 quarrels had transmuted into violence. Contemporary reports of their outbursts set husbandly abuse against drunken wifely vitriol: Bulwer hit and kicked his wife, threatened her with a knife and on one occasion bit her cheek so badly the blood flowed freely.

Rosina was Mary Anne's closest friend and won her support even while Mary Anne judiciously reported to John that there was blame on both sides. Rosina was not an easy friend: she was quick to take offence and her moods and whims were unpredictable. In letters written during the period of their friendship she accused Mary Anne of 'irritability of temper' and of saying things 'both coarse, and ill bred'.[26] When Mary Anne borrowed a book, Rosina wrote in a panic to reclaim it before Bulwer discovered its absence, despite having authorised the loan. She described Bulwer repeatedly to Mary Anne as 'your Edward', introducing a note of suspicion about her friend's allegiances. Rosina never believed anyone to be indisputably on her side and she needled and pushed her friends in order to test their loyalty. In December 1835 Mary Anne copied a character sketch of herself by Rosina; its emphasis on her good fortune suggests that Rosina struggled to accept the disparity in their circumstances. 'When I think dear ——— really loves me – tho I have reservations – thought she was too happy – was too well off – as far as this world goes – to be capable of paying the tax of genuine friendship . . . her faults she has borrowed from others – but her youngness of feeling – and <u>kindness</u> of disposition – are her own – and they must have been of the nature of the ash – to have gone unscratched – thro the fiery ordeal of prosperity.'[27]

Rosina's example, like that of Eleanor Pigott, illustrated the dangers for a woman of her marriage failing. The events of 1834–6 triggered a war between Rosina and Bulwer that blighted the lives of both and in which Rosina had to defend herself from the might of the establishment ranged against her. She was separated from her children and prevented from being with her daughter Emily at her death. She was not an affectionate mother and for years she, like Bulwer, used the children as a weapon, but the howl of rage with which she accused Bulwer of murdering Emily through wilful neglect was genuine. Her ire was focused not just on Bulwer but on Disraeli, with whom she claimed Bulwer committed acts of sodomy. In 1857, when her campaign against Bulwer escalated, she recalled an incident that took place in 1831, just after Disraeli's return to England: 'I also recollected how some years before, the loathsome monster had (the first day his confrère Acrobat Disraeli returned from the East and came in – just as we were going to Dinner) dared to pollute my ears – when I asked him when he came up at three in the morning what had kept him so long below? by saying "By Jove! Dizzy has been making me wild to go to the East & & & and he says – one never would look at a woman again."'[28]

The precise nature of Disraeli's relationship with Bulwer has been the subject of much debate. Until the late twentieth century biographers dismissed or ignored the rumours of sodomy; more recently William Kuhn has written at length of his conviction that Rosina's accusations were founded in fact.[29] When Rosina circulated her allegations in 1858, Disraeli responded by reminding Bulwer of the need to pay her allowance, which has been read by some as a covert instruction that she should be bought off,[30] and both men went to considerable efforts to recover letters she held. Byron described the Turkish bath as 'that marble paradise of sherbet and sodomy',[31] and it is quite possible that Disraeli, like Byron before him, had sex with men during his Eastern travels. In many ways, though, the question of whether he and Bulwer had a sexual relationship is anachronistic, since it relates to a period when male sexuality was less rigorously categorised than it is now; when the figure of the dandy licensed a certain ambiguity and ardent friendships between men were common. Throughout his life Disraeli was attracted to young men and older women, and Bulwer was among the friends with whom he identified most closely. Rosina – dismissed at the time as mad, bad, and dangerous to know – may well have had reason to perceive him as yet another threat to her marriage and security.

~

In letters to John, Mary Anne contrasted her fortunes with Rosina's, highlighting the stability of her own marriage. In April 1834 she reported, in a detail calculated to embarrass her brother, that 'No married people go on better than we do Wyd still the <u>lover</u>.'[32] It mattered to her that John should think she was happy and thus protected by an attentive husband from his failures and betrayals. But by the mid 1830s Mary Anne was an isolated figure. Rosina figured so largely in her life partly because she had few other female friends, especially after her neighbour Mary Dawson followed her husband to a government apartment in Whitehall. That she felt this lack is suggested by the reappearance in her circle of the Bennett sisters, with whom she began once again to exchange visits. To John she wrote of Ethel's unhappiness with Lord Charles Churchill and of rumours, printed in the press, that Ethel's child was not Lord Charles's. Lucy Bennett she announced to have at last found a husband: an illegitimate younger son with no money. The couple were unable to afford a house so lived with Mr Bennett at Pythouse, waiting for his death to give them freedom and a space of their own. Anna Bennett had no husband but instead acquired new religious fervour, which, Mary Anne told John, made her behaviour so odd that the prospect of her marriage seemed more remote than ever. Later Anna gave up religion and became, in Mary Anne's words, a 'regular <u>she-rascal</u>'.[33] Meanwhile Uncle Viney undressed before a maid in a provincial hotel and asked her to cut off his head. He was put under the care of doctors, who gave no hope of his recovery. Mary Anne believed him to have been driven to madness by debt and was determined to protect her mother from any knowledge of his fate. She and Wyndham found a keeper for him, a woman named Mrs Shaw, and then tried to get rid of her when they discovered she kept her patient tied down. Before they could replace her, James Viney died, and for years thereafter Mary Anne received letters from individuals claiming to be his illegitimate children or to have been duped out of money by him.

Insanity, illegitimacy, religious mania: none were phenomena with which Mary Anne could publicly be associated, and she told John about them all.

Gossip about mutual acquaintances was one of the ways she sustained a relationship with her absent brother as, over the years of separation, stories of wayward relations gave her something to say and, in the contrast they offered, bolstered the presentation of her own security. Yet while she deployed gossip to frame her own circumstances, she simultaneously made herself vulnerable to it, despite the warning offered by the case of her cousin Eleanor.

Lady Charlotte Guest held a dinner party in 1834 at which Mary Anne told 'a shocking story' and made her hostess furious. 'All the Mammas looked grave and the young ladies shocked, and I was red with anger that such a thing should have happened in my house.'[34] Meanwhile Mary Anne occupied herself laying bets against the chances of a foreign prince winning her heart and in mocking the 'fools . . . [who] chuse to fall in love with me'. One such fool wrote that without her his 'remaining moments in life' promised to be 'gloomy & comfortless'; another, who signed himself only 'B', that he wished her 'happiness, notwithstanding of your cruelty'. B's peroration was desolate: 'if you don't hear from me, you could say: the person adored me 13 months, is no more'.[35] 'Wyd as usual my confident', she emphasised to John.[36] Yet she hated women, she confessed elsewhere, and was surrounded by 'envy & jealousy'.[37]

～

The philosopher William Godwin met Mary Anne in 1834 at a dinner given by his daughter, Mary Shelley. His diary entry for 25 August, written in his usual elliptical style, read 'Dine at MWS's; adv Mrs Wyndham Lewis and George Beauclerk.'[38] George Beauclerk was a friend of Mary Shelley and a near neighbour of Mary Anne, who was eleven years his senior. He had a reputation as a fortune-hunter but thought of himself as a Romantic figure, another latter-day Byron. Writing to Mary Shelley, he outlined the similarities between himself and the poet: 'The same ardent feeling The same secluded retiring habits . . . The same invincible love of independence and scorn for slavery and meanness and the same serious and almost mordant cast of mind.'[39] After 1834 he and Mary Anne were frequently spotted in one another's company. Their friends believed them to be having an affair.

George Beauclerk always denied that his relationship with Mary Anne was a sexual one, although at times his denials were equivocal. Whether or not they slept together is ultimately less relevant than the fact that Beauclerk represented Mary Anne's most emotionally significant attachment since her marriage. Their connection lasted months, possibly years, and was quite different from her dalliances with gentlemen in London ballrooms. Beauclerk accompanied Mary Anne in the evenings when the nature of the company permitted him to do so, and was at her side whenever possible. It was he, for example, who took her to dine with Mary Shelley, a woman whose history precluded wide social acceptance. Throughout the period of their relationship he made use of the proximity of Upper Grosvenor Street to slip in and out of Grosvenor Gate unobserved.

The main sources for Mary Anne's liaison with George Beauclerk are drafts of letters he wrote to her after the relationship ended, which she retrieved with the help of his brother Charles, who was her ally in the aftermath of the affair and who appears to have chosen to adopt the most charitable reading of her behaviour. Most unusually for a woman who hoarded every scrap of paper, she did not keep the original letters she received from Beauclerk, presumably because the risk of them being found was too high. Wyndham exercised his right to read his wife's letters, as the poste restante system with John illustrated, and Eleanor Pigott's bleak Parisian exile stood as a warning of the fate a woman faced if her marriage collapsed. When Charles Beauclerk returned the drafts, he reassured Mary Anne that 'they entirely remove from your intimacy with my Brother all grounds for any ill natured scandal that the world may have cast upon it', and he also paid her a backhanded compliment: 'they prove you a most good-natured person and not half a quarter so vain a one as the world takes you to be, otherwise you could not have put up goodnaturedly for so long with such very uncomplimentary epistles'.[40] Charles Beauclerk favoured gallantry over truth when he pronounced the draft letters to be proof of Mary Anne's innocence. She remembered enough of their contents to want to recover them, her sense of their importance greater than her sense of caution. When fear of discovery was over, she marked the packet containing the drafts 'Mr Beauclerk to be kept'. George Beauclerk was a singular actor in her drama and her urge to curate and catalogue all parts of her story overrode her desire to erase the traces of infidelity.

Beauclerk's letters suggest theirs was a tempestuous partnership. 'I never will be the slave of the touchiest female on Earth', he wrote in the first draft of the sequence. 'There is no extent to which my intimacy with any woman ever caused me, that gave her the right to Tyrannise over me.' Later in the same document he informed her he had decided against visiting her, 'for when I do go to see people I like to find them as all hosts & hostesses should be if they let in Visitors – in a good humour'. He continually berated her for the company she kept, warning that the world was ready to make fun of her house and reputation and that while riches would bring her admirers, they would not earn her friends. 'You defy the Opinion of the world which no woman can do without one day suffering from it.' Elsewhere he raged at the damage her reputation did to his own standing. 'I told you the Plain truth when I asserted that my intimacy with you had, in many instances, been the cause of my not visiting at houses where I used to visit and who don't visit you.' He recognised that his lectures were hardly those of the lover, and in a moment of prescience foretold Mary Anne a future without him, 'with a man more ardent in his imagination less addicted to tell you your faults'.

Beauclerk skirted around the precise nature of his relationship with Mary Anne, working through a series of characterisations designed to prove its virtue. Early on he claimed that they never 'passed the boundary of matrimonial rights' and later argued that he had a right to limit her friendships with other men, since 'I am far too Proud to be coupled up with such characters as your admirers.' But in later drafts he invoked his concern for Wyndham as proof that they should continue to meet – 'I highly respect your husband and I cannot bear that he should see your inconstancy nor fancy mine in this suddenly giving up our acquaintance' – and noted that the world thought of him as her 'Cavalier Servante'. He recalled his decision to abandon 'all idea of ever going beyond Platonism' when he first met Mary Anne, but also how that decision was then overturned as she cast her spell over him. He evoked memories of thrice-weekly visits, each an hour in length, which had to be conducted in secrecy and difficulty, 'your door . . . facing, as it does, the most common egress and ingress to the Park'.[41]

Writing long after their friendship ended, Rosina Lytton Bulwer described how Mary Anne would show her Beauclerk's letters and laugh over them. To another correspondent Rosina explained that her low opinion of Beauclerk sprang 'from the toadying and violent love letters he used to write to Mrs Disraeli during the life of her first Husband some times two a day! although he saw her every day! – hoping no doubt thereby to step into Wyndham Lewis's shoes when he died'.[42] She even inserted a reference to the correspondence in her novel *Very Successful*, also written in the 1850s. All Rosina's novels took aim at Bulwer; in *Very Successful* she also attacked Disraeli (who appears as 'Mr Jericho Jabber') and Mary Anne. The novel features a rogue called Gorge Beaucherche and relates how 'one of the many strings to his bow (a *very* long one it was) had been Mrs Jericho Jabber during the lifetime of her first husband, when she very foolishly, and not very honourably, used to shew and laugh over his voluminous diurnal epistles'.[43]

Rosina was not a reliable witness since she declared both Mary Anne and Beauclerk her enemies long before she mocked them in public. But she was right that Beauclerk had his eye on Wyndham's money and one reason he harangued Mary Anne was that he believed gossip about their relationship harmed his hunt for a rich wife. 'My circumstances are such that unite myself I infallibly must to Some one with money or Power.' Writing to Mary Shelley of his many disappointments, he attributed his lack of success to the 'Aristocratick chain which binds down all intellects . . . in a Country where Money and influence are the Great friends of fame'.[44] Rosina's anecdotes also support the supposition that Mary Anne did not take Beauclerk's criticism of her conduct seriously. But she was nevertheless attracted by his romance and passion. Beauclerk challenged an enemy to a duel in the early 1830s, an affair about which Mary Anne took Bulwer's advice, and his letters depict a man who felt deeply and shared his emotions with the world. He offered Mary Anne excitement, the chance to be part of a drama, and she seized both with outstretched hands.

~

Two days after Mary Anne dined with Godwin and Mary Shelley, Disraeli wrote to Lady Blessington. 'As you are learned in Byron do you happen to know who was the mother of Allegra?'[45] Allegra's mother – and, briefly, Byron's mistress – was Claire Clairmont, Mary Shelley's stepsister. The stories of the second generation of Romantic writers exerted a fascination for men in precarious positions like Disraeli and Beauclerk, because they were stories in which talent cut through prejudice. Shelley's poetry was still a minority taste in the 1830s, although it was beginning to be discovered by figures such as Browning and Tennyson, but *Frankenstein* was widely read and Mary Shelley was a compelling figure for men and women attempting to live according to the dictates of their hearts. Her story, like those of Byron and Shelley, suggested ways that one might shape one's relationships and hinted at the adventure possible in rejecting convention. Mary Shelley's attempts to rehabilitate her reputation ensured that by the 1830s she was no longer so scandalous a figure as to prevent women like Mary Anne, who pushed against norms of social acceptability, from associating with her. For Disraeli, meanwhile, the Romantics offered an example of an intellectual as well as an emotional mode of being, in which one's private life coloured one's politics and public persona. Questions informed by a Romantic elision of public and private, politics and poetry and passion and power all fed into his first great love affair, with Henrietta Sykes.

Henrietta was the wife of Sir Francis Sykes, a baronet with a substantial income. She lived on Upper Grosvenor Street like George Beauclerk, just along the road from Grosvenor Gate. She and Disraeli met in April 1832 and were unashamed in their passion for each other. Sir Francis was away, travelling in Europe for his health, and in any case had his own mistress, Mrs Bolton, a former lover of Disraeli's. Sykes knew of Disraeli's relationship with his wife and permitted him to live in his house during his absences. Upper Grosvenor Street became Disraeli's base, and he and Henrietta appeared everywhere together, including at Mary Anne's parties. He took her to visit his family at Bradenham, throwing Sarah into a state of confusion. How many servants would Henrietta bring? How on earth were they to entertain her? 'I am so afraid that it will rain & that Lady Sykes will die of ennui, for how can we amuse her of an evening as it is, & the long mornings too. She will hate us.'[46] Henrietta took Disraeli, accompanied by Sir Francis and Mrs Bolton in an uncomfortable *ménage à quatre*, to Sir Francis's house in Southend. She introduced him to Lord Lyndhurst, with whom she was also rumoured to have had an affair.

Disraeli's letters to Henrietta have been lost, almost certainly destroyed by cautious executors anxious to protect his name. The sources for what happened are the fragmentary diary he kept between 1833 and 1837, and

Henrietta's letters to him. These reveal their affair to have been physical, passionate and couched in terms of high romance. 'Think of the happy ten minutes on the Sopha', she reminded him after one parting. 'How delicious would be the wandering of Henrietta & himself, thro' the friendly domain, and the happiness of returning to the peaceful Cot, & reposing in each other's arms . . . most idolized, I love you, adore you, worship you with fond idolatory & the blood gushes in torrents when I tell you so.'[47] In a letter of December 1833 she explicitly figured herself as a actor in a drama, mourning separation from her lover. 'I went into your room today, arranged your wardrobe, kissed the Bed, swallowed my tears & behaved as a heroine.'[48]

Like Mary Anne, Henrietta was born in 1792 and was thus twelve years older than Disraeli. At times she adopted a maternal demeanour in her letters, signing herself 'your Mother'. The affair also offered an instance of a private connection leading to professional advancement, as Henrietta effected the crucial introduction to Lord Lyndhurst. It allowed Disraeli to perform a grand romantic narrative, to himself and to the world that witnessed their love. 'One incident has made this year the happiest of my life', he wrote in his diary for 1833. But despite his professed happiness, he was sceptical about the permanence of his passion. 'How long will these feelings last?' he asked. 'They have stood a great test, and now absence, perhaps the most fatal of all.'[49]

In the end it was not absence but the presence of another man that brought the episode to a close. Henrietta sat for her portrait with the painter Daniel Maclise and embarked on a relationship with him. Disraeli discovered her betrayal, there was a bitter argument, and he took refuge at the Carlton Club. Bulwer had the misfortune to meet him there and made a tactless remark about Henrietta, prompting another dispute. Later Disraeli wrote to apologise, explaining that he had 'fled to a club for solace and then, from what I heard, it seemed to me that all the barriers of my life were simultaneously failing, and that not only Love was vanishing but Friendship also'.[50]

During the peak of his passion for Henrietta, Disraeli had begun a novel about his feelings; now he finished it in a different vein. *Henrietta Temple* tells the story of Ferdinand Armine, a Catholic aristocrat who falls in love with Henrietta Temple despite being engaged to his cousin Katherine. The novel relates the heady early days and bitter end of Disraeli's romance, drawing heavily on his correspondence with Henrietta. When Sarah edited her brother's works for reissue in the 1850s, she cut some of *Henrietta Temple*'s more explicitly amorous exchanges, but the first edition, published in 1837, gives a vivid picture of how Disraeli experienced his emotions and how they shaped his perception of himself. 'All the troubles of the world were folly here; this was fairy-land', he wrote in a description of being in the same room as his heart's desire. Henrietta transforms Ferdinand into a 'knight who had fallen from a gloomy globe upon some starry region flashing with perennial lustre'.[51] Elsewhere he composed meditations on love that suggest he was as entranced by the idea of passion as by its actuality:

What a mystery is Love! All the necessities and habits of our life sink before it. Food and sleep, that seem to divide our being, as day and night divide Time, lose all their influence over the lover. He is, indeed a spiritualised being, fit only to live upon ambrosia, and slumber in an imaginary paradise. The cares of the world do not touch him; its most stirring events are to him but the dusty incidents of by-gone annals. All the fortunes of the world without his mistress is misery; and with her all its mischances a transient dream. Revolutions, earthquakes, the change of governments, the fall of empires, are to him but childish games, distasteful to a manly spirit.[52]

In this instance, *Henrietta Temple* presents a fantasy of love that bears little resemblance to the reality of Disraeli's story, despite its autobiographical basis. The period of his affair with Henrietta Sykes coincided with the period of his political awakening, when he stood for Parliament, published political pamphlets and, through the agency of Henrietta herself, became Lord Lyndhurst's chief aide. Ferdinand responds to his emotions intuitively, allowing his actions to be dictated by passion. Disraeli was neither cold nor calculating, and when he offered love it was complete and all-encompassing, but he nevertheless wooed in a manner that was strategic as well as passionate, always assessing the political and intellectual implications of affairs of the heart. In *Henrietta Temple* he explored responses to love: both his own and those of an ideal figure. He experimented with ways of articulating passion, with how to characterise oneself as an emotional entity. Completing the novel in the aftermath of his break with Henrietta, he used fiction to explore how other people mould and change you. In so doing he constructed a myth of himself as not merely a Byronic dandy but a Romantic hero who loved, as Claire Clairmont did her daughter, 'with a passion that almost destroys my being'.[53]

~

Disraeli parted from Henrietta in mid December and retreated to Bradenham for Christmas. 'You must not bring any one down with you', Sarah warned, 'as you will spoil Tita's holiday.'[54] Sarah did not know the affair was at an end but was weary of juggling the household to accommodate Henrietta and her train of children, pug dogs and servants, and of having her brother's happiness flaunted before her. Earlier in the year a local man who wanted to marry her died and Isaac wrote to Disraeli of the loss of 'a possible contingency of happiness in store for our Angel – her last and secret hope'.[55] Sarah was thirty-four in 1836 and knew she would never marry. Disraeli returned from the East promising to be everything to her but had instead discovered politics, powerful friends and women. He was bad company that Christmas, maudlin and bitter, but at least he was alone. Sarah no longer called him 'Ben', the name bestowed by his parents, but 'Dizzy', the name he made for himself.[56]

Writing to her beloved brother at the end of 1836, Mary Anne boasted, 'I have as many lovers admirers & friends as usual.' Yet, she warned John, 'you will see us all looking older'.[57] She was forty-four that Christmas, Wyndham was fifty-nine: 'how much you will have to see & hear when you first come to England'. 'Keep thyself single until we meet', she ordered. 'I will get thee a wife, who shall be the joy of thy life.'[58]

CHAPTER FOUR

Fairy Story

MRS KENT

In 1833 the peace of Bradenham was disturbed by passion below stairs. The villain of the story was the lady's maid Mrs Kent, who won Tita's heart and then abused his devotion. 'Kent', as she was known, already had a husband from whom she was estranged, and a son (or a daughter) on whose behalf she planned to entrap Tita into paternal care. To this end she threw herself at him and did her best to persuade him that together they should leave the family's employment. The D'Israelis rallied round to protect their charge, an innocent giant apparently quite unable to defend himself against the wiles of women. They took him to London, hoping to distract him with a holiday and sightseeing, and dismissed another servant who dared to taunt him. Kent, faced with insuperable opposition from her employers and separated by them from the object of her affections, announced her intention of leaving Bradenham for good. Its inhabitants breathed a collective sigh of relief, and Tita was saved.

~

This was the version of the story that Sarah told Disraeli, in a letter written to prepare him for the arrival in London of Tita, Isaac and Maria. To leave Bradenham with Kent 'would be his ruin', she insisted. 'Besides we want him to stay.'[1] When Kent handed in her resignation, Sarah was dismissive of her motivation: 'Of course to be in town with him.' No one had any interest in Kent's version of events or in her future as a single woman with a dependent child and no reference. History as related by the D'Israeli family cannot confirm the sex of Kent's child, or where that child lived while its mother slept in servants' quarters at Bradenham. The D'Israelis were generous, liberal employers, more interested than many of their contemporaries in the welfare of their staff, but there was no place in their household for an adventuress determined upon the pursuit of a good man. No one had any doubt that Tita was the innocent party or that it was their responsibility to 'take care' of him. A man who had faced imprisonment and exile in his years with Byron was cosseted and comforted. A woman who dared to assert her right to an independent emotional existence and to pursue that existence despite the ridicule of others was left to face the world alone.

In the first weeks of 1837, stories of Byron and Shelley occupied Disraeli's every moment. An influenza epidemic swept London at the beginning of the year, and in an attempt to escape it Disraeli sought refuge with Byron's friend and biographer Lady Blessington at Kensington Gore, then slightly removed from the city. 'People die here by dozens', he told Sarah from the comfort of Lady Blessington's drawing room. 'D'Orsay and myself however defy the disorder with a first rate cook, a generous diet and medicated vapour baths.'[2] A first-rate cook and a generous diet were expensive commodities, and Lady Blessington spent her days writing furiously, generating as much income as possible from her pen. Inspired by her example, Disraeli began a new novel entitled *Venetia*, a fantasy in which the heroes of second-generation Romanticism survive into middle age. His 1834 letter to Lady Blessington enquiring about the identity of Byron's mistress suggests he had been contemplating a novel about Byron for some time, and proximity to Lady Blessington herself appears to have given him the necessary focus. He lingered at Kensington Gore until mid February, spending the mornings at leisure, the afternoons at work and the evenings engrossed in conversation with his hostess on all things Romantic. When he returned to Bradenham in March, these conversations continued by letter. Surrounded once more by his family, he could not help but compare his father's painstaking progress with monumental works of scholarship (in this case a history of English literature) with his own endeavours. Work of Isaac's calibre, he told Lady Blessington, was 'hewn out of the granite with slow and elaborate strokes. Mine are but plaster of Paris casts, or rather statues of snow that melt as soon as they are fashioned.'³

There is some truth in Disraeli's characterisation of his fictions, but *Venetia* stands apart from the other novels of the 1830s, in large part because of the complexity of its engagement with Romanticism. Its heroine Venetia Herbert is a cipher, her story a vehicle for extended portraits of a reimagined Byron and Shelley. Byron is represented in the novel as Lord Cadurcis: a man of genius, celebrated and then spurned by society, a keeper of a bear, a lover of wild Whig women and a suitor of Venetia. Venetia is the daughter of Marmion Herbert, another man of genius with a story based on that of Shelley as well as Byron, who has abandoned his wife and daughter in order to fight against the British in the American Revolution. Venetia's mother knows from her own history that genius is incompatible with domestic felicity and is determined not to let her daughter repeat her mistakes. She whisks Venetia away to Italy, where, in one of the plot's many improbable turns, they bump into Marmion Herbert, now living a life of sobriety and virtue. The reunited family move to the Gulf of Spezia, where they find their own version of domestic bliss. Domestic bliss is now possible for the Herberts because Marmion has grown up, repenting of youthful folly to become a respectable man. Disraeli's image of the reformed Romantic is derived from Lady Blessington's portrait of Byron, and suggests that he thought the virtuous Byron might be rather a bore. 'It is perhaps scarcely necessary to remark', he notes, his narrative voice tinged with regret, 'that Herbert avoided with the most scrupulous vigilance the slightest allusion to any of those peculiar opinions for which he was, unhappily, too celebrated.'⁴

Into this model of respectability enter Lord Cadurcis and his heir, dependable cousin George, who sail into the Gulf of Spezia one sunny day on their way back from Greece. Everything is now set for a happy ending. Herbert and Cadurcis become friends, a plot development about the friendship between men that mirrors the conventional romantic plot of Venetia and Cadurcis's story earlier in the novel. They have long conversations about love, just as Shelley and Byron did at Lake Geneva, and having seen that even poets can reform, Venetia's mother makes no objection when Cadurcis and Venetia renew their vows. But their location in the Gulf of Spezia is against them. On a hot and ominously calm day, Herbert and Cadurcis take their boat out to sea and, like Shelley before them, are drowned in a sudden storm. With their death, Disraeli's vision of a mature, responsible Romanticism is cut short. Venetia has to make do with cousin George, even though he is no radical poet. The ending of the novel is a coda, a disappointing finale to a tale of Romanticism reborn. 'Perhaps the reader', runs its muted conclusion, 'will not be surprised that, within a few months, the hands of George, Lord Cadurcis, and Venetia Herbert were joined in the chapel at Cherbury . . . Peace be with them.'[5]

The critical consensus about *Venetia* says that Disraeli kills off his Romantic poets and their associated trails of destruction and misery in order to allow the respectable family unit to triumph. In this analysis, the marriage between Venetia and George Cadurcis represents the triumph of Victorian over Romantic values and is symptomatic of Disraeli's incipient conservatism. But this reading of the novel ignores the fact that its final marriage plot is a practical afterthought, a consolation rather than the ending of a tale of passion. And the portrait Disraeli paints of the mature Marmion Herbert, a domesticated hybrid of Shelley and Byron, is that of a wrecked man who is compelled to suppress his radical idealism in order to keep his wife happy. *Venetia* suggests that domestic happiness arises only when genius succumbs to its fate in the Gulf of Spezia, and that this is a poor compromise. Writing to his friend Lady Caroline Maxse at the end of 1837, Disraeli reiterated his unwillingness to exchange his visions of greatness for conjugal joy. 'I am not married, but any old, ugly and ill-tempered woman may have me tomorrow. I care for no other qualifications. A wretched home makes us enjoy the world, and is the only certain source of general happiness.'[6]

In *Venetia* Disraeli wrote a flawed fantasy; in 1837 he lived one. At Kensington Gore D'Orsay and Lady Blessington amassed unpayable debts while pretending their position was unassailable, and while Disraeli took refuge in writing romance and dreamed of a glittering career, his own debts threatened to suffocate him. By the spring of 1837 he was facing ruin. At Bradenham in March he wrote to a creditor begging him not to have him arrested in Buckinghamshire, where he was trying to extract money from Isaac. 'My arrest at this moment, especially in the county, will entirely put an end to this most vital affair.'[7] That creditor, a Mr Collins, heeded his request: another, a Mr Davis, did not. On market day at High Wycombe the local sheriff's officer received a warrant for Disraeli's arrest and Mr Davis himself arrived in the town to see him taken. At least it was not magistrates day, Disraeli told his agent William Pyne. 'I was therefore not "executing justice and maintaining truth" on our bench, where I believe the rebellious tribe of Davis anticipated nabbing me.' The sheriff's officer was a friend of Disraeli's and tipped him off, and his brother James signed a bail bond, averting disaster. 'What is to be done?' Disraeli asked Pyne. His debts were so mountainous he could no longer keep track of what he owed, and the threat of Isaac discovering the truth was too much to be borne. Not only would he never help if he knew the full extent of his son's disgrace, Disraeli insisted, 'I really believe he never wd. forgive me. Indeed I do not think my family cd. hold up their heads under the infliction.'[8]

Somehow, Disraeli stumbled through this crisis. Isaac advanced money, Disraeli borrowed more, the angriest of his creditors were temporarily placated. Disraeli had long wanted a seat in Parliament, but now he needed one in order to avoid prison, or at the very least, exile and permanent disgrace. (MPs were immune from arrest for debt.) Early in the morning of 20 June 1837, William IV died and nineteen-year-old Victoria was woken to be told she was Queen. For the final time in British history, the accession of a new monarch triggered a general election, and Disraeli's hunt for a winnable seat began once more, this time driven by acute financial imperative. He was offered a seat in Devon but turned it down, thinking it not safe enough. He watched developments at Wycombe, hoping against hope that Charles Grey, his opponent from 1832, would decide not to stand. It was not however until 30 June, ten days after the King's death, that he was able to write to Sarah with his news. 'My darling', read his letter. 'The clouds have at length dispelled, and my prospects seem as bright as the day. At 6 o'ck this evening I start for Maidstone with Wyndham Lewis.'

Wyndham's 1837 campaign was already well under way when he invited Disraeli to join him at Maidstone. Buoyed by the strength of his support, the local Conservatives decided to field a second candidate, and a deputation was assembled to travel to London and find someone suitable at the Carlton Club. Mary Anne told John that it was at her instigation that Wyndham nominated Disraeli as his second, and was full of praise for her new candidate, in her view 'one of the greatest writers and orators of the day'.[9] She glossed over the fact that Disraeli was not the campaign's first choice. Wyndham wanted to find a man rich enough to pay his own election expenses, and local Conservatives were in favour of asking George Dawson to stand. In the end, they decided Dawson was not a sufficiently good speaker, and that their need for an inspiring orator outweighed their desire for additional funds. So in Maidstone Disraeli joined Wyndham and Mary Anne on their canvass, introducing himself to the electorate with a long speech in opposition to the new Poor Law, the legal framework passed by the Whigs in 1834 to abolish outdoor relief and drive the poor into segregated workhouses. He told Sarah that it was 'the best speech I ever made yet' and that it allowed him to canvass on his own merits, but he also acknowledged that Wyndham's 'influence and munificence is very great'.[10] It was a good combination. Wyndham was known in the constituency and was rich enough to purchase support with bribes and gifts, and Disraeli's powers of persuasion and intellect injected the campaign with promise and energy. Mary Anne adorned herself, the candidates and their carriages with purple ribbons and made friends with every voter she met, spending the canvass, she told John, in a 'tumult of joy & bustle'. She passed her days driving about the town, 'playing the amiable to a pitch of distraction', and she and Disraeli shrieked with laughter when women in the street enveloped Wyndham in embraces to his visible discomfort, heaping blessings on his head as they did so.[11]

After Disraeli's death in 1881, the *Maidstone and Kent County Standard* published the recollections of a man who witnessed the 1837 election. 'Mr Hodges', announced the newspaper, 'retains a boy's recollection of the scenes on the hustings at Maidstone.' He remembered Disraeli as an impressive figure; a pale-faced, dark-haired maker of stirring speeches. 'Mrs Wyndham Lewis stood on the hustings by his side, "covered in purple ribbons"', the paper continued. 'Mr Wyndham Lewis was also there, and the trio were familiar to everyone in Maidstone, so constantly were they together in the streets during the election.'[12] Another elderly witness, a fierce radical in his youth, wrote to Disraeli in 1880 of his memory of the campaign: 'I see you and Mr and Mrs Lewis now, as plain as I did on the day when I stood by the hustings . . . there is no working man in the land who entertains a higher opinion of you as a statesman, orator and writer.' The old man, one Henry Lott, described himself as Disraeli's 'converted opponent and grateful admirer' and as a 'poor prophet in my day', but noted correctly that 'calling bad names was in vogue then'.[13]

Lott's letter points to one aspect of the Maidstone campaign ignored in Mary Anne's letters to John and Disraeli's to Sarah: the anti-Semitic insults hurled at Disraeli on the hustings. The mob handed up bacon and ham and his speeches were interrupted by cries of 'Shylock'. Supporters of his opponent, the radical Colonel Thompson, publicly queried the pronunciation of his name to draw attention to his otherness. But despite the abuse, and thanks in large part to Wyndham's deep pockets, Disraeli won his election. Wyndham received 728 votes, Disraeli 668 and Colonel Thompson 529. As the votes were tallied, Disraeli scribbled a hasty note to Sarah, relating his triumph through a short table of election results. Two days later Mary Anne wrote John a letter that illuminates the particularly personal nature for her of this latest political success. 'My own dearest Brother', she began. 'You will be delighted to hear that on Thursday the 27th of this month I was safely deliver'd of all my anxieties & produced a pair of twin members with whom I returned to town in triumph on Friday morning.' At the end of her letter she abandoned such maternal imagery to present herself instead as a political oracle. 'Mark what I prophecy', she wrote. 'Mr Disraeli will, in a very few years, be one of the greatest men of his day – his great talents back'd by his friends Lord Lyndhurst & Lord Chandos with Wyndham's power to keep him in Parliament will insure him success – They call him my Parliamentary protégé.'[14]

~

A few weeks after the Maidstone victory, Mary Anne paid her first visit to Bradenham, in the company of Disraeli and Wyndham. She described the house and its inhabitants to John: 'rooms 30 & 40 foot long, plenty of servants, horses dogs & a library full of the rarest books'. Sarah was 'handsome & talented', the two younger brothers full of praise for each other, and Isaac was 'the most loveable perfect old gentlemen I ever met with'. Maria she did not mention. Disraeli himself ('our political pet') she compared to the Tory leader, describing him as 'the finest creature next to Sir R Peel'. Disraeli's election to Parliament shifted his relationship with Mary Anne, drawing them together in common purpose. She invited him to join her in her box at the opera; he haunted Grosvenor Gate, working on constituency business with Wyndham. To Mary Anne he wrote letters: short notes when he was in London and unable to call; longer epistles during a quiet September at Bradenham. These were letters born partly of friendship but partly from necessity. He owed Wyndham his share of the Maidstone election expenses, and when Wyndham pressed for repayment he had no way of obliging, but Mary Anne remained loyal to him and did her best to persuade Wyndham against calling in the loan.

She retained her faith in her protégé even as debts remained unpaid and his maiden speech in the House of Commons went disastrously awry. Disraeli chose to speak on Irish matters. He was shouted down by Radicals and Irish MPs and received little encouragement from his own side. In the end he was forced to sit down without finishing his speech, although his final cry – 'I sit down now, but the time will come when you will hear me' – has since been much quoted. Veteran politicians were kind in the moment of humiliation, the Whig Richard Sheil consoling him with the fact that no one would now be unaware of him, and advising him to rebuild his reputation within the Commons with a series of short, dull statements. Disraeli took Sheil's advice, laying aside at the same time the bright colours and gold chains of the dandy and adopting instead a darker and more statesmanlike mode of dress. After the speech he told Mary Anne that he was comforted by the cheers of Robert Peel, who had already showed some support for his new MP by inviting him to a political dinner at his house. Sarah received a proud report of the invitation: 'The dinner to day is merely a house dinner of 14: all our great men . . . It has created some jealousy and surprise; but W[yndham] L[ewis] is delighted and says "Peel has taken him by the hand in the most marked way."'[15] His creditors were thwarted by parliamentary privilege, powerful men asked him to dinner, and he could write to a friend that he lived 'amidst a tumult of politics, and can scarcely find time even to scrawl this'.[16] 'Amidst a tumult of politics': he was where he was meant to be.

For Mary Anne too, the autumn and winter of 1837 were filled with good omens. She and Wyndham had a holiday in Paris, and George Dawson published verses in her praise in Lady Blessington's society journal, *The Book of Beauty*. Disraeli's presence in her house and her opera box gave her pleasure, as did her visit to Bradenham. In 1826 she had copied sections of *Vivian Grey* into her commonplace book; now she urged John to reread it, convinced he would be struck anew by its brilliance.[17] In September she received news that John's regiment was to return to England after a decade in Mauritius. John's letters about his return were punctuated with requests for a new loan from Wyndham to enable him to purchase a lieutenant colonelcy and so command his regiment, and a secret letter to Mary Anne contained a frantic assessment of his outstanding debts in England. He owed £400 and was in danger of arrest the minute he stepped ashore. 'For Gods sake', he told his sister, 'permit me to land in England with all the happiness I anticipate in seeing you and my mother once again without any burthen on my mind.'[18]

Mary Anne was jubilant at the thought of John in command of his regiment and went to work to put together the funds, as she had done so many times before. Meanwhile Wyndham, for so long an absent figure in her story, wrote with renewed affection when business parted him from her. Immersed in work in Wales, he complained of being uncomfortable without her, and in a separate letter, of how much he wished she was with him, 'then I sh'd not be in such a hurry to return – my only comfort is to hear from you'. This second letter also contains an enquiry after George Beauclerk, known to Mary Anne and Wyndham as the 'Superlative', suggesting that either Wyndham remained in ignorance of the intensity of Beauclerk's relationship with his wife, or that he chose not to notice it.[19] At Christmas, business took him back to Wales, and he and Mary Anne agreed that she would visit the D'Israelis at Bradenham rather than make a long journey in the depths of winter. 'I trust you are now much amus'd by the happy family by whom you are surrounded', he wrote. Their partnership emerges with renewed clarity in these letters as affectionate, mutually supportive and respectful. At Maidstone, Wyndham arranged for beef, bread and beer to be distributed to a thousand families on Christmas Eve, bearing out the truth of Mary Anne's later insistence that he bought relief as well as votes with his income. And on 1 January 1838 he sent a further letter, containing good wishes to the D'Israelis and an instruction for 'Dizzy' to return to London for the start of parliamentary business by the end of the week. For Mary Anne herself, his wife of twenty-three years, he had a particular message. 'My own darling, I was delighted to receive your letter last night, it made the old year run out in Happiness – I now wish you a happy new year & that we may live together many more years with equal solace to each other as heretofore.'[20]

~

On 14 March 1838, Mary Anne and Wyndham were passing a quiet morning in his library at Grosvenor Gate. Mary Anne's papers show that he settled a tradesman's bill and she cut a lock of his hair. Wyndham, who had been feeling mildly unwell for two days, was sitting at his desk when he slumped forward and fell from his chair. A frantic Mary Anne summoned servants and doctors but he was already dead, killed by a heart attack. Friends rallied round and Mary Dawson, living next door once more, came to protect Mary Anne from curious enquiries. She could not prevent a visit from George Beauclerk, paid within two days of Wyndham's death. Beauclerk reported Mary Anne's state to Mary Shelley, who replied in a letter full of sympathy for a fellow widow. 'I think of my own tragedy', she wrote. 'Completed so early – so disastrous in its consequences & feel the more for her – though she will not have to struggle as I have done through long years of poverty & solitude.' Mary Shelley also told Beauclerk she was glad Mary Anne had him to rely on, but used an avowal of her faith in him to strike a note of caution about the need to treat Mary Anne with propriety. 'I verily believe', she wrote, perhaps more in hope than expectation, 'in your distinterested-ness.'[21]

In addition to Beauclerk, Mary Anne had to receive a visit from a depu-tation of Maidstone Conservatives, who brought her an address of sympathy signed by 1,500 people to which she made a dignified reply, subsequently published in the local newspapers. Her response, read on her behalf by George Dawson, was formal and brief, but since no letters from her have survived for the period immediately following Wyndham's death, it is the only source we have for her own assessment of her state. (In addition to reading the statement, Dawson may well have helped her craft it.) She spoke of her 'heavy and most unexpected affliction' and of her gratitude on hearing praise of her 'late dear husband'. 'It is the greatest consolation to me to find that his virtues are justly appreciated', she continued. 'I can offer no greater tribute of attachment to his memory than to cherish with the fondest recollection, the sympathy which his kind friends have shewn towards me.'[22] Writing to Disraeli in mid May, two months after Wyndham's death, she made the only other surviving reference to her grief. 'My heart is too full & anxious & <u>at times</u> to bear up against the misery which almost destroys me the moment I have nothing to do', she wrote. 'His perfect sweetness of temper & love, & now I know not where to seek for comfort. My brother, cannot love me as he did you know.' John's return to England was now imminent, but without Wyndham, Mary Anne feared the meeting, a fear articulated through a comparison of husbandly and brotherly love. 'I have never been accustomed even to an impatient word', she confessed. 'I know not now, how to bear one, he thought me perfect, my brother <u>must</u> see a thousand faults.'[23]

On the day of Wyndham's death Disraeli wrote one dismissive note to his money agent, triggered by the realisation that the Lewis estate would press for quick repayment of his debts, and then, recollecting himself, wrote to Sarah that the news left him 'overwhelmed and incapable of any exertion'.[24] The day after, he saw Mary Anne and wrote again to Sarah, asking her to invite Mary Anne to Bradenham and reporting the result of a snatched conversation with Mary Dawson about Wyndham's will. The will named Mary Anne and William Price Lewis (Wyndham's elder brother) as executors, and made William Lewis the heir, but left Mary Anne a life interest in the whole of the estate. Grosvenor Gate was hers for her lifetime, as were dividends from Wyndham's many investments, which amounted to an income of about £5,000 a year. The house and money were hers unconditionally, including in the event of her remarriage.

William Lewis proved reluctant to run Wyndham's estate in conjunction with his sister-in-law and she had to stand her ground in order to secure her inheritance. In April she travelled to Wales to negotiate with Lewis and view her property, and eventually reached an agreement with Lewis that she would give up various portions of her interest – chief among them Greenmeadow, which she had no wish to retain – in return for guaranteed annuities. John Guest was appointed to safeguard her interests and make sure the value of the annuity accurately reflected the value of the estate, and she was assisted too by her lawyer, Thomas Loftus. But it was she who hammered out the terms of an agreement with Lewis and she who fought for her house and income. From Bradenham Disraeli wrote with advice about how to proceed. She should not attempt to do too much after the shock and fatigue she had borne, he warned, and she should not sign anything she did not fully understand. He feared she would find his instructions 'stupid and prosy' but he considered that circumstances had placed her under his charge. 'As your brother is not here, and you are a lone lamb in this world, I think it but proper to write this, even at the hazard of boring you.'[25] Mary Anne did not dispute Disraeli's characterisation of her as a 'lone lamb', but nor did she need advice about how to conduct her financial affairs, especially not from men – either brothers or friends – who were themselves mired in debt.

~

One person reacted so oddly to Wyndham's death that it marked the end of her friendship with Mary Anne. On 5 April Rosina Lytton Bulwer wrote a letter of condolence that started promisingly: 'My poor Darling I have been very anxious to know how you are.' She had been unable to write earlier, she continued, because she had herself been too unhappy, following the death of her spaniel, Fairy. It was a loss, she reported, 'that I shall not get over – for many a day – my heart literally feels torn up by the roots'.[26] Mary Anne was deeply offended by Rosina's lack of interest in her suffering and by her segue from the loss of a husband to the loss of a dog. When she received the letter, she was with Lady Charlotte Guest and her protégé from next door, Robert Dawson. They were as taken aback at its contents as she was and mentioned it to their friends; before long, gossip about Rosina's conduct was circulating in the London clubs. When Rosina discovered she was the subject of talk, she wrote again to Mary Anne, this time in an angry letter to 'Mrs Wyndham Lewis', accusing her of slander and denying that she had shown more concern for her dog than for her friend's bereavement. She had written every day to Mary Anne's maid to ask after her, she protested, until she became so unhappy and bedridden as to be forced to deputise the task to a friend. Besides, she continued, Fairy was 'the only faithful, true, and disinterested heart I possessed'. She also accused Mary Anne, still recently widowed, of never knowing 'a days unhappiness, and never a day's misfortune'.[27]

Mary Anne responded robustly to Rosina's accusations. The two had met briefly in Bath when Mary Anne stopped in the city on her journey to Wales in April, and at that point, Mary Anne noted, 'so far from being unhappy you were the gayest of the gay'. She chided Rosina for refusing to bear her company in Wales when 'I only wanted gentleness & kindness' and cited her long support of Rosina in her battle with Bulwer. 'If we are not to continue as friends', she warned, 'remember it is by your own desire.' But she was also conciliatory. Rosina was her oldest friend outside her family, and she should 'take me as I do you – as I find you'. 'We have known each other too many years for either of us to alter & we must be perfectly aware of each others respective faults & virtues.'[28]

Rosina would not be placated. She accused Mary Anne of blackening her name whenever she heard her praised, and maintained that her apparent gaiety in Bath was a mask assumed to hide a broken heart. And rather than being a support in her battles with Bulwer, she attested, Mary Anne was the cause of her marital misery. 'One of his chief sources of quarrel with me, was for being so fond of and so much with you and in those days he was wont to lump you with . . . other disreputables.'[29] At this point Mary Anne ceased the correspondence, and her eighteen-year friendship with Rosina came to an end. Rosina was not content to leave matters there. She wrote the dog incident into her 1839 novel, Cheveley, and sent Mary Anne an abusive poem, entitled 'False Heart Beware', in which she asked whether she had been well served for enduring Mary Anne's 'wayward madness' for so long.[30] When Rosina felt she had been betrayed, she never forgave. Writing to a friend in 1873, the year after Mary Anne's death, she castigated her ignorance, asserting that when Jonathan Swift came up in conversation, Mary Anne asked if she had ever met him at Rosina's house. She maintained that Mary Anne and Disraeli were engaged in an affair before Wyndham's death, and that all that attracted Disraeli to her was her money, since he found her a 'vulgar illiterate woman'. She also claimed to have arrived at Grosvenor Gate at the moment of Wyndham's death (she was in fact absent from London at the time) to be greeted by the coroner's men and a jubilant Mary Anne, flushed with delight at already having accepted an offer from Disraeli. In a scattergun attack she even accused Mary Anne of showing a 'brutal want of feeling, about her poor brother', conduct which Rosina found 'revolting'.[31]

Rosina's animus stemmed from more than a dispute about the appropriate levels of mourning for a dog. Disraeli was chief among the ranks of her enemies and was in her eyes a deviant who had engaged in immoral acts with her husband. Mary Anne's friendship with him, after years of support for Rosina against Bulwer and his friends, represented a shift in allegiance. Despite her protestations of affection for Rosina, Mary Anne could not remain loyal to both her and Disraeli. Disraeli's dislike of Rosina was almost as active as hers of him, although he had greater command of his pen and his emotions. In the first of her July letters Rosina had warned Mary Anne that her imminent remarriage was freely discussed, making a mockery of her pose as a grieving widow. Mary Anne reacted angrily to the suggestion, but her denial was partial. 'In the last six weeks my house has been filled by those who have claims on me in every way – I again repeat – I have not yet been a widow five months – no one has had the indelicacy of even hinting marriage.'[32] Hints of marriage might be avoided, but the same was not true of a new relationship. Rosina's actions made it easier for Mary Anne to jettison her, but when the time came to choose between her and Disraeli, there was really no choice at all.

~

In the narrative of Mary Anne and Disraeli's romance, there are two versions of what happened next. Both are fictions. The first version of the story appears in the letters they wrote to one another in the year following Wyndham's death. This story charts the emergence of love out of mutual grief and tells of passion winning the day to allow for the union of two soulmates. It requires us to take both letter-writers at their word. In the second version of their story, apparent in an alternative reading of the letters, debt, deception, sibling loyalty and other lovers are hidden in order for a marriage of convenience – a marriage crucial for Disraeli's survival – to take place.

The truth probably lies somewhere in between. Neither Mary Anne nor Disraeli could reconcile their conception of themselves or each other with the cynicism of a marriage of convenience, and it mattered to them both that they should be, and appear to be, swept up in a grand romance. That romance's fictional quality gave them an emotional context for their courtship, endowing it with the drama denied them by circumstances. Their correspondence imitated the patterns of epistolary novels such as Frances Burney's *Evelina* and *Cecilia*, in which Mary Anne, as a young woman in the 1800s, first witnessed a literary version of herself. For women like her with limited prospects, literary representations of possible biographical plots were particularly significant because they suggested futures in which reason and passion could be reconciled. The Bennett sisters had to confront the failure of reality to give them the chance to inhabit such plots; Mary Anne's first marriage also involved serious emotional compromise. Disraeli offered her the chance to be wooed like the heroine of the silver-fork novels he wrote, and she responded in kind. And epistolary and silver-fork novels were not the only literary models for their romance. In their letters to each other, Mary Anne and Disraeli enacted the conventions of the marriage plot of the emergent realist novel, their relationship self-consciously mirroring the emotional arc of the form. The heroines of these novels were not usually forty-seven-year-old widows; nor were their heroes routinely thirty-five-year-old dandies. But for Mary Anne and Disraeli, who derived expressions of emotional authenticity from their reading and writing, it didn't matter.

~

The tone of their letters changed within a few weeks of Wyndham's death. In April, while Mary Anne was in Wales, Disraeli wrote from Bradenham of his great anxiety about his father's health. His greatest wish, he confessed, was that Isaac should live to see him settled. It was a clear indication that he was thinking of marriage and that he wanted Mary Anne to know it. Her first surviving letter to him following Wyndham's death dates from May, written while she was in Bristol helping her mother organise her financial affairs. In a postscript she implicitly chided Disraeli for spending too much time with Lady Londonderry, an old friend and a powerful social figure. He shot back a retort: he was not passing any more time with Lady Londonderry than with anyone else, and in any case, Mary Anne appeared to be so merry in Bristol as to have no time to write to him. She was outraged by the suggestion that she was enjoying herself when she spent her days immersed in a tangle of business and her evenings in a state of exhaustion. But at least while he was with Lady Londonderry – a married woman – he was less likely to think of marrying himself. 'I hate married men, I would as soon you were dead <u>rather</u> selfish!'[33]

While Disraeli and Mary Anne staked their claims to each other's time and loyalty, Mary Anne kept up a separate correspondence with Augustus Berkeley, one of the 'disreputables' (Bulwer's word) of Lord Worcester's set with whom she had been acquainted in the 1820s. Berkeley wrote to her as 'Rose', a name that usually signals a romantic alliance in her correspondence. In April he was full of self-pity as he watched Mary Anne begin a new life. 'Free, unshackled, your <u>imprisoned</u> passions set loose.' He warned her that passions could deceive and yoke her into 'wedding misery'. He was worn down by debt and hardship, but were he 'untrammelled like thyself, I would enter the lists, Win and wear thee'. Following the pattern set by Rosina, he threatened her with the same degree of ridicule that saw the lady's maid Kent expelled from Bradenham for daring to follow her heart. 'The babbling World already gives you to the Tory Novelist.'[34] Berkeley wrote to Mary Anne through the summer of 1838 and she replied, but her letters have been lost. His professed disappointment at her taste erupted in a letter in which he invoked a cacophony of Shakespeare and Milton to denigrate her. 'He who best can play the Fool to amuse the present hour becomes <u>for that hour</u> the God of your idolatry. Continue to play your fantastic tricks; "till Angels scorn to weep." "To a Nunnery go" – you know the rest.'*[35] Mary Anne annotated this letter 'Augustus Berkeley 1838', but it did not mark the end of their acquaintance, and Berkeley still dined intermittently at Grosvenor Gate in 1839, to Disraeli's chagrin.

Disraeli continued to write to Mary Anne throughout April and May, both before and after her return from Wales. She was on tenterhooks about John, whose arrival in England was expected every day. She nevertheless had time to have Wyndham's watch chains reset with Disraeli's seal. The gift was ready by the time of a grand banquet held by Lord Chandos, and

---

* 'Let me play the fool / With mirth and laughter let old wrinkles come', *Merchant of Venice*, I, I; 'Or, if thou wilt, swear by thy gracious self, / Which is the god of my idolatory, / And I'll believe thee', *Romeo and Juliet*, II, ii; 'His glassy essence, like an angry ape, / Plays such fantastic tricks before high heaven / As make the angels weep', *Measure for Measure*, II, ii; 'Get thee to a nunnery; why woulds't thou be a / breeder of sinners?', *Hamlet*, III, i. In *Paradise Lost*, Satan also cries 'thrice in spite of scorn, / Tears such as Angels weep'. Book I, 619–20.

Disraeli's response acknowledged the symbolism of her offering. 'For the first time in public, I wore *your chains*. I hope you are not ashamed of your slave.'[36] The watch chains were the first of many objects Mary Anne and Disraeli invested with significance in order to realise a concrete expression of passion. Both of them were back in London by the end of June, when the Queen was crowned. Disraeli had planned not to attend the coronation since he did not possess Court dress but was persuaded to change his mind by his brother Ralph, and hastily assembled a borrowed outfit. He gave his corona-tion medal to Mary Anne. Sarah, the recipient of such objects in the past, had to make do with the reports of Tita, whom the D'Israelis sent to London to witness the coronation on their behalf.

In the weeks before the coronation, Disraeli became involved in a legal dispute relating to allegations of bribery during the Maidstone election. A petition was brought before the Houses of Parliament and the petitioners' lawyer Charles Austin alleged that corruption at Maidstone was worse than elsewhere; that Disraeli had reneged on the sums he promised as bribes and that his election agent had made additional payments on his behalf. Maidstone was known to be a rotten constituency, and no one doubted that bribery was part of usual election practice there, but Disraeli refused to let the allegations stand. He published a letter in the *Morning Post* denouncing his detractors and accused Charles Austin and his fellow lawyers of taking money to circulate lies. Austin's statement he characterised as 'the blustering artifice of a rhetorical hireling, availing himself of the vile license of a loose-tongued lawyer, not only to make a statement which was false, but to make it with a consciousness of its falsehood'.[37] He expected his letter to result in a challenge to a duel; Mary Anne feared the same and was deeply distressed. Austin elected to fight with the law rather than pistols and sued for libel. 'I wo[ul]d have preferred a more expeditious and cheaper process of settling the business', Disraeli told Mary Anne, 'but at any rate it may save you some suffering.'[38] Mary Anne paid handsomely for her relief when Disraeli lost his case and she settled the damages and his legal bills.

Disraeli's sleight of hand, in impugning lawyers rather than answering the charges against him, succeeded in diverting the attention of the public from the allegations of bribery, but not everyone was so easily distracted. George Beauclerk called at Grosvenor Gate and poured poison in Mary Anne's ear about Disraeli's conduct. She refused to listen and afterwards Beauclerk wrote mournfully of the injustice of her anger. He had only repeated what he read in the papers, he insisted, and she was only angry because he was not – unlike her – wilfully blind to the faults of those he admired. It was not cruel to assert that Disraeli was poor, he protested, nor to point out that a poor man could hardly afford to buy his election himself. He warned her to stop defending Disraeli publicly, at least to those who were ignorant – unlike him – of the full extent of her partiality. 'Instead of convincing the world that nothing but Mr Ds superior acquirements and the Good People of Maidstone's true Patriotism were the Levers by which that Gentleman was forced into his Parliamentary Seat, you will but the more induce them to believe that it was nothing but Mr Wyndham Lewises Influence and money directly or indirectly which accomplished this feat.'[39] Beauclerk maintained that he wrote from a position of neutrality, but his sarcasm exposed him. Like Augustus Berkeley, he watched Mary Anne's blossoming relationship with Disraeli from the sidelines, jealous and angry at the idea of an interloper winning the widow's fortune but unable to do anything to stop him.

∼

The relationship between Mary Anne and Disraeli has often been described as unequal: she was too old for him, unable to give him children and far from being his intellectual equal. In this assessment he married her for her money and then repaid her for the affection and security she gave him through gallant loyalty. But the letters from the summer and autumn of 1838 give the lie to the suggestion that she was his for the taking. The Austin libel case shifted the dynamic between them by emphasising Mary Anne's power. She chose to rescue Disraeli from his legal entanglements, just as she chose, as Wyndham's executor, not to call in his election debts (she appears to have persuaded William Lewis to follow her lead, and the loan was never repaid). Thereafter the relationship evolved on her terms. She knew Disraeli was an adventurer even though she was ignorant of the depth of the financial precipice on which he stood, and she knew how much, of both money and emotion, she had to give. She knew too that there were other men who wanted to marry her.

By July they were sleeping together, apparently indifferent to gossip. Mary

Anne's jointure was secured to her regardless of her conduct, and she seems, for a brief period, to have let her guard down. Disraeli wrote that he wanted their life as it was to last forever; she noted in her commonplace book that 'love-making after marriage is the best way of reconciling me to love-making before'.⁴⁰ He dressed in a hurry at Grosvenor Gate, leaving his watch and seal behind, and had to write afterwards asking her to post them. Sitting in the debating chamber in the House of Commons, he wrote of romantic dreams that he experienced as a latter-day Coleridge, half wakeful. 'I passed a dreary and tumultuous night, in which your image was never absent from my sight, though acting in distressful and harrassing scenes.'⁴¹ He insisted on their happiness, refusing to countenance the idea that it might be illusory. But he acknowledged that there was something unreal about their drama. 'You know in how strange, and how sweet a mode my days now vanish. Your heart must be my excuse.'⁴² Writing in 1922, Constance de Rothschild recalled her mother's memories of the pair at about this time: 'the little intimate nods and smiles interchanged by the two friends sitting on opposite sides of the table, and the way they drank to one another's health'. As a young girl her mother had viewed Disraeli as a 'joyous, fantastic, captivating acquaintance' while Mary Anne 'looked and seemed very much older'.⁴³

At the end of August Disraeli made his first determined attempt to trans-late their affair into a plan for a marriage. He wrote to Sarah that he would not abandon Mary Anne to come to Bradenham but would postpone his visit until she was able to travel with him. He claimed that since Mary Anne was quite alone he could not leave her in solitude; he did not say that it was Mary Anne's male friends rather than her loneliness that he feared. In the end he went to Bradenham a few days before Mary Anne and wrote immediately to plead for her company. His family, so long his refuge during times of stress, seemed insipid after her 'vivacious sweetness',⁴⁴ and when she arrived the next day, he marked the moment with a sonnet celebrating the sound of her step 'in my fathers hall' and the echo of her voice 'within the chambers of my youth'. 'Is there not a spell / Of rare enchantment on my raptured life?' 'Ah! sweet one', the poem concluded, 'once to sigh / That such a face might love me, was a dream / Might well become a poets fantasy; / And on me now, say, can it deign to beam?'⁴⁵ More 'poets fantasies' followed and Mary Anne pronounced all his lines 'perfect'.

Some of his efforts were perhaps more perfect than others; one poem wished he 'were the flea / That is biting your knee'; another mourned the fact that he was simply 'poor Diz / With a secondrate phiz / and all I can do / Is to love you most true.' His verses praised the sight of moonbeams alighting on Mary Anne's brow, her presence in Bradenham's 'glades and sylvan bowers' and the natural beauty of her voice in which 'birds warble'. At one point even such stock poetic conceits deserted him and he was reduced, like a love-lorn adolescent, to writing out her name over and over again. 'My Maryanne Mary-Anne Mary-Anne Mary-Anne Mary-Anne Mary Anne.'[46]

It is Disraeli's voice that speaks from September 1838; no documents by Mary Anne for this period have survived. The notes he sent to her room each morning give some idea though of an evolving maternal theme in their relationship, in which Disraeli wrote of himself as Mary Anne's 'child'. 'How is his darling?' ran one such note. 'And when will she come and see her child? He is up and in the little room.'[47] They came to use 'child' interchangeably, both signing themselves in this way when they wanted to enforce a notion of emotional or physical vulnerability, and in September it was Disraeli who needed to convince Mary Anne of how much he loved her and how much he longed for the security of marriage. Writing to his money agent William Pyne at the end of the month, he was confident they would be wed early in the new year. 'Don't let this letter be lying about your table', he warned.[48] Marriage offered financial relief both because he believed he could use Mary Anne's income to pay his debts and because Isaac had indicated he would settle money on him on the occasion of his marriage. In the meantime, he suggested to Pyne, perhaps he should approach his brother James, in charge of the profitable Bradenham farms, to act as security against a further loan.

Disraeli spoke too soon when he announced that the date of his wedding was fixed, and Mary Anne became angry at being pushed into a new marriage less than a year after the death of her husband. She had already settled Disraeli's legal bills and forgiven his debt, and believed his desire for a dash to the altar to be motivated by mercenary concerns. She also became wary of being accused of impropriety. They quarrelled and she announced her intention of leaving Bradenham immediately. Disraeli was told to make her excuses to Sarah and she would not be softened by letters of apology. He tried to persuade her to stay and then, recognising defeat, asked her not to leave angry. 'Our last hours should be passed in peace, if not in pleasantness. Pray let us meet, and look happy, even if we be not.'[49]

The next day Mary Anne was back in London. Disraeli wrote of his misery at her absence: 'All is dull, silent, spiritless; the charm is broken, the magic has fled!' He invoked Shakespearean comedy to console himself that 'the course of true love / never did run smooth' and tragedy to articulate his premonitions. 'Alas! alas! mine I fear will be wild and turbulent. May it not terminate in a fatal cataract. Remember! O.'* 'O' stands here for a shape that appears in this letter for the first time and then recurs again and again in their correspondence, a cross between a heart, a rose, a kiss and a root vegetable. It had a particular significance for both Disraeli and Mary Anne, expressing things otherwise unspoken, a symbol of constancy even when their language revealed their thoughts about the future to be irreconcilable. Mary Anne responded in a conciliatory but firm letter in which she instructed Disraeli to prove his love by looking after his physical health by eating properly and walking every day rather than indulging in an orgy of unhealthy self-pity, and also by putting in serious work on his new literary endeavour, a tragic play about wife-murder entitled *Alarcos*.

Throughout the autumn they played a shadow game, writing of their love but also of exploits calculated to inspire pity, jealousy and fear of a lonely future. From Bradenham Disraeli reported that the dahlias, symbols of their blossoming September amour, had been caught by an early frost, to Tita's great distress. He described himself in mournful solitude, embracing Mary Anne's letters a thousand times. Sitting in a hot courtroom on the magistrates' bench at quarter sessions, he mused on his love and his doubts, drawing again on the dream imagery that pervades his letters to her. 'I cannot believe, now that we are *separated*, that all our love is not a romantic dream.'[50] Mary Anne, while less self-consciously literary, also invoked the natural world in her account of herself, writing of lying awake during lonely nights at Grosvenor Gate listening to the wind whistling. But her letters also gave every impression of a rejuvenated life in London. She recounted a merry

---

* 'The course of true love . . .' is from *A Midsummer Night's Dream*, I, I; in *King Lear* Lear dares 'you cataracts and hurricanoes' to 'spout / Till you have drench'd our steeples, drown'd the cocks!'. III, ii.

day's shopping with Mary Dawson, and the news that Lord Charles Churchill was suing Ethel for divorce. She told of amusing dinners at Grosvenor Gate with Augustus Berkeley, and her delight at her new friends, one Captain Neale and one Miles Stapleton. Neale took snuff, a horrid habit, but Mr Stapleton was also writing a tragedy and making excellent progress: was Disraeli doing any work on his? 'Mr Stapleton called during my walk should he be here again tomorrow, (of course he will) I shall ask him to dine.' But she missed Disraeli and longed 'to see your dear kind eyes fixed on me as they always are when I sing & at all times when she is naughty.'[51] This swift movement from first to third person is another recurring stylistic trick of both Mary Anne and Disraeli's letters, and has a distancing, dramatising effect, allowing for the presentation of the self as an epistolary character as well as a living being. 'Fortunate Berkeley, thrice happy Stapleton, cursed Neale!' Disraeli replied. 'What is it to you, whether he takes snuff or not?' He dashed off a poem of passion denied: 'Parted, can Love remain?' 'Visions of woe arise / Full of gloom as the skies: / I have no hope!' He ended by drawing the O shape, their 'mystical mark', 'but my hand trembles as I sketch it, and my lips grow pale'.[52]

Mary Anne was full of disingenuous surprise at this reaction to her news: 'I thought you would like me to find out bad habits & to feel almost a dislike to all but yourself.'[53] Disraeli was only partially consoled, although he insisted he was not jealous. 'When the eagle leaves you, the vultures return.'[54] Peace was restored, but only temporarily. Mary Anne wrote that Mr Stapleton had told her the plot of his play as a great secret. 'I do not like him so much as I used', she confided, 'and I suppose he does not me, naturally – but he calls here much the same.'[55] Disraeli fired a letter back, doubting her constancy and prophesying for them fading emotions and estrangement. He prayed that 'the future may be different to what my prophetic soul paints it'; she retorted with a reproach for his cruelty. Just because she could not come to Bradenham as soon as he asked, 'you allow the darkest doubts & unkindest thoughts of me to fill your heart'. She attacked him for writing to her in the drawing room, surrounded by his family, rather than in the privacy of his room, a betrayal that 'unidealized' his letters. In any case she was ill and deserving of a little sympathy, but since he no longer cared for her she would say goodbye, turning his rhetoric against him. 'Adieu for to use your own words there can be no love where there is no confidence.'[56] Realising he had gone too far, Disraeli sought to explain his actions. 'Your assurance that there was no one there who interested you and kept you from me, seemed to my jaundiced eye, coldblooded. I conjured up Stapleton like the serpent in Paradise "*Whispering in the ear of Eve, familiar toad!*" reading to you his damned trajedy (damned I am sure it will be in every sense of the word); and you charmed, interested, and forgetting your captive victim.'[57]

Disraeli and Mary Anne spun their affair into being through dreams, prophecies and symbols. They wrote of each other and themselves as characters, beings seen externally as well as inhabited. The dramatisation of Mr Stapleton illustrated the dangers of such an approach, as the introduction into their drama of a new player, depicted by one as a confidante and the other as a villain, threatened a disunity in their fictional constructions. Mary Anne represented herself as Disraeli's child, a lone figure grateful for the support of kind friends. Stapleton consoled her but Disraeli had her heart. Disraeli categorised himself as the victim, compelled by circumstance to stand by while interlopers ensnared his love. Mr Stapleton wrote a character of Mary Anne that implies that he resented Disraeli's influence on her manner during the period of her courtship. 'Naturally gifted with a warm heart and ardent disposition, she is capable of sincere affection and even of extraordinary devotion', he wrote. 'But from the circumstance of having been constantly in the society of (soi-disant) literary people, and adopting the language they sometimes employ, she gives to the expression of sorrow a harshness which destroys the attractive softness of one in affliction, and often diminishes the full force of a natural thought by the over-strained language in which it is clothed.'[58]

Disraeli returned to London in November, drawn by continuing trouble over outstanding Maidstone debts. Storms lifted tiles off the roof at Bradenham and blew in the windows at Grosvenor Gate, allowing both him and Mary Anne to colour their depictions of emotional upheaval by evoking the elements. New attempts to reach an understanding about their future failed; Mary Anne left London and 'ruffled feelings' marred their parting.[59] She spent November and December with friends, first with the Milner Gibsons at Theberton Hall in Suffolk and then with her girlhood companion Dolly Whitmore Jones at her house in Oxfordshire. Thomas Milner Gibson was an MP who had been at school with Disraeli and, like his schoolfellow, entered Parliament as a Conservative in 1837. He was committed to free trade and by the end of 1838 found himself a marginalised figure in his party. In 1839 he resigned his seat to stand as a Liberal, and thereafter became a driving force in Liberal politics. His wife Arethusa was a notable figure, a hostess who was intimate with men of letters as well as diplomats and politicians. Thackeray was her friend, as was Dickens, who listed her among his own ideal guests, and her drawing room was the scene of some crucial Liberal power-broking in the middle decades of the century. Her friendship with Mary Anne, which appears to date from about this time, was long and loyal. Some eighty letters from her to Mary Anne survive, spanning a thirty-year period of gossip, political reports and news of her children (she had eight, but only four survived infancy, and Mary Anne was a source of support during these multiple bereavements).

The winter of 1838 saw Mary Anne's first visit to Theberton, from where she wrote to Disraeli at the end of November, promising to behave herself. 'On my word Dizzy not a word or look of love to me from any one.'[60] The company was plentiful, with an agreeable number of unattached lords, officers and untitled gentlemen to flirt away the hours with. She rode out with Arethusa in her carriage, watched as paper fire lanterns were set off from the lawn and enjoyed the bustle of the company as they prepared for balls and tableaux. She was particularly full of praise for Mr Wombwell, an heir to a baronetcy and a fellow guest. 'I Like Mr Wombwell better every day', she told Disraeli, two days after her arrival. 'He has such good useful sense, & an abundance of good humour.'[61] After the Gibsons' ball most of the company left but Mr Wombwell stayed and obligingly drove Mary Anne and a pregnant Arethusa around the surrounding countryside. 'You have no idea how amusing I find Mr Wombwell', Mary Anne reported in her next letter. And then, a day later, 'I continue to find Mr Wombwell agreeable, remarkably so, he is so sweet tempered & does everything to please me.' She was full of praise too for her host and hostess, in a manner that suggests that while Disraeli and Milner Gibson had known each other from school, they were no longer close. 'The more you know of the Gibsons the more you will like them', she wrote. 'Dizzy we always agree about people dont we.'[62]

Wise after the Mr Stapleton affair, Disraeli did not make the mistake of attacking Mr Wombwell, but nor did he agree with such praise of a rival. He ignored all references to Mary Anne's gaieties and wrote instead of his own illness, which struck as soon as he reached Bradenham. He took to his bed and was nursed by Maria, to whom he wrote a rare sonnet of gratitude. In letters to Mary Anne he had figured himself as his lover's child; now he invoked his mother as his spouse. 'As becomes a faithful wife, / Art thou a nursing parent; when we flee / The struggling world, and its tumultuous strife, / In thy fond breast a harbour from the sea / Of troubles welcomes us.'[63] Maria is an all but absent figure in Disraeli's story, and his biographers have frequently drawn the connection between his near motherlessness and his attraction to older women. Given the recurrence of images of childhood and maternity in his love letters – both those to and from Mary Anne and also those from Henrietta Sykes – there is a good deal of logic to this reading. But it is nevertheless open to question how much Disraeli experienced Maria as an absent figure. She was always there at Bradenham: not his chief correspondent or confidante, but a steadfast presence nevertheless. When he felt abandoned by Mary Anne and sank into lethargy, he turned back to her, even as he signed himself in letters as Mary Anne's child. Mary Anne was persuaded by his suffering to arrange a visit to Bradenham, drawn by the prospect of mothering him back to health. 'I know not why', she wrote, 'but I always love you better (if possible) when you are ill.'[64] She returned to London, and on 7 December arrived at Maidenhead, where she was met by Disraeli, who 'cd. not give up the delight of being with her *alone* at first and immediately'.[65]

Mary Anne was accompanied to Theberton by Eliza Gregory, her Cardiff singing pet. Eliza was nineteen or twenty in 1838 and had spent much of her adolescence in and out of Mary Anne's house. Her position in the Grosvenor Gate household was uneasy. She was not a servant but nor was she an adopted daughter. She was a companion but she was too young and from too modest a background to be admitted into the company kept by her employer. Mary Anne told Disraeli that Eliza could share a bedroom with his mother's maid as she prepared for a journey to Bradenham, but made clear that despite this she was not to be treated as one of the staff. 'Eliza does not eat with the servants but her dinner is our luncheon time & she can eat her supper in the housekeepers room & sit in mine except in the evening's when we might like her to act [or] sing.'[66]

After Mary Anne's marriage to Disraeli, Eliza left her service. The two of them evidently parted in anger: a year later she wrote to Mary Anne to confess that 'I have too strong a recollection of your early kindness to me to be quite happy till I have told you that I regret the circumstances attendant to our separation.'[67] She wrote again a few years later to tell Mary Anne that she was happily married to a Mr Riches and had two children. But a decade after the Theberton visit Eliza attempted to blackmail Mary Anne by revealing details of her conduct during this period. She alleged that her employer, along with Arethusa Milner Gibson, had allowed herself to be corrupted by 'a demoralising set of demireps' and owed 'the tiny remnant of respectability' left to her to Eliza.[68] Arethusa dismissed the suggestion that this diatribe was based in fact, but Eliza was one of several people – including, at times, Disraeli – who accused Mary Anne of consorting with rakish men and of damaging her own reputation in the process. When Mary Anne left Bradenham in the third week of December to travel to Chastleton in Oxfordshire, where she was to spend Christmas with the Whitmore Joneses (again in the company of Eliza), the rhetoric of Disraeli's letters suddenly escalated. On first reading these are the letters of an adventurer attempting to snare an elusive prize, but it is also possible that he may have been more alert to Mary Anne's equivocal reputation and the threat posed to his plans by her circle of raffish admirers than he was prepared to admit.

Mary Anne arrived at Chastleton on 19 December; three days later Disraeli had not heard from her. He wrote formally, not to 'sweetheart' or 'mine own', but to 'dearest Mary-Anne' to protest at her unaccountable silence. He had her ring as a talisman hung near his heart. Without it 'I should . . . think that for the last ten months I had been dreaming.'[69] Still he received no letter and so he wrote again, angrily this time. They had parted with love so why did she now ignore him? 'Above all persons, you who alone occasion our painful separations, are the last who should grudge me the only solace under such circumstances.' Given that he knew her to be writing other letters (he had received one for her, from her lawyer), her conduct was all the more extraordinary. 'It does indeed appear to me more than unaccountable, that a person, who can have found time to write to her lawyer or her trustee, and probably to many a corpulent beau, or seedy second rate dandy, should have allowed nearly a week to elapse with[ou]t sending a line to the individual to whom she professes to be devoted.'[70] Mary Anne's reply was robust. He had expressed no anxiety to hear from her, and she would not send letters where they were not wanted. 'I do not like to send coals to Newcastle. A woman should never be fonder of a man than he is of her except when he is ill or lonely and then you will find me devoted & affectionate.'[71] She had nothing to say of the corpulent beaus or the seedy second-rate dandies. Her silence on the subject, in a letter otherwise full of her fellow guests at Chastleton, made two things clear. She was not accountable to Disraeli for her friends and nor would she be lectured by him.

In the face of her defiance he changed tack. Now he wrote once more to 'My beloved and adored Mary Anne', and even slid into his letter an oblique apology. He had not meant to be unkind, he insisted, but had merely written under the influence of strong feelings. Thank goodness they did not have many lovers' quarrels. 'Truly they are not loveable things, and should only be adopted by those, whose flagging affections require stimulus.'[72] Quarrels had proved to be too dangerous for the stimulation of affection, so Disraeli relapsed into theatrical descriptions of his own state, written in a register borrowed from his tragedy *Alarcos*. On 29 December he wrote that he had passed one of the worst weeks of his life, spent prostrate on the sofa, 'utterly wretched'. 'Not a wink, no not a single wink did I sleep last night. I thought all was over between us, that you loved me no more, that I was doomed for ever to have my heart crushed. Indeed it is not exaggeration to say that this morning my life seemed on a thread.' 'You must love me', he concluded. 'My heart is too full, my head too weak to say anything but I bless and adore you.' A postscript reinforcing this trailed off mid sentence, the phrase 'I am so nervous I can . . .' followed only by a wobbly line.[73]

The authenticity of this performance of emotion can be judged by the fact that on the same day Disraeli wrote an elegant and lively note to Lady

Blessington, following a 'charming' visit by Count D'Orsay to Bradenham.[74] (He told Mary Anne that the visit had been a failure, since his plight left him quite unfit to entertain guests.) Mary Anne, however, was convinced. 'My own very dear Dizzy', she replied, 'your sad, kind, dear dear, letter I can only weep over & kiss – I will be with you my love as soon as possible . . . Your impatience to see me cannot be beyond mine to be clasp'd to your dear faithful heart again.'[75] She asked him to make sure they had a sitting room at Bradenham available for their private use, and wrote of her pity for Count D'Orsay, trapped with a grieving host. But she was also puzzled by the extent of his desperation, and full of practical concerns. Her mother's pension needed attention, and she would be bringing both her mother and Eliza to Bradenham. Also accompanying her would be her brother, now back in England and restored to the bosom of his family.

Disraeli's reply was a triumph of high-flown eroticism: overwritten, over-blown, sexualised and calculated to work Mary Anne, even before her arrival, into a peak of acquiescent anticipation:

My beloved, thrice beloved,

I am mad with love. My passion is frenzy. The prospect of our immediate meeting overwhelms and entrances me. I pass my nights and days in scenes of strange and fascinating rapture. Till I embrace you, I shall not know what calmness is. I write this to beg you to take care to have your hand *ungloved*, when you arrive, so that you may stand by me, and I may hold and clasp and feel your soft delicious hand, as I help your mother out of the carriage; now mind this, or I shall be insane with disappointment.[76]

History does not relate whether Mary Anne arrived at Bradenham gloved or ungloved, although given her love of drama and romance it seems likely that in this, at least, she did as she was asked. But when she left for London two weeks later she was still unengaged. Disraeli wrote of his misery at her absence, and his ill health following a late evening with boring visitors, but she was more concerned by her elderly mother's actual ill health than these imaginary maladies, particularly since they were his own fault. 'I cannot say I am sorry you have had a bad night', she wrote at one point, 'as it was in consequence of taking too much wine. Shame Shame, Dizzy, no human being not even your own dear self could cause me to eat or drink the least thing that disagreed with me.'[77] He swallowed the reproach and continued to write of his love, insisting on its strength in every letter. He had promised not to return to London until he had finished *Alarcos*, but at the end of the month he announced he could no longer bear to be apart from her. She was tired by the effort of caring for her mother and worried about her brother, who lurked at Grosvenor Gate, living at her expense and pleading with her to fund another promotion. 'I come', Disraeli announced, 'to console my soft and precious treasure.'[78]

Disraeli did not tell Mary Anne of a letter from D'Orsay that acted as the real spur for his return to London. 'When I read in the beginning of your letter, The Trajedy is finished', D'Orsay wrote, 'I thought that you were married, but on reflection I supposed that if it was so, you would have said, The Comedy. How is it that you leave her in London by herself. I saw her driving alone a few days ago in Pall Mall.'[79] At a dinner party at Grosvenor Gate on 3 February Disraeli met the Milner Gibsons, George Wombwell and Mr Stapleton, the presence of two of the despised demireps apparently confirming the prescience of D'Orsay's warning. Four days later, on the 7th, matters between Mary Anne and Disraeli finally erupted. Protestations of passion, devotion and constancy were abandoned as at Grosvenor Gate they had a grand row, the worst of their affair. Disraeli marched out of the house leaving behind a distraught Mary Anne, and all seemed over.

~

Four letters from Disraeli to Mary Anne survive from 7 February, as do three notes from her to him. She evidently wrote more letters but these have been lost, so the testimony for that day comes overwhelmingly from him. In the morning she wrote asking him to call; he replied that he would do so as soon as he was dressed. In this first short note he denied that he had allowed his friends to influence his conduct towards her (D'Orsay's letter notwithstanding) and dismissed the suggestion that she had enemies waiting to condemn her behaviour. They had only themselves to blame for their predicament and he was gloomy about their future. Having sent this missive ahead and given Mary Anne some indication of his state of mind, he then went to Grosvenor Gate, where the row took place. From the letters he sent afterwards, we know that it centred on her persistent refusal to fix a date for their marriage and her belief that he only wished to marry her for her money. She called him a 'selfish bully' and told him to get out of her house. He left; she sent a lost note speeding after him in which she appears to have asked him not to be angry and to return; he replied in a coldly furious letter. He was not angry, he insisted, only sorrowful. But he was used to disappointment and would recover from being so bitterly disappointed by her. She had every material thing she needed to make her life delightful (unlike him, ran the unspoken reproach) and would soon forget him. He deployed the dream image of earlier letters, this time to doubt her loyalty. 'You will find life delightful and full of enjoyment, altho' not illumined by the love of one, who will soon be to you a dream.'[80]

If Mary Anne replied to this letter, then that reply too has been lost. Later that evening Disraeli wrote again, either in response to a further communication from her or because he was unable to contain himself. Everyone talked of their marriage as a settled thing except her, he protested. He was placed in absurd situations, forced to turn down offers of the country seats of friends as honeymoon destinations because he did not know if a honeymoon would ever take place. Mary Anne used to talk of their marriage: did she feel she had to do so in order to keep his attention? As a woman of the world she ought to understand that her vacillation placed him in an impossible situation. 'The continuance of the present state of affairs, could only render you *disreputable*; me it wo[ul]d render *infamous*.' He was already talked of as 'Mrs Wyndham Lewis's De Novo', a reference to a contemporary adventurer dismissed by one journal as a 'he-prostitute'.[81] In any case, did Mary Anne really think she was that much of a matrimonial prize?

I avow when I first made my advances to you, I was influenced by no romantic feelings. My father had long wished me to marry; my settling in life was the implied, tho' not stipulated, condition of a disposition of his property, which would have been convenient to me. I myself, about to commence a practical career, wished for the solace of a home, and shrunk from all the torturing passions of intrigue. I was not blind to worldly advantages in such an alliance, but I had already proved,

that my heart was not to be purchased. I found you in sorrow, and that
heart was touched. I found you, as I thought, amiable, tender, and yet
acute and gifted with no ordinary mind; one whom I co[ul]d look upon
with pride as the partner of my life, who could sympathise with all my
projects and feelings, console me in the moments of depression, share
my hour of triumph, and work with me for our honor and our happi-
ness.

Now for your fortune: I write the sheer truth. That fortune proved
to be much less than I, or the world, imagined. It was, in fact, as far
as I was concerned, a fortune which co[ul]d not benefit me in the
slightest degree; it was merely a jointure not greater than your station
required; enough to maintain yr. establishment and gratify your private
tastes. To eat and to sleep in that house, and nominally to call it mine;
these could be only objects for a penniless adventurer. Was this an
inducement for me to sacrifice my sweet liberty, and that indefinite
future, which is one of the charms of existence? No; when months
ago I told you one day, that there was only one link between us, I felt
that my heart was inextricably engaged to you, and but for that I
would have terminated our acquainted. From that moment I devoted
to you all the passion of my being. Alas! it has been poured upon the
Sand!

So there Mary Anne had it, to read, reread and contemplate in solitude.
The early protestations of devotion were a charade, played out for practical
benefit. As he discovered her good qualities he discovered too that he had
been deceived about her fortune, which was hardly big enough to merit the
attentions of a fortune-hunter. And when at last he gave his heart to her
she proved an unworthy recipient, quite incapable of recognising or cherishing
the extent of his passion.

Having worked himself into a state of blind self-righteousness, Disraeli
veered into outright disingenuousness. 'Had we married', he told her, 'not one
shilling of your income sho[ul]d have ever been seen by me; neither indirectly
or directly, wo[ul]d I have interfered in the management of your affairs. If
society justly stigmatises with infamy the hired lover, I shrink with equal
disgust from being the paid husband.' Mary Anne accused him of selfishness;

how could she when he was on the point of repaying her the expenses of his libel trial? 'By heavens, as far as worldly interests are concerned, your alliance could not benefit me.' And in any case, 'I wo[ul]d not condescend to be the minion of a princess; and not all the gold of Ophir sho[ul]d ever lead me to the altar. Far different are the qualities which I require in the sweet participator of my existence. My nature demands that my life sho[ul]d be perpetual love.'

If only, he continued, he had listened to the friends who had warned him to be wary in his dealings with her. 'Coxcomb to suppose that you wo[ul]d conduct yourself to me in a manner different to that in which you have behaved to fifty others!' Had she enjoyed sporting with his heart? 'Was there no ignoble prey at hand, that you must degrade a bird of heaven?' Would not Captain Neale have made a more fitting target? She had broken his spirit and poisoned his life, and he hoped she was satisfied. The world would mock him, but he would be upheld by his self-respect. Finally he concluded:

Farewell. I will not affect to wish you happiness, for it is not in your nature to obtain it. For a few years you may flutter in some frivolous circle, and trifle with some spirits perhaps as false and selfish as your own. But the time will come when you will sigh for any heart that co[ul]d be fond; and despair of one that can be faithful. Then will be the penal hour of retribution – then you will think of me with remorse, admiration and despair – then you will recall to your memory the passionate heart that you have forfeited, and the genius you have betrayed.[82]

Why did Disraeli write like this to a woman he had spent months wooing? He was angry, and having half convinced himself of the veracity of his feeling, he was hurt by the suggestion that his passion was somehow in-authentic. But he was also frightened. By the beginning of 1839 the Whig government of Lord Melbourne was on the point of collapse; in May Melbourne would resign, prompting the Bedchamber Crisis in which Robert Peel declined office after Queen Victoria refused to replace her Whig ladies-in-waiting. Melbourne was forced to limp on as a powerless Prime Minister, but throughout 1839 the threat of governmental collapse and parliamentary dissolution hung over the country. For Disraeli, dissolution before marriage meant the end of his career and his life in England. He could not stand for re-election with his Maidstone debts unpaid and was only protected from the bailiffs by parliamentary privilege. The moment Parliament was dissolved, he would lose that privilege and would be faced with the prospect of debtors' prison or permanent European exile. He lied when he said he was not an adventurer and that he had no intention of touching Mary Anne's money, but he did so because he was terrified. Theatrical passion had failed to win her. Now, intuitively, he tried to shift their dynamic once and for all, spurning her in the unkindest way in order, perversely, to demonstrate the power of his feelings.

Apparently, Mary Anne told Disraeli he was 'cruel'; in his fourth letter of the day, written late in the evening, he flung the word back at her. 'I wrote what I felt', he insisted. 'I think it must have been *true*; and I wrote as much for your sake as for mine.' She had asked him to come to her; he would not, but only because he was 'wearied, harassed, and exhausted; unfit for any converse'. Although they could never be together, she still had his affection, and he would visit her tomorrow to assure her of it. Again he returned to her accusation of cruelty; truly, he had never meant to be so. But he was full of equivocation, apparently unsure even of the contents of a letter written in the white heat of rage. 'I am certain I never meant to write a *cruel* letter; but is it a *true* one? That is the question; and if you think, that I have expressed the truth, shun that Disraeli whom you perhaps still love.'[83]

Mary Anne's response to this letter does survive. She did not write pages of reproach or self-justification; she did not continue their argument. She had none of his literary skill, none of his powers of argument or persuasion. But she wrote directly and powerfully, paving the way for reconciliation. 'For Gods sake come to me', she implored. 'I am ill & almost distracted – I will answer all you wish – I never desired you to leave the house, or implied or thought a word about money I rec[eive]d a most distressing letter & you left me at the moment not knowing from the house. I have now been a widow a year & the world knows not how I was situated with him & you cannot understand my bitter s[h]ame – I often feel at the <u>apparent</u> impropriety of my present position. I am devoted to you.'[84]

The next morning he wrote that he would call that afternoon, and praised her tenderness. He would be the most unfortunate man should circumstance deprive him 'of a heart which I believe to be unrivalled for the profundity and the pathos of its affections'.[85] In return she wrote, one line only: 'I am too ill to see any one but yourself to day, oh come.'[86] Again he was moved, and the sequence of letters ends with one from him, written as if his long, vitriolic letter had never been. 'My darling and my life, I will come to you *immediately* I am dressed. I found her dear note of yesterday and kissed it very much. She is the joy of my life and I wish to be her solace.'[87]

The events of 7 and 8 February 1839 left their mark on Disraeli and Mary Anne's relationship. No longer did she equivocate, the threat of losing him for good having shown her how much she wanted to marry him. He understood this. Gone now were the literary invocations of passion: he had won her and did not need to keep winning her. Before he had pleaded with her; now she deferred to him and asked for expressions of reassurance and affection. His letters became more akin to those of a busy husband to his wife of long standing than those of a lover. There continued to be problems at Grosvenor Gate, where Mary Anne's mother and brother lingered, fighting with each other and her about Disraeli's presence in the house. He knew he was at the root of the tensions but remained aloof, secure now in the knowledge that Mary Anne would not be dissuaded from marrying him by disapproving relations. To Sarah, still his chief confidante even in matters of the heart, he described the scene. 'The broils bet[wee]n mother, brother and dau[ghte]r rage so terribly and continuously, that I hardly know what it will end in.' It was most inconvenient, since it prevented him from asking Ralph to dine. 'I suppose my constant presence, tho' not confessed, is at the bottom of it on their side . . . I of course never open my mouth, and am always scrupulously polite: but what avails the utmost frigidity of civilisation against a brother in hysterics, and a mother who menaces with a prayer-book!' Others among Mary Anne's relations preferred the interloping lover to the censorious brother, but that too caused problems. Uncle William Scrope, Mary Anne's smartest relation, asked her to dine with Disraeli, specifically excluding John. 'The mother', Disraeli told Sarah, 'is of course frenzied.'[88]

John Evans returned to his regiment in the spring of 1839 after a long leave of absence, and in May wrote to thank Mary Anne for purchasing his promotion to colonel. He was now forty-nine and in command of the regiment he had joined at seventeen. On 8 May he was leading his men on a march along the Cheddar Cliffs into Bristol when the young soldier carrying the regimental colour was taken ill. The march halted and John took the colour himself, telling the lines of men that it was the first time he had carried his regimental standard since the Battle of Vimiera, in which he had fought as a volunteer. It was a moment of gallantry recorded in military histories: the old soldier, a fighter from the lost world of the Napoleonic wars, relieving a young man in distress and doing so with dignity and honour. In his private life John let down those around him again and again, and he showed scant regard for Mary Anne's feelings during decades of unstinting support. But to his fellow soldiers he was a hero and a leader of men.[89] That night, after the regiment had arrived in Bristol, he fell ill and travelled to London to stay at Grosvenor Gate while he consulted a doctor. He wrote to Mary Anne to warn her of his arrival, his handwriting faint and unsteady. Eleanor Yate was also staying at Grosvenor Gate, but Mary Anne hid the presence of her ill brother from her mother, afraid that he would cause her anxiety. Two weeks later John was dead.

Disraeli told Sarah that John had been suffering from 'brain-fever': the most likely explanation for his sudden decline is that he had malaria, contracted in Mauritius.[90] Throughout his illness Eleanor Yate remained ignorant of the fact that her son was dying in an upstairs bedroom, and even after his death Mary Anne contrived to remove her mother from London without telling her that she had been in the same house as John's body. The strain of concealment and of watching her brother die reduced Mary Anne to a state of collapse, and she and Eleanor took refuge with one of the Clutton sisters in Bedfordshire. Disraeli moved into an empty Grosvenor Gate, dealing with servants, the distribution of John's possessions and the arrangements for the funeral. His wedding was again postponed, but Mary Anne wrote every day to assure him of her improving health and her confidence in their shared future. With her brother dead and her mother fragile, her emotional dependence on Disraeli grew stronger. She signed herself his 'devoted grateful Child & Wife' and called him her 'darling husband'. He responded calling her his 'sweet, dear wife' and dwelling once more on his love. He still wrote of her in the third person, but his premonitions for their life together were direct and grounded. 'The more I think of Mary-Anne, the more I love her. Now she has gone, I feel quite lone, but I am cheered with the prospect of coming joy, and with the certainty of her admirable qualities.'[91] 'Dizzy I have the most perfect confidence in you', she responded. 'Your fond affection & goodness will form the future happiness of my life – My heart is bursting to prove how well I love & how highly I value you.'[92]

A week after their arrival in Bedfordshire, Mary Anne plucked up the courage to tell her mother the truth about John's death. According to Mary Anne's account, Eleanor understood that her daughter had acted out of concern for her, and said only that she was comforted by the knowledge that John had been loved and cared for at the end of his life. With her conscience unburdened, Mary Anne prepared to return to London, even as she and Disraeli continued to exchange promises of love and happy lives. 'I hope we shall never again part', he wrote on 11 July, in a letter containing sentiments completely unlike those of the previous winter. The bluster and the storm had gone; what was left feels, even at a historical distance, genuine. 'I can not pretend that I love you more than I did, but absence has made me feel how necessary you are to my existence.'[93] In London they paid a ceremonial call on Lady Blessington. Mary Anne had not met her before, since her company was usually barred to women, but Disraeli wanted his future wife to meet his friend and Mary Anne now acceded to his every request. He wrote to Sarah asking her to send a button from the Bradenham servants' livery so his crest could be copied for the uniforms of the Grosvenor Gate servants, and lawyers were instructed to draw up a marriage settlement. A date for the ceremony was set: 28 August 1839.

~

A cluster of documents shades in the period immediately surrounding the wedding, among them the marriage settlement itself, drawn up on 23 August. As was common for women of substantial property, the settlement designated Mary Anne a 'femme sole', meaning that all her property remained hers and did not become Disraeli's. All interest on the Lewis estate was to be paid to her 'for her sole separate and peculiar use', and could not be subject to

Disraeli's 'debts control interference or engagement'. Importantly, she could dispose of her property as she wished, meaning that she was free to pay Disraeli's debts if she wished to do so. The protection offered her was in this respect limited, but it did at least indemnify her against liability for his debts and it ensured that she, not he, received her income. The settlement named George Dawson and John Guest as her trustees, both of whom had known her for longer than Disraeli and whose first loyalty was to her.

The marriage settlement lists Mary Anne's possessions in their entirety, and itemises every single object at Grosvenor Gate, down to the kitchen utensils. None of it was Disraeli's, and the future he rejected on 7 February, in which he slept and ate in her house and nominally called it his, became on paper a reality. But Mary Anne had already shown generosity with both her house and her money, and Disraeli was in no position to quibble about the disposition of salt cellars. The settlement also lists Mary Anne's jewellery, in a section entitled 'Brilliants', which runs for several pages. A few lines give a sense of its fantastic colour. 'Brilliant tiara in two parts (weight sixty carat) one large oriental carbuncle set with sixty large brilliants – one garnet bracelet – one pair brilliant earrings emerald suit of a necklace brooch and earrings set with brilliants – One turquoise snap-mounted with brilliants – One pair diamond and turquoise earrings to correspond – one oval brooch composed of small brilliants and rubys.'[94] After Wyndham's death Mary Anne had had to pack her jewellery away, but her marriage to Disraeli allowed her to wear it once more, and for the rest of her life she sparkled in a blaze of precious stones.

That the caution of Mary Anne's trustees demonstrated by the marriage settlement was justified is clear from a letter Disraeli wrote the day before the wedding to his agent, William Pyne. 'During the honeymoon and travel, it is possible that letters may be occasionally *read*', he warned. 'I think it right to say that Mrs D. is aware that I am about raising a sum of money, but is ignorant of the method. There will be no harm therefore, if necessary, of your writing to me on the subject generally but avoid *details* as to the *method* of security – which are unnecessary.'[95] To Mary Anne herself he wrote a poem in which he confessed that he could not rationalise the depth of his love for her. The letter to Pyne suggests this was untrue, but the poem itself reads as an attempt not to deceive but to assure Mary Anne he would make

her happy. It suggests too that even while he married from mercenary moti-
vation, he had come to appreciate the qualities others loved in her: spon-
taneity, a merry disposition, sound judgement and a conversational style as
surprising as it was quick:

> I love her since her heart is true
>   And knows no guile;
> Her spirit high, yet tender too;
>   And all the while
> Tho' she may love, her judgment clear
>   As chrystal mines;
> And quick as in the summer sphere
>   The lightning shines.
> I love her wit that artless flows,
>   Her dulcet voice;
> Her face that with expression glows;
>   I love my choice.[96]

No letters from Mary Anne survive for this period, but she too made
wedding preparations. At Grosvenor Gate the servants were put on board
wages for the month of the honeymoon, and she told Mary Dawson of her
imminent remarriage. Mary Dawson replied that Mary Anne's kindness,
especially to her children, caused them all to rejoice on her behalf. 'I have
so long considered you as one of my own family', she wrote, 'that if you were
my Sister I could not be more interested than I am in your welfare.'[97]

The wedding itself was a small affair. Mary Anne was given away by her
uncle William Scrope and the best man was Lord Lyndhurst. The D'Israelis
did not leave Bradenham to attend and there were no additional guests,
probably in deference to the fact that it was Mary Anne's second marriage
and grand festivities were not appropriate. Disraeli's journey to the church
had a moment of comedy when one of Lord Lyndhurst's horses was seized
with the staggers, but a replacement was found before Mary Anne was handed
into the carriage after the ceremony in front of a crowd of onlookers. During
the ceremony itself Disraeli was nervous and tried to put the ring on the
wrong finger, but Mary Anne was cool and collected, garbed in a 'travelling

dress of exotic brilliancy'.[98] From the church they travelled to Tunbridge Wells to begin their honeymoon, and from there both wrote letters to the family at Bradenham. Disraeli sent his first letter to his mother, describing the ceremony, and Mary Anne wrote to Isaac. 'My only & dear Papa', ran her epistle. 'I wish you could see your happy children – We exemplify lifes <u>finest tale</u> – to eat – to drink – to sleep – love & be loved.'[99] In Tunbridge Wells she also put her name to a letter to a Maidstone creditor drafted for her by Disraeli, in which she maintained that Wyndham had settled all election expenses and Disraeli had no outstanding debts in the constituency. And in her account book she penned a brief memorandum of the day. 'Married on the 28th (1839) of August. Lord Lyndhurst & Mr Scrope (my uncle) were present at the ceremony at St Georges Church Hanover Square. dear Dizzy became my Husband.'[100]

At Bradenham the wedding was marked with celebrations. The village church bells rang all day and the D'Israelis allowed the servants to hold a dinner and dance. 'It was half past one the next morning', Sarah told Disraeli, 'before we could persuade Tita to dismiss them to their repose.' Tita himself was overjoyed that the man who had found him an English home finally had a home of his own too. 'I wish I could do justice to the polyglot wishes for your happiness & that of your fair lady, which Tita has entrusted to me', wrote Sarah. 'You well know that however unconveyable they are as sincere as any breathed at Bradenham – & what more can be said for any.'[101]

Part Two

Ever After

(1840–1867)

CHAPTER FIVE

On Heroes and Hero-Worship

MISS LYSON

Miss Lyson was engaged to the Reverend Mr Mynor, a reforming curate of some prominence. On the day of her wedding, villagers garlanded the church gate with flowers and local children scattered petals in her path. Miss Lyson meanwhile remained out of sight, waiting for her bridegroom. When it became clear that he was not going to appear, she retreated, giving sudden illness as an excuse. Detectives were summoned from London, the canal was dragged and rumours circulated. The bridegroom had been spotted the day before the wedding enquiring in Gloucester about trains to Devon; another witness reported seeing him in the company of sinister priests, fuelling speculation that he had gone over to Rome. A militiaman who was caught destroying old clothes was arrested on suspicion of his murder but released without charge. One of the detectives told Mr Mynor's father that absconding bridegrooms were a surprisingly common occurrence, citing the example of a young man so frightened by elaborate wedding preparations that on the morning of his marriage he boarded a ship to the West Indies. The village thought the matter straightforward, whispering to each other that one only had to look at the bride to solve the mystery. She was not attractive, her temper was uneven and it was an open secret that her stepmother wanted to be rid of her. She was possessed of a fortune but, her neighbours agreed, a man needed more than money to make him happy.

~

The Reverend Mr Mynor performed his disappearing act in October 1855, when Sarah Disraeli was staying nearby with friends. Her host took part in the search for him and she visited the Lysons with her hostess in the week before the wedding. She was gripped by the story's nexus of revelations about marriage, money, families and betrayal, and related its details in two animated letters to Mary Anne. The saga was also covered in *The Times*, in an article entitled 'Mysterious Disappearance of a Clergyman', but *The Times*, unlike Sarah, refused to discuss the 'rumours of a strange character' circulating about the reasons for Mr Mynor's flight. 'I knew that the missing Bridegroom would excite your interest', Sarah told her sister-in-law. 'I believe that nothing has been heard of him really, but we are away from the authentic news & in the midst of the rumours & reports which abound – every body has a fresh story'.[1] Of the fate of the bride, chosen for her money and then abandoned in spite of it, we know little. The combined efforts of metropolitan detectives and local searchers failed to find any trace of her affianced husband, and together they vanish from the historical record at the point at which the trail on him runs cold.

Mary Anne – another woman chosen for her money – next appears in her story on her honeymoon, shimmering with colour and life in the letters Disraeli sent home to Sarah. From Calais the Disraelis drove to Ostend, where their carriage was hoisted on to a train to Brussels. After a night to recover from a rough crossing and a long journey, they drove onwards, moving steadily through Belgium and Germany by road and then steamer until they reached Baden-Baden in the Black Forest. Baden-Baden was a spa town and for a few days they were content to sink into the comfort of 'the most picturesque, agreeable, lounging sort of place of idleness you can imagine'. The season was coming to an end, though, and they quickly grew tired of the town's dilapidated gentility. Mary Anne thought it no better than Cheltenham, Disraeli reported. 'Public dinners, balls, promenades, pumps, music and gambling.'[2] Disraeli too thought it 'too faded wateringplacish to please',[3] and so they made their way through the Black Forest to Munich, joining in festivities organised by the King of Württemberg en route. At Munich they toured galleries and churches before departing for Paris, where they arrived at the beginning of November. Together they threw themselves into Parisian life, appearing at the opera and the theatre, exchanging calls and invitations with English visitors and catching up with political news in the pages of *Galignani's*

Messenger and Paris fashions in the shops of French *modistes*. 'Mary Anne is particularly well', Disraeli wrote, 'and in her new costumes looks like Madame Pompadour, who is at present the model of Paris at least in dress.'[4]

At the end of November they arrived back in England, drawn home by Disraeli's sense of gathering political momentum against the Whigs and concern for Isaac, whose sight was failing alarmingly. The doctors Disraeli consulted believed Isaac's blindness to be caused by sedentary habits and an overburdened digestive system, and he summoned his father to Grosvenor Gate to listen to the experts. They prescribed abstinence from food and drink, and pills of an unspecified nature, but Isaac nevertheless ceased to see, bringing to an end decades of reading in low light. Sarah became her father's eyes, spending hours each day reading to him and taking dictation. Meanwhile at Grosvenor Gate Mary Anne and Disraeli performed the rituals expected of a newly married couple. They paid an uncomfortable visit to Disraeli's Basevi cousins in Highgate, Disraeli's fruitless attempts to borrow money from his relations precluding friendship between them and his bride. They took delivery of a splendid breakfast set of Worcester china from Mrs Meredith, mother of Sarah's lost love William. And they dined with Disraeli's acquaintance Mrs Montefiore, having been invited to meet her Rothschild connections. 'There were Rothschilds, Montefiores, Alberts, and Disraelis', Disraeli told Sarah. 'Not a Xtian name, but Mary Anne bearing it like a philosopher.'[5] Peel sent his congratulations on the marriage, and Mary Anne lost little time in exerting a wifely influence over her husband's unhealthy habits by calling in a new doctor to attend him. 'Too much health and the over indulgence of an appetite of tremendous constancy had somewhat deranged my liver', he conceded.[6] She also assumed responsibility for his hair, which she trimmed every two weeks and, when grey started to appear, dyed with indigo, or black henna.

In addition to Disraeli's letters to Sarah, the records of various shared projects give us an insight into the dynamic of the Disraelis' marriage in its first months. In Mary Anne's commonplace book Disraeli transcribed some of the poems written by former suitors, suggesting mutual enjoyment of bad rhymes and doggerel rhythms. He drew up a reading list of novels for her, encompassing work by Austen, Mary Shelley and Bulwer, and copied in riddles and epigrams on the nature of woman. 'Fickleness is in Woman of the world, the fault most likely to result, from their situation in society', ran one such *bon mot*. 'Well! we deserve no better of them: And after all, the flame is only smothered, by society, not extinguished: give it free ventilation & it will blaze.'[7]

Disraeli also copied into the commonplace book a list of his and Mary Anne's characteristics, drawn up by her shortly after their marriage. The double presence of this list in their papers, in her hand in loose-leaf draft and in his in the book in which they exchanged anecdotes and ideas, suggests something of its significance, for Mary Anne as she attempted to understand the contrast between them, and for Disraeli as he read and responded to her account of their partnership. The list opens with a couplet suggesting something of the physical pleasure Mary Anne took in her husband ('His eyes as black as sloes / and oh so <u>beautiful</u> his nose'). Disraeli's characteristics occupy the left column, hers the right:

Very Calm	Very effervescent
Manner grave & almost sad	Gay & happy looking when <u>speaking</u>
Never irritable	Very irritable
Bad humoured	Good humoured
Warm in love but cold in friendship	Cold in love but warm in friendship
No self love	Much self love
Very patient	No patience
Very studious	Very idle
Very generous	Only generous to those she loves
Often says what he does not think	Never says anything she does not think
It is impossible to find out who he likes or dislikes from his manner	Her manner is quite different to those she likes
He does not show his feelings	She shows her feelings
No Vanity	Much vanity
Conceited	No conceit
No self love	Much self love
He is seldom amus'd	Every thing amuses her
He is a Genius	She is a Dunce
He is to be depended on to a certain degree	She is not to be depended on

So that it is evident they sympathise only on one subject – Maidstone much like husbands & wives about their Children.[8]

This list of qualities has been more widely quoted than anything else Mary Anne wrote, in part because of its disarming frankness and its open avowal of how ill suited she was to be the political wife of a man of intellect. 'He is a genius – She is a Dunce': many have agreed with her assessment. At first glance the list reads simply as a celebration of Disraeli, whose striking qualities are emphasised by proximity to his wife. 'Very studious – Very idle', 'No self love – Much self love' (repeated twice), 'Very patient – No patience'. But Mary Anne does something more complicated than simply praise her husband as she sets up her oppositions. Disraeli appears as a chameleon, shifting opinions and manner according to circumstance, keeping his true feelings hidden. She appears initially as a creature of the moment, easily amused, happy and warm. But she represents herself as two beings, one seen by the world and one witnessed only by those closest to her. 'Her manner is quite different to those she likes'. Disraeli, meanwhile, combines in her account patience with bad humour; his calmness translates into coldness to friends and a refusal to be amused. He is to be depended on, but only 'to a certain degree'. Yet he is 'warm in love' while she is 'cold', belying the inference that their public personae mirror the roles they occupy as lovers. Mary Anne's conclusion, that they sympathise over his constituency as other couples do over their children, is deliberately undermined by her presentation of them as the personification of contrasts. Her list is not merely a joke against herself but an exploration of the structural relationship of the pair, defined by each other. Its portrait is optimistic, of husband and wife as two parts of a whole, a balanced, harmonious union.

~

On 10 February 1840, the Queen married Albert of Saxe-Coburg and Gotha at the Chapel Royal, St James's Palace. Disraeli spent the day 'Prince hunting' and eventually battled through crowds to catch sight of the bride and groom travelling through Kensington as they made their way to Windsor.[9] A week later he formed part of a procession of MPs who followed the Speaker to Buckingham Palace to congratulate the Queen on her marriage. He looked so marvellous in his Court costume, he told Sarah, it was generally agreed he should never wear anything else. It was his first visit to Buckingham Palace, and although it compared badly to the Bavarian castles visited during his honeymoon, he was nevertheless impressed by the scene, all 'busy and brilliant'. 'The Queen looked well', he related, 'the Prince leaning on her left in high military fig very handsome.'[10] The royal marriage was famously happy but in its early years it was not without its problems. Victoria would not permit her husband to interfere with her rule, and initially his power in his adopted country and his houses was limited. 'In my home life I am very happy and contented', he wrote to a friend three months after the wedding. 'But the difficulty in filling my place with the proper dignity is, that I am only the husband, and not the master in the house.'[11]

Over time Albert carved out a role for himself at home and in the country, paying particular attention in the early years of his marriage to the moral standing of the royal family, damaged by generations of dissolute Georgian monarchs, and to the living conditions of the urban poor. During his first year in Britain, Chartist cries for reform made explicit the extent of suffering in the country. The People's Charter, calling for six reforming measures including universal manhood suffrage and a secret ballot, had been drawn up in May 1838, and by 1840 Chartist protests were a feature of British political life. 'Last night all the town was terrified with expected risings of the Chartists', Disraeli told Sarah in January. 'The troops ordered to be ready, the police in all dir[ecti]ons, and the fire engines all full as incendiarism was to break out in several quarters.'[12] Disraeli was broadly in sympathy with the Chartists, believing that the repressive measures taken against them were the actions of a weak government, and he was one of very few MPs to oppose the punitive treatment meted out to their leaders. But in most matters he was loyal to his party leadership, and throughout 1840 he courted Peel and other Tory grandees, waiting for a Whig collapse and subsequent Tory ascendancy.

Disraeli's campaign to be part of that ascendancy was given new energy by his marriage. For the first time in his adult life he had a permanent London home, somewhere he could entertain colleagues and from where he could build his own power base. In 1827 Grosvenor Gate had allowed Mary Anne to establish herself as a Tory hostess; now it had the same transformative effect for her husband. The interior of the house remained unchanged from

1827, Mary Anne's vivid colours and fabrics, looking a little faded now, still present in every room. Mary Anne was always concerned with keeping her wardrobe up to date but she was less concerned that her house should be fashionable. It was comfortable, to her taste, and it mattered little to Disraeli that its interior was a decade behind the times. In January and February he held eight political dinners to which he invited all the most prominent members of his party. Predominantly male dinner parties were a staple of the political landscape in the 1840s, although the hosts of such events were usually political leaders, not backbench MPs. 'I have asked nearly sixty MPs to dine with me and 40 have come', he told Sarah in mid February. 'There is scarcely anyone of station in the house or society that I have not paid this attention to, which was most politic.'[13] His guests were also drawn from the House of Lords and one of his most successful parties was that attended by the Duke of Buckingham, who lavished praise on Mary Anne's china and her opulent style of entertaining.

The bills for these parties were met by Mary Anne, as were all the running costs of Grosvenor Gate, now home once more to a political couple. In 1838 and 1839 her position as the widow of a rich man gave her an unusual degree of financial autonomy, and her account books for this period show her living comfortably within her income of £5,000 a year, meeting her expenses promptly and investing surplus funds in government stocks, the performance of which she monitored carefully. But at the end of January 1840 she wrote to Lady Blessington for advice about how to cut her household expenditure while maintaining the appearance of largesse. Lady Blessington, drowning in debt among the splendour of Gore House, sent back a detailed salary scale for household servants as well as other housekeeping tips. 'I am trying a new plan for altering old lamps', she reported, 'by which common oil of three shillings and sixpence a yd can be used instead of sperm oil, without smell, and giving an equally brilliant light.' 'How our dear good Dis would laugh at this.'[14]

Dear good Dis might be above such minor concerns as the cost of lamp oil and the per-head price of his dinner parties, but Mary Anne made careful lists of how much their guests ate and drank and exerted tight control over kitchen supplies and tradesmen's bills. If she bought Disraeli new clothes, she wrote it down; the budget for her servants' board was written into the agreements they signed when they entered her service. 'One pound of sugar ought to last five days for Mama & Dizzy', she noted in March 1840. Lady Blessington recommended paying an under housemaid £18 a year; a year later Mary Anne paid her new housemaid only £13. Lady Blessington thought a lady's maid should receive £25, from which she should meet her own laundry costs; Mary Anne offered her new maid £18. Her cook received only £25 a year; Lady Blessington's earned £40. When the Disraelis were absent from Grosvenor Gate the servants had their wages reduced, their consumption of household supplies was minutely detailed and the footmen were told to conserve their hair powder until their employers' return. If servants did not please, they were sent on their way. In 1842 a housemaid called Jane Farrell was dismissed for 'this day behaving very outrageous', and Elizabeth Ashe lasted only one day as a lady's maid before being sent away for 'bad behaviour'.[15] Mary Anne was easily offended by servants who were sloppy or disrespectful and she struggled to retain staff. For the most part Disraeli remained oblivious, avoiding all conversation with the servants even during Mary Anne's occasional absences. If she was present, he left the management of Grosvenor Gate absolutely to her; if she was unavoidably engaged during a crisis, he acted only according to written instructions. After a great quarrel between the servants left Grosvenor Gate unexpectedly denuded of staff in October 1840, he confided to Sarah that his 'domestic ministry' was 'as troublesome as the French' but he played no part in the negotiations for peace.[16]

In this he was not unusual. Grosvenor Gate was Mary Anne's domain and she neither sought nor encouraged his involvement in its internal politics apart from at times of real trouble. What was unusual was the contrast between their experiences of their house in the first months of their marriage. Disraeli did not make a home to which he brought his wife but rather became an expensive member of an existent household. Like Prince Albert he was a husband but not a master; unlike Albert he was indifferent to this. The male spaces at Grosvenor Gate – the dining room and library – became a kingdom in which he could see friends, negotiate with colleagues and write his way to fame without worrying about how much it cost to keep the decanters filled and the lights on. Mary Anne now had to fund a dual establishment and to support the political career of a husband still mired in debt. Her fixation with the cost of things became legendary but few knew the full scale of his financial disarray, or that she had grown up in a straitened household where the habit of ferocious economy became inculcated. Few knew too that she had spent her first marriage scrimping and saving in order to fund the career of a brother whose debts were nowhere near as monumental as Disraeli's.

~

The Queen's wedding in February set the tone for a brilliant social season, and once the labour of hosting and paying for political dinners was over, the Disraelis joined the crowds at Court, at the opera and in the ballrooms of aristocratic friends. They were invited to grand parties, Mary Anne received calls from the wives of Tory peers and was, according to Disraeli, 'happy in her successes'. At a Court drawing room held to celebrate the Queen's birthday in May, Mary Anne's dress was 'second to none – at least to us commoners'. The Queen was dressed in white but Mary Anne's outfit, described in the *Morning Post*, included 'A manteau of rich pale green satin, lined with white' and 'body and sleeves of la Medicia, superbly ornamented with a profusion of the finest diamonds'. The costume was completed by 'headress, feathers and blond lappets; ornaments, a splendid suite of diamonds and emeralds'. Ladies did not usually upstage the Queen by displaying their wealth in diamonds sewn on to their sleeves, but Mary Anne's love of fine feathers outweighed her desire to imitate the costumes of her peers.[17]

Ladies of quality usually refrained too from berating Napoleonic princes, but when Mary Anne and Disraeli found themselves victims of the poor oarsmanship of Louis Napoleon, afterwards Napoleon III, he received a scolding. Bulwer was giving a breakfast party at Craven Cottage on the Thames, and when the Disraelis and Louis Napoleon arrived late, they discovered the company had taken to the water in a steamer. Louis Napoleon volunteered to row down the river to meet them, only to steer his craft on to a reed bank in the middle of the river. Mary Anne sat in the prow, castigating him for his folly. 'You shd. not undertake things, wh: you cannot accomplish – You are always Sir, too adventurous.'[18] Disraeli wrote about the incident in autobiographical notes in the 1860s in which he recalled that he had been impressed by the good temper with which the future Emperor received his chastisement.

Some among Disraeli's circle refused to associate with his overdecorated wife, and in the months following the wedding his marriage was the subject of gossip and whispers in many a drawing room. His old friend and correspondent Lady Londonderry was angered by the match, and it was several years before she warmed towards Mary Anne. The salon of Lady Jersey was closed to her and *The Satirist* was scathing about Disraeli's attempt to convince the world that his wife was 'a young and beautiful female instead of a middle-aged, comfortable, matronly-looking dame' with a 'rubicund and good-natured face', which the artist of her portrait in *The Book of Beauty* failed to torture 'into anything approaching angelic form and grace'.[19] Her closest friends remained the women who had supported her before her marriage, principally Mary Dawson and Arethusa Milner Gibson. She also renewed her correspondence with Miles Stapleton, who inherited the title of Lord Beaumont in the summer of 1840. On hearing of her marriage Stapleton wrote that she had made a happy choice, since Disraeli's 'disposition seems to be as noble as his mind is replete with the highest order of genius'. 'You will I am sure be happy with a person of such good qualities and great talents', he continued. 'Allow me to add that to witness the happiness of both of you will equally increase my own.'[20]

They were together for most of their first year of marriage, and very few letters by Mary Anne from this period survive. Disraeli told Sarah of his wife's contentment, and his notes gesture towards an affectionate marital conversation about activities and plans. In August he commemorated their first wedding anniversary with a poem in which he celebrated Mary Anne as the 'most perfect wife'. 'The seasons change, sweet wife, but not our love.' 'The revolving year, that all its moons / Hath counted since thy bridal hand I pressed, / Brings us yet moons of honey.' He described her somewhat improbably as 'A graceful sprite' but his account of her all-encompassing interest in his pursuits rings true, despite the hyperbole. 'Hovering o'er all my fortunes; ever prompt / With sweet suggestions; and with dulcet tones / To cheer or counsel.' She was, he insisted, his 'star of inspiration'. 'On this day, / That made thee mine, I bless thee.'[21]

❧

During their courtship, poetry was one of the means by which Disraeli enacted the role of the courtly hero, wooing and winning his lady. Yet the act of writing and presenting verses signified dissimulation as well as gratitude, and was designed to convince Mary Anne of the emotional validity of their affair. After their marriage the poems he wrote on her birthday and their wedding anniversary performed the same function, papering over the cracks of a relationship marred by secrecy and double-dealing. The chief confidante of Disraeli's heart in 1840 was not Mary Anne but Sarah, a fact he took great pains to conceal from his wife. When he wrote to Sarah from Grosvenor Gate he addressed his letters to 'My dear Sa', but in the privacy of the Carlton Club she was always 'My dearest'. She followed the same pattern, writing to 'My dear Dis' at Grosvenor Gate and 'Dearest' at his club.

Mary Anne had no idea Disraeli wrote Sarah long, gossipy letters from the Carlton, or that Sarah sent the bulk of her replies there. 'All your letters to the C[arlto]n arrived safe but you sho[ul]d occas[iona]lly write to Grov[esno]r Gate, or the sudden ceasing of the correspondence may produce surprise', he warned in February.²² This secret poste restante system (which mirrored that used by Mary Anne and John to deceive Wyndham in the 1820s) lasted for two decades and allowed Sarah to preserve her place as her brother's most important correspondent. Disraeli destroyed Sarah's Carlton letters but it seems likely that her private communications amplified themes only hinted at in her Grosvenor Gate bulletins and that they kept Disraeli more closely connected to his family than would otherwise have been the case. Mary Anne was jealous of Disraeli's familial bonds and was particularly alert to the degree of attention he paid Sarah. She knew the damage that could be wrought on a marriage by intrusive siblings and the supremacy of old loyalties, and she sought to contain Disraeli's links with his family. When she had written to John, however, she had been reliant on Wyndham's willingness to frank her correspondence and had no private space in which she could receive letters. Disraeli had his club, his own frank, and, after parliamentary franking privileges were abolished early in 1840, the ability to post a letter without having to account for his actions, and of all these he made full use.

In May Sarah wrote to the Carlton Club in some agitation about a local creditor who had written to Disraeli at Bradenham demanding payment of a debt. Disraeli was dismissive, claiming to have settled the creditor's account by using his influence to secure a living for his son. Besides, he wrote, 'the affair is only trumped up in consequ[enc]e of my marriage'.[23] News of his marriage to a wealthy lady spread quickly among his creditors, and fending off their demands taxed his ingenuity. He used the Carlton Club for a second secret correspondence with his agent William Pyne, in which he continued his efforts to borrow money to repay old loans. Since he dared not tell Mary Anne the extent of his indebtedness, he could not ask her for help, and in any case his debts far exceeded her annual income. In September 1840 he managed to borrow £5,500, and still the creditors came.

In November 1840, fourteen months after their wedding, the marriage hit its first serious hurdle. A writ was delivered in Disraeli's absence to Grosvenor Gate and Mary Anne opened it. This, 'and other circumstances', he told Pyne, 'have at length produced a terrible domestic crisis'. He could not visit Pyne in his office for fear of running into yet another creditor, so begged him to call, but also to disclaim all knowledge of the row. 'You need know nothing of what has occurred, but may call on other, and more important business, of a very different nature.'[24] Mary Anne demanded to know the full extent of his debts and he told her enough to convince her that affairs were critical. But in March 1841 there was another crisis when the bailiffs threatened to invade Grosvenor Gate and Disraeli wrote to Pyne reproaching him for 'allowing judgment to be signed ag[ain]st me, and an executive virtually put in my house, without even apprising me that an action had commenced'.[25]

By the middle of their second year of marriage both Mary Anne and Disraeli were suffering under the strain of financial uncertainty. In March 1841, a week before the arrival of the second writ, Disraeli wrote from Grosvenor Gate to Sarah that their Easter plans were uncertain. They would come to Bradenham but only 'if Maryanne finds any benefit' . If not they would move on to Tunbridge Wells. 'She wants quiet more than anything else.' Later in March Disraeli made a passing reference to Mary Anne having given up her box at the opera, demonstrating further retrenchment on her part. She was unwell, he told Sarah, and was trying to alleviate her symptoms through a newly fashionable home-cure version of hydrotherapy. A shower bath was installed at Grosvenor Gate; one should be installed at Bradenham, he directed, in order to facilitate their visit there. 'Write to me at Gros[vesno]r Gate about it,' he told Sarah, 'in case you have anything to say.'[26] Physical illness for

Mary Anne often accompanied bouts of strain, and although Disraeli called in new doctors and she followed their prescriptions, real relief came to her when she had physical and emotional security – security not to be found in shower baths and pills.

~

By the middle of 1841 the Whigs were in disarray and Disraeli was again living in fear of a dissolution and arrest. His Maidstone election accounts were still unsettled, making it impossible for him to stand there again, and in any case he had nothing like the wealth needed to campaign in a corrupt constituency. In May he told Pyne that he was in urgent need of £500: three weeks later Parliament was dissolved and with £500 in cash he was able to evade his creditors and stand as the Tory candidate for Shrewsbury. Mary Anne paid for the campaign. 'I must now into the city and get the *argent* and lodge it at Drummonds', he wrote from the Carlton Club in June. 'Thank God and you, 'tis all ready.'[27] In her account book Mary Anne recorded the transfer of £700 from her account to Disraeli's and on 14 June she and Disraeli arrived in Shrewsbury to campaign, not waiting for the end of the parliamentary session. Four days later he issued his election address, in which he attacked the 'self-interested doctrines' of the government,[28] and from then until polling day he and Mary Anne canvassed from eight in the morning until sunset. One newspaper reported that she was assisting her husband 'with all the energy of despair'.[29]

On 24 June a broadsheet was posted around Shrewsbury listing the outstanding judgments against Disraeli. Parliament was now dissolved, so he had no protection against arrest. The broadsheet was explicitly anti-Semitic, calling Disraeli a 'Child of Israel' who owed money to 'Tailors, Hosiers, Upholsterers' and 'Jew Money Lenders'. 'Honest Electors of Shrewsbury', it asked, 'will you be represented by such a man? Can you confide in his pledges? Take warning by your brethren at Maidstone, whom Benjamin cannot face again. He seeks a place in Parliament merely for the purpose of avoiding the necessity of a Prison, or the benefit of the Insolvent Debtors Act.'[30] The broadsheet listed debts totalling over £21,000 and prompted Disraeli to issue a second election address declaring its contents to be 'UTTERLY FALSE'. Disingenuously he avowed that he would not have solicited votes had he not had an income 'which renders the attainment of any Office in the State, except as the recognition of Public Service, to me a matter of complete indifference'.[31]

His bravado worked, and on 30 June he won his election. Back in London he reported to Sarah that he had been out of Parliament (and so vulnerable to arrest) for only five days. To his mother he reported that Mary Anne had 'done wonders'.[32] 'One thing she alone did; namely to make me from a somewhat unpopular, to one of the most popular candidates in her Majesty's dominions.'[33] In Disraeli's speech to the electors he thanked them 'for their kindness to her who was nearest and dearest to him',[34] and on the day of the poll Mary Anne threw flowers into the crowd as he processed through the town. Mary Dawson wrote to congratulate Mary Anne on a joint success and Disraeli's friend Caroline Maxse also applauded her presence on the campaign trail: 'a woman is always so useful'.[35]

All the witnesses to the Shrewsbury election are silent on the subject of Mary Anne's reaction to the judgment broadsheets. They represented her first exposure to the true scale of Disraeli's debts, more than she could ever settle herself. They revealed to her how close they stood to ruin, that in marrying him she had condemned herself to live under perpetual threat of bailiffs entering her house and confiscating their joint possessions. Her response was uncompromising and generous. She directed Disraeli to consolidate his debts and gave the man who took them over, the money-lender Samuel Ford, a charge on her estate. In March 1842 she signed a deed from Ford for £5,000 and she also paid the expenses of fighting a petition against Disraeli's election in May that year. She saved his career and his future in England, imposing yet more thrift on her household in order to do so. Yet still she remained excluded from his financial arrangements, aware after 1841 only of the debts of which he chose to tell her.

The general election of 1841 increased the Tory majority in the House of Commons to seventy-eight. Governments did not automatically resign when they lost elections in the mid nineteenth century, and so the Whig ministry limped on until August, when Lord Melbourne lost a confidence motion and left office. Peel became Prime Minister and both Disraeli and Mary Anne were convinced that Disraeli would be at the heart of the new Tory administration. On 31 August Peel presented the Queen with his

Cabinet appointments and Disraeli lurked at the Carlton waiting for news of a sub-Cabinet role. 'All about appointments in the papers moonshine',[36] he told Sarah: two days later he was still waiting, and he scribbled a note to Mary Anne announcing that he could stand the atmosphere at the Carlton no longer. On 4 September the newspapers published complete lists of government appointees; Disraeli was not among them.

That night Mary Anne wrote to Peel begging for office. The excuse she gave for writing was straightforward: 'My husband's political career is for ever crushed, if you do not appreciate him.' She emphasised that Disraeli had abandoned literature for politics and asked Peel not to let such a sacrifice be in vain. 'Do not destroy all his hopes, and make him feel his life has been a mistake.' She reminded him too of the expense to which both she and Disraeli had been put by their support of the party. 'May I venture to name my own humble, but enthusiastic, exertions in times gone by, for the party, or rather for your own splendid self.' She closed by begging Peel not to answer her letter, 'as I do not wish any human being to know I have written to you this humble petition'.[37] Mary Anne claimed that Disraeli was in ignorance of her letter, although this has been called into question by his biographers. It has been suggested that he encouraged her to write, or even drafted her letter in order to avoid the ignominy of being seen himself to ask for office. Yet the letter's tone and gesture are characteristic of Mary Anne. In it she expresses her anxiety as 'overwhelming' and argues that intensely felt personal loyalty excuses an act of social indecorum. Even the date, given simply as 'Saturday night', implies that the letter was an emotional petition rather than an act carefully thought through.

The next day there was still no news, and now Disraeli wrote to Peel himself asking to be spared the humiliation of being overlooked. He reminded Peel that he had fought loyally under his banner, even when faced with hate and malice meted out to no other politician (a rare direct reference to the anti-Semitism he faced on the hustings). 'I have only been sustained under these trials', he wrote, 'by the conviction, that the day would come when the foremost man of this country would publickly testify, that he had some respect for my ability and my character.'[38] Peel's reply was premised on the argument that no member of his Cabinet had any authority to offer Disraeli a position. Disraeli replied refuting the suggestion that he was holding Peel to another's promise. 'Not to be appreciated, may be a mortification: to be baulked of a promised reward is only a vulgar accident of life, to be borne without a murmur.'[39]

Disraeli would later deny he had asked Peel for office, but at the time his failure to become part of the government was shattering. 'All is over', he wrote to Sarah. 'The crash wo[ul]d be overwhelming, were it not for the heroic virtues of Mary Anne, whose ineffable tenderness and unwearied devotion never for a moment slacken.' 'It was principally to honor her', he continued, 'that I aspired to this baffled dignity.'[40] The dignity he wanted for himself, not Mary Anne, but he had certainly never been more grateful for her support.

They fled to France, abandoning Parliament and politics in order to recover. Disraeli was once again battling to keep the bailiffs out of Grosvenor Gate and spent the two weeks before his departure organising loans with Pyne. 'Fortunately my household Gods have not been desecrated', he told Sarah from Pyne's office. 'I have the consolation to leave England with the conviction that that catastrophe can't happen in my absence.'[41] They settled themselves in Caen and for two months Disraeli was virtually silent. On Mary Anne's birthday he wrote her an 'Impromptu'. His voice was broken, he declared, but for her 'would I could call back its ancient fire! Then might I do some justice to thy charms, / And quick devotion, that surround my days / With joy and safety.' At his lowest ebb since their marriage, and deprived of the company of friends and family, he recognised her value as never before, and the tribute he paid was more direct than those of previous years. She was 'My stay in woe, my councillor in care!' 'O! mayst thou only joy in future share!'[42]

Mary Anne recorded her delight at this poem in a letter to Sarah in which she described finding it at the breakfast table on the morning of her birthday. Her mother was staying at Bradenham and she had put Grosvenor Gate at the disposal of the D'Israeli family, so her letters from this period are full of domestic details and instructions. But they also testify to the peace she found alone with Disraeli for the first time since their honeymoon. 'I know they all love me at Bradenham', she told her mother. 'Indeed dear Mama I deserve it – for Dizy is so strong & well now & we are so happy.'[43] It was easier to be happy when she was not competing for her husband's loyalty, and easier too to be affectionate towards his family when separated from them. For her it was a liberating autumn, a manifestation of all that was best in their partnership. Disraeli needed her and she had his company and attention. Together they rode and walked, explored chateaux and grew round on fine French cooking. 'They think me here a most robust little lady', she wrote in November to her mother.[44] And then again in December: 'Dizys love, he is got so fat, & in such fine health & spirits.'[45]

~

Eleanor Yate, Mary Anne's mother, was seventy-eight in 1841. At the beginning of 1842 she began to fail, and Mary Anne took her to Bradenham to nurse her. For almost four weeks she and Disraeli were apart, and their letters show him marooned at Grosvenor Gate in her absence, surrounded by servants he did not know and responsible for relaying her dictates about the house and his own health. He must tell the new maid to be 'very careful' of fire; occasional tables should be moved so his papers were not disturbed during breakfast; he must order a hot-water bottle to be brought to his bed every morning with tea and bread and butter. He also was responsible for paying the servants: 'let me know if you want more money'.[46] That he missed her is clear, and he wrote of his devotion to physical symbols of her – violets sent from Bradenham and kisses inscribed in letters. 'We have been nearly a week apart', he lamented on 21 February. 'If I wanted instruction, it has taught me the value of the sweet one I have lost.' She had written that she considered his letters to be private, not for consumption by his family. He approved of her reserve, he replied. Their letters were 'sacred, secret, mystical'.[47] Her responses were similarly ardent. 'How transported I shall be, to be clasp'd in your dear arms again, for there is nothing else to console or cheer me.'[48]

Tired from the effort of caring for her mother, Mary Anne reacted hastily to small slights from her in-laws. When a letter to Disraeli was forwarded from Bradenham to Grosvenor Gate without her knowledge, she wrote angrily that they had no reason to behave badly to her. 'All this cheapens me so Dizzy', she protested. 'It cannot be your wish, and after so much has been said on similar subjects and do I deserve it?'[49] At this he was irritated and he wrote coldly, not to his 'beloved' but 'dearest Mary Anne'. He denied any illicit correspondence with Bradenham, and all correspondence with Sarah. 'I did not write to my sister . . . because as correspondence be[twee]n her & myself has entirely ceased, it is to me by no means agreeable to resume it.' 'I perceive', he continued, 'that nothing can remove the perverted view in which you persist to consider my relations with my family. My correspondence, almost my cordial intercourse with them has ceased.' As for Bradenham, he never visited 'but with disgust & apprehension'.[50]

This disavowal of Bradenham and Sarah may appear rather breathtaking in its disregard for reality, but it was born of alienation. With Mary Anne installed at Bradenham, an illicit correspondence was impossible. At least she had his family caring for her at a time of crisis, he wrote; he was alone in a household of warring servants who would not meet his eye. He needed her home in order to feel less weary of life. Barred from government in the party of power, he was, he confessed, 'utterly isolated. Before the change of Government, political party was a tie among men, but now it is only a tie among men who are in office. The supporter of administration, who is not in place & power himself, is a solitary animal.'[51]

Their separation dragged on through March and Mary Anne grew fragile and exhausted. At the beginning of April she brought her mother back to Grosvenor Gate in a customised invalid carriage and for two months more she devoted herself to her care, seeing few friends and writing few letters. One of Disraeli's creditors whose debt had been bought by Ford (and so was insured by her estate) wrote her a threatening letter: she responded by instructing Ford to terminate negotiations with the offender. 'Mr Ford is authorised, on her part to adjust any claims on me, preferred in a decent manner', Disraeli wrote. 'But the menaces of ruffians she treats with contempt.'[52]

At the end of May Eleanor Yate died, and now it was Mary Anne who was vulnerable. Eleanor was her last link to her childhood and to her brother John. With her mother gone, Disraeli became her world. She had signed her property over to Ford in order to service Disraeli's debts; her security and happiness were dependent on him. In her absence at Bradenham that spring, Disraeli had allowed Ford's bailiffs into Grosvenor Gate to catalogue and value its contents, ownership of which he then transferred to Ford in order to raise more money. Ford agreed to take a single chair in lieu of a houseful of furniture and Mary Anne was not told that everything in her house now belonged to somebody else.

In August Disraeli wrote Isaac a letter designed to be read only in the event of his death. With his debts consolidated by Ford and Mary Anne aware of their magnitude, if not their full extent, he felt free from the threat of disaster for the first time. He attributed his emotional and physical stability to Mary Anne and wanted Isaac to know the depth of his gratitude. 'I am entirely indebted for this position & this state of mind . . . to the unexampled devotion of my beloved wife.' 'Since our marriage', he continued, 'she has defrayed either for those parliamentary contests so indispensable to my career, or for debts incurred before our union, no less a sum than thirteen thousand pounds sterling, & is prepared to grapple with claims & incumbrances to an amount not inferior.' He wanted this to be recognised in Isaac's will, but also in 'the affection & gratitude wh: every member of my family must feel towards her to whose ceaseless vigilance & unbroken devotion I am indebted for even existence'.[53] He was aware that she had no one left other than his family, and, an outsider himself, he knew that her background, manner and costumes marked her out from her contemporaries, leaving her alone in the world in which she appeared to glitter. In the wedding anniversary poem for that year he credited her with rescuing him from his demons, 'spirits of envy, strife & hate'. ''Tis woman's mind these marvels worked, / Heroic, wise & fond.'[54]

~

In *Coningsby*, the novel he published in 1844, Disraeli produced a manifesto for how to be a hero. His main character is endowed with a 'noble ambition . . . which will not let a man be content, unless his intellectual power is recognised by his race, and desires that it should contribute to their welfare'. This, Disraeli writes, is the 'heroic feeling; the feeling that in old days produced demi-gods; without which no State is safe; without which political institutions are meat without salt; the Crown a bauble, the Church an establishment, Parliaments debating-clubs, and Civilisation itself but a fitful and transient dream'.[55] *Coningsby*'s subtitle is *The New Generation* and the novel depicts a generation of new politicians determined to reform a broken system.

In Paris in 1842, the year of Mary Anne's fiftieth birthday, Disraeli had met two members of that new generation. They were George Smythe and Alexander Baillie Cochrane, two young Conservative MPs who, along with a third MP, Lord John Manners, were attempting to yoke themselves into a parliamentary group called Young England. Over dinner in Paris, Smythe and Cochrane asked Disraeli to join them. Young England aspired to inject honour and romance back into politics, and for Disraeli, the chance to lead a parliamentary grouping of idealistic young men offered a way back into the centre of public life.

Young England were never a wholly unified group and its four main characters would take up different positions on specific issues throughout the period of their alliance. What united them was the belief that England was a country badly in need of heroes. They advocated a return to a romanticised feudalistic assumption of responsibility by the aristocracy for those who laboured under them and they attacked a corrupt Whig oligarchy that they believed had poisoned the country during a century and a half of political dominance. They sought to reawaken the idea of a national community through an imaginative re-creation of networks of sympathy which they argued had disappeared from British society. And in both their political and literary writing they proclaimed the need for figures who would inspire the populace through their genius, creativity and capacity for imaginative understanding.

Young England drew on three interwoven strands of thought. Manners and Smythe were heavily influenced by the preacher Frederick William Faber, and from the start the movement was tinged with a High Church aesthetic as well as a more general mid-nineteenth-century turn to the feudal past. Disraeli injected it with Romanticism in novels whose Young England heroes have all Byron's charisma combined with a determination to prove that Shelley's figure of the poet as the 'unacknowledged legislator of the world' can be transformed so that the poet, the imaginative and sympathetic man, becomes the world's acknowledged legislator. The third strand shaping Young England came from the work of Thomas Carlyle, who in 1840 gave a series of lectures 'On Heroes, Hero-Worship & the Heroic in History'. Carlyle traced the history of the hero from Norse mythology to Napoleon, asking questions about the nature of heroism and the impulse to worship great men.

Among his heroes were both writers and kings. Poets are prophets, he argued, who endow a nation with a voice. Shakespeare he described as 'an English King, whom no time or chance, Parliament or combination of Parliaments, can dethrone!' It is truly a great thing, he wrote, for a nation to 'produce a man who will speak forth melodiously what the heart of it means'. The heroic leader, meanwhile, whether king, emperor or politician, he characterised as a figure of sincerity who brings passion and intensity of feeling to his cause. In this account Napoleon is a lesser hero than Cromwell because his sincerity is of an inferior type, and Cromwell a greater man than his contemporaries because they fail to inspire the imagination of the populace. 'What man's heart does, in reality, break forth into any fire of brotherly love for these men?' Carlyle asks of the other Roundhead leaders. 'They are become dreadfully dull men! . . . One leaves all these Nobilities standing in their niches of honour: the rugged outcast Cromwell, he is the man of them all, in whom one still finds human stuff.'[56]

The impact of Carlyle's thinking on the Young Englanders is evident in the literature all four produced, but particularly in the work of Disraeli. In Paris in 1842, having agreed to join forces with Smythe, Manners and Cochrane, he pursued the question of how the man of genius should shape himself as a leader of men. He had an audience with the French King and long conversations with leading French politicians and thinkers, chief among them Adolphe Thiers and François Guizot. With the King he established a rapport and together they discussed British foreign policy, even though Disraeli had no authority to speak for his government. Mary Anne recovered her spirits away from the cares of home, sending messages to Sarah about Paris fashions and her social activities. She was always fonder of her sister-in-law when she was not competing with her for Disraeli's attention, and it was cheaper to live in a hotel in Paris than keep Grosvenor Gate open. Mary Anne's account book suggests she took satisfaction in the cuts she was able to make to her housekeeping budget by living abroad. Their separate spheres were well established, with Disraeli concerning himself with matters of state and Mary Anne with the shape of bonnets and the wages of servants, but in Paris the distance between their daily pursuits lessened. The relationship between their social and political life there was intimate, with connections forged and solidified over dinners and morning calls, and in Paris Mary Anne's acquaintances were not so attuned to the subtle markers of class difference her appearance and manners revealed.

When the Disraelis arrived back in England in January 1843, the links between her social life, his political ambitions and his developing conception of the ideal leader grew stronger. With a parliamentary coterie behind him, Disraeli's prominence increased: newspapers reported on the activities of Young England and news reached Bradenham that his quiet opposition to Peel was receiving much praise. Mary Anne's dinner parties and breakfasts were well attended by powerful people intrigued by the prospect of a new grouping within the Tory Party, and she was, Disraeli told Sarah, 'tho' too much worked, amused – wh: is for her, everything'.[57] At a ball in Shrewsbury in May, Mary Anne was the grand lady of the night, dressed in white, adorned with velvet flowers and diamonds, and Disraeli reported that she 'got even more cheering than I did'.[58]

In July they were invited to a fete at Gunnersbury, the country home of Lionel and Charlotte de Rothschild. It was the start of two of the most important friendships of either of their lives, Mary Anne with Charlotte and Disraeli with Lionel. The Rothschilds had a young family, and after this first meeting the Disraelis frequently spent Sunday evenings dining *en famille* at their house in Piccadilly. Both Charlotte and Lionel were aware of the eccentricities of their new friends and were inclined to be suspicious of Disraeli's professed commitment to Jewish emancipation (Lionel's ambition to become an MP was blocked until the late 1850s by legislation requiring new MPs to swear an Anglican oath). But they appreciated the good qualities of both and understood through close acquaintance that the Disraelis felt their isolation, and the equivocal nature of the positions they occupied. In his autobiographical notes, Disraeli attributed the Rothschilds' great success to their loyalty to each other, delineating their prosperity as 'as much owing to the unity of feeling wh: alike pervaded all branches of that numerous family as on their capital & abilities'.[59]

In the autumn of 1843 the Disraelis visited Henry Hope at Deepdene, his Italianate house in Surrey. Hope was an influential supporter of Young England, and under his roof Disraeli began to translate its political philosophy into fiction. *Coningsby*, his first novel since *Venetia*, told the story of Young England's rise. George Smythe appears as the eponymous hero; Manners and

Cochrane as his boyhood friends. Its plot is secondary to its cry for political leaders who are also heroes. Coningsby is a story about aristocrats and Disraeli was not suggesting that the old order should be stripped of its traditional power. Rather he argued that that order needed to reform itself and its relationship with the people in order to make Britain great once more. 'There is no influence at the same time so powerful and so singular as that of individual character', he writes in a disquisition on Lord Liverpool's administration.[60] That influence can be exercised for good or for ill; it is the responsibility of the new generation to ensure it is a positive force. The novel has a Jewish visionary, Sidonia, who some critics have suggested was modelled on Lionel de Rothschild, and he makes a powerful case for the role of emotion in public life. 'Man is only truly great when he acts from the passions; never irresistible but when he appeals to the imagination.'[61]

In order to fulfil the potential of his passion Coningsby requires the sympathy of like-minded men; friendship allows him to be great. 'Often, indeed, had he needed, sometimes he had even sighed for, the companionship of an equal or superior mind.'[62] He also needs the love of a woman to whom he can be a hero. The romantic plot of Coningsby has sometimes been characterised as an irrelevance inserted to placate market demands for an emotional narrative, and in one of his notebooks Disraeli himself dismissed the idea of writing a domestic story on the grounds that 'for the middle class marriage often the only adventure of life'. He also noted that heroes are often 'Impotent or averse to women' but that 'Private Life' was 'more important than public leading to greater results'.[63] In Coningsby he attempted to reconcile these competing ideas by demonstrating that a political and a romantic plot could exist in harmony, each complementing the ideology of the other. He is critical of the separation between the lives of men and women, noting wryly that 'while ladies are . . . performing all the singular ceremonies of a London morning in the heart of the season; making visits where nobody is seen, and making purchases which are not wanted; the world is in agitation and uproar'.[64] Yet by the novel's conclusion it is clear that Coningsby needs to win his heroine in order to achieve his promise as a political and intellectual redeemer. At the end he is ensconced in his own home, with a beautiful wife at his side and his hearth enlivened by the friends of his youth. 'They stand now on the threshold of public life', Disraeli writes. 'What will be their fate?' 'Will they remain brave, single, and true; refuse to bow before shadows and worship phrases; sensible of the greatness of their position, recognise the greatness of their duties; denounce to a perplexed and disheartened world the frigid theories of a generalising age that have destroyed the individuality of man, and restore the happiness of their country by believing in their own energies, and daring to be great?'[65]

Mary Anne, the first reader of Coningsby, was most excited that her husband was writing again. From Bradenham in November she wrote to her uncle William Scrope that Disraeli was engrossed in a new project. 'We must remain here for some time longer', she informed him, 'for reasons I will tell you when we meet.' After leaving Deepdene they had paid a triumphant visit to Manchester, where Disraeli made a speech at a grand meeting – 'literary not political', Mary Anne hinted.[66] A number of notes from Disraeli to Mary Anne survive from this period, demonstrating how intimately she was involved in his writing day. 'I feel a great desire for a cigar, but will not smoke one, unless you approve', ran one such note. 'I propose to go out NOW; I have written 9 pages', promised another. 'Darling, I wish you wo[ul]d come up & talk a little over a point, if you are not particularly engaged.' 'I have finished the vol: & am inclined for a stroll. Are you?' And finally, 'My darling – I must tell you that I am very well, & writing to my hearts content, D.'[67]

Mary Anne brought more to Coningsby than an appreciative eye and occasional permission for its author to smoke a cigar. In wooing her Disraeli had tried to be a hero, to use the conventions of literary romance to win her heart. Her house set him free to pursue public ambitions, her money rescued him from disaster and her love and loyalty protected him from doubt and anxiety. Coningsby himself was modelled on George Smythe, but the novel's depiction of the crucial relationship between love and leadership stemmed from Disraeli's own experience. Mary Anne's unquestioning, intuitive responses to his claims of genius bolstered those claims and revealed the public possibilities of private happiness. In the aftermath of his rejection by Peel, Disraeli had written to D'Orsay that 'Mary Anne sends to you vows of real friendship – and says that nothing in the world would delight her more than to extricate us both from all our Scrapes. She is, as you know, a heroine, and as I have ceased to be a hero, it is fortunate that one of us has some great qualities.'[68] In 1844, with creditors at bay, a novel completed and his political ambition rekindled by the allegiance of a coterie of idealistic young men, he was able to contemplate the possibility that he could become a hero once more.

~

1844 was a momentous year for both the Disraelis. In May *Coningsby* was published and the reviews Mary Anne clipped and filed reveal the debate it generated. *Punch* mocked its celebration of Sidonia and Jewish history and many of the journals criticised Disraeli for writing about real people, only thinly disguised. 'It is bitterly personal, satirical, political', wrote the reviewer for the *Literary Gazette*. 'It treats of aristocrats lately dead or still living, or ministers and opposition, of members of parliament of all opinions, of cotton lords, actresses, demireps, and others belonging to the world of fashion.'[69] Thackeray, writing in the Whig *Morning Chronicle*, characterised its heroes as dandies and marvelled at the sight of such men 'made to regenerate the world – to heal the wounds of the wretched body politic – to infuse new blood into torpid old institutions'. Thackeray sympathised with Disraeli's characterisation of Peel's Conservative Party, 'which conserves nothing, which proposes nothing, which resists nothing, which believes nothing', but disputed the suggestion that a new generation could reanimate it so that 'we are one day to reorganise faith and reverence round this wretched, tottering, mouldy, clumsy, old idol'.[70]

Coningsby sold well, and together with the attention attracted by Young England, it thrust Disraeli back into the heart of public discourse. Smythe, Manners and Cochrane toiled at Grosvenor Gate, preparing speeches and writing newspaper columns at Disraeli's bidding, and he was invited to chair a grand literary meeting in Manchester. In the summer of 1844 he travelled to Shrewsbury to shore up constituency support and was apart for the first time from Mary Anne on their wedding anniversary. She sent him on his journey with a hot-water bottle, sleeping draughts, biscuits and a bottle of cognac, but even with the hot-water bottle 'in constant use & a great comfort to me . . . I feel very lonely at night'.[71] He wrote that the people approved of his literary and political efforts, and that while he was assured of their support, she was much missed by the town. 'Wherever I go, I hear of nothing but "Mrs Disraeli" & why she did not come':

Among the shopkeepers, whom I wish most to please, your name & memory are most lively & influential. 'Such a gay lady! Sir; you never can have a dull moment, Sir' & I tell them all that you are a perfect wife as well as a perfect companion; & that separated from you for the first time after five years, we are (alas! alas!) parted on our wedding day! The women shed tears, wh: indeed I can bearly myself restrain.[72]

Disraeli was among the first generation of politicians who needed to appeal to a middle-class electorate and he understood the power of giving himself a personal narrative about love and loneliness with which his recently enfranchised constituents could identify. In his notebook he had written of marriage as the great adventure of life for the middle classes, and his decision to put his own marriage at the heart of his election campaign reflected this conception of middle-class preoccupations. In an age when public figures did not routinely display their emotions in order to curry favour with their public, his presentation of himself as a bereft husband marked him out from his contemporaries. The deployment of the personal story as a political tool would become a commonplace of British political life, but Disraeli was among the first to harness its power. The mythology that he and Mary Anne developed in order to smooth their marriage now became instrumental in enabling Young England to align itself with its supporters. In *Coningsby* he depicted a political genius fulfilled by his emotional existence, and in Shrewsbury that summer he presented himself as that genius: a writer of brilliance, a political leader, and an ardent lover.

In October the Disraelis visited Fryston Hall in Yorkshire, home of the family of Richard Monckton Milnes, a Young England acolyte. Among their fellow guests was Elizabeth Spencer-Stanhope, who wrote an account of her visit to her husband. She was charmed by Disraeli, whose manner she described as 'half foreign', and who won her approval 'with his singularity and good-nature which he exerted in dressing truffles for me'. Mary Anne she thought was a surprising character, 'in a lace dress, looped up on each side, over pink satin, and a wreath on her head, though I should think near fifty'. 'However', she continued, 'she is very amusing and off-hand, saying everything that comes uppermost and unfeignedly devoted to her D'Izzy. She does not give herself airs and seems very good-natured. This morning she has been giving us an account of the scenes between Sir Lytton Bulwer and Lady Bulwer, and her own ineffectual attempts to reconcile them.' A day later she was still trying to work out Mary Anne. 'Mrs D'Izzy I like quite as much as her husband, and think her *equally* clever *in her way*.' 'She would idolise you for your admiration of her D'Izzy, as she calls him, for only my simple and *sincere* tribute this morning brought tears to her eyes.'[73]

The success of the *Coningsby* year came to a head at Stowe in January 1845. Both Disraelis were invited by the Duke of Buckingham to a ball to meet the Queen. Mary Anne sent a long description of their evening to Sarah, which started with a lengthy wait 'like a flock of sheep . . . not light enough, no seats no fire, a little hot bit & a great deal of cold wind, a marble floor – Fancy poor shivering Dizzy & cross looking Mary Anne, in black velvet hanging sleeves, looped up with rosetts of blue & diamond buttons, head dress bows of the blue velvet fastened with diamonds.' The Queen arrived to receive the bows and curtsies of her chilly subjects and thereafter the evening was a triumph. Peel was cordial to them both and the Duke of Buckingham himself escorted Mary Anne to the supper room, 'The Queen & your delighted Mary Anne being the only ladies so distinguished'. Afterwards Mary Anne retired to a sofa with the Duchess, who revealed that the Queen herself had 'pointed out Dizzy saying theres Mr Disraeli'. The next day the Duchess asked her for lunch and gave her a private tour of the Queen's quarters. The rooms were beautifully appointed but Mary Anne was less interested in fine china and Old Masters than in the domestic arrangements. The Queen and Prince Albert slept 'Without pillows or bolster': was not this odd? Even more interesting were the prim protocols surrounding the Queen's water closet. 'The Queen asked the woman, where the Prince could go – but there was no second convenience.'[74] Disraeli too wrote of their triumph to Sarah. 'Her Majesty, Peel, Aberdeen, and all equally distinguishing us by their courtesy. The whole scene sumptuous and a great success for the Duke.'[75]

∼

The ball at Stowe ruined the Duke of Buckingham. His finances had been on the point of collapse for years and Disraeli had long been involved in negotiations to help shore up the estate. After the ball the bailiffs arrived and in 1848 Stowe was sold. The Buckingham crash revealed the speed with which disaster could envelop an individual in a world where one could be hosting the Queen one minute and bailiffs the next.

The Disraelis began 1845 at a high point, secure in their partnership and in their home. Disraeli began to mount sustained attacks on Peel in the House of Commons before finally voting against him on a measure which signalled the breakup of Young England and the end of all hopes of a reconciliation between Disraeli and Peel. In February and March he was working constantly, drafting speeches and speaking in the House while racing to complete a new novel, Sybil. Sybil is Disraeli's great 'Condition of England' novel. It tells the story of the Chartist uprisings of 1839 and is brilliantly acute in its observations of both high society and the abject suffering of the working poor. In it he gave Britain the concept of 'Two nations' 'between whom there is no intercourse and no sympathy; who are as ignorant of each other's habits, thoughts and feelings, as if they were dwellers in different zones, or inhabitants of different planets; who are formed by a different breeding, are fed by a different food, are ordered by different manners, and are not governed by the same laws'. These 'Two Nations' are 'THE RICH AND THE POOR' and Disraeli is clear that the governing classes need to have sympathy for those who labour under them if Britain is to be regenerated. As in Coningsby he presents a country in need of heroes, but now his heroes are radicals, men who reveal injustice and fight its evils even as they assert the healing power of the imagination.[76]

In his review of Sybil Douglas Jerrold contexualised Disraeli's ouvre within a tradition of political fiction. It 'is a work', he wrote, 'worth perusing and worth analysing. It will scarcely gain its object so well as the works of many other authors, who have sought to delude the frivolous into philosophy, and at the same time please the child and the man. Its purport is too evident. The politics outweigh the fiction, and the mere novel reader will hardly get over the dissertation on history that immediately follows the vivid and animated opening.'[77]

Sybil is an experimental, ambitious work, with a heroine and a plot that require considerable suspension of disbelief from even the merest of novel readers. In it Disraeli tested the limits of fiction, using a romantic narrative to articulate serious concerns about the state of the nation. The novel depicts once again the venal Whig oligarchy of Coningsby, contrasting its families with a hero and heroine who are passionate, brave and committed to the care of the people. Disraeli dedicated the novel to Mary Anne, articulating his own private happiness and his model marriage in the process and providing an additional contrast to *Sybil's* portrait of a domestic structure that has failed to regulate the scions of dynastic houses. 'I would inscribe this work to one whose noble spirit and gentle nature ever prompt her to sympathise with the suffering; to one whose sweet voice has often encouraged, and whose taste and judgment have ever guided, its pages; the most severe of critics, but – a perfect Wife!' This dedication met with ridicule in one literary review. What wife, asked *Fraser's Magazine*, would wish to be so honoured? Mrs Disraeli 'may be as shocking a shrew as ever stood in need of a Petruchio to tame her; but it does not therefore follow that she is a "perfect wife". In the names of all the women of England, single as well as married, we enter our protest against the insinuation, and deny its justice.'[78]

The dedication to *Sybil* represented Disraeli's most public declaration of Mary Anne's perfection. That both were ridiculed for it highlights the extent to which their marriage challenged contemporary preconceptions about ideal matches. Mary Anne was older, less educated and richer than her husband and she did not belong to the political class. Their peers understood their union as a marriage of convenience and their extravagant declarations of devotion threatened to undermine the inculcated codes of the marriage market.

In the summer of 1845 the Disraelis appeared triumphant, absorbed in a frenetic social life. Lady Londonderry unbent sufficiently to be courteous to Mary Anne, who, Disraeli told Sarah, 'suddenly finds herself floating in the highest circles & much fêted. She is of course delighted. Lady Jersey, who meets us everywhere, in a stupor of malice & astonishment!'[79] In private, the strain on both was once again immense. Disraeli's financial problems became newly urgent: the editors of his letters note that this happened in two-year cycles, suggesting a series of temporary measures to placate his creditors.[80] He needed to raise between three and five thousand pounds and in July attempted to sell the copyright of his literary work to one James Crossley, who was told to communicate with him at the Carlton, not at Grosvenor Gate.[81] Simultaneously he tried to insure his life to secure further loans and he was, he told Sarah 'harassed to death'. Mary Anne, meanwhile, was 'exhausted': code, in Disraeli's letters to Sarah, for a wife in a precarious emotional state. She spent her days packing for a European autumn with frightening intensity. She was working, he told Sarah, 'with now almost fatal rapidity, for unless affairs quietly mend . . . it will be quite impossible for me to go; & I know not what excuse to make for my staying in town & for many other things'. After a period of harmonious partnership Mary Anne was again shut out of one part of her husband's life, kept in ignorance of the crisis enveloping him. He could not be honest with her about money without revealing the great deceptions at the heart of their courtship and marriage, and so he turned for support to Sarah, leaving his wife puzzled and anxious. His wedding anniversary poem for 1845 opened '"Henceforth confide in me" she smiling said, / "My sunlit destiny shall glance on thee, / In spite of all thy gloom."'[82] But writing poetry in which Mary Anne appeared as his chief confidante and support was a poor substitute for allowing her these roles in reality.

At the beginning of September the Disraelis were still in London, but he was able to tell Sarah that 'the clouds are dispelling'.[83] Financial relief came from an undisclosed source and Disraeli wrote two days later that he was in a position to leave. 'I think it *quite impossible* that any letters can arrive', he told his sister, who was to act as his de facto agent in his absence. 'You must howr. use yr. discretion. The moment we are settled, we will write & apprise you when you are to commence yr. duties.'[84] He lamented the fact that he was unable to visit Bradenham before leaving for France, but wrote that 'there is no alternative. I can keep MA. here no longer.' At the last minute their departure was delayed by Mary Anne's health. In his letter of instruction he told Sarah that they were forced to remain in London an extra day to allow her to recover: two days earlier he had described Mary Anne as 'very low & shattered, not slept for the last week & must have change of air & scene immediately'.[85]

One reading of Mary Anne's state during this period is that she was on the verge of a breakdown. Since her marriage she had contended with debt, deceit, the death of her mother, creditors at her door, increased public prominence and increased public mockery and she had few friends who truly understood her character or the particular difficulties of her situation. One such friend was Charlotte de Rothschild, who in September sustained a visit by Mary Anne so extraordinary that it lends credence to the theory that she stood on the verge of nervous collapse. Charlotte's account of what Mary Anne said cannot be bettered by paraphrase:

> I am quite out of breath, my dear, I have been running so fast, we have no horses, no carriage, no servants, we are going abroad, I have been so busy correcting proof-sheets, the publishers are so tiresome, we ought to have been gone a month ago, I should have called upon you long ere now, I have been so nervous, so excited, so agitated, poor Diz has been sitting up the whole night writing, I want to speak to you on business pray send the darling children away.

'It would, without any exaggeration,' Charlotte told her sister-in-law, 'take more than ten pages to put down conscientiously all the lady's words not noting exclamations & gestures, & tears . . . I have never seen her in such a state of excitement before, and all I could do was gasp out "has anything happened"':

> Mrs Disraeli heaved a deep sigh, and said: "this is a farewell visit, I may perhaps never see you again life is so uncertain . . . Dizzy & I may be blown up on the rail-road or in the steamer there is not a human being that loves me in this world, and besides my adored husband I care for no one on earth, but I love yr. glorious race, I am rich I am prosperous, I think it right to entertain serious thoughts, to look calmly upon one's end &c &c. – Mrs Disraeli's conversation is not exactly remarkable for clearness of thought, concision of language or for a proper concatenation of images, ideas, & phrases, never the less I had always been able to comprehend, and to reply, but on that memorable Friday, I was quite at a loss to understand her meaning . . . I tried to calm & quiet my visitor who after having enumerated her goods & chattels to me, took a paper out of her pocket saying: "this is my will, and you must read it, show it to the dear Baron, and take care of it for me. – I answered, that she must be aware of my feelings that I should ever be truly grateful for such a proof of confidence, but could <u>not</u> accept so great a responsibility. "But you must listen" replied the inexorable lady, she open'd

the paper & read aloud: "In the event of my beloved husband preceding me to the grave, I leave & bequest to Evelina de Rothschild (she interrupted herself to put in "that beautiful dunce") all my personal property.

Evelina was Charlotte's daughter and a particular favourite of Mary Anne's. Charlotte tried to protest but reported that Mary Anne 'would hear no answer, no objection':

Away rushed the testatrix leaving the testament in my unworthy hands, I pass'd a miserable night . . . The next morning I breakfasted in a hurry, dressed in a hurry, walked in a hurry to the abode of genius & his wife to whom I returned the will, there was a scene, a very disagreeable one, and then all was over, <u>the dream & the reality</u>.[86]

Charlotte's account captures the difficulty of reasoning with Mary Anne when she became excited or emotional and she writes of her friend as a creature of impulse: not clever or easy but loyal in friendship and in love. She captures too Mary Anne's loneliness as, without a family of her own, she attempts to become part of other people's families, and the mother of other people's children. That Mary Anne felt the rejection of her gesture is evident from the fact that the 'scene' that followed her visit was 'very disagreeable'.

Jane Ridley has suggested that Disraeli was extricated from financial disaster by Lionel de Rothschild, who put up more than the £5,000 so urgently needed. This suggestion is given credibility by Mary Anne's account book, which records that in August the Disraelis asked Lionel to take charge of their investments, thereby involving him in their financial future.[87] Ridley notes that Mary Anne's will was made in Disraeli's hand and argues that 'there was a characteristically shrewd method in Mary Anne's madness'.[88] Charlotte would have had no knowledge of the financial arrangements between her husband and Disraeli and so no context for Mary Anne's conduct. But if Ridley's hypothesis is correct, it complicates Charlotte's account of Mary Anne's instability. In this reading she appears simultaneously fragile and practical, brought low by the revelation of yet more deceit and the prospect of disaster, involved in the search for a remedy, and finally made giddy by relief and gratitude towards her saviour.

~

On 9 September 1845 the Disraelis closed their house and made their way to Dover. The servants' rations were recorded and measured out; Mary Anne's diamonds were lodged in the vault at Drummonds Bank. She had £195 in her purse and all the household bills were paid. Shortly after they left, one of Disraeli's admirers delivered a live turtle to Grosvenor Gate and the bemused servants, not knowing what to do with it, sent it on to Bradenham. The carrier stopped on the road to display the animal to curious passers-by, charging a shilling a head for the privilege of touching it. Exhausted by the attention, the turtle grew sick and died shortly after reaching Bradenham. Tita took charge of its carcass, quartering it, he told the family, in the manner approved by Byron. It was made into soup and so, Sarah wrote to both her brother and sister-in-law, 'we think we did very well & acknowledge we owe you two quarters of that nectar & ambrosia combined.' 'So much', she concluded, 'for your affairs.'[89]

CHAPTER SIX

Household Words

DOLLY WHITMORE JONES

Dolly Whitmore Jones's husband John was heir to Chastleton in Oxfordshire, an imposing Jacobean house built by his ancestors in 1612. As Mrs Whitmore Jones, Dolly became the chatelaine of Chastleton, producing ten children and immersing herself in the life of the house and surrounding countryside. When John died, she became both lord and lady of the manor, overseeing its farms and stock of valuable timber as well as the household. She was not the owner of the house: that privilege rested with her brother-in-law Arthur, who was mentally disabled and for whom she acted as guardian. After Arthur's death Chastleton passed to her eldest son Willie, a weak man who disappeared to Bermuda before returning to claim his inheritance. Willie evicted his mother and siblings from the house and proceeded to strip the estate to fund disreputable living. After more than three decades at Chastleton, Dolly was made homeless, forced with her younger children to take refuge with her relations. Her exile lasted for two years, ending when Willie fell ill and summoned his family back to care for him. One of his unmarried sisters became his housekeeper, but although Dolly visited Chastleton and forgave Willie, she elected to remain in the house she had rented at Kew. Chastleton had been her kingdom, but in the end the security it offered was contingent on the whims of men, and consequently provisional.

~

Mary Anne was never threatened with eviction from her house and thus had physical security of which her childhood friend Dolly could only dream.

But in the 1840s the nature of home nevertheless became fragile and contested in her story too. At Grosvenor Gate Mary Anne, like Dolly, was both lord and lady, managing the finances, provisioning the kitchen and wine cellar, appointing the staff. In France in the autumn of 1845, released from the care and expense of housekeeping, she found rejuvenation. She and Disraeli rented a house in Cassel in Flanders and for two months kept no company and saw few English newspapers. They adapted to the agricultural rhythms of the village, getting up at five with the light and going to bed at seven. They employed a Flemish cook, who stewed pigeons and did delicious things with eggs, cloves and onions, while Mary Anne kept chickens and attempted to train stray pigeons as pets. As in 1841 she was made happy by cheap living and the uncontested company of her husband. They drove around local villages, admiring church spires and mocking Catholic idolatry, and they walked miles each day – 300 in total, Mary Anne estimated. 'MA. is looking extremely well', Disraeli reported to Sarah, 'quite recovered from the trying season of London & scales styles and even leaps ditches.'[1] Mary Anne's letters were full of roads so thick with mud they sank in it to their ankles and the beneficial effects of the Cassel air. 'I am got so fat & Dizzy likewise', she told Sarah, suggesting that the Flemish cook made more of an impression on their waistlines than did the daily walks.[2]

In between the walking, eating and fowl-training Disraeli began a new novel, the third in his Young England trilogy. *Tancred* starts as a political novel, resuming the story of Coningsby and his friends, but then becomes an extended meditation on Jewish history and culture. It is an uneven book, hardly read now, in which Disraeli set out his conception of a pan-European Jewish aristocracy richer in history and intellect than the Whig oligarchy governing Britain. It reveals the intellectual significance of his friendship with the Rothschilds and the emotional importance of Mary Anne's whole-hearted embrace of Jewish history – the feature of her thinking that so embarrassed Charlotte de Rothschild during the episode of the will. In the poem Disraeli wrote on Mary Anne's birthday in Cassel he described her as 'Partner of all my thoughts, whose vivid brain / Rich with suggestive sympathy, can aid / My struggling fancy!'[3] Her influence is apparent both in the novel's romanticised account of Jewish history and its portrait of the Coningsbys' marriage. Endowed with money and political success, the hero and heroine of *Coningsby* have responsibilities in separate spheres, since Coningsby counts 'entirely on Edith to cherish those social influences which are not less important than political ones'. 'What time', asks *Tancred*, does this leave for romantic love? 'They were never an hour alone. Yet they loved not less; but love had taken the character of enjoyment instead of a wild bewitchment; and life had become an airy bustle, instead of a storm, an agony, a hurricane of the heart.'[4]

Once *Tancred* was complete, Disraeli laid novel-writing aside. He was at points in his life a compulsive writer of fiction, producing page after page at great speed, making few corrections along the way. But novels always functioned as a respite for the moments when real life failed him. *Vivian Grey*, *The Young Duke*, *Contarini Fleming* and the other creative works of the early 1830s were products of the directionless years following 1826; *Henrietta Temple* was a response to the failure of a romance with Henrietta Sykes; and *Venetia* a project returned to after multiple failed attempts to become an MP. Similarly the Young England trilogy – *Coningsby*, *Sybil* and *Tancred* – allowed Disraeli to articulate a political vision at a time when his influence with his party was negligible. The effect of the trilogy was to strengthen his voice and to assure him a hearing among his contemporaries in Parliament. After 1846 he had no need to channel his intellect and energy into fiction. His novelist's voice did not fall silent after *Tancred* but spoke instead through other genres: speeches, letters, articles and campaigning prose. The result was a political voice of animation and power – and a long period of quiet in his literary career.

~

The respite from the 'airy bustle' of separate spheres restored Mary Anne's equilibrium too. At the end of November the Disraelis moved to Paris, where Disraeli was able to receive newspapers and letters quickly and from where he watched developments in British politics closely. They took up the strands of friendship established during their visit to the city a year before and Disraeli had several audiences with the King. 'We are so happy', Mary Anne told Sarah in mid December, 'I know not where to begin or end.' They dined with the Parisian Rothschilds and Mary Anne revelled in the practicality of their grandeur. 'My dear', she insisted to Sarah, 'even

Dizzy himself could give you no idia of the splendour of that gorgeous banquet. The table I was told is made of an extra strength to support the innumerable groups of silver and china works of art.'⁵ 'MA. made a most brilliant toilette last night', Disraeli wrote, in a letter crafted for the eyes of his wife as well as his sister. 'Indeed I passed her off as my daughter & she found many admirers.'

'Politics seem more wild & confused than ever', he continued in the same letter. 'It appears to me that Peels difficulties are insurmountable.'⁶ By the autumn of 1845 Peel had become convinced by the famine in Ireland that the Corn Laws (protectionist trade restrictions that maintained the price of British corn) must be repealed. Defence of the Corn Laws was a Conservative shibboleth, a central plank of the party's identity as the champions of agriculture. Peel himself had long been a supporter, and the high-handed manner in which he attempted to impose a major shift in policy on his party made him enemies. In the House of Lords, Lord Stanley, previously Peel's Colonial Secretary, became leader of a Protectionist group of Tory peers, and in the Commons, Lord George Bentinck, the hunting-mad younger son of the Duke of Portland, gave up his stud to devote himself to bringing down Peel. Bentinck had made little impression in Parliament prior to 1846, but he was a messianic defender of the agricultural interest and he flung himself at Peel with a vengeance born of ideological purity.

Disraeli did not share Bentinck's single-mindedness on the matter of the Corn Laws, but he too detested Peel and had been sharpening his opposition to him since 1841. The Corn Law debates offered the perfect opportunity to slay an old foe, backed this time by Bentinck and the Tory squirearchy. Their detractors labelled Bentinck and Disraeli 'the Jockey and the Jew', but they formed a potent partnership. Bentinck brought passionate conviction to their cause; Disraeli rhetorical firepower. On the floor of the House of Commons Disraeli framed his destruction of Peel as an attack on political apostasy, and men on both sides of the House were taken aback by his venom. He called Peel 'a burglar of others' intellect' and dismissed his life as 'one great appropriation clause'. 'The right hon. Gentleman tells us, that he does not feel humiliated', he mocked. 'I will tell the right hon. Gentleman, that though he may not feel humiliated, his country ought to feel humiliated. Is it so pleasing to the self-complacency of a great nation, is it so grateful to the pride of England, that one who, from the position he has contrived to occupy, must rank as her foremost citizen, is one of whom it may be said, as Dean Swift said of another Minister, that "he is a Gentleman who has the perpetual misfortune to be mistaken!"'[7]

Although Peel managed to pass Corn Law repeal, Disraeli's attack ended his leadership. As the Bill passed in the House of Lords, Disraeli and Bentinck inflicted a governmental defeat over a separate issue and Peel stepped down as Prime Minister. 'The Ministry have resigned', Disraeli told Mary Anne in a note scribbled from the Carlton Club. 'All "Coningsby" & "Young England" the general exclamation here.'[8] His victory came at a high price. The Tory Party splintered into two factions, Peelite and Protectionist. Both groups went into opposition and Lord Stanley immediately began to work towards reunification. Disraeli and Bentinck were in no mood to compromise. In August they embarked on a triumphal tour of agricultural constituencies, seeking to shore up electoral support for their stance. Stanley was dubious about the wisdom of such a tour but Disraeli relished the approbation of the crowds and his reception by Protectionist Tory grandees inclined to extend friendship to the man who had brought down Peel.

His travels culminated at Belvoir Castle in Leicestershire, seat of the Duke of Rutland (the father of Disraeli's Young England contemporary, Lord John Manners). Belvoir, he told Mary Anne, was 'Coningsby to the life', and he luxuriated in the sensation of finally inhabiting the scene of his silver-fork novels. He was in the thick of the political action and he saw at first hand the way in which a great house produced power and influence of a kind that a man with no country house of his own could ever achieve. He missed Mary Anne, and his daily letters were full of assertions of love and complaints of loneliness. 'I grew very dull, & rather dispirited, towards twilight, & find the solitary nights very unhappy.'[9] But the dukes, political conversation and power-broking of Belvoir were outside Mary Anne's world. The wives of the Tory statesmen who gathered there were not invited to join their husbands, and when Disraeli wrote political gossip to Sarah from Belvoir he included the cautionary line: 'I shan't say I wrote this.'[10] Mary Anne sent dutiful reports of her social activities but the balance of power between them is evident in her plea for news: 'I shall not expect long letters, but just to say how you are.'[11] Alone at Grosvenor Gate, she read and reread reports of his speeches in the newspapers and his letters. 'Your dear letter my darling husband made me very happy this Morn'g . . . but say more about your dear self – do you sleep well – and what people say to you – The compliments, five lines will do.'[12]

~

In his wedding anniversary poem for 1846 Disraeli paid tribute to a relationship that could withstand trials and remain unchanged. 'Seven long years . . . find us still the same', he wrote. They were 'Knit in the same affection' by 'A life of proved devotion, where two hearts, / Amid the tumult of the world, sustained / Their course by sympathy.' Yet his focus in this poem was on his own gathering strength as much as his marriage.

> Beloved wife!
> Onwards I feel my way; the breath of fame
> Supports my progress, & the watchful eye
> Of nations nerves my heart – & yet alone,
> Reft of thy still small voice, that gently guides
> And aids with quick perception, I should sink,
> My spirit lose its valor, & my life
> Become as blank & dreary as the days
> Wherein I was not thy most happy spouse.[13]

His birthday poem that year continued this theme, celebrating 'St. Mary Anne' as 'a spirit canonized / To reign o'er happy marriages', a provider of 'Support & solace', and the creator of 'a happy home'.[14] But the Belvoir interlude marked the beginning of a new phase in their marriage, in which a 'happy home' was no longer a certainty. By the beginning of 1847 Mary Anne and Disraeli were effectively leading separate lives. He rarely dined at Grosvenor Gate, preferring to remain at the House of Commons with colleagues or at the Carlton Club. There are few letters from her for this period, but an ominous phrase creeps into her account book: 'pas content'. It appears for the first time as early as March 1846, during the period of the Corn Law debates: 'Dizy dined at the House 4 times a week & we dined out 3 or 4 times, pas content.' It recurs in June 1847: 'one months housekeeping no company Dis from home 5 or 6 days pas content'. And in February 1848, 'no company & Dis at the House 4 times a week pas content'. With Disraeli so frequently absent, Mary Anne's ability to fill her house with friends over dinners and grand breakfasts was restricted, and 'pas content' refers to the absence of guests as well as the absence of a husband. 'One dinner with ourselves five – no other company. Pas cont.'[15]

One source for Mary Anne's activities and manners during this period is the diary of Louisa de Rothschild, sister-in-law of Charlotte. Louisa was intrigued and a little worried by both Disraelis, and in a diary full of minute analyses of self and others she attempted to characterise them. 'Mrs Disi talked well as one who possessed grand powers of observation, strange that she should be blind to her own absurdity', she wrote after dinner at Charlotte's house in 1847. 'However notwithstanding them all I like her, for she has a warm heart.' In November Mary Anne was 'as usual an odd mixture of good sense & nonsense of amusing humour & gaity & of no less amusing absurdity'. Again and again Louisa returned to the contradictions in Mary Anne's character: 'an odd mixture of hardhearted shrewdness & nonsense'. 'In her constant smile there is perhaps a want of sincerity but her enthusiasm is truthful & genuine, her heart is really kind & her talents of no ordinary description.' Disraeli was no less perplexing, although Louisa, a devout woman, doubted his commitment to the Jewish cause. 'Disi was extremely affected with the children but in good spirits & not too grand to be amiable. He spoke of the Jews' bill in his strange Tancredian strain, saying we must ask for our rights & privileges, not for concessions & liberty of conscience. I wonder if he will have the courage to speak to the House in the same manner.'[16]

In the election of June 1847, Lionel de Rothschild was elected as the Liberal MP for the City of London. New MPs were required to swear an oath of allegiance on the New Testament, and Lionel's refusal to do so and subsequent inability to take up his seat brought the issue of Jewish discrimination to the centre of British politics. George Bentinck was committed to passing an Act repealing Jewish disabilities but found himself at odds with his party over the issue and stepped down as Tory leader in the House of Commons. With his departure, Disraeli edged closer to power. As his Belvoir visit made clear, however, it was quite unthinkable that a

ISAAC D'ISRAELI.

Isaac D'Israeli. Isaac's literary works, Disraeli told a friend, were 'hewn out of the granite with slow and elaborate strokes'.

Maria D'Israeli. In later life Disraeli had almost nothing to say about his mother, a silent figure in a family of opinionated letter writers.

Bradenham House, Buckinghamshire. Isaac rented Bradenham on a long lease in 1829, fostering an enduring connection between the family and the countryside around High Wycombe.

Disraeli as a young man. 'His eye is black as Erebus', wrote one observer at this time. 'His mouth is alive with a kind of working and impatient nervousness, and when he has burst forth … it assumes a curl of triumphant scorn that would be worthy of a Mephistopheles.'

Sarah Disraeli. Disraeli's older sister was an intelligent, independent-minded woman, with unbounded faith in her brother's talents.

Giovanni Batista Falcieri. 'Tita', as he was universally known, had been Byron's gondolier and major-domo. Disraeli was captivated by him, and installed him as servant-in-chief at Bradenham.

George Gordon, Lord Byron. Byron was Disraeli's hero, the figure on whom he modelled himself.

John Evans. Mary Anne adored her brother, shown here in his regimental finery. His behaviour, however, caused her great pain.

Mary Anne Lewis as a young woman. This portrait, which dates from the period of her first marriage, gives some indication of the petite vivaciousness which attracted the attention of so many lovelorn admirers.

The farm at Brampford Speke near Exeter, where Mary Anne spent her childhood.

Wyndham Lewis. Mary Anne's first husband is a shadowy figure in her story, and this silhouette is the only authenticated surviving image of him.

Edward and Rosina Bulwer Lytton. In the years before the Disraelis' marriage Edward was Disraeli's closest friend, and Rosina Mary Anne's.

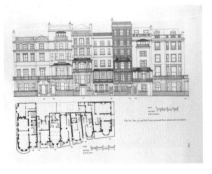

Developer's drawings showing the plan and elevation of No. 1, Grosvenor Gate on the far right.

Marguerite, Countess of Blessington. Disraeli formed an enduring friendship with Lady Blessington, a fellow writer and biographer of Byron.

The comparative list of characteristics that Mary Anne drew up shortly after her marriage to Disraeli. The list shows Mary Anne's clear sense of the differences between her and her new husband, as well as her odd, sloping handwriting, which one correspondent likened to 'hieroglyphics'.

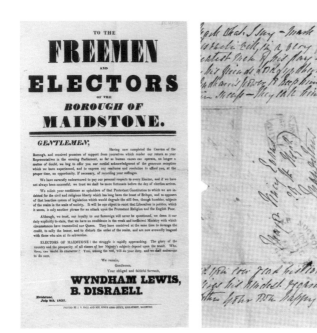

Maidstone election address, 1837. After several unsuccessful attempts to become an MP, Disraeli was finally elected to the House of Commons after running for election alongside Wyndham Lewis at Maidstone.

Letter from Mary Anne to John Evans, 29/07/1837. 'Mark what I prophecy', Mary Anne wrote to her brother after the Maidstone election. 'Mr Disraeli will, in a very few years, be one of the greatest men of his day … They call him my Parliamentary protégé.'

Drawing by Edward Buckton Lamb, 1862, showing a proposed design for Hughenden. Lamb assisted Disraeli and Mary Anne as they transformed Hughenden from a simple eighteenth-century building to the fairy-tale house of their dreams, complete with ornamental Ds in the stonework.

The drawing room at Hughenden, photographed in the early 1880s.

The parterre and south front of Hughenden today, where the gardens have been replanted to reflect Mary Anne's horticultural vision. Disraeli loved the garden she made, and considered it her greatest creative achievement.

Mary Anne in a posthumous portrait by James Middleton, made from a contemporary miniature. Disraeli commissioned this portrait after Mary Anne's death to fill the empty space above the fireplace at Hughenden.

Disraeli in 1873. At Mary Anne's funeral in 1872 onlookers commented on the strange sight of a grey Disraeli, but he never appeared in public uncurled or undyed again.

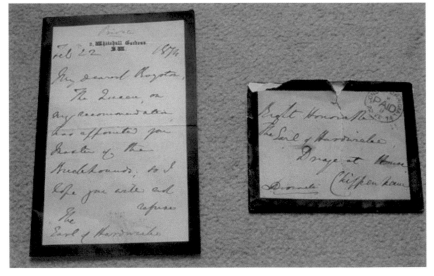

Letter from Disraeli to the Earl of Hardwicke, 1874. Disraeli would go on after Mary Anne's death to become Prime Minister for a second time and to fall in love again, but for the rest of his life he wrote his letters on thick-black-edged paper, in memory of her.

representative from an urban constituency with no property could ever be leader of the country party. In June 1847 he resigned his Shrewsbury seat and stood as the Tory candidate for the county seat of Buckinghamshire, where he was elected unopposed. He started negotiations to buy the estate of Hughenden, which sat within the constituency. Bentinck offered to guarantee the purchase and so enable Disraeli to assume the role of agricultural landlord and member of the landed gentry. The sale was complicated and the ownership of Hughenden remained unresolved for almost a year, but the promise of Bentinck's support enabled Disraeli to take a further step towards his reinvention as man of substance.

Mary Anne might write 'pas content' in her account book, but 1847 therefore promised much for the Disraelis. *Tancred* was published and received a good deal of press attention, Disraeli gained powerful friends in the parliamentary party, a county constituency and the prospect of a country house of his own. At Bradenham, affairs were less stable. On 20 April Sarah wrote to Mary Anne to alert Disraeli to the sudden illness of their mother. The next day, as the Disraelis were leaving for Bradenham, an express arrived from James telling them of Maria's death. Sarah was distraught and James left it to Disraeli to break the news to Isaac on his arrival. Shortly before Maria died, she read *Tancred*, and Sarah reported that 'Mamma at last confirms that she never before thought Dis was equal to Mr Pitt – so you see it pleases all varieties of hearers or readers.'[17] It was a rare insight into Maria's view of her eldest son, which confirmed she was not among his circle of female acolytes. But while Disraeli and Mary Anne saw little change in their lives after Maria's death, Sarah and Isaac felt it deeply. For the remainder of 1847 Isaac's spirits were low, brought down by grief and infirmity, and Sarah now carried the burden of his care alone.

The Disraelis spent Christmas at Bradenham and were still there at New Year when Isaac contracted influenza. He died on 9 January, aged eighty-three. In contrast to his wife's passing, about which there is little in the historical record, Isaac's death prompted an outpouring of emotion and mourning from his children. Letters of condolence arrived daily, Disraeli began work on a memoir of his father to accompany a memorial edition of *Curiosities of Literature*, and to his friends he wrote of his terrible grief. 'Your letter poured balm into the bruised spirits of our circle', he told John Manners.

'My only consolation for the death of my father is his life.'[18] A week after Isaac's death, Mary Anne learnt that her old friend Mary Dawson had also died. Her son Robert, Mary Anne's favourite during her first years at Grosvenor Gate, wrote a brief note telling her the news. 'I trust this will be the first to inform you of a loss which to us is irretrievable.'[19]

Isaac did not own Bradenham but rented it on a long lease, and while Disraeli and Mary Anne returned to London, Sarah was left to disassemble the house. Her younger brothers showed no inclination to help her as she cleared cupboards and paid off tradesmen, and her best support came from Tita, made homeless, as she had been, by the death of his employer. Disraeli assumed temporary financial responsibility for the house and its occupants, sending Sarah money to settle bills and adjudicating in decisions about the disposal of property. 'Dis' brilliant speech brings a balm & consolation to my heart, tho' alas! I have to read it alone', wrote Sarah in February.[20] When Tita left in March to take up a new position in London, she remained behind to plan her own departure and a future unanchored by parents or children. In the summer she set off on travels to family friends before renting a house on a hill outside Hastings overlooking the sea. Disraeli disapproved of her decision to settle so far from London and in such a lonely house, but Sarah's letters suggest she actively sought a refuge where she could experience the totality of her separation.

Isaac's death prompted all the Disraeli siblings to renegotiate their relationships with one another and with Mary Anne. They were all now in or approaching middle age: Mary Anne was fifty-six, Disraeli forty-four, Sarah forty-six. Old disputes, previously smoothed over by parents and a shared history at Bradenham, flared into the open. James objected to Disraeli's control of the Bradenham finances, and quarrels about money and possessions became common. In the interregnum between Sarah's departure and the final disposal of Bradenham, she had to intervene by letter in a dispute between Mary Anne and one of the servants after Mary Anne attempted to lower the staff's salaries. But Isaac's death also paved the way for the final purchase of Hughenden. With Isaac's inheritance and Bentinck's backing, Disraeli was able to complete the purchase and to write to Mary Anne, on 6 September 1848, 'It is all done – & you are the Lady of Hughenden.'[21] Two days later Mary Anne recorded the purchase of 'a Rustic hat for Dis'[22] to signify his transformation from scribbling author to country squire.

~

Hughenden sits on a hill in the Buckinghamshire countryside outside High Wycombe, among rolling fields and parkland. The building Disraeli bought dated from the mid eighteenth century and had a classical stuccoed exterior, but over the years the Disraelis made significant changes to both the house and the park, most of them overseen by Mary Anne. They employed the architect Edward Buckton Lamb (an ardent exponent of Gothic Revival) to bring the house up to date in a way that combined his and their tastes. Lamb added crenellations and gave the house a new facade, and Mary Anne scattered Ds through its stonework. Outside she created an Italian formal garden, complete with fountains and bright flower beds, and planted an ornamental forest intersected by walks and groves.

To the modern eye Hughenden is not an attractive place, its exterior heavy and ponderously overdecorated. Today visitors approach the house from its dark north side and via a chilly entrance hall, shaded by conifers in the circular driveway. Despite this, there is something unexpectedly lovely about it. The house has changed a good deal since the Disraelis' day, but it is still possible to feel the love Mary Anne lavished on it and the relaxed, private air she and Disraeli strove to create. Many of the Disraelis' furnishings and possessions remain, cared for and documented by the National Trust. The two of them lived in rooms on the sunny south side of the house, using the north-facing formal spaces of dining room and library predominantly for entertaining in the evenings. The ground-floor sitting room looks out over the garden, and in the panelled hall a modest wooden staircase leads up to the private spaces of bedroom, boudoir and study. All three rooms are above the big south-facing sitting room and in the mornings are filled with warm light. In the bedroom the curtains and bed-hangings are cream and gold, the furniture is picked out in gilt and white and the bed – a compact four by six double – faces the window. Next door is Mary Anne's boudoir, dominated by the desk in the big bay window from where she could oversee work on her garden while planning future alterations. Here she sat in the mornings briefing her staff, writing letters and keeping her accounts. Blue carpet runs through from the adjoining bedroom, and chintz curtains and furnishings splash colour throughout the room.

Today Mary Anne's boudoir remains the prettiest, lightest room in the house, making an effective contrast with Disraeli's study next door. Here the colours are darker and richer, pinks and reds dominating the windows and chairs. Disraeli's dispatch box and waste-paper basket are still present, and every other room in the house holds objects that recall the Disraelis' presence. On the dressing table in the bedroom stand Mary Anne's delicate brushes and nail files; in the sitting room paintings of family, friends and heroes – Isaac, Maria and Sarah, Bentinck, Lady Blessington, D'Orsay, Tita and Byron – line the walls. In the strongroom, usually hidden from view, is Mary Anne's wedding ring, a tiny gold band too small for modern fingers and too small for her when her hands swelled up during her final illness. The guides in the house and garden are proud of Mary Anne and they tell the story of her marriage and her accomplishments at Hughenden with enthusiasm. It is the place where that story belongs and from where both her and Disraeli's characters emanate from colour schemes and prized possessions. It is a large house but an intimate one, despite the stone Ds in the battlements. When the sun shines, it feels as if there are few more peaceful places on earth.

~

On 21 September, less than three weeks after Disraeli wrote to Mary Anne to tell her that Hughenden was theirs, George Bentinck died of a heart attack. His death threw the financing of the purchase into disarray and for a time it seemed as if the house must be sold before the Disraelis had even moved in. In her account book Mary Anne wrote that after the funeral at Marylebone Old Church, 'Dear Dizzy went & sat alone, in his deep grief.'[23] Bentinck's death deprived Disraeli of his chief supporter in the party as well as threatening Hughenden. Writing to Bentinck's brother Lord Henry, Disraeli described the news (and this in the year of Isaac's death) as 'the greatest sorrow I have ever experienced'. He was shaken by the loss and he mourned his friend for years. Yet, as he told Lord Henry, 'I can neither offer, nor receive, consolation. All is unutterable woe!' 'I only write this', he continued,

'because, when the occasion is fitting, there are reasons, wh: make it neces-
sary I should see you.'[24]

On 18 October Henry Bentinck went to Grosvenor Gate, where he and
Disraeli spent four hours in conversation. Bentinck proposed that Disraeli
should accept a loan of £25,000 from his father, the Duke of Portland, in
return for which Portland would take a mortgage on Hughenden and receive
the rents directly. Disraeli refused this suggestion, arguing that he could not
be the representative of another master in his house and on his land. The
Portlands believed it to be crucial that Disraeli should assume the possessions
of a Conservative Party leader and thus save the Protectionists in the House
of Commons from annihilation. So when he threatened to resign his seat
and retire from public life, they compromised. 'I went on the state of my
affairs', Disraeli told Mary Anne, 'observing, that it wd. be no object to them
& no pleasure to me, unless I played the high game in public life; & that I
cd. not do that witht. being on a rock. And then I went into certain details,
showing that I cd. not undertake to play the great game, unless your income
was clear.'[25] Eventually the Portlands agreed to loan the money on the
understanding that the loan could be recalled at any time and Disraeli would
collect the rents and make them over to the Duke. In public Disraeli would
appear as a secure landowner quite fit to lead the party of agricultural interest;
in private he would, in effect, be a tenant in his own home, required to
vacate if the Portlands decided they wanted their money back.

It was an imperfect arrangement, but it allowed Mary Anne and Disraeli
finally to take possession of their house. They slept at Hughenden for the
first time in November, and then Disraeli returned to town while Mary Anne
oversaw the final dismantling of Bradenham. Much of the Bradenham furni-
ture was moved to Hughenden along with the unsold portions of Isaac's
library. 'We have passed the last six weeks in moving from Bradenham to
this place – a terrible affair', Disraeli told Lady Blessington at the end of
December. 'I seem to have lived in waggons like a Tartar chief.'[26] But at least
they were installed and Bradenham was no longer an expensive, sad drain
of time and money. There were teething problems as they worked out how
to live among their new neighbours. Disraeli objected to the sight of children
and their nurserymaids littering his private road on their way to the vicarage,
and neither he nor Mary Anne cared for the vicar, whose house they could

see from their east-facing windows. The living of Hughenden was in their gift and the vicar was answerable to them, but he did little to ingratiate himself, at one point writing to Disraeli to reprimand him for setting a bad example to the parish by travelling on a Sunday. This drew a stern reply from Disraeli, which Mary Anne copied and kept in a sign of how seriously both took the impertinence. Urgent affairs of state had called him away, Disraeli wrote, prompting him to deviate from his usual practice, as the vicar would have known had he 'made any temperate enquiry'. Moreover, he added, 'I would venture also to observe, that my object in attending Divine service is not merely or principally to set an example to others.'[27]

At Hughenden Disraeli played the part of Anglican paterfamilias, over-seeing his farms, his tenants, his home and his church with an assumed authority more usually derived from many generations on the land. In print he situated himself in a Jewish lineage of age and distinction. Both were gestures of defiance, calculated to confront the continuing anti-Semitism of his depiction in *Punch*, which portrayed him in cartoons as a greasy-haired Fagin, and a political Shylock. His memorial edition of *Curiosities of Literature* was published on 1 January 1849, and in the memoir of Isaac he wrote for its preface, he invented the Venetian history for his family and sketched out his great-grandfather's decision to settle one of his sons in England. He described his grandfather's passage to greatness and Isaac's difficult youth as the dreamy, writerly son of a man of ambition and enterprise. The portrait of Isaac upset Sarah because it contained no mention of their mother. Sarah herself Disraeli did celebrate, describing her heroic assumption of the role of Isaac's eyes following the onset of his blindness. He celebrated too Isaac's connection with Bradenham, represented by his long residence in Buckinghamshire and his burial in the village church. And writing about Isaac's *Life and Reign of Charles I*, he made a claim for the importance of the retired literary life. *Charles I* was published between 1828 and 1831, when, Disraeli wrote, 'the principles of political institutions, the rival claims of the two Houses of Parliament, the authority of the Established Church, the demands of religious sects, were, after a long lapse of years, anew the theme of public discussion'.[28] Men were attracted to a writer who could produce parallels for the contemporary scene, he insisted, and who could thereby illuminate the particulars of his own historical moment.

He was writing about Isaac but also about himself: the dreamer propelled into public life by the acuity of his vision, his intellect stemming from a grand Jewish history, his social status intimately associated with the English countryside and the Anglican church. As he reinvented himself as an appropriate leader for his party, he still held fast to the myth of his Jewish heritage, the thing that made him different from other Tory MPs. He needed to be a man of property in order to conform to the model demanded by his party and so fulfil his political ambitions. But in order to conform to his own conception of the political leader, he needed too to be the descendant of an aristocracy of culture, faith and intellect older and more distinguished than that which ruled Britain.

~

At the beginning of 1849 Disraeli left Mary Anne at Hughenden and travelled back to London for negotiations about the Conservative leadership of the House of Commons. Lord Stanley, who as Protectionist leader in the House of Lords was charged with selecting a Commons chief, knew of Disraeli's power in the debating chamber and understood that large sections of the parliamentary party were expecting him to be crowned. Disraeli had appeared as de facto leader when he summed up the parliamentary session in August 1848 in a speech that received much praise, and he and Stanley had met socially over dinner at Grosvenor Gate in July. But Stanley was nevertheless unwilling to anoint a Jewish upstart reliant on the patronage of others who had not yet proved himself loyal or trustworthy, even though his colleagues warned him of the danger of cutting Disraeli loose from the ties of party. Writing to a supporter, Disraeli rearticulated his ultimatum to Stanley. 'I am prepared to follow any leader, whom my party may elect, provided always that the leader is able to lead. I will not undertake the burthern of debate in a subordinate position, because the inevitable & humiliating inference from such conduct on my part, would be, that I was a man fit to be used, but not to be trusted.' The very fact that he was not an aristocrat, he continued, 'renders it, to my mind, still more necessary, that my position sho[ul]d be assured, & my character enforced & sustained'.[29] At the end of January Stanley and Disraeli met and Stanley proposed a compromise by which Disraeli would form a trio of leaders with John Manners's elder brother

Lord Granby, and John Herries, an elderly Protectionist who had served in Lord Liverpool's government. Stanley's suggestion, Disraeli told Mary Anne, was that he should be the 'real leader' of the trio and that once the jealousy and distrust of his party had dissipated he could assume sole command. Stanley bolstered Disraeli even as he asked him to accept a lesser prize. 'Says it is all over with the party if I retire.'[30]

Disraeli initially refused this offer and then, when Stanley reminded him that he would lose all influence if he retired, and of the antagonism towards him in some sections of the parliamentary party, he tacitly withdrew his refusal. As with the purchase of Hughenden, it was an imperfect arrangement, but it kept Disraeli within the Conservative fold, placated his opponents and restored some measure of control to the party in the Commons. As Stanley predicted, Granby and Herries proved to be ciphers, and by the end of the year Disraeli had become the acknowledged Leader of the Opposition in the lower House. He and Stanley gradually came to respect each other as, with the leadership question resolved, they began the process of rebuilding the Conservative Party and presenting a united front against the government. On 22 February Disraeli was able to write to Sarah that 'Things, publickly, look very well. After much struggling, I am fairly the leader, & gave notice tonight, amid the cheers of the Squires, of a grand motion, wh:, I hope, will rally all the farmers to my standard.'[31]

The leadership negotiations meant that Mary Anne and Disraeli were apart for almost a month. She remained at Hughenden in January, overseeing an army of carpenters, painters, plasterers, bricklayers, gardeners and chimney sweeps. 'My darling, you have, I am sure, done at Hughenden what no other woman, or man either, cd. do', Disraeli wrote. 'You have gained a year in our enjoyment of that place, where I trust every year we shall be happier & happier.'[32] She left Hughenden only to travel along frost-hardened roads to High Wycombe to post him papers, but despite the distance between them she was as usual absorbed by details of his conversations, health and bodily functions. 'It is of the greatest importance <u>before</u> parliament meets that something should be settled about the Leadership', she wrote on 6 January. '<u>No time is to be lost</u>.' Grosvenor Gate was being repainted in their absence and she was full of concern about the effects of the paint on his health. She gave him permission to move from Grosvenor Gate to a hotel if the paint made him feel sick, 'as it sometimes affects the bowels'. Disraeli's digestion was a subject of much discussion during this period and prompted a series of specific instructions from her. He should keep himself warm: particularly important when 'the bowels are in a tender state. Get the round table in the bed room, put near the fire, not left in the corner near the window.' He should eat mutton chops or a fowl for dinner. 'Tell Ann to put a hot bottle in yr bed at night.'[33]

Disraeli obeyed all these instructions even as he lamented her absence, but while their letters were affectionate their experiences were increasingly separate. The news that Tita had at last found love and was to be married at St George's, Hanover Square made Disraeli long for his own wife. 'Come to me as soon as you can', he implored on 24 January. 'I much miss you – & it appears to me you must have now formed your administration, & can leave things without anxiety.'[34] As his prominence increased it became politically necessary for Mary Anne to represent them socially, and he valued her instinctive reading of society feeling. 'Baroness Brunow is at home on the 30th, & has sent us an invitation' ran his letter of 25 January. 'I don't particularly want to go, but very much wish you shd., & maintain yr position in society, & feel the public sentiment on many affairs.'[35]

$\sim$

At this point, Mary Anne's voice in the archive falls silent. Almost no letters from her survive for the first months of 1849, so we have to glimpse her in the letters she received, acting as godmother to Robert Dawson's new baby in April, visiting her infirm uncle William Scrope in March, running around town in search of new servants in February. Louisa de Rothschild paid her a morning call in early February and found her 'in high spirits but not as tender as usual'.[36] Later that month Mary Anne wrote an irritated note about her housekeeper's 'total want of abilities' in her account book, and in the same letter that related the progress of his public pursuits, Disraeli told Sarah that 'private affairs . . . are very cross, & much annoy me'. He himself was absorbed in parliamentary business, struggling with a volume of work heavier than he had ever known. His life, he told Lady Londonderry, was now 'confined to Committees, house of Commons, &, when at home, to the gay study of statistics'.[37] To John Manners he wrote that his leadership was gradually becoming secure but that there were great problems in managing an 'army without officers'.[38]

In March the precariousness of Disraeli's financial arrangements was again exposed when a loan was recalled and he was forced to borrow money secretly from Sarah. Then Mary Anne's assets were temporarily frozen following a lawsuit related to the will of her brother-in-law William Price Lewis and she was, for the first time in their marriage, dependent on Disraeli for money for her housekeeping expenses and domestic renovations. In previous years Disraeli would send her notes throughout the day, brief bulletins relating parliamentary gossip, his activities and the state of his health. Now, quite suddenly, those notes fell away, written only when he needed something from Grosvenor Gate or to inform her of a change of plan. The one exception to this dated from June 1849 and related news of the sudden death of Lady Blessington. In April that year Lady Blessington's debts had finally overwhelmed her and she and D'Orsay had fled to Paris to escape their creditors. She was heartbroken and died the day after moving into her new house. Her death and the flight of D'Orsay severed another link with Disraeli's youth, adding to his sense of isolation within his marriage. He began to call with increased frequency on Lady Londonderry, to confide once more in his sister rather than his wife and, as in 1847–8, to treat the House of Commons as a refuge from his home.

'The storm wh: has, more or less, been brewing in my sky for the last 12 months, burst rather suddenly yesterday.' Thus Disraeli told Sarah that the sparks of resentment and mutual mistrust had finally ignited. 'At present I am residing in an hotel, leaving Grosvenor Gate to its mistress.' It was jealousy that had brought matters to a head, he insisted. 'I found all my private locks forced – but instead of love letters, there were only lawyers bills & pecuniary documents. Had I not been taken unawares, I shd have secured these papers, wh: may produce some mischief – but I hope may not.' His case was clear, he insisted, 'tho' between ourselves, it might have been otherwise':

There is only one point in wh: I felt a little embarassed, & used yr. name to carry me thro'.

I said that I was going out of town last Thursday to Bucks Assizes

– but I did not, & Meyer Rothschild unintentionally let the cat out of the bag.

I have replied that I went out of town to see you – & that after the last rows, I was resolved that yr. name shd. never be mentioned by me to her again – & that the 'deceit', as she calls it, is the necessary consequence of her violent temper & *scenes*, wh: I will bear no more. So remember this – LAST THURSDAY.

I don't know how all will end: I shall not give up a jot, whatever tides. I am rather confused & shaky of course, having had a bad night, in a strange bed, without my usual conveniences, so pardon this rough epistle, & believe me, yr affec brother D.[39]

Disraeli also wrote that day to his agent Philip Rose, explaining that he had called 'to consult you on a domestic point'. 'I only write this to say that if Madame consults you upon it, or, rather, wishes to do so, you will confer with me before you see her.'[40]

As with other moments of crisis in the Disraelis' relationship, here we have to rely on the accounts produced by Disraeli for his supporters. Mary Anne had no one in whom she could confide. She had no close family living and her oldest friend, Mary Dawson, was dead. Despite her money, she was now dependent on Disraeli for her position in the world, and her power to change his behaviour was limited. It seems likely that her rage was born of powerlessness as well as from the conviction that she was being duped. Disraeli's letter to Sarah makes it clear that Mary Anne believed him to be engaged in an adulterous affair with another woman; the note to Rose demonstrates that financial deception still marred their relationship. That Disraeli's devotion to Sarah herself was a further cause of rows is made explicit here, as is the fact of Disraeli's deception. He was not with Sarah and was not in Buckinghamshire: the crucial phrase in his letter, for those concerned with biographical detection of adultery, is this: 'My case is very clear, tho' between ourselves, it might have been otherwise.'

In his 1994 biography of Disraeli, Stanley Weintraub mounted the case for the prosecution. His argument ran as follows: Disraeli was lonely and in need of consolation, Mary Anne was silly and quite unfit to be his wife, he had various opportunities to philander and two children were born in the

1860s who could have been his. One was the younger son of Lady Dorothy Nevill, a near neighbour of the Disraelis and great friend of both; the other was a young woman called Kate who was adopted as a child and who believed herself to be Disraeli's daughter based on family myth and physical resemblance.[41] Neither account, as Weintraub himself acknowledged, is conclusive. And in many respects the question, while intriguing, is irrelevant. Disraeli may have strayed during his marriage and would not have been unusual had he done so. He maintained intense relationships with young men as well as women throughout his life, one of whom, George Smythe, seduced Dorothy Nevill, prompting her hasty marriage to a middle-aged cousin. The presence or absence of illegitimate children neither confirms nor refutes the possibility of extramarital sex, and in any case to define adultery purely as sex in this case misses the point about what so upset Mary Anne. Disraeli's letter reveals that it was the deception she minded, the sense that his loyalties lay with women other than her. One such woman was Sarah; another was Lady Londonderry, with whom he renewed a chivalric correspondence in 1849. The frequency of his epistolary communication with Lady Londonderry drops around the time of the July row and the editors of his letters have suggested that it was unlicensed visits to her that prompted Mary Anne's anger.

Disraeli told Sarah he would not compromise; a week later he wrote that they were planning to leave town for Hughenden. He did not refer directly to the row again but implied they had patched up their differences. If Disraeli held firm and refused to apologise then perhaps Mary Anne wavered and sought forgiveness for her jealousy, her isolation leaving her with no option to do otherwise. On 4 August Disraeli wrote that he was 'very busy & harassed about going to Hn. wh: must be done, but wh: for many reasons is distressing'.[42] The house, schemed for by him and worked on by her, now threatened to throw them together without a programme of political and social activities to mask the differences between them. Throughout the autumn of 1849 Mary Anne's voice remains silent, but their mutual unhappiness is everywhere apparent in Disraeli's correspondence. He was 'sick at heart', he told Sarah shortly after their arrival.[43] 'I doubt whether I can bear this life much longer', he wrote a week later. 'But I suppose something will turn up; only visiting at country houses seems to me even something worse: constant dressing & indigestion. I suppose I must find refuge in blue books: I have piles ready.'

But even the thrill of planning parliamentary battles failed to absorb him: 'God knows where I shall be the next campaign, & I don't much care.'[44]

They remained at Hughenden through September and October, Disraeli burying himself amidst parliamentary papers in his study; Mary Anne escaping the house each morning to spend the day in her garden, fighting misery by throwing herself into physical activity. There were no wedding or anniversary poems that year and when Disraeli was absent, at meetings in London or Aylesbury, his letters home were short and to the point. At the beginning of October he travelled without Mary Anne to the house of a Protectionist MP in Essex for a party meeting and then made ill health an excuse to linger in London on his way home. From Aylesbury he told her he was 'jaded *to the last degree*' but he sought neither her advice nor news of her activities, writing only to inform her of his delayed return.[45] To Sarah he reported himself 'very unwell' but stressed that this should remain 'between ourselves'.[46]

~

In November Disraeli attempted to escape. Mary Anne was forced inside from the garden by short days and bad weather, and he described himself to Sarah as 'hipped & dispirited beyond expression'. 'Indeed I find this life quite intolerable – & wish some earthquake wd. happen, or something else of a very decided nature occur, that wd produce a great change.'[47] That day he wrote to Rose to beg him to '*write me a line to say, that you want me in town*'.[48] While he waited for a response a letter arrived for Mary Anne from Arethusa Milner Gibson, containing the revelation that Mary Anne's former companion Eliza Gregory (now married to a Mr Riches) was attempting to blackmail them both over their relationships with men in 1838. A friend wrote on Eliza's behalf that Mary Anne was Eliza's debtor 'both peculiarly and morally'. 'Mrs Riches hopes that you may be allowed lucidity enough to comprehend this.'[49]

It seems likely that Eliza's reappearance in Mary Anne's life did not aid domestic harmony at Hughenden, but it is also possible that, attacked from without, the Disraelis drew closer together. That Mary Anne told Disraeli of Eliza's threats is implied by a line in a letter from him written once he arrived in London: 'I have done nothing about Miles or anything yet, & shan't till you arrive when we will consult.'[50] 'Miles' is the reading of an illegible name preferred by the editors of Disraeli's letters, but they note that the name could be read as 'Riches', a supposition borne out by examination of the original manuscript. At Hughenden Mary Anne kept her counsel on both Disraeli's absence and Eliza. She wrote calmly of her progress in clearing dead trees and assured him that if he wished to return accompanied by 'political friends' she would have bedrooms ready for them.

This letter appears to have reconciled Disraeli to the company of his wife, for the next day he wrote asking her to join him at Grosvenor Gate while he completed his business in town. It is possible that he needed her in London in order to resolve the question of how to respond to Eliza, about whom the archive at this point falls silent. Mary Anne arrived to find the house empty and Disraeli dining at the Carlton Club, and again she neither mourned his absence nor demanded his company. She assumed he was having dinner 'at the Carlton, with some useful friend', she wrote, and so would sit up and wait for him until eleven, at which point she would go to bed.[51] The care with which she avoided any suggestion that she required his company is notable and suggests that the rows of the summer and the gloom of the autumn had made her wary in her dealings with him. They returned to Hughenden together, and in December Mary Anne quarrelled with James, prompting the younger Disraeli brothers to spend Christmas with Sarah in Hastings. Mary Anne and Disraeli were invited to spend Christmas at a country house in Cheshire but declined. 'I cannot stand it', he told Sarah. 'Bad as this is, nothing is so terrible as the constant parade & pageantry of a Xmas week in a great house in the country, witht. the slightest object of interest, yr. health destroyed with the stupid excitement, & your time wasted: no ease, repose, or refuge.'[52] Instead they immured themselves at Hughenden and Mary Anne made a cold the excuse for a retreat to her room, where she stayed for ten days. The result, Sarah learnt, was 'a most severe & unamiable Xmas'.[53]

~

Household Words, Charles Dickens's weekly journal, was published for the first time on 30 March 1850. It was the result of a long-held ambition of Dickens's, to 'conduct' a journal through which he could speak directly to his readers. Although many writers contributed to its pages, it was distinguished by Dickens's voice, both in his own contributions and in the style he imposed elsewhere. 'We aspire', he wrote in his 'Preliminary Word', 'to live in the Household affections, and to be numbered among the Household thoughts, of our readers.' *Household Words* celebrated domesticity, familial loyalty and the communal hearth. 'We have considered what an ambition it is to be admitted into many homes with affection and confidence', the 'Preliminary Word' continued. 'We know the great responsibility of such a privilege; its vast reward; the picture that it conjures up, in hours of solitary labour, of a multitude moved by one sympathy.'[54] But the title of *Household Words* was double-edged, acknowledging the scope and reach of Dickens's words and making a claim for the influence in ordinary homes of famous men. Dickens took the phrase from the St Crispin's Day speech in *Henry V*: 'then shall our names / Familiar in his mouth as household words . . . Be in their flowing cups freshly remember'd. / This story shall the good man teach his son; / And Crispin Crispian shall ne'er go by, / From this day to the ending of the world, / But we in it shall be remember'd.'[55]

Household Words brought together three narratives that by 1850 had gained widespread prominence. One told the story of the affectionate Victorian family, epitomised by Victoria, Albert and their children. Another celebrated the home as the site of that affection, a space that exemplified the possibility of retreat from the world but that also permitted economic engagement with the consumption of domestic commodities, the imperial patriotism of which was made concrete by the Great Exhibition of 1851. The third narrative contextualised the power of the Victorian leader of men, representing him as a figure whose influence could be felt in every household in the land. That leader was himself a creature of the domestic hearth, defined by his allegiance to middle-class values of uxoriousness and moral probity. Disraeli understood the power of this image, championing 'the happy and celebrated homes and hearths of England' in a speech in 1847.[56] Yet he and Mary Anne embarked on their eleventh year of marriage imprisoned in each other's company by their house and the status with which it endowed them. In 1846 Disraeli had written to a friend who was contemplating separation from his wife about the absolute necessity of avoiding such a course. 'Some of the best friends I know, & whose menage is now an example, are persons who mutually behaved in a very wild manner in their youth – but tho' they had doubtless many scenes, they never permanently separated – & now in the extreme maturity of life, they enjoy each others society, & what is more, assist each other in obtaining & enjoying the society of other people.'[57]

At the beginning of 1850 he and Mary Anne had little choice but to hold fast to the belief that the same would eventually be true for them too. Separation was unthinkable. His modest background and notorious history meant his career relied on him performing the role of upstanding master of home, land and party to perfection: to show aristocratic disdain for bourgeois values was impossible. Mary Anne's position in society and at Hughenden was dependent on her marital status. Without Disraeli she would keep her house at Grosvenor Gate (which made her more fortunate than Dolly Whitmore Jones and most of her contemporaries), but as a separated woman she would be debarred the society of her friends. So as the year began they made a concerted effort to present a united front to the world. A great honour was conferred on Mary Anne when she was invited to join Disraeli at the Conservative gathering at Belvoir Castle in January; afterwards she returned to London while Disraeli travelled onwards to a further meeting of grandees at Burghley House outside Stamford in Lincolnshire.

In June they were out driving together when a messenger on horseback brought the news that Disraeli's nemesis Robert Peel had been thrown from his horse and was badly injured. Peel died four days later, and while Disraeli wrote of his sorrow at his passing, he and Stanley were nevertheless alert to the possibilities inherent in a changed political landscape. Both hoped that without Peel as their standard-bearer his followers might rejoin the Protectionists, injecting some much-needed talent into the party. Chief among the Peelites was William Gladstone, whom Stanley and Disraeli badly wanted back in the Protectionist fold and who after 1841 emerged as one of the most brilliant men in the House of Commons. Disraeli was always more unwilling than others to recognise Gladstone's talents ('there were no "household words" in his speeches'),[58] but even he acknowledged that it was impossible to imagine a strong Protectionist government without him.

Disraeli no longer needed to make excuses to linger at the House of Commons. His burden of work was now so heavy that he went out only rarely, spending his spare hours reading papers and attempting to cajole his MPs. Only one letter from Mary Anne survives from this period, written to

Disraeli during his absence at Burghley. She had seen her uncle William Scrope, who had been very affectionate towards her. 'I was almost crying', she reported. 'You know how grateful I feel to those who really appear to love me and every hour of my life I am more sensible of this.'[59] It was a reminder to her husband of the devotion of which she was capable and an implicit plea that he might once more show her his love.

In March 1851 the Whig government of Lord John Russell resigned. Stanley and Disraeli were not prepared to take office. The government defeat that prompted Russell's resignation was inflicted by Radicals rather than Tories, and Disraeli knew that Stanley would struggle to find qualified members of the House of Commons for his Cabinet. Nevertheless, the Queen asked him to form a government and gave her consent to Disraeli becoming its leader in the House of Commons. In the 1860s Disraeli wrote an account of Stanley's audience with the Queen, based on conversations with Stanley and a little novelistic embroidery. From this account comes the story that the Queen objected to Disraeli's inclusion in Cabinet, citing his conduct towards Peel as proof of bad character. Stanley is reputed to have made the following reply: 'Madam, Mr Di[sraeli] has had to make his position, & men who value their positions will say & do things, wh: are not necessary to be said or done by those for whom positions are provided.' 'That is true', acknowledged the Queen. '& all I can now hope is, that having obtained this great position, he will be temperate – I accept Mr Disraeli on yr guarantee.'[60] Since the source for this exchange is Disraeli himself, it needs to be treated with caution. By the time he recorded it he had won the Queen's admiration, and in this context its inclusion in his memoirs is indicative of some satisfaction at having moved from royal pariah to favourite. It is indicative too of his pride at having achieved greatness from obscurity, which reads Stanley's excuses on his behalf as testament to his genius. But even with these caveats it still suggests that both Stanley and the Queen believed Disraeli's background to be problematic and his temperament unreliable. It suggests too that Stanley now saw Disraeli as essential to the party and that he understood the difficulties Disraeli experienced as a result of his social position and un-English origins.

The morning after Stanley's audience with the Queen he called at Grosvenor Gate in a jubilant mood to tell Disraeli, 'Well, we are launched!'

But his optimism was misplaced. Gladstone refused to be part of a Cabinet that supported protectionism, and other potential ministers followed his lead. Stanley was forced to return to the Queen with the news that he did not have sufficient support to form an administration, and Disraeli had to relinquish the possibility of office. The interlude convinced Disraeli that if the Protectionists were ever to form a government, they would have to abandon the principle of protection and so pave the way for a reconstructed Conservative Party. 'The ludicrous catastrophe of 1851 determined me no longer to trifle with the question', he wrote in his manuscript memoir. Gradually he persuaded Stanley that protectionism was dead, and for the remainder of the parliamentary session of 1851 both men devoted their energies to propping up a weakened Russell until they were fit themselves to hold office.

Mary Anne's account book for the season of 1851 records a marked increase in her social activities, suggesting that she made a decision to become less dependent on the presence of her husband. 'MA is out a good deal, but the H of C. absorbs me', Disraeli told Sarah in March, the balance of his phrasing indicating his awareness of a subtle shift in power as Mary Anne reduced her reliance on him. On 8 February her carriage was knocked sideways by an omnibus and she and her servants narrowly escaped serious injury. Three days later Disraeli dispatched a rare note on the progress of his day from the House of Commons, addressed to 'My dearest'.[61] Tiny hints only, but they give the impression of a frost giving way to a partial thaw, and this is supported by a letter Disraeli wrote in late March to his old friend John Manners, who was engaged to be married. 'My own experience tells me,' he wrote, 'that domestic happiness, far from being an obstacle to public life, is the best support of an honorable ambition, & I am sure, that you will prove no exception to this satisfactory result.'[62]

But in August, as the Disraelis prepared to leave for Hughenden, there was another 'row'. Again we have only Disraeli's account of what happened, but from his letters it is clear it was triggered by Mary Anne's continuing animosity towards James. Sarah had recently moved from Hastings to Twickenham and so was nearer her brothers and sister-in-law. 'MA. proposed this morning to dine with you on Sunday, if you were "alone"', Disraeli wrote to her from the Carlton Club. 'She did not mean Ralph, but, of course, Jem.

– This led to one of our frequent rows upon the subject & I sd. that I shd. not write, or attempt to ascertain.'⁶³ A week later they were at Hughenden, where Mary Anne's dispute with James rumbled on, its cause unclear. James Disraeli had become the most difficult of the siblings, seemingly unable to settle to any satisfactory occupation. He farmed at Bradenham and subsequently badgered Disraeli to use his influence to secure him government appointments, which Disraeli did with reluctance and limited faith in his brother's abilities. James's relationship with Mary Anne was fractious, and since both were easily offended, arguments between them were a common occurrence. 'I have not succeeded in terminating the Jem quarrel, wh: greatly annoys me', Disraeli told Sarah in September. 'I can hardly expect him to come on here, & it is a great effort for me to go to him.'⁶⁴

Disraeli was ill for much of August and September, establishing a pattern of frenetic political activity in London followed by illness and nervous collapse at Hughenden that would recur yearly as his political prominence increased. Mary Anne meanwhile was forced once at Hughenden to reveal to Disraeli that she had sprained her foot in town '& cannot walk ten yards. It does not get better, & sometimes, tho' I can hardly intimate it, I think 'tis the gout. However it completely knocks up her principal resour[c]es & terribly taxes me.'⁶⁵ Her housebound state made it harder for her and Disraeli to avoid one another's company, and her sensitivity to any suggestion that she was suffering from gout (a disease of increasing age) is evident in Disraeli's warning to Sarah of 1 September: 'Don't allude any more to MA's sprain; let her assume that I have told you it has recovered – wh: it has not.'⁶⁶

In addition to preparing for the parliamentary session of 1852, Disraeli had another occupation that autumn. He had decided to write a 'political biography' of Lord George Bentinck, which would both celebrate his friend and provide a comprehensive account of the Corn Law schism. *Lord George Bentinck* represented Disraeli's attempt to impose narrative coherence on the events of 1846–51 and so prepare himself and his party for office. It was designed to celebrate the defenders of protectionism but simultaneously to acknowledge the end of their campaign. Written as he surveyed his own position and the distance he had travelled from 1846, it was also an acknowledgement of how much he owed to Bentinck and the Portland family.

In October the Bishop of Oxford stayed at Hughenden, a visit that occasioned extensive preparations by Mary Anne. On her birthday that year Disraeli expressed his gratitude, sending her verses for the first time in five years. The poem was a single stanza of four lines: 'This is an offering to a perfect Wife / Long may this day illume my happy Life. / Long may the Sun upon this bright day shine, / And Long may I, this day, call thee, Love, mine.'[67] He had bestowed the accolade of 'perfect wife' many times before: here in a stanza shorn of hyperbole it is an elegy for past happiness that holds out hope for a better future. 'Long may I, this day, call thee, Love, mine.' Disraeli's lines are qualified, their rhythm broken by the contingency of their phrasing. The poem is not a prophecy but a plea for a broken relationship to be repaired; for the reappearance of light in their home.

~

As Christmas approached, Mary Anne and James patched up their differences, to Disraeli's relief. 'Now the talk is of a grand family party at Xmas', he told Sarah. 'Dont say I told you, as I wish the grace of the affair to be with her.'[68] Two weeks later he wrote again to urge Sarah to join them. 'You must make the exertion of paying us a Christmas visit if you can, that we may all be together. This house is wonderfully warm for a country house, and your room is the prettiest in the world, and the sunniest aspect.'[69] But Sarah elected to stay in her own home, protected from any possibility of family strife. Those of her letters to Disraeli that survive make no reference to the quarrels he recounted or the bitterness of his portrayal of his wife, presumably because he destroyed all correspondence not fit for Mary Anne's eyes. But that Sarah dreaded being surrounded by family tension is evident from her refusal of invitations to Hughenden and consequent sacrifice of her favourite brother's company. As in 1850 Ralph and James joined her that Christmas, and together, Sarah wrote, 'we all three unite in kindest love & good wishes to you & to Mary Anne'. It was for the pleasure of offering these wishes that she wrote at all, she concluded, 'having as you perceive nothing to say'.[70]

CHAPTER SEVEN

Princess Nobody

When Miss Scott decided to disappear, she left her acquaintances in no doubt as to the seriousness of her intent. To her particular friends she wrote letters warning that they would never again hear from her; a year and a half after she vanished, her lawyer had no idea what had become of her. Suicide might seem an obvious possibility, but Miss Scott did not disappear alone. She took with her her maid, a nameless Frenchwoman, and together they appear in the historical record only as they vanish, the circumstances of their lives unknown. Of the maid we know nothing except her nationality; of Miss Scott we know only her surname and that she was an unmarried woman of means, the possessor of both a lady's maid and a lawyer. We know too that something in her life convinced her of the need to erase herself from her world. Did she part company from her maid and seek oblivion on her own? Or did they together make new lives far away from home, framed by new identities and concocted histories? Were they in fact found, their recovery kept secret by scandal-scarred relatives? In death as in life they elude discovery, fading into the past at the moment Miss Scott asserts her right to control her own destiny, and her maid – we presume – follows her.

～

It was Sarah Disraeli who reported Miss Scott's story to Mary Anne, in a letter dating from the autumn of 1859. Sarah was drawn to tales of domestic mystery, such as the saga of the runaway bridegroom she related in 1855. She existed in the shadows, spending much of the year quietly in her rented house in Twickenham, kept company by her maid and her dog. Her brothers came and went, visiting when they needed sympathy or the comfort of familial rituals, writing to her to complain about each other when squabbles suspended direct contact. On her sitting-room wall hung portraits of her parents and a sketch of the library at Bradenham, the space in which she had been her father's eyes and scribe. Each autumn she left her home to visit the houses of others, passing several weeks with friends in Herefordshire, Worcestershire and Wales, and at Hughenden. In these houses she effaced herself in spare beds and strange drawing rooms, slipping into the rhythms of her hosts' days. In the 1850s the ideal of the selfless woman bound up in her home and her husband assumed new power following the publication of Coventry Patmore's *Angel in the House*. It gained further momentum as the quiet heroines of *Little Dorrit* and *A Tale of Two Cities* were embraced by a Dickens-hungry public. In contrast to these figures, and in keeping with other women whose stories intersect with Mary Anne's in the 1850s, Sarah had no husband and no permanent home of her own. 'You know the line "most women have no character at all"', she wrote to Mary Anne in 1853. 'That is certainly not your case.'[1] It was not her case either, but she lived as if it were, taking care to erase herself from the homes and thoughts of others whenever she believed her presence to be becoming inconvenient.

In February 1852 Disraeli's star grew suddenly more luminous when Russell's ministry fell and the Queen once more invited Stanley (now elevated following his father's death to the title of Earl of Derby) to form a government. This time there was no possibility that the Conservatives would decline office. Derby managed to put a Cabinet together, although its paucity of experience and talent was so apparent it became known as the 'Who? Who?' Cabinet, a nickname derived from the deaf Duke of Wellington's incredulous reaction to the announcement of appointments in the House of Lords. As had happened the year before, Derby offered Disraeli the position of Leader of the House of Commons and Chancellor of the Exchequer: when Disraeli demurred on the basis that he had no knowledge of the economy, Derby is reputed to have replied, 'they give you the figures'.[2]

Disraeli went to Buckingham Palace to be sworn in as a member of the

Privy Council alongside sixteen other appointees also new to government office. 'I had to grant perpetual audiences yesterday to people who want something', Sarah told Mary Anne as news of the appointment became public. Her postman asked her to arrange a transfer for him in 'a very tremulous voice which impressed me strangely with a sense of my extraordinary power'; a friend implored her to persuade Disraeli to read a pamphlet on the state of the currency; a stranger wrote asking for a government job for her husband. Mary Anne herself scribbled a note to the 'Right Honble The Chancellor of the Exchequer', suggesting that in success the memory of earlier misery faded. 'Bless you my darling, your own happy devoted wife, wishes you joy & hopes, you will make as good a Chancellor of the Exchr – as you have been a husband to your affectionate Mary Anne.'[3]

At Grosvenor Gate dozens of letters arrived congratulating Mary Anne on Disraeli's success. 'May you long enjoy your present high position', ran Dolly Whitmore Jones's letter from Chastleton, just a hint of mockery underlying her good wishes.[4] 'I can no longer refrain from congratulating you on the present happy event, I hope it is all that Mr Disraeli can wish', wrote Dorothy Nevill from her new home in the country before adding that her brother needed a job – could Disraeli oblige?[5] Charlotte de Rothschild arrived home from Paris and immediately sent a note to say she sympathised with all Mary Anne felt; her sister-in-law Louisa had written of Mary Anne two years earlier that 'it must be intoxicating to see one we love achieve great things, forcing the unwilling world to give him fame & applause'.[6] Even a spurned lover forgot his animus against the 'Tory novelist' amid the prospect of a government sinecure. 'My dear Lady', wrote Augustus Berkeley, 'let me heartily congratulate you on the high position you are destined to attain through the brilliant talents of your Husband.' He did not write for form's sake, he insisted, but because 'I must ever feel the deepest interest in all that concerns you.' Incidentally, 'if anything should offer to suit a man of <u>moderate</u> fortune & but of moderate intellect' perhaps she would put in a good word for an old friend? 'I do not mean exactly now, but something might turn up.'[7]

The manner in which Mary Anne wore her triumph irritated some among her acquaintance. The Queen met her properly for the first time at a dinner at Court in April 1852 and thought her 'very vulgar, not so much in appearance, as in her way of speaking'. (After subsequent meetings she softened her position, writing that Mrs Disraeli was 'wonderful – telling me her husband was "so fond of children & flowers", & that children were so fond of him & all call him Dizzy!!!')[8] In March Charlotte Guest (who had met her husband John through Mary Anne) wrote that her old friend was making herself ridiculous. 'They say Mrs Disraeli's absurdities are beyond everything', she recorded in a private meditation on the Derby ministry. 'She called herself "the Prima Donna" of the affair, says she gave away all the appointments herself and that now they all come to her to write their election addresses!'[9] If Mary Anne noticed or was hurt by the sneers, she left no record of it. Instead she sent her servants into 11 Downing Street to measure the drawing rooms and loaned Disraeli £479 (to be reimbursed by the Board of Works) for the redecoration and furnishing of his official residence. Mary Anne believed that she and Disraeli would both move to Downing Street once the refurbishments were complete, and in March wrote to Dorothy Nevill of their imminent departure from Grosvenor Gate. But Disraeli resisted relocation, knowing that Derby's ministry was far from secure and valuing the refuge from Whitehall afforded by Grosvenor Gate. Deprived of a move to administrate, Mary Anne collected poems in praise of the new Chancellor, undaunted by stanzas more concerned with taxation than poetic merit. 'If Benjamin, can but devise / An equitable Rate, / In Fame unsullied, he will rise, / Main Pillar of the State.'[10]

Disraeli was dealing with a volume of work that left him little time to do anything but sleep. 'I am very well', he told Sarah, 'but I literally have not time to take my meals.'[11] But he was finally in government, in charge of one of the great departments of state, right-hand man to the Prime Minister and at last a nationally important figure. It was his responsibility as Leader of the House of Commons to send reports of its business to the Queen, and for his sovereign he painted the actions of his political opponents with the eye of a novelist. A 'dull debate' in April was enlivened by a speech by Russell, 'statesmanlike, argumentative, terse & playful'.[12] His dispatches were partisan ('the discomfiture of the opposition is complete'), but Victoria was charmed. Her hostility to Disraeli lessened as he wooed her in letters that were courtly, chivalrous, ornately respectful and often funny. 'Mr Disraeli (*alias* Dizzy) writes very curious reports to me of the House of Commons proceedings

– much in the style of his books', she told her uncle the King of the Belgians.[13] Meanwhile Disraeli entered into Prince Albert's plans to transform South Kensington into a site of scientific and artistic discovery, and stayed for the first time at Windsor Castle as a Privy Councillor and guest of the Queen.

He no longer had any time to take part in the social season, but Mary Anne flung herself into its balls and visiting rituals, knowing that she was acting as his emissary and husbanding the connections vital to his political success. 'MAnne however is very gay and ubiquitous', he told Sarah three weeks after his appointment.[14] And in June, 'MA keeps you *au fait* to her brilliant campaign in wh: I share very little: sitting 14 or 15 hours a day in H. of C. almost continuously, besides having the cares and labor of govt.'[15] That Mary Anne took her responsibilities as wife of the Chancellor seriously is evident in a letter to her from Viscountess Ponsonby. 'I have just seen a Person who I believe to be the best authority – a Ministers Wife certainly ought to go to every Drawing room – & I was quite right in saying not in the same dress – I write these few lines for fear any thing I might have said yesterday might make you decide on not going.'[16] So Mary Anne appeared at Court in dresses of crimson and white satin; in blue skirts and gold lace petticoats almost as wide as she was tall; with feathers, flowers and diamonds in her hair.

To recover a semblance of the Disraelis' emotional existence during this period of activity and excitement we have to listen closely to the rhythms of their letters and to throwaway remarks. 'MA. I suppose keeps you a little au fait to our, or rather to her life,' writes Disraeli to Sarah in June, the balance of his sentence registering the gulf between the spheres of husband and wife. 'Mine you know by the newspapers. I go nowhere.'[17] And then a week later he writes again. 'I have half promised M.A. to go with her to a ball in the evening at Lady Wiltons. Yr. letters to D.S. are sometimes sent to G. G. None have *miscarried* – but it is better, if anything important, to send them under cover to T. P. Courtenay Esqr 11. D.S.'[18] Here in the things not said are the old moments of tension and hints of marital distance: a promise of company, reluctantly given; a warning about the fallibility of a secret postal system; a reassurance that no letter has been seen by anyone for whom it was not intended; advice about how to ensure communications reach only their recipient. But in October he writes again to Mary Anne in the old style. 'A very busy morning . . . I only write this line to tell you I love you.'[19] Mary Anne gives no indication of her feelings in her account book, her most intimate record of household affairs, but from the diary of Charlotte Guest we learn that her position in Conservative circles was still isolated even when she appeared within the citadel of Grosvenor Gate, a hostess apparently able to command the company of London. 'To a wonderful crowd at Mrs Disraeli's. Everybody was there, especially all the high Tories, but it was really shameful how they turned the poor woman into ridicule in her own house, and almost within her own hearing.'[20]

Mary Anne is silent too on the entrance into her story of a new object of Disraeli's affections. Lord Henry Lennox was the second son of the Duke of Richmond, MP for Chichester and, at Disraeli's instigation, a Lord of the Treasury. He was young, emotional, witty and quite prepared to be Disraeli's disciple. He gained Disraeli's confidence and then became the recipient of some strikingly intimate letters. From Hughenden in August Disraeli wrote to Lennox as 'my beloved', lamenting their parting. 'I think very often of my young companion, and miss him sadly, for his presence to me is always a charm, and often a consolation.'[21] By the beginning of September stylised regret had given way to expressions of devotion. 'I cannot let another day close without thanking you for your letter, but I am so tired that I can only tell you that I love you.'[22] Two weeks later, the same again: 'Adieu, my dear Henry, and write to me whenever you can and like: even a line is pleasant from those we love.'[23] It would be easy, reading these letters, to overlook the extent to which men in the mid nineteenth century expressed mutual friendship and admiration in language we might now more commonly expect to find in the letters of lovers. Nevertheless it is notable that it was Lennox who received many of the most personal letters Disraeli wrote over the course of 1852 and it was Lennox whose company he sought when he came to London to see his Treasury staff that autumn. 'I shall be in D. S. tomorrow by two o'clock', he wrote in mid August. 'I apprehend that my morning will be very much engaged, but I hope we may dine together, alone.'[24]

At the end of September Lennox made a ten-day visit to Hughenden, arriving two days after the departure of Lord Stanley, Derby's son and an undersecretary in Foreign Affairs. The new Lord Stanley was another young man drawn to Disraeli and another recipient of affectionate letters. Derby looked on his heir's admiration for Disraeli with disquiet, believing that it indicated a lack of familial loyalty as well as the insidious nature of the influence Disraeli wielded over younger members of the government. Derby still did not trust Disraeli, and Disraeli found Derby's aristocratic withdrawal from political discussions at the end of the parliamentary session an irritant. At Knowsley in Lancashire Derby was the master of a great estate before he was Prime Minister, more occupied in his sporting acres than in his study. 'Statesmen', Disraeli wrote to a friend, 'do not much meddle with politics in September, & my despatches from Knowsley have only taken the shape of haunches of venison.'[25] Although his affection for Hughenden was undiminished and he and Mary Anne had discovered a degree of emotional equilibrium there, he nevertheless found the business of Budget preparations more arduous while immured in his woods. 'I shall be in D. S. on Tuesday morning', he told Stanley with some relief. 'Dear D. S. The country is only fit for boys & girls, sportsmen & poets – not for men.'[26]

Parliament reopened on 4 November, and on 3 December Disraeli presented his Budget to the House of Commons. He was recovering from a bout of influenza and so Mary Anne took him in her carriage to the Palace of Westminster. It was probably on this drive that an incident occurred that was afterwards held up as an example of Mary Anne's devotion. She is reputed to have trapped her hand in the carriage door and badly injured her fingers but to have kept her injury a secret until Disraeli had left the carriage, in order not to distract him from his speech. The Chancellor was undisturbed, the Budget was presented and Mary Anne's friends wrote to congratulate her on her husband's genius. But Disraeli knew that the passage of the Budget through Parliament was fraught with difficulty. The debate opened on 10 December; three days later Disraeli told the Queen that the result was 'very doubtful.'[27] On the final night of the Debate, 16 December, Gladstone rose to attack the Budget and the Chancellor in a speech of brutal brilliance. Gladstone had remained loyal to Peel after the Conservative schism of 1846 and had no love for the Protectionist government. He was Disraeli's equal in the House of Commons in age, intellect and oratorical power, and in the long term his Budget speech of 1852 marked the beginning of an open rivalry between the two men unlike any political joust before or since. In the short term it sealed the Government's defeat. The Budget was rejected by the

House of Commons, and three days later the Derby ministry resigned. Disraeli returned his seals of office and wrote to the Queen to thank her for her 'gracious & indulgent kindness' during 'an unequal contest',[28] and he and Mary Anne held a dinner party at Grosvenor Gate to console their particular friends, 'a very few disconsolate ex-officials or partizans'.[29] On Gladstone, the new occupant of 11 Downing Street, Disraeli took revenge by refusing to hand over the Chancellor's robes first worn by Pitt and still on display today at Hughenden. He also dunned Gladstone for repayment for the furniture at Downing Street, ensuring that a dispute that started in the House of Commons quickly became personal. From Twickenham Sarah wrote to Mary Anne. 'The End! – You had led me to expect, but there is consolation even in defeat – I am told that never was Dis more <u>triumphant</u> never more completely flayed his enemies.'[30] Louisa Rothschild, watching like Sarah from the sidelines, wrote in her diary that she pitied Mary Anne. 'Poor Mrs Disraeli, I feel grieved when I think of what her feelings must be today – But where there is triumph, fame & glory there must sometimes be blights & shadows it is only the obscure who know not the pangs of wounded ambition.' Yet writing a month later Louisa could not help feeling that there was a lesson to be learnt from the Disraelis' dejection. Disraeli 'looked perfectly wretched' and Mary Anne 'was also much out of spirits'. 'Had Disraeli ever wished to carry out any great triumph', she wrote, 'or to bring forward some truly useful measures, he would not be so cast down; he would feel that in or out of office he had high, noble duties to perform and that his talents need never be unused – but his own elevation having been his only aim he has nothing now to <u>sweeten</u> the bitter cup of ill success.'[31]

For the next seven years the Conservatives remained in opposition. They came close to forming a government in 1855, but Derby declined office (to Disraeli's chagrin), believing that Palmerston was the only man the people would accept as their leader. The great developments in foreign affairs of the 1850s are therefore tangential to the Disraelis' story. He had little power in negotiations over the management of the Crimean War between 1853 and 1856, or in shaping an official response to the Indian Mutiny of 1857. His political position was never fixed and in the long years of opposition he minded more about returning the Conservatives to power than about pursuing a particular political programme. But he was only Derby's deputy, and at times he struggled to convince his chief to adopt his strategies for unseating the government. He was increasingly impatient for office but as second-in-command of the Opposition had relatively few outlets through which to channel his energy. He occupied himself in trying to strengthen the position of the Conservative Party by founding a sympathetic newspaper, *The Press*, to counteract a perceived anti-Conservative bias in the pages of rival papers. He wrote many unsigned articles for *The Press* but was not its editor, and although he was instrumental in its establishment he deliberately kept news of his involvement as quiet as possible to minimise suggestions that it was merely a Conservative propaganda sheet. His relationship with Derby came under further strain as his influence over Stanley increased and Derby began to doubt his suitability for the role of Leader of the Opposition. Disraeli clung on to his position, knowing as he did that he lacked the support of both his chief and his party. For his part he was sceptical about Derby's political intelligence. Visiting Knowsley in December 1853, he described it to Mary Anne as 'a wretched house' and mourned their parting. 'I feel separation very much, & am in rather low spirits.'[32]

Throughout the autumn and winter of 1853–4 Mary Anne was struck by multiple bouts of influenza. At Grosvenor Gate Disraeli coaxed her into seeing a doctor, and once they arrived at Hughenden she seemed to recover, throwing herself into work on the house and garden. But she became ill again, suffering from what Disraeli termed 'a state of nervous debility', a phrase that in his letters usually suggests a period of emotional volatility. He felt the lack of her active presence. 'As she is the soul of my house, managing all my domestic affairs, it is, irrespective of all other considerations, a complete revolution in my life', he told Lord Londonderry. 'Everything seems to me to be anarchy. She has not left her sofa for a fortnight, & I have been obliged, almost at the last moment, to put off those friends, whom we hoped to receive here, because she would not credit the necessity of so doing.'[33] Over time Mary Anne recovered her health and her equilibrium, but she was sixty-one in 1853, and the physical and emotional effects of serious influenza were no longer setbacks she could easily conquer. In October Disraeli described her as 'a great invalid';[34] the following January he reported to Lord

Londonderry that 'at one moment, the physicians hardly gave me a hope'.[35] She was still unwell in April, but Disraeli was able to write that she did appear to be improving, although he reported that a prevailing east wind made progress slow.[36] By the summer she was herself again, but the illnesses left their mark, confronting him with the realisation of how much he needed her and forcing her to acknowledge the reality of the twelve-year gap between them. Two years later, after more winters dominated by illness, she wrote Disraeli a letter to be opened after her death. 'And now God bless you, and comfort you, my kindest dearest – you have been a perfect husband to me, be put by my side in the same grave. And now farewell my dear Dizzy, do not live alone dearest, someone I earnestly hope you may find as attached to you as your devoted Mary Anne.'[37]

As Mary Anne grew older she became a more demanding employer, and the progress of staff through both Hughenden and Grosvenor Gate was rapid. A new cook-housekeeper was given a trial in June 1854 but dismissed as 'very bad'; an under-butler was discharged 'for improper conduct about 2 women'. A potential coachman failed to secure his position because he had 'disagreeable manners, & he wanted a new great coat as well as new morn'g suits'. Even if staff did nothing wrong they could still be sent on their way. Mrs Rowles left Mary Anne's service in 1858 'for no fault only she is too young to be competent for housekeeping sweet tempered & dresses beautifully, perfectly honest'.[38] Sometimes domestic trouble was sufficiently serious to require the intervention of the nominal master of the house. During one of their absences from Grosvenor Gate the coachman's wife was arrested for stealing a diamond ring from a neighbour: 'All this, tho' not very serious, was very disagreeable', Disraeli told a friend.[39] The affair was both serious and disagreeable for the coachman and his wife: she was sentenced to three months' hard labour and he was dismissed from Mary Anne's service 'for no fault', she recorded, 'but from his wife's misconduct'.[40]

With friends too Mary Anne's relationships occasionally became irascible. Edward Bulwer Lytton (the order of his name changed after his mother died in 1843, according to the inheritance arrangements set out in her will) spent an afternoon in the drawing room at Grosvenor Gate in the summer of 1852 lamenting the behaviour of his estranged wife Rosina and raising the question of whether Rosina would live through the winter, since her health was known to be fragile. Several months later he wrote to reprimand Mary Anne for misreporting him in conversations with others. He had not suggested 'that Lady L's death was <u>daily</u> expected', he protested, and she had no right to tell her friends he had. He claimed to have Rosina's best interests at heart, arguing that if she knew he was aware of her illness 'it might produce a state of mind at war with the least chance of better emotions left to the mother of my only surviving child'. Could Mary Anne therefore kindly keep their conversations private in future? He thought it 'impossible' that she had deliberately sought to make mischief between him and Rosina, but nevertheless demanded that there be no 'further misrepresentations' on her part.[41]

From subsequent letters by Bulwer it is evident that Disraeli issued an invitation to Hughenden as a peace offering that Bulwer first accepted and then declined. Yet although Mary Anne is silent on the subject of Bulwer and his marriage, it is possible in this phase of her life to glean a sense of her independently of Disraeli through two relationships charted in her papers. The first was with a twenty-three-year-old novelist called Elizabeth Sheppard, who sent Disraeli the manuscript of her novel *Charles Auchester* in May 1853, asking him to help place it with a publisher. *Charles Auchester* was inspired by *Contarini Fleming*, and Mary Anne took up Sheppard's cause, sending the novel to Henry Colburn and then effectively acting as her agent when Colburn proposed an agreement with the firm of Hurst and Blackett. She negotiated more favourable terms for Sheppard, gave her permission to dedicate the novel to Disraeli and dispensed advice about the title. Correspondence from Sheppard herself as well as from Hurst and Blackett demonstrates Mary Anne's financial acumen and her command of the detail of business agreements throughout the episode. Sheppard's gratitude was expressed in her letters to Mary Anne from 1853, and Mary Anne's letters from her friends were full of praise for *Charles Auchester*, suggesting they understood the pride she took in the work of her latest protégée.

In 1854 Sheppard brought out a second novel, entitled *Counterparts*, this time dedicated to Mary Anne herself. Shortly afterwards she became convinced that Mary Anne disapproved of her changing publishers. She wrote a frantic letter to Sarah (whom she believed lived with the Disraelis) demanding to know why Mary Anne had not acknowledged her most recent communication. Sarah was taken aback by the letter but consulted Mary

Anne and wrote to Sheppard reassuring her of Mary Anne's approval while warning her against allowing 'your too susceptible imagination to conjure up shadowy evils'.[42] Sheppard failed to heed this warning and instead took to loitering on the street outside Grosvenor Gate in the hope of meeting her patroness. When this failed, she wrote directly imploring Mary Anne to see her. 'May I ask you not to tell Miss Disraeli that I have asked permission to see you for she will think me actually insane.'[43] More agitated letters followed in September 1854 as Sheppard became convinced that Mary Anne was offended by the unauthorised dedication to *Counterparts*: she wrote, she insisted, not 'to renew any communication with you', but in 'self-defence'.[44] Mary Anne was made sufficiently angry by this to instruct one of her servants to send a reply protesting the insinuations of Sheppard's 'very extraordinary letter' and to keep a copy of her reprimand.[45] It was the last communication between them.

A second relationship documented in letters dating from the 1850s paints a different picture of Mary Anne. Her correspondent was Sarah Brydges Willyams, a rich widow of Jewish descent who began an epistolary relationship with Disraeli at some point before 1851. In the memorandum Disraeli's lawyer Philip Rose wrote on Mrs Brydges Willyams after Disraeli's death he described her as 'a lady of advanced age [and] of moderate fortune, inherited from her own family, but of great intelligence, and considerable intellectual powers, and . . . an enthusiastic pride in the race from which she sprung'. This, Rose explained, 'was the tie that first attracted her to Mr Disraeli, and secured her devoted attachment to him'.[46] The correspondence started sporadically, Mrs Brydges Willyams writing to Disraeli of her family history; he responding with copies of his novels. In 1851 she wrote asking him to act as her executor and offering in exchange to make him heir to her estate. In his memorandum Rose described the Disraelis making early visits to Torquay to meet their benefactress, and then how these visits led to friendship between the three and resulted in Mrs Brydges Willyams making a new will in Disraeli's favour in 1857. Christmas visits to Torquay became a feature of the Disraelis' year and a ceremony they appear to have anticipated with pleasure. They would stay in a hotel but spend their days with Mrs Brydges Willyams, taking her for drives in Mary Anne's carriage and dining at her house in the evening.

Throughout his life Disraeli needed sympathetic female correspondents to whom he could write of politics and his thinking without fear of reper-cussion: Sarah was one such correspondent, as, during the 1830s, were Lady Londonderry and Lady Blessington. From 1851 Sarah Brydges Willyams fulfilled this role and was the recipient of some of Disraeli's most frank accounts of his activities, his duels with the government and the state of the Conservative Party. Philip Rose was exaggerating when he described their correspondence as 'a brilliant specimen of social and political gossip written in the freedom of private friendship – such as has been rarely equalled' (he was not privy to Disraeli's correspondence with Sarah), but he was right that something about Mrs Brydges Willyams made Disraeli feel he could depend upon her discretion and write of public affairs to her with confidence.

Disraeli's letters to Sarah Brydges Willyams have received a great deal of attention from his biographers. More rarely commented on are the sixty-three letters Mary Anne sent to Torquay between 1851 and 1863. These letters are unique among her papers because they reveal her epistolary voice over a period of years in letters written to someone other than her husband. They allow us to see her in her own words at parties, at Grosvenor Gate and at Hughenden. Her letters usually focus on the exploits of her husband, the subject most likely to interest Mrs Brydges Willyams, but rather than limit her pen, this focus suggests that Mary Anne was grateful to have the ear of another woman who participated in her devotion to Disraeli but whose age (Mrs Brydges Willyams was in her eighties) lessened the possibility that she might compete successfully for his attentions. Mary Anne oversaw the posting of game from Hughenden and newspapers from London and was quick to thank Mrs Brydges Willyams for the flowers that arrived week after week to adorn her dressing table and scent Disraeli's dispatch box. 'Your constant kind & affectionate thoughts of him adds much to the happiness of our lives',[47] she wrote in February 1855. In May she related news of a third invitation to a ball at Court, 'which proves we are in favour does it not'.[48] Two weeks later, in the midst of a frenetic social season, she reported ruefully that 'my time is employ'd in dressing & undressing'.[49] She described prepara-tions for a grand breakfast at Grosvenor Gate and delighted in conveying news of the extremity of new fashions. 'The dresses this season are so vast & grand looking, such an immense quantity of trimming.' Mary Anne's ability to skid between subjects is particularly evident as a sentence describing enormous dresses transmutes into a tale of domestic woe: 'it is almost impossible to get footmen they are all on the Rail Roads or the army a general complaint Lady Londonderry has only one in her house & cannot get any nor can we'. Evident too in this letter is her complete identification with the Conservative cause. Lady Derby and the Duke of Northumberland were giving weekly parties, presumably, she argued, because 'they think there is a chance of our coming into office'.[50]

In August 1856 the Disraelis escaped Conservative Party squabbles and slipped across the Channel to Spa in Belgium, informing no one of their departure. Disraeli told Mrs Brydges Willyams that they deliberately left no forwarding address at Grosvenor Gate so that no letters could follow them. 'This complete breaking of the perpetual chain of public circumstances & the cares & trouble of business, has perhaps done me as much good, as the waters.'[51] Mary Anne also wrote to Mrs Brydges Willyams dwelling on things Disraeli chose not to convey. 'Dizzy takes these wonderful tonic walks & baths with great perseverance & benefit, I am rejoiced we came here', she wrote on 20 August. 'The place is full of gaily dress'd ladies & cavaliers of all nations . . . The second night after our arrival we were awoke by a blaze of light & beautiful music – a Serenade, with torches, in honour of Dizzy.'[52] At the end of the year they travelled abroad for a second time to spend December and January in Paris, where Mary Anne reported that they dined out 'almost every day, with celebrated people'. The Disraelis themselves were among the celebrated. Disraeli received much 'homage',[53] according to Mary Anne, while he told his brother James that at dinner at the Tuileries they were accorded a signal distinction. 'Mary Anne had the honor of sitting on the right hand of our Imperial host, & I the scarcely less distinguished post of being next to the Empress, who was very agreeable, & sparkled almost as much as her necklace of colossal emeralds & diamonds – as large as the precious stones in Aladdin's cave.'[54] Mary Anne took the opportunity to remind the French Emperor of the scolding she had given him on the Thames two decades earlier, and the Empress, hearing the sorry result of her husband's overconfidence, remarked, 'just like him'.[55]

In February 1853 Mary Anne wrote to a Miss Richardson in Dublin. Miss Richardson claimed to be able to discern character through handwriting, and Mary Anne sent samples of her script and Disraeli's to put her to the test. Miss Richardson thought that Mary Anne's slanting hieroglyphics were a product of 'an ardent quick & versatile mind . . . little restrained by rule method or discipline', 'intuitive insight', and a nature that was 'generous & warm-hearted but impulsive hot & excitable'. Their author, she concluded, had 'more of elastic buoyancy & cleverness than steadiness in pursuit much active energy, much shrewd & quick though careless perception'. The sample of Disraeli's handwriting, meanwhile, demonstrated 'a marked individuality'. 'The mind is aspiring elevated & of disinterested views, & speculative & of many ideas, earnest though vivid impressions what is once grasped here is rarely lost or forgotten.' Miss Richardson also deduced 'a generous spirit & by no means an easy temper – can be courteous bland & conciliatory – but is naturally irritable if not obstinate has a resolute will'.[56]

All the Disraeli siblings were struck by the accuracy of the readings (the possibility that Miss Richardson knew of Disraeli and Mary Anne by repute and saw through Mary Anne's cloak of anonymity appears to have escaped them). Ralph called at Grosvenor Gate to make copies of the reports for Sarah, and Sarah herself wrote that she felt 'as if I had been in communication with a witch'.[57] 'I should like to send for mine', she wrote in a separate letter, 'but fear if as true as yours it will not be flattering to my self-love.' It was in this letter that Sarah suggested that Mary Anne made nonsense of the theory that 'most women have no character at all' and she was pleased that Miss Richardson recognised this. 'The lady evidently delights in your hand-writing; it must be a treat when she receives one full of originality among all the common place penmanship of characterless persons.'[58]

Sarah and Mary Anne shared a fascination with coincidences, disappearances and the uncanny, and the exchange of anecdotes focused on these themes drew them closer together over the course of the 1850s. Disraeli still wrote privately to Sarah, but the pace of his letters had slowed and she was no longer his most important correspondent. Instead the bulk of communication between Twickenham and Grosvenor Gate was carried out via Mary Anne. But while they were fond of each other, the contrast between the two women was absolute. 'Thank you for your pleasant history of all your gaieties', Sarah wrote to her sister-in-law in July 1854. 'I think I enjoy [them] as much as you do, & without any fatigue which I fear you must suffer from – how many costumes you must have put on last Monday!'[59] While Mary Anne shone in diamonds and silk dresses, her strength of character noted by strangers and her eccentricities recorded by friends, Sarah's life continued to be characterised by stillness. Her letters to Mary Anne suggest she was not unhappy, although she felt vulnerable to isolation during the occasional absences of her maid and entirely cut off from her brother's world of politics and bustle. Yet they also suggest she was self-conscious about her invisibility. When she caught a bad throat infection she was at least able to write that 'living all by oneself has at least the advantage of curing this complaint – I am already better from not speaking a word from morning till night'.[60] After the excitement of Disraeli becoming Chancellor in 1852, meanwhile, she described herself falling 'from the excess of light into such profound darkness & repose, that I am bewildered'.[61]

As had been the case for Mary Anne in the 1830s, gossip was one of the ways Sarah sought to bolster her position. It gave her something to say and increased her visibility. The stock gossips of the nineteenth-century novel are often single women with no secure place in their communities, such as Miss Bates in *Emma*. Such women invest in the narratives of others because their own lives are accorded little social importance. Sarah's retellings of the stories of the disappeared – Miss Scott, for example, or the runaway bride-groom in Gloucestershire – reflect her experience of being a bit-part player in the lives of others. She appears in her letters as a woman of charisma, wit and intelligence, a rock for her brothers and a foil for her volatile sister-in-law. Her existence is isolated, yet it is also independent, and she remains, at all times, her own mistress. But after the death of her parents, she is turned by her world into Princess Nobody, a woman who operates outside the structures of bourgeois family life and who is therefore rendered invisible by a society that calibrates the value of women according to their domestic position. Princess Nobody is the heroine of Andrew Lang's 1884 fairy story based on Richard Doyle's illustrations in *Fairyland: A Series of Pictures from the Elf-World* (1870). It is composed of fragmentary narratives structured around Doyle's illustrations, which Lang cut, rearranged and coloured to suit the threads of his fiction. It owes its figuring of Nobody in part to the moment in *Little Dorrit* when Amy Dorrit tells Maggy the story of the woman who sits alone in her house, tending the shadow of Nobody, an inversion of the Somebody who has passed from her life. Lang's heroine is a fairy princess who vanishes from her parents' arms in order to escape marriage to a hideous dwarf. She can only be recovered by a prince, but even to him her real name must remain unknowable. 'Let us offer to give our daughter for a wife, to any Prince who will only find her and bring her home', proclaim the distraught fairy king and queen.[62] Prince Charming does eventually find Princess Nobody and her tale ends with a quotation from *Twelfth Night*: 'Journeys end in lovers meetings, and so do Stories.'[63] Lang's work offers an intriguing lens through which to see the cases (as represented in letters and other sources) of Mary Anne and the Princess Nobodies in her history; women whose biographies do not end in lovers' meetings like *Princess Nobody* and the marriage plot of the nineteenth-century novel, but in the more absolute form of erasure experienced by the shadow and the heroine of Amy Dorrit's fairy tale.

One such woman was another Mrs Disraeli. On 14 August 1856 James Disraeli wrote to Mary Anne to announce his engagement to Isabella Cave, a lady from Gloucestershire with a fortune of £1,000 a year. Isabella was twenty-eight in 1856; James forty-three. 'You must please tell all to Dis', he directed Mary Anne. 'I only came to Town yesterday intending to come to you directly, but my courage failed me.'[64] James had good reason to fear his elder brother's disapproval of the match, since although Miss Cave was from a good family and promised to make a charming wife, James did not promise to make a good husband. In the year of his engagement his housekeeper Mrs Bassett (the 'Mrs' an honorific title) gave birth to a daughter, Annie, whom James acknowledged as his. Mrs Bassett went on to have a second daughter by James and lived openly as his mistress.

Sarah, who was unaware of the nature of James's relationship to Annie and with Mrs Bassett, was hurt by Disraeli's silent refusal to give his blessing to the marriage to Isabella. She threw herself into arrangements for the wedding, making friends with Isabella and her family and negotiating on James's behalf the delicate arrangements caused by the Caves' decision to marry off two of their daughters on the same day. Disraeli and Mary Anne chose not to attend the wedding and left Sarah to placate fellow guests by concocting excuses for their absence. She tried to provoke a response from

Disraeli to the news of the engagement and marriage, asking for his views on the match and, when that produced no answer, to effect introductions to smooth the path of the newly married couple. When that request too was ignored she wrote her only surviving angry letter to Disraeli, reprimanding him for the pain his silence caused. 'A few words of recognition from your pen to James – or at least some kind message to them both through me – would have more than satisfied all', she insisted. 'But you have totally ignored our existence in a manner that must lower us in the eyes of those with whom we have been necessarily thrown into contact.' For James's bride she had nothing but praise. 'I feel so strongly her merits, & the advantages which must arise from her judicious character, & her refinement of habits & feelings that perhaps I may be usually sensitive, but I think under any circumstances we should have been surprised as well as grieved at your being the only person from whom we heard not a word of kindness.'[65]

From Isabella herself there is only one surviving letter, written to Mary Anne in January 1857. 'I wish I could give you a more favourable answer to your kind inquiries after my health but it seems that Bronchitis is no easy tenant to get rid of when it has once taken up its quarters.'[66] Isabella's complaint was not bronchitis but consumption, or tuberculosis. She became pregnant immediately after her wedding and the strain of the pregnancy caused her health to deteriorate. By the beginning of March she was bedridden and Sarah oversaw the process of moving her from London to St Leonards on the south coast, where it was hoped sea air would restore her. Six weeks later Isabella delivered a premature daughter, who lived only for a day, and on 20 June she herself died, looked after until the end by her sister-in-law. 'Yesterday was a most oppressive day here, all day an impending thunderstorm', Sarah wrote of the day of Isabella's death. 'She seemed gradually to sink under the weight of the atmosphere – Poor dear James is at this moment quite overwhelmed.'[67] Further familial disunity threatened when an incorrect rumour reached Sarah and James that Mary Anne and Disraeli had been seen dancing at a ball five days after Isabella's death.

Two months after Isabella was buried, Sarah wrote again to Disraeli, asking for advice about the correct wording for the dead woman's tombstone. 'Will you please to tell me if the word <u>Marriage</u> . . . is English? – would not <u>wedded life</u> be too pedantic? . . . I hope these queries will not trouble you much, but I have to decide, as the words are waited for, & have no head & no one to consult.'[68] It was Sarah, not James or the Cave family, who organised Isabella's tombstone, just as it was Sarah who took on the exhausting task of her care. '"Marriage" is a state of union, as well as the act of being united, & good English in the sense you use it', Disraeli replied. 'It is preferable to "wedded life": indeed, it is quite unobjectionable, & the right word.'[69]

~

In 1857 the new Duke of Portland called in the Hughenden loan. Disraeli was out of office and so had no salary; Mrs Brydges Willyams's promised bequest offered security only for the future. In January Disraeli drew up a confidential schedule of Mary Anne's income for a moneylender called Henry Padwick, who was instructed not to communicate with Grosvenor Gate 'except in person'.[70] For Padwick he also itemised debts still amounting to over £25,000 in addition to the Hughenden mortgage. Mary Anne's investments continued to yield an income of about £5,000 a year, and rent from the Hughenden farms brought in an additional £1,200, but for Disraeli the financial necessity of returning to government was acute, particularly since he needed to serve as Chancellor for only a few more months to be awarded a pension of £2,000 a year in perpetuity. His efforts to reform the Conservative Party and make it once again a serious electoral force therefore had personal as well as political impetus. When Palmerston's government was defeated on a measure in February 1858, both Derby and Disraeli knew they had to accept the task of leading a minority government or risk presenting their party as perpetually unfit for office.

Disraeli returned to the Treasury, able once more to claim a government salary, and in June Edward Bulwer Lytton was offered the Cabinet position of Colonial Secretary. Ministers of State had to stand for re-election when they accepted government office. This was usually a formality, but Rosina Bulwer Lytton, harassed by spies employed by her husband, was determined to disrupt his progress to high office. Rosina's life in the years following her break with Mary Anne was very hard. Her daughter died and in death became yet another weapon deployed by husband and wife against each other. Rosina was poor but had no way of forcing Bulwer to pay her an allowance, and her animosity towards him consumed her and poisoned her relationships with others. She wrote several novels attacking Bulwer, which he tried to have suppressed, and periodically sought to embarrass him by deluging his house, Parliament and his clubs with letters addressed to 'Sir Liar Coward Bulwer Lytton'. She and Bulwer were locked into their marriage by mutual antipathy, since although obtaining a divorce became easier after the passing of the Matrimonial Causes Act in 1857, it was only granted if one party was an innocent victim, and both Rosina and Bulwer had spent too many years blackening each other's reputations for either to convince the court of their innocence. Bulwer also dreaded the additional publicity divorce would bring. Rosina, in contrast, thrived on drawing attention to his sins. On the day of his re-election she travelled to Hertford from the Taunton hotel where she lived, having arranged in advance for the town to be plastered with placards warning of her arrival. As Bulwer reached the end of his hustings speech, concluding with what one newspaper described as 'a fervent tribute of admiration to the womanly beauty exhibited in the long line of open carriages', Rosina pushed her way through the crowds claiming she had come to expose the wrongs perpetrated against her. 'Recognised as soon as observed', ran one press report, 'her voice was nearly drowned out by the shouts of Sir Edward's supporters, but Sir Edward's eye caught hers, and his face paled.' Bulwer turned his back on his wife and disappeared below the hustings platform, leaving Rosina to lecture the gathering on his cowardliness. During her speech she announced she would confront her husband every time he appeared in public, and demanded the use of the town hall to make a public statement on his sins. This was denied and she retired to Taunton, triggering 'the greatest possible excitement in Hertfordshire'.[71]

Two weeks after the Hertford election (in which Bulwer was returned unopposed), Rosina came to London for a meeting to discuss her allowance. Waiting for her at the house of Bulwer's intermediary were the keeper of a lunatic asylum, two nurses and two policemen. Press reports drawn from the testimony of Rosina's friend Rebecca Ryves, who was with her at the time, reported that Rosina caught a glimpse of Bulwer himself as she was shown a 'certificate' of her insanity and constrained to enter the asylum keeper's carriage. She was taken to a private asylum in Brentford, Essex. 'The pre arranged programme, evidently is that my statements, are not even to be listened to, much less investigated', she wrote to Rebecca Ryves in a letter passed by the asylum's censor. 'With every other person in the kingdom, – before they can be kidnapped, and incarcerated <u>numerous</u> witnesses are examined where they are <u>well known</u> and have lived as to their <u>conduct</u>, <u>character and capability of marrying their affairs</u>, and the <u>truth</u> or falsehood of the allegations which have made their known enemy, and oppressor vote them insane!!'[72]

Bulwer aimed to make Rosina vanish from public consciousness by simultaneously halting her campaign of embarrassment and humiliation and removing her as an obstacle to his political career. But although he was able to effect her physical disappearance to a place where she had no rights and no recourse to the law, his actions rebounded against him. Rosina's circle of female friends went to work on her behalf, advertising her incarceration and ensuring that it was reported widely in the newspapers. The people of Taunton designated themselves her defenders and formed a committee to work for her freedom. 'There is a firm belief that Lady Lytton is the subject of a horrible and appalling injustice and wrong', read a long article in the *Morning Chronicle*. 'While perfectly sane, she has been shut up in a lunatic asylum merely in order that a woman, who has, no doubt, been a constant cause of annoyance to her husband, may be prevented for ever from giving him similar trouble, or in any way again molesting him.'[73] 'Publicity, <u>is</u> the soul of justice', Rosina wrote to a friend, quoting Jeremy Bentham.[74] Three weeks after entering the asylum, she was released on condition she would go abroad with her son, and to this demand she acceded.

～

In one of the press reports of Rosina's incarceration, there is an indication that Bulwer's actions had a specific motivation. Her 'morbid resentments' were not directed against Bulwer alone, the *Manchester Times* reported. 'It is because of the recent development of these against other persons, political as well as private friends of Sir Edward's, that restraint has been deemed necessary.'[75] The political and private friend was Disraeli; Rosina's allegation was that he and Bulwer had together committed sodomy. 'It would appear that the tack these wretches are on, is something I said of Disraeli', she told Rebecca Ryves, 'which was something as <u>told</u> me by Sir Liar himself.'[76] In June, as Rosina's letter-writing campaign against Bulwer escalated in the run-up to the Hertford election, Disraeli wrote to his friend complaining of her conduct:

> I thought you had tamed the tigress of Taunton – but, unhappily, this is not the case.
>
> She is writing letters to your colleagues, & friends, of an atrocious description, such as, I thought, no woman could have penned, accusing you of nameless crimes, at least wh: only can be named by her, & threatening aggravated hostilities.
>
> This is not very pleasant to your friends: I should think, hardly, to yourself.
>
> What can be the explanation? Is it possible, that your agent has been so negligent, or so imprudent, as to leave her allowance in arrear?[77]

It has been suggested by some commentators that this letter contains in its last paragraph an instruction that Bulwer should buy Rosina's silence; a supposition supported, runs this line of argument, by an episode in 1864 when both Bulwer and Disraeli attempted to purchase various letters relating to Rosina from a third party.[78] That Rosina's allegations were an embarrassment to Disraeli is without question. She wrote to Queen Victoria outlining her theories, and in December 1858 to Lord Derby. 'Indeed if you would study the propensities of your loathsome Colonial Secretary, and Chancellor of the Exchequer', ran her letter to Derby, 'you would make one King of Sodom, and the other King of Gomorrah, they having run the gauntlet of every vice.'[79]

The suggestion that Disraeli's letter of June 1858 contains a veiled instruction to Bulwer to silence Rosina with money is not borne out by its timing. The letter dates from two weeks before the Hertford election and several weeks before coded references to Rosina's accusation of Disraeli began to appear in the press. Nevertheless the episode raises a question about Disraeli's relationships with men. The allegations arose during a period when Disraeli was surrounded at Downing Street by young male acolytes, including Henry Lennox, Lord Stanley, and his new secretary Ralph Earle. The admiration of these young men was evidently important to him, even if it complicated his cultivated public persona of domesticated master of the house. But evidence of emotional attachments to young men is not evidence of sexual relationships with them. Moreover, Disraeli's reliance on the men who were his aides and political supporters was born of circumstance. He led the Conservatives but was still not of them, and he knew he did not have their loyalty. 'My friendships, tho' I have to deal with many men, are rare', he told Stanley in 1857, after the younger man had disappointed him by refusing an invitation. 'I counted yours among my chief & most enduring possessions, & notwithstanding the many circumstances, public & private, wh: might, for the moment, modify, or diminish, our intimacy, I had such confidence in the depth & stability of your character, that I have ever looked forward to our mutual relations as furnishing, during the remaining years of my life, one of my chief sources of interest in existence.'[80]

~

The social season of 1858 began with festivities to mark the marriage of the Queen's eldest daughter Princess Victoria to Prince Frederick of Prussia, and ended with the 'Great Stink', when hot weather combined with overflowing open sewers to suffocate London in a miasma of malodorous gases. At a ball to celebrate her wedding, Princess Victoria was seen in tears at the prospect of leaving her home; at the Palace of Westminster that summer parliamentarians draped lime-soaked curtains across the windows to protect themselves from the smell. The pressures of office meant that the Disraelis were at Hughenden less than usual and Mary Anne ended the year planting and pruning by torchlight, refusing to let early evenings and dark days interfere with her work. While the style of her dresses and conversations was much criticised, no one disputed Mary Anne's taste as a gardener, and visitors to Hughenden spoke with one voice in praise of a garden created with passion and skill. In keeping with the ideals of nineteenth-century garden design, she cultivated geometric blocks of colour in her planting, relishing bright patterns and striking effects. Disraeli loved the garden and made a point of displaying the results of Mary Anne's horticultural talents to his friends. Letters from her to him are rare for this period, but his to her are affectionate, intimate and uncomplicated, a continuation of shared conversations. 'You gave me the most delicious sandwich I ever tasted – I think I know what it was', ran one note from Downing Street to Grosvenor Gate. 'I hope you have had a fine day's campaign, & will tell me many tales, when we meet, of yr exploits.'[81] When he travelled alone to London that autumn to see his staff, her memory accompanied him. 'As I came in the Cab thro' all the Hyde Park Streets & squares, I thought of my dear companion in days of trouble & incognito – always faithful & always fond.'[82] They spent Christmas in Torquay with Mrs Brydges Willyams and then in January Disraeli went alone to Windsor to dine with the Queen and stay for two days. 'My dearest Wife', he wrote in some consternation from the castle, 'I have not got my right dress. Give James, breeches, drawers, silk stockings & shoes. This is the only time you have tripped since our marriage – &, therefore, I send you, as punishment, only one kiss.'[83]

In Parliament, the great subject in the session of 1859 was Reform. In February Disraeli commended a Conservative Reform Bill to the House of Commons; in April the measure was defeated. Parliament was dissolved, a general election called and the result left the Conservatives still short of a Commons majority. In June a coalition of Whigs, Liberals, Peelites and Radicals met at Willis's Rooms on St James's and there Palmerston and Russell announced their willingness to work with each other and to cease competing for votes and the Premiership. Out of that meeting grew the Liberal Party, a group with more MPs and more power than Derby and Disraeli could hope to muster. In June the government was defeated on a foreign policy bill and the ministry resigned. Disraeli was less disconsolate at being ejected from office than in 1852. He had his pension, and his efforts to reform the Conservative Party had produced a more unified body than that which had taken power the year before. He and Mary Anne retreated to Hughenden and for once he was content to accept the desultory political pace of his social superiors. He sent grouse to Mrs Brydges Willyams and in an accompanying letter wrote that Hughenden offered 'a most wonderful contrast, after the late scenes of our life – so green, so still, so sweet!' 'There is no news', he continued, 'the world is so well-bred, that nothing happens when Parliament is not sitting – only, now & then, a revolution or so; perhaps a congress; perhaps a war?'[84]

At the end of October the Disraelis made their way north to Knowsley to stay with the Earl and Countess of Derby. Disraeli and Derby were due to speak at a great Conservative banquet in Liverpool and Disraeli and Mary

Anne were invited to sleep at Knowsley the night before, Mary Anne for the first time. At dinner Derby became impatient with Mary Anne and humiliated her in front of the assembled company. In an account of the incident in his *Rambling Recollections*, Sir Henry Drummond Wolff described an unnamed Conservative magnate passing the evening 'in what is called chaffing Mrs Disraeli, for the amusement of his guests, but much to her distress. An eye-witness told me that Mr Disraeli sat perfectly still, and apparently without emotion; but the next day he made the use of some pretext to leave the house, and never returned, though frequently invited, and though he was working in the closest and most continuous manner with the politician in question.'[85] Disraeli never again visited Knowsley, even when circumstance would have made it convenient to do so, and the incident was a sign of his loyalty to Mary Anne, a moment when personal loyalty triumphed over political allegiance. But it was a sign too of Mary Anne's continued struggle to win acceptance among political elites and in the great country houses of England. Stories of her offending starched hostesses abounded and usually focused on her frank references to Disraeli in his bed or in his bath. Such anecdotes categorised her as silly and insignificant and smoothed over the complications of her character and position, rendering her true self invisible despite her apparent visibility. One commentator summarised the view of her held by parts of her acquaintance when he credited Disraeli with carrying into 'the charmed circle this uncultivated and graceless woman'. Mary Anne's existence in that circle was never straightforward. The Knowsley episode suggests she was hurt by the disdain with which she was sometimes treated – and that Disraeli would brook no impudence to or about her in his presence.[86]

~

Among the Disraelis' visitors at Hughenden in the late summer of 1859 was Sarah, who arrived on 24 August and left to visit friends in Wales on 13 September. Earlier that year she had given up her house in Twickenham and moved back to London to take up residence with her brother Ralph at his house in Gloucester Place. She kept up a steady correspondence with Mary Anne and helped with preparations for large Grosvenor Gate dinner parties by drawing up lists of guests and sending out invitations. Autumn travels to the houses of others remained a feature of her life, but in 1859, the year of her fifty-seventh birthday, she felt the strain of her journeying. In September Mary Anne described her as 'delicate';[87] in October Sarah herself told Mary Anne that she had been very unwell for the past three weeks and that it was a 'bad end to three months' health seeking'.[88] Winter came on suddenly and from Gloucester Place in November Sarah wrote to Mary Anne that the fog was so dense it was as thick inside the house as out. On 3 December she wrote again inviting Mary Anne and Disraeli to dinner.[89] Two days later Disraeli told Mrs Brydges Willyams that Sarah was seriously unwell and Mary Anne was with her; the next day Ralph told Mary Anne that the doctor thought their dinner party should be postponed. Sarah's symptoms were severe bowel pain and constipation; two days after the cancelled dinner party another doctor suggested that only surgery would save her, and a day later, on 9 December, she made a will leaving all she possessed to be divided equally between her three brothers.

Cancer of the bowel is one possible diagnosis for Sarah's illness; another is an abscess that burst, triggering infection.[90] 'I have had a sleepless night, & so have you', Disraeli wrote to Ralph as the seriousness of Sarah's condition became apparent. 'Language cannot describe what this sudden, & by me never contemplated, catastrophe has produced on me.' Sarah was still alive but Disraeli acknowledged that her case was hopeless, speaking of her in the past tense. 'She was the harbor of refuge in all the storms of my life, & I had hoped she wd. have closed my eyes!'[91] By 17 December Sarah was in a terrible state of delirium and agitation, although the sound of Ralph's voice seemed to calm her. Mary Anne, worn down by long days and nights at her sister-in-law's bedside, was seized with neuralgia and ordered home by the doctors. Throughout 18 and 19 December both Disraeli and Ralph sent bulletins from Gloucester Place – Sarah was sleeping, had rallied a little and seemed calmer. Disraeli went home to rest for a few hours and Ralph sent another note to Grosvenor Gate. 'Our dear Sister died this morning a little after 3. She seemed to be in no pain.'[92]

Disraeli described Sarah to Lady Londonderry as his 'nearest & dearest relative'. 'She was a person of great intelligence & charm – one of those persons, who are the soul of a house & the angelic spirit of a family.'[93] In 1853 he had described Mary Anne in the same terms to Lord Londonderry, but while the phrase was recycled, his grief was fresh and bitter. 'She was my first, & ever faithful, friend, & I am quite overwhelmed', he wrote at the end of the year.[94] Mary Anne remained housebound on the orders of her doctor, anxious for the welfare of her husband and brothers-in-law. Ralph had carried the strain of Sarah's final hours and for him Mary Anne was particularly concerned. Sarah's funeral took place before Christmas, and on Boxing Day Ralph told Mary Anne that he and James were preparing to walk to the cemetery to visit her grave. Sarah was 'the soul of the house' but she had no permanent house of her own; she was the 'angelic spirit of a family' but her family gathered about her only at her death. While their loss was raw, her brothers tended her tombstone; today no record of that grave survives and the site of her burial has been lost.

The final letter from Sarah in the Disraelis' papers is to Mary Anne and dates from the first part of 1859. 'I hope you will not think this is a great intrusion on your privacy, nor grudge a few moments from your sweet fresh air – I can't say I have any news to offer as an excuse.' She had been visited the day before by the wife of a new Conservative MP and so had a snippet of gossip to relate that she knew would please her sister-in-law. Her visitor, she reported, 'said the Party were in the greatest spirits & that the Chancellor of the Excheqrs speech was the finest thing in the world & surpassed even the expectations of his new followers – My love & thoughts are with you both. God bless you dear Mary Anne and Dis. Your ever affec SD.'[95]

CHAPTER EIGHT

The Rose and the Ring

MRS BEAUCLERK

Mrs Beauclerk's husband kept her existence a secret. Her wedding took place in Scotland, away from official registers, and for the first three years of her marriage she lived a double life in the house of her mother, pretending to be an unmarried woman. Only when she became a mother herself did the fiction fracture, compelling her husband to undergo a second wedding in London and thereafter to maintain her and her daughters in an establishment of his own. Captain Beauclerk claimed it was not shame of his wife that prompted his secrecy but rather the prejudices of society. Mrs Beauclerk was neither well-born nor well-off, and he would not risk the wrath of rich and ageing relations. Without their money he held little hope for the future; without his wife he stood, he believed, more chance of securing an income. Whether Mrs Beauclerk was subject to the slights and slanders foretold by her husband when she was finally revealed as his wife we do not know. Whether she was happy, as a bride in the house of her mother or as a mother in the house of her husband, is also a mystery. Her husband boasted of domestic contentment and, once the secret of his marriage was out, of his success in finding a wife who was at least fertile. Life might be monotonous, he told an old friend, but at least it was free from the excitements, mortifications and disappointments that had in the past made him wretched.

～

The letter Mary Anne's former suitor George Beauclerk wrote in 1867 to tell her of his marriage broke decades of silence between them. He wrote that he was in her debt, and sent her £20 in recompense. That this money was meant as a bribe is evident from his request that she use her influence to find him a government job. Such pleas were not unusual in Mary Anne's correspondence by the 1860s, although few other petitioners were brazen enough to accompany their pleas with money, or to remind her of her inability to have children. Beauclerk wrote that he might have been content had he married without the hope of children, although this seemed unlikely given the bliss fatherhood brought him. Moreover, had he married a woman 'accustomed to luxuries, carriages, sweets, flowers, and the opera and fine dressing, she never could have sat down in my humble home, content to be the wife of a man . . . too poor to dress her with the extreme and to me disgusting prevalence of gaiety'.[1] He also wished to inform Mary Anne that he had a large packet of letters from her that would prove damaging to both her and Disraeli were they ever to be circulated. Would she care to have them back? To this Mary Anne made no answer. By 1867 her position was immeasurably stronger than that of the unfortunate Mrs Beauclerk and she would have no truck with the threats, bribes and pleas of a man who had once called her 'Rose'. Her reply was limited to a single sentence: 'Mrs Disraeli returns the enclosed cheque for 20£ to Capn Beauclerke, because she cannot remember any reason why it should have been sent to her.'[2]

The January of 1860 was a long, hard month at Grosvenor Gate. The fog that had invaded Ralph Disraeli's house as Sarah lay dying lingered on into the new year, and for Mary Anne and Disraeli, kept in London by the impending parliamentary session, it was of little consolation to receive reports that Hughenden was alight in rare winter sun. They gave no political dinners and saw few friends. Some of Disraeli's critics thought his bereavement provided a useful excuse to avoid a party angry at being ejected from office, but they did not know the centrality of Sarah to his emotional existence. From his study he planned and plotted for the new session, but, he told Derby, he worked with difficulty, 'living in perpetual fogs, to say nothing of moral vapors'.[3] Relations with Derby were strained following Mary Anne's humiliation at Knowsley, and Disraeli felt the weakness of his parliamentary support. Mary Anne's voice too is muted during this period, recording only 'one month no company' in her account book and, in a letter to Lady Salisbury, that she would ever mourn Sarah's loss.

But as the fogs receded the Disraelis picked up the threads of the public life in which Sarah had only ever played a minor part. Disraeli and Derby steered their troops through a series of parliamentary manoeuvres designed to unsettle but not unseat the government. They knew the difficulties of holding office while in a minority in the House of Commons and the dangers of political stasis to party strength and unity. The Queen and Prince Albert demanded stable government and Derby believed intuitively in the wisdom of keeping the Liberals in power while the Conservatives rebuilt their strength. Disraeli was less committed to this strategy but had neither the influence nor the will to oppose it. In May Mary Anne told Mrs Brydges Willyams that he was 'never on better terms with his party', a message she reiterated in June.[4] It was a fiction, and in the same month Disraeli wrote to a party elder threatening to stand down. He was unable to mask his exasperation with rank-and-file MPs who failed to understand the impossibility of governing effectively with a minority of 120: dissolution had been inevitable, he insisted, and the only way to restore Conservative strength. Yet he was left alone to take the blame for a party-wide failure to hold on to power. 'I have, however, to bear the brunt of disaster, & the measures of the Cabinet, are called my measures, & I am held as alone to blame for their production.' Only one course was therefore available to him. 'I must resign a Leadership, which I unwillingly accepted, & to which it is my opinion, that fourteen years of unqualified devotion have not reconciled the party.'[5] The prospect of losing their most formidable political presence in the House of Commons prompted the party grandees to reassure Disraeli of their support and convince him to withdraw his resignation, but although he continued at the helm of his party he did so under sufferance, maintained in office by the absence of rivals and despite the mistrust of both troops and commanders.

The truce that Sarah's death prompted between her brothers proved short-lived. With Ralph, Disraeli exchanged terse letters; with James he had little contact. For both he chastised Ralph. 'We have never had a line from you since yr visit here – &, of course, we never hear from James. This is not the way to keep the family together – poor darling Sa's last hope & prayer.'[6] At moments of crisis the siblings still came together, and when James was threatened by serious illness in 1863 Disraeli and Mary Anne cut short a visit to Lord and Lady Salisbury at Hatfield in order to rush back to London. But they were uninterested in the rhythms of each other's lives and even Ralph's marriage prompted little comment. Ralph was the only one of the Disraeli siblings to have legitimate children of his own, and he named his son Coningsby, hoping to win support for the child from his famous uncle. Yet Disraeli and Mary Anne, who were affectionately interested in the children of their friends, showed little desire to become better acquainted with Ralph's offspring. 'Heaven descended is what Mr Disraeli affects to be', Charlotte de Rothschild wrote to her son in 1866, 'though London is full of his relations, whose existence he completely ignores.'[7]

Mary Anne might tell Mrs Brydges Willyams that Disraeli was secure in the affection of his party, but that she recognised the danger in which he stood is evident from the manner in which she marked her re-entry into the social season of 1860. She invited 350 guests to watch a grand review of volunteer troops in Hyde Park from her roof, which she had boarded, carpeted and furnished with chairs and sofas for the occasion. Her style of entertaining was lavish but practical: refreshments were ordered from Gunters at £1 a head and extra staff were employed to prepare and clean up. Her guests for the review of June 1860 were listed in the *Morning Post* and included diplomats, politicians of both parties, members of the royal family and all the smartest London hostesses. After such parties Mary Anne went through the published lists of her guests with minute attention, crossing off those who had failed to appear, recording excuses received and marking mistakes introduced by newspaper editors. Both she and Disraeli knew that political influence was socially derived, that it originated in dining rooms and on drugget-covered roof tiles as much as in the committee rooms and lobbies of the Houses of Parliament. To be able to command the presence of everyone who mattered in London to your rooftop on a Saturday afternoon in June was therefore a sign that you still held political fortune in your hands, and it acted as a warning to potential rebels of the might of the man they attempted to cross.

The underlying strength of Disraeli's position was evident too in outward signs of royal approval. Both the Queen and Prince Albert had warmed to him over the course of the 1850s, although they continued to be sceptical about his professed desire to shore up a Liberal government. In January 1861 Mary Anne was invited to dine at Windsor Castle for the first time, to both her and Disraeli's delight. 'It is Mrs Disraeli's first visit to Windsor, & is considered very marked on the part of Her Majesty to the wife of the leader of the Opposition, when many Cabinet Ministers have been asked there *witht* their wives', he told Mrs Brydges Willyams.[8] Various anecdotes of this evening, however, suggest that Mary Anne was snubbed by a monarch who continued to think her vulgar, and she was not invited to join Disraeli on subsequent overnight visits to Windsor and Osborne. These visits were almost the only occasions on which the Disraelis were apart now, since they came and went to Hughenden together and visited country houses exclusively in one another's company. Disraeli's letters during his absences at Court reveal that he shared Mary Anne's fascination with the minutiae of royal living, and were full of details of the food he was given, the compliments he was paid and the stratagems he employed to protect himself against royal draughts. After the death of Prince Albert from typhus in 1861 plunged the Court into mourning and turned the Queen into a recluse, Disraeli consolidated his sovereign's approval through the devotion he showed to Albert's memory. He supported plans for a grand memorial to the Prince in South Kensington and spoke eloquently in the House of Commons about the loss the country had suffered. The Queen responded by sending Disraeli engravings of herself and the Prince, which were hung at Hughenden amongst the portraits of Isaac and Maria, Lady Blessington, D'Orsay and Tita.

Mary Anne was seventy in 1862, Disraeli fifty-eight. They embraced technological developments with the vigour of those half their age. Disraeli was photographed for the first time in 1861 and Mary Anne was an active presence during his session with the photographer, instructing him on what to wear and how to stand, and tidying and arranging the curls she dyed black every few weeks. She would never allow herself to be photographed but was proud of Disraeli's image, sending the first copy of his photograph to Mrs Brydges Willyams. 'It is the first & I enjoy sending it to you – his faithful friend – some more will be out in a short time, & in a few weeks the man says all over the world.'[9] A few months later they were invited to witness a second portent of a shrinking world at a party hosted by Samuel Gurney, chairman of the London and Provincial District Telegraph Company.

'Telegraph communications', promised the invitation, 'will be interchanged during the evening between England and Egypt, Africa, &c. Tea and Coffee at 9 o'clock. Conversation and Electric Correspondence from 10 to 12 o'clock.' 'I enclose you . . . an American card', wrote Mary Anne to Mrs Brydges Willyams of the invitation, 'which I think looks so <u>American</u>.'[10]

With age and fame came new kinds of scrutiny. When they drove around London in their open carriage, people pointed and waved; at the South Kensington exhibition, Mary Anne reported, Disraeli's reception was marked. 'You would be amused at the peoples anxiety to see him . . . great numbers take off their hats.'[11] In March 1863 Disraeli was asked to become a Trustee of the British Museum, which, as Mary Anne noted, was 'one of our greatest honors, as it is never given but to first rate abilities position charact[er]'.[12] Disraeli accepted with an unusual degree of emotion, confessing to the Prime Minister, Lord Palmerston, that there were few distinctions he would value more. 'My father', he wrote, 'was the first man of letters who, much more than half a century ago, began to turn its MS wealth to account; in the illustration of our history; & I have been brought up in a due appreciation of its treasures, & a due reverence for its authorities.'[13]

Meanwhile putative biographers began to turn their gaze towards him. The first approach came in March 1860 from Francis Espinasse, author of the *Imperial Dictionary of Universal Biography*, and Disraeli was sufficiently flattered to put together a memorandum of the 'facts' relating to the 'mythic period' of this history. He would do so, he told Espinasse, in spite of the fact that 'my life, since I emerged from the crowd, has been passed in a glass-house'.[14] In a subsequent letter he wrote a brief account of this 'mythic period': his childhood and life before he rose to political prominence. He related the history of his early election contests, the dates on which his novels appeared and the scenes of his foreign adventures. 'In these days of rapid locomotion, my travels go for nothing', he acknowledged, 'but I was in Syria, Asia Minor, & ascended the Nile to Nubia.' His election in 1847 as MP for Buckinghamshire was the public event that had brought him greatest satisfaction. His marriage, meanwhile, had brought him nothing but 'complete domestic happiness . . . which has mainly sustained me in a career of considerable trial'. In contrast to Mary Anne, with her stories of milliners' shops and factory work, Disraeli took pains to emphasise the grandeur of his wife's lineage, stressing her connection to the Scrope family of Wiltshire and General Sir James Viney rather than her father's relatives. Still he professed himself doubtful of the feasibility of Espinasse's task. 'Details in contemporary biography', he warned, 'can hardly be touched witht. great delicacy & reserve.'[15] Later that year he received a second approach, this time from Thomas Kebbel, who would go on to publish a life of Disraeli in 1888. To Kebbel Disraeli was more uncompromising. 'I am not an admirer of contemporary biography, and I dislike to be the subject of it.'[16] Yet he nevertheless agreed to see him and became gradually convinced of the merit of controlling his biographical reputation by engaging with a supporter like Kebbel, who won the privilege of an invitation to Hughenden in 1864.

A further sign of Disraeli's public status came in the spring of 1863, when both he and Mary Anne were invited to attend the wedding of the Prince of Wales and Princess Alexandra of Denmark at the Chapel Royal, Windsor. They owed their invitation to Lord Palmerston, who asked the Queen to extend the honour to them as well as Lord and Lady Derby, but they did not know this. 'The chapel being very limited, the invitations are still more so', Disraeli told Mrs Brydges Willyams. Mary Anne's inclusion ('by the Queens particular command', he insisted) prompted howls of outrage from her rivals.[17] 'There is no language, wh: can describe the rage, envy & indignation of the great world', ran his account of the wedding. 'The Duchess of Malboro' went into hysterics of mortification at the sight of my wife, who was on terms of considerable intimacy with her, & said it was really shameful . . . & as for the Duchess of Manchester, who had been Mistress of the Robes in Lord Derby's administration, she positively passed me for the season witht recognition.'[18] Mary Anne took the honour of her invitation seriously, writing to the Marchioness of Ely for advice about the protocol of what to wear. 'We wear no train but feathers and lappetts, not long however & not many feathers', came the reply, which suggests that Lady Ely was anxious at the prospect of Mary Anne appearing in her usual jewelled and feathered splendour.[19] The wedding itself was an occasion to remember. The Queen, still in deep mourning, sat alone high above the crowds, playing no part in the pageantry. Disraeli thought her distance added an additional layer of majesty to the proceedings. 'The presence of the imperial & widowed mother, in her Gothic pavilion, watching everything with intense interest, seeing everything, tho' herself almost unseen, was deeply dramatic, & even affecting.'[20] The ceremony was followed by a wedding breakfast at Windsor Castle, after which there was an unedifying scramble for places on trains back to London. Ladies in diamond necklaces were mobbed at the station and in the melee the French ambassador's wife was separated from her husband. 'I rescued her', Disraeli wrote, '& got her into a railway carriage with my wife & some other grand dames, who had lost their husbands – I think I had to sit on my wife's lap.'[21]

~

In Torquay Sarah Brydges Willyams devoured accounts of the royal wedding and the glittering social season that followed as the Prince of Wales and his new Princess established their own court, alleviating the gloom emanating from the Queen's household. Mrs Brydges Willyams was ninety-three in 1863 and she lived for the Disraelis' letters and their annual visits. As Disraeli became ever more prominent, both he and Mary Anne developed new appreciation for the peace Torquay offered. Mrs Brydges Willyams made no political demands and was disconnected from the tangled world in which friends were colleagues and everyone wanted something from somebody else. As in the 1850s, Mary Anne's voice during this period of her life comes through strongly in the letters she sent to Torquay. A story doing the rounds in London she describes as 'unmitigated nonsense'; a political dinner at Grosvenor Gate 'gives me so much trouble, & makes the house so uncomfortable, as everything must be moved to make room for 40 people'. At Hughenden the 'owls make such a noise as soon as it gets dark, you might hear them at dear Mount Braddon'. Mrs Brydges Willyams is always 'my dear' to Mary Anne and her desire for her company is consistently expressed. 'How much I wish you could be here & with us', she writes in February 1862. 'Say yes & I will take such care of you, as much as I do of Dizzy.'[22]

Torquay offered one kind of respite from political conversations and the cares of housekeeping, but Hughenden offered something more – a space for peace and regeneration, even when the house itself was anything but peaceful. In 1860 Mary Anne embarked on an ambitious programme of works in the grounds, planting forests and making walks and a new Italian garden. In 1863 she turned her attention to the house, reworking its exterior and interior completely. In October 1860 she told Mrs Brydges Willyams that she was overseeing the creation of two walks and a trout stream and planting 600 evergreens; a year later she reported having 'eight or ten navvies to superintend, my favourite occupation you know'.[23] While only the garden was in chaos the Disraelis could still entertain at Hughenden, and in September 1862 Disraeli reported that they were preparing to receive fourteen overnight visitors in ten days. 'Its as hard work as having a playhouse – or keeping an Inn.'[24] When Mary Anne's workmen invaded the house, Disraeli found even his sanctuaries of study and library difficult to maintain, but he admired the romantic aesthetic of her scheme. At the end of September 1863 he was able to write that 'we have realised a romance we had been many years meditating: we have restored the House to what it was before the civil wars, & we have made a garden of terraces, in wh: cavaliers might roam, & saunter, with their ladye-loves!'[25] He was grateful too for the pleasure the work brought Mary Anne, writing to a colleague that 'she has been very much amused, wh: is something for your money'.[26]

As Hughenden underwent its transformation into the house of the Disraelis' dreams, they settled with renewed security into the roles of country landowners they had assumed fifteen years earlier. Mary Anne hosted fetes for village children; Disraeli oversaw the building of a new school. They installed cygnets on the terrace, named Hero and Leander. They were present at harvest homes, which had become, Disraeli noted, 'a novel feature, as now practiced, of our English country life'. He was still not quite of the country and so could observe its rituals with an anthropological interest. Instead of individual farmers holding boozy suppers for their workers to celebrate the end of the harvest, he told Mrs Brydges Willyams, all the farmers of the parish were bringing their labourers to massed tents with banners and bands before processing to the church to give thanks, each man with a stalk of corn in his buttonhole. 'The Clergy are at the bottom of this movement: it connects the harvest with religion, & the Church. Even a *dissenting* farmer can scarcely refuse to walk in the procession on such an occasion. Unconsciously, all are reviving pagan rites, & restoring the Dionysian festivals.'[27] After the church service marking the first harvest home, the procession marched up the hill to the manor house. Mary Anne greeted them from a window before retiring with the revellers to the tent for dinner, where toasts were drunk to the health of the royal family and Disraeli.

Secure in his role in the community around Hughenden, Disraeli finally fell in love with the house. Memories of the periods in the 1850s when it seemed to offer only bitterness, isolation and unhappiness faded as it came to symbolise the distance he had travelled from the uncertain days of the 1830s. Constance de Rothschild visited Hughenden as a child and remembered the intensity of Disraeli's pleasure in his grounds as well as the strange incongruity of his country costume. 'How he loved the place!' she wrote in her memoir. 'And how he tried to act up to the character he had imposed upon himself, that of the country gentleman! for, dressed in his velveteen coat, his leather leggings, his soft felt hat, and carrying his little hatchet, for relieving the barks of trees from the encroaching ivy, in one of those white hands, which probably hitherto had never held anything heavier than a pen, Mr Disraeli was *the Squire* of the Hughenden estate, the farmers' friend and their representative in Parliament.' She remembered too Disraeli's insistence that all his visitors should admire Mary Anne's work. 'Over and over again "Dizzy" bade us pause and admire the sylvan scene, as he expressed it, evidently relishing that sweet-sounding word "sylvan." He lingered over it and repeated it more than once. "And," he added, "this is all owing to the cleverness of Mary Anne; she devised the walk, and she made it with the help of her two old men of the soil."'[28]

For Disraeli the romance of Hughenden was immanent not just in its woods and walks but in 'the 'men of the soil' who worked his land. 'I like very much the society of woodmen', he wrote in private reflection in 1860. 'They are healthy – their language is picturesque, they live in the air, & nature whispers to them many of her secrets.' To see his head woodman fell a tree was 'a work of art', he continued. 'No bustle, no exertion, apparently not the slightest exercise of strength – He tickles it with his axe, & then it falls exactly where he desires it.' The romance of woodmen could take a less mystical vein, as another story from 1860 illustrates. 'An old, but very hale, man told me today, that he was going to be married, & that his bride would not be very much younger than himself, but he had lodged in her cottage now for more than a year, & he thought she wd. do for him.' Disraeli reported this story to Mary Anne, who promptly sent a wedding dinner to gladden the table of the happy couple.[29]

Inspired by the turn to antiquity in Mary Anne's reworked Hughenden and freed by a political lull from the demands of work, Disraeli turned to the subject of his own past, writing a series of autobiographical notes and sketches towards a memoir over the course of several Hughenden autumns. His memory took him back through the ranks of men he had known, men who led him to recall a saying of Mary Anne's: 'manners change even more than features'. He wrote of the 'vigour and flexibility' of Lord Lyndhurst's mind; Derby's report of the Queen angrily insisting in the early days of her widowhood that Prince Albert died 'from want . . . of pluck'; the way that Peel's voice swooped downwards so that 'wonderful' became 'woounderful' – a result, Disraeli thought, of him managing his elocution like his temper ('neither was originally good'). He passed comment on the grim oddity of Derby's mansions in London and at Knowsley, both furnished 'like a second-rate lodging house . . . in itself essentially mean: all this not from stinginess, but from sheer want of taste'. Lady Jersey, in contrast, had succeeded in establishing in her elegant drawing rooms a *salon*; something no other hostess had been able to achieve. 'It requires the acme of social position, knowledge & tact – great self-command – If a bore comes, & however importunate, you must never by your reception of him let him suspect that he is a bore, or he will go about, & tell, & prevent others coming.'[30]

Mary Anne too revisited her past in the early 1860s, although the manner in which she did so differed from Disraeli's. At Hughenden she set about the creation of a monument to Isaac D'Israeli, commissioned, designed and built without Disraeli's knowledge. The monument was to be a column on a hill on the estate, visible from the house and for miles around, but despite the difficulties of concealing news of its development, she was determined it should be a surprise for her husband. It was erected over the course of the summer of 1862, and Disraeli's lawyer Philip Rose was employed as a go-between to coordinate its installation with both Mary Anne and the architect. Rose wrote a memorandum of the affair in which he listed the steps he took to preserve the secret, including ordering that the stone should be wrought away from the site and that its installation be fast and not reliant on the labour of local men. He also conceded that Disraeli did in fact hear news of the monument before he arrived at Hughenden but that Mary Anne never learnt the truth. From Hughenden Disraeli wrote of finding 'a monument to my father, raised by my wife, and in my absence. It is quite finished and really, whether I consider the design, the execution or even the material – I think it one of the most beautiful things in England.' The monument's inscription celebrated Isaac's connection with Buckinghamshire, a connection now continued by Disraeli, 'Knight of this Shire'.

A year before the Hughenden monument was erected, a dispute with the Lewis estate brought Mary Anne into contact with a different chapter of her story. In March 1861 she discovered that Wyndham's heirs were underpaying a dividend deriving from colliery shares left to her, and together with Disraeli she travelled to Wales to enquire into the matter herself. The only reference in her papers to this visit comes in a letter to Mrs Brydges Willyams, in which she denies newspaper reports that she went to meet her relations. 'Like you, I have none.'[31] Disraeli was more forthcoming about their Welsh experiences, and was particularly struck by the contrast between the Cardiff of Mary Anne's memory, a sleepy country town with fewer than 8,000 inhabitants, and the city of 40,000 souls they beheld. From Cardiff they went to Greenmeadow, which Disraeli had never seen. He was struck by the grandeur of its setting, 'a picturesque house, beautifully situate at the gorge of a valley of Welch mountains, richly wooded, with the river Taff raging through its wild & shaggy bottom'.[32] Their pilgrimage took place three decades after Mary Anne's last visit to Wales, and almost half a century after she became mistress of Greenmeadow.

∽

On 15 August 1863, Disraeli and Mary Anne were driving back to Hughenden from Wycombe Abbey, where they had been dining with Lord and Lady Carrington. It was approaching midnight and dark outside. As they entered their parkland, Mary Anne noticed sparks outside the windows of the carriage, glittering in the blackness. As the sparks grew closer, they revealed themselves as fireflies, illuminating the carriage as brightly as a single spotlight. Unable to believe their eyes, the Disraelis turned all the mirrors in the carriage inwards to cancel out the reflection from the lamps, but still the sparks grew brighter. The driveway up to the house was steep and the fireflies followed them as they pulled up the hill, lighting their progress home before vanishing in a globe of colour at the gates of the pleasure gardens. Disraeli and Mary Anne were mystified by the spectacle and vowed to take the carriage out the next night to witness it once more. But the next night it rained, and the night after, and the summer came to an end. Few of their friends believed that creatures more usually found in Mediterranean climates had illuminated their way home. But Mary Anne and Disraeli held fast to their story, their certainty of their seduction by the fireflies bolstered by the presence of the other; the magic of the scene figured and celebrated in their papers as a joint experience.

~

The Rose and the Ring, William Thackeray's Christmas book for 1854, is a comic tale of star-crossed lovers, cantankerous fairy godmothers, magical talismen and ageing monarchs. The rose and the ring of its title are objects that render their possessor irresistible to members of the opposite sex, no matter how ridiculous they are. So the King of Paflagonia is smitten with his silly Queen despite the fact that she is fond of flattery, scandal, cards and fine clothes and has grown stout with the passing years. The twists and turns of the story are only resolved when its hero and heroine are forced by circumstance to confront the fact that they love each other even when deprived of the magical assistance of the rose and the ring, and that they do so in spite of their physical faults and character flaws. 'What care I', says the heroine to her prince as she vanquishes her enemies, 'if *you* think I am good-looking enough?'[33]

The Rose and the Ring combines the magical and the ordinary in ways that are both funny and touching. Characters vanish and fairies fight battles but the old King and Queen eat muffins and eggs for breakfast and squabble amiably over pocket money for their favourites. Theirs may be a marriage forged on a fiction (the Queen has entrapped her husband with the aid of the ring), but it is nevertheless a solidly affectionate relationship, at least until the malign magic of others temporarily forces them apart. A bad-tempered fairy godmother can wreak havoc with the rose and the ring but is also the possessor of much common sense, who recognises the dangers of the gifts she gives. Made wise by experience, she will give to the hero and heroine only 'a little misfortune' on the grounds that this is more likely than magical objects to equip them for married life.

It is this combination of the magical and the ordinary, along with its commentary on the things that do or do not make people beloved, that makes *The Rose and the Ring* a fitting companion text for the Disraelis' story in the 1860s. Mary Anne's days as 'Rose' were now far behind her; Disraeli too had travelled a long way from dandified suitor attempting to win the hand of his ludicrous princess. Yet both retained an allegiance to these antique versions of themselves. Writing to Mrs Brydges Willyams of the deposition of the Greek King in December 1862, Disraeli termed it 'a privilege' to 'live in this age of rapid & brilliant events. What an error to consider it a Utilitarian age! It is one of infinite Romance. Thrones tumble down, & crowns are offered, like a fairy tale, & the most powerful people in the world, male & female, a few years back, were adventurers, exiles, & demireps.' In talking of royal upstarts and political pretenders he was talking also of himself: the adventurer who stormed the citadel of power, the demirep who became a statesman of international renown and the emperor of his own domain. 'An estate is a little Kingdom', he wrote of Hughenden in the same letter. 'There is almost as great a variety of interests, & characters, & parties, & passions, on these acres, as in Her Majesty's realm.'[34] And as Mary Anne grew older, her pride in the romance of her youth only increased. She kept George Beauclerk's letter in spite of its veiled threat, just as she kept his compromising missives from the 1830s, annotating them to ensure they would not be destroyed. It was at about this time too that she began to spin fairy stories about her rags-to-riches girlhood, pointing out the mythical milliner's shop in which she had worked to bemused companions during a visit to the south-west in 1862. And at a Rothschild dinner in 1864 she talked at such length of the thirty-two proposals she had received that she prevented the gentleman sitting next to her from eating.

Moreover, in Sarah Brydges Willyams the Disraelis acquired a fairy godmother of their own. Charlotte de Rothschild wrote during a visit to Torquay that Mrs Brydges Willyams was a fantastical creature, a 'female Croesus'. 'She has piercing black eyes, wears a black wig with an enormous top knot, no crinoline, is quite a miser, starves herself into a skeleton, except when her adored Disraeli is here, is ninety-seven years of age, keeps neither horses, nor carriages nor men servants – only an enormous watch-dog to protect her and her gold.'[35] Charlotte exaggerated Mrs Brydges Willyams' age but, judging by other contemporary accounts, little else.

By 1863 Disraeli's financial situation had reached equilibrium courtesy of a Conservative supporter who bought his debts and charged only a modest rate of interest. But when news came from Torquay in November 1863 that Mrs Brydges Willyams was failing, the Disraelis and their friends knew that their hour had come. They arrived just too late to see her and were sincere in their sorrow at her passing, faithfully ensuring the granting of her final wish, to be buried at Hughenden. Mrs Brydges Willyams kept her promise to make Disraeli her heir, and her death left him better off to the tune of approximately £40,000. The legacy meant his debts could be paid and his self-presentation as a well-heeled country gentleman finally became a reality. Charlotte de Rothschild wrote of the incongruity of the Disraelis appearing in her drawing room 'as black as crows – I mean in deepest mourning – but in joyous spirits'. To her son she wrote of the difficulty of composing a letter to Mary Anne on Mrs Brydges Willyams's death, 'which sincerity prevents me from making one of condolence, and which from motives of feeling & delicacy cannot be one of congratulation'.[36] Disraeli was himself less bashful, writing with unusual frankness to Derby from Torquay, 'It would hardly be frank to let yr assumption, that the business, that keeps me here is "unpleasant", pass over in silence. I have lost a kind & faithful friend, but I have lost her in the fullness of years, & she has made me the heir to her not inconsiderable fortune.'[37]

It would be easy to read Sarah Brydges Willyams's legacy as a fairy tale come true for the Disraelis, a magic charm causing a mountain of debt and a lifetime of financial anxiety to melt away. And in many respects this reading seems accurate. Mary Anne talked at length of the labours the legacy entailed, but both she and Disraeli always spoke of their benefactress with gratitude. Yet it had one unlooked-for effect on Mary Anne's position. Her talisman or magic charm, the thing that had made Disraeli marry her, was her money. For decades it had been her income that supported their houses and financed his political career. Now the value of her jointure was proportionally less significant and her power consequently diminished. Disraeli's position too during this period continued to be under threat from disconsolate MPs and a lack of energy and action on the political stage. With his finances secure, he had less of an imperative to campaign for a return to office and a government salary, and became a withdrawn figure.

In October 1861 he described himself as 'an actor without an audience'[38] and in February 1863 he characterised the role of Leader of the Opposition as 'at present, an office more of thought than action'.[39] In the summer of 1865 he once again offered Derby his resignation, which was once again refused. But to Mary Anne he wrote that his troops remained dispirited. To keep his spirits up, he told her, 'I think of you, wh: always sustains me, & I know we shall find many sources of happiness without politics – if it comes to that.'[40]

The unorthodox manner of the Disraelis' financial liberation did little to ease a continuing sense among their landed contemporaries that there was something vulgar about them. To many, Mary Anne appeared to become more, not less, of an overdressed oddity as she grew older, and stories about her behaviour continued to circulate in drawing rooms and dining rooms. Several of these stories were collected by William Fraser in his 1891 volume *Disraeli and his Day*. Fraser knew both the Disraelis and complemented his own memories with the tales of those who remembered them. He was generous towards Mary Anne, writing that although she 'had the reputation of uttering gauche sayings; and of being remarkable for the want of good sense in her remarks', he failed to observe this. But he could not resist including one much-repeated story of her scandalising a prim country-house hostess by announcing at breakfast that the house was full of indecent pictures. 'There is a most horrible picture in our bedroom: Disraeli says it is Venus and Adonis: I have been awake half the night trying to prevent him looking at it.'[41] The journalist Henry Lucy centred his recollections on Mary Anne's reputation in High Wycombe, where tales of her stinginess abounded. These stories were framed by an implicit assertion of Mary Anne's fundamental failure to be an acceptable lady of the house. One such tale had her refusing to pay the band who played for a visiting dignitary to Hughenden more than half a crown: there was, Lucy wrote, 'a pretty row about it . . . Mrs Disraeli wanted to fight it out in court, but Dizzy wouldn't let her, and quietly arranged the affair'.[42] And in an anecdote that had many variants, all of which undermined Mary Anne at the expense of praising Disraeli's loyalty, the MP William Gregory related the snub earned by George Smythe when he ventured to ask Disraeli what kept him with his wife. 'George, there is one word in the English language of which you are ignorant', Disraeli is reputed to have replied. "'What is that?" asked Smythe, somewhat taken aback by his manner. "*Gratitude*, George" said Dizzy, in his deep, solemn voice.'[43]

A more generous contemporary assessment of Mary Anne came from the young Lord Rosebery (Liberal Prime Minister from 1894–5), who met her at Raby Castle in 1865. Raby was the seat of Rosebery's stepfather, the Duke of Cleveland, and as the eighteen-year-old son of the house, Rosebery was given the task of entertaining Mary Anne at dinner. In his diary he called her a 'half-crazy, warm-hearted woman' and he took pains to set her conversation down as accurately as possible, feeling he had met an 'uncommon specimen'. His account captures the pace of Mary Anne's conversational style as well as her devotion to Disraeli. Their conversation opened with Rosebery praising *Coningsby* – praise Mary Anne found unsurprising for a novel 'written by a clever man like him'. It then turned to Mary Anne's activities at Hughenden, where, Rosebery reported, 'she managed everything, even to ordering Dizzy's clothes'. Mary Anne talked of her labours in the garden, describing how she stayed out all day, taking a light lunch for her and beer for her workmen. 'Is not that very fatiguing?' Rosebery enquired. 'Ah, but the mind overcomes the body – and then he is so glad to see me when I come back, and he comes out and sees what I have done, when it is all finished, and says sometimes, "This is delightful, better than anything you have done yet." And then I feel quite intoxicated for the moment, and quite rewarded.' 'I never allow Dizzy to come and see me while I am planting', she continued, 'because he would lose the *coup d'oeil* of seeing it when it is finished.'

Rosebery then asked Mary Anne if she cared for politics. 'No, I have no time, I have so many books and pamphlets to read and see if there is my name in any of them! and I have everything to manage, and write his stupid letters. I am sorry when he is in office, because then I lose him altogether, and though I have many people who call themselves my friends, yet I have no friend like him. I have not been separated from him since we have been in the country, except when I have been in the woods, and I cannot lose him.' Mary Anne's assertion that she had no friend like Disraeli touched Rosebery; in his account she appears a lonely figure, surrounded by people yet with few real confidantes. Rosebery freely confessed to being star-struck by Disraeli, but even given his reporter's bias, the prevalence of Disraeli in

Mary Anne's conversation is striking. 'I am looking to see if Dizzy is sitting next any pretty woman that he would like to sit next and admire', he recorded her saying after they had exhausted the conversational possibilities of politics.[44] He took Mary Anne into dinner for the next two nights and made assiduous notes of her view of Lord Derby (who, she insisted, 'gave hardly anything to the Conservative Election funds'); her disingenuous account of the Brydges Willyams legacy ('The old lady at Torquay who left Mr Disraeli 40000£ never told him her intentions') and her praise for Rosebery himself: 'Mrs Disraeli promised to give me a set of Mr Disraeli's studs which she said she had taken away from him to give to young men that she liked.'[45]

Rosebery's diary is an illuminating source of information about Mary Anne's preoccupations and conversational style because he did not reduce her utterances to a series of eccentric bon mots. Instead he attempted to capture the rhythm of her speech and the apparently unselfconscious manner in which it pointed to her separation from her contemporaries. He recognised too that there were things about Mary Anne that were easy to ridicule and that it was tempting to draw her into exchanges for the fun of waiting to hear what she would say. 'I cannot help quizzing her by talking in this way', he acknowledged after relating their conversation. But after three evenings in her company he detected a depth to her not accessible to those who listened only for her eccentric sayings. His final judgement was unambiguous. 'I really like her.'[46] Several years later Mary Anne introduced Rosebery to his bride, Hannah Rothschild, one of the great heiresses of the nineteenth century, repaying his attention during her Raby visit and solidifying his affection for both her and Disraeli.

Another person who felt great affection for Mary Anne was Charlotte de Rothschild, whose letters are a valuable source for Mary Anne's manners, conversation and appearance during the 1860s. That Charlotte was fond of her is clear, as is the fact that she frequently found her exasperating. Charlotte referred to Disraeli as Mary Anne's 'illustrious husband', a label that captured his fame while poking fun at the importance he ascribed to himself and the seriousness Mary Anne accorded him. Her letters suggest that inviting seventy-year-old Mary Anne to formal dinner parties was a risk, since she was inclined to fits of ill-humour and to fall asleep when conversation stuttered. Sometimes in Charlotte's letters Mary Anne is Dizzy's 'decidedly worse half'; at other points she appears as 'a bore at tea-time' and her conversation is 'dreadful'. 'Dizzy has the gout', she writes in 1864, 'and reads French novels to while away the heavy hours spent near Mrs Diz.' Yet at other points Mary Anne is Disraeli's 'shrewd, good-natured wife' and Charlotte stresses her own devotion to her. No matter how rude Charlotte was about Mary Anne in her private letters, she continued to invite the Disraelis to private Sunday evening dinners, to accept invitations to Hughenden and to treat both Mary Anne and Disraeli as part of her own family: sometimes inconvenient, sometimes embarrassing, but always loved. Also noticeable in her letters is her sympathy for Mary Anne, an old lady out of step with the modern world. The Mary Anne of Charlotte's letters is tired but quite unwilling to accept the reality of her own ageing. 'Ladies, who have no children consider them-selves young, handsome and fascinating for ever – they lack the admonishing hands which mark the flight of time', Charlotte writes in 1865. In October that year Mary Anne is 'very cross. Lady Carrington says she must be nearer eighty than seventy, that she is the most wonderful woman in the world, but quite the most tiresome one.' Mary Anne told no one her real age, not even Disraeli, but in Charlotte's account few are fooled by her performance of eternal youth. She is 'pale, thin & wrinkled' and she struggles in London drawing rooms, 'where she grows weary & dissatisfied because men & women listen to her great husband & pay little attention to her; and where she says odd & startling things to arrest the eyes & ears of men & women'. No matter how much sense Mary Anne talks, her 'shrewdness of observation is always marred by a spice of the ridiculous'.

Mary Anne in her finery as described by Charlotte is a startling creature, at one point 'beautifully attired in an old evening dress, wearing, like the savages, a wreath of red feathers' and at another appearing in a wig 'adorned with sky blue velvet folds and gold butterflies'. 'Not ridiculous', Charlotte adds loyally, 'but very becoming.' And while she might be marginalised in the social seasons of the mid 1860s, her determination to be part of them remains unabated. In July 1864 Charlotte writes that Disraeli is longing for the repose of Hughenden 'but Mary Anne wants a continuation of London and the world'. Charlotte regrets Mary Anne's devotion to London, believing her to be happier at Hughenden, 'where she can be out in the open air from morning till night, and to have trees & flowers & shrubs – which harmonize with all ages'. In society, in contrast, 'the younger & most agreeable or the most gifted, & fascinating often turn away from poor Mrs Dis, whom they find tiresome, and leave very cross at their neglect'. This is a theme repeated a few months later, when Mary Anne returns from Hughenden in an admirable temper, 'the prolonged life among her beautiful beech-trees & evergreens suiting her far better than her existence in the brilliant world'.[47]

~

Vying with Mary Anne for attention in Charlotte's letters is her eldest daughter Evelina. In 1865 Evelina married her cousin Ferdinand de Rothschild, repeating the family habit of intermarriage, which kept the fortune consolidated. It was a happy match, celebrated in June 1865 by a happy wedding at which Disraeli made a speech. Evelina, he said, had been 'long admired and so long loved'. Addressing Lionel and Charlotte directly, he confessed he felt no need to console his old friends on the loss of their daughter to a home of her own, since the couple planned to 'build their nests, if not in the same tree, at least in the same grove'.[48] After their honeymoon tour Evelina and Ferdinand did indeed settle near her parents, and Charlotte's correspondence is full of pride in her daughter as she took her first steps in society as a married woman. But in December 1866 Evelina died in childbirth alongside her baby. Ferdinand retreated to Buckinghamshire, where he built at Waddesdon a palace of mourning dedicated to his lost love. Charlotte and Lionel were paralysed with grief from which neither ever fully recovered. In the first days after Evelina's death, only Mary Anne, unconstrained by manners or social ritual, could offer comfort. 'I was, of course left', Charlotte told her son Leopold, 'with the good, kind-hearted Mrs Dizzy, who cried with me and then tried to tell me many things, which would have interested darling Eve had she been at my side, all mirth & fun & wit & humour.'[49] 'Come to me', she asked Mary Anne. 'I wish to thank you and to speak to you not of my sorrow, not of my darling's sad end, but of her beautiful life; I want to tell you how much she appreciated your card how gratified she was for all your kindness.'[50] Throughout that winter Mary Anne and Disraeli were constant in their support of their friends, sitting with them on Sunday afternoons, talking politics to distract and entertain, and allowing both Charlotte and Lionel to speak of their grief unimpeded. The things that were comical about Mary Anne were rendered irrelevant by the unconditional loyalty and sympathy she offered.

Evelina's death took place six months after the Conservatives returned to power. In October 1865 Lord Palmerston died aged eighty. His Liberal successor as Prime Minister, Lord John Russell, was less popular in the country and had a weaker grip on his party. Russell's ministry was defeated over the question of parliamentary reform, struck down by a newly emboldened Derby and Disraeli. Disraeli returned to the Treasury, Reform unsettled and his relationship with Derby fundamentally altered. Derby was sixty-seven in 1866 and for years had been disabled intermittently by gout, which was becoming a serious obstacle to office. For months at a time he was forced to retreat to his sickbed at Knowsley, leaving Disraeli in charge of the party and the country. Derby was Prime Minister in name; in reality he shared the role with Disraeli, who was now the most visible and powerful politician in the government. His fractious party fell behind him, calmed by once more being in power and by the stature of Disraeli's public profile. 'Mrs Dis beams like the disk of the sun', Charlotte reported in 1867. 'She speaks perpetually of the enthusiasm which her illustrious husband excites wherever he goes; he talks politics with justifiable pride.'[51]

Now firmly in the ascendant, Disraeli made a crucial appointment. At Raby Castle in 1865 he had walked into the drawing room to find a fellow guest named Montagu Corry singing comic songs for the entertainment of the assembled ladies. Corry was mortified at being so discovered; Disraeli amused. 'I think you must be my impresario', he is reported to have said. Corry was twenty-eight when he met Disraeli. He was a dapper young man who took great pleasure in life, was well connected and popular with young women ('What a Lothario Monty is' was another remark attributed to Disraeli). In June 1866 Corry wrote a hesitant letter to Disraeli outlining his credentials to serve in government as a private secretary, and his commitment to the Conservative cause. 'I can scarcely presume to ask for the honour of being Private Secretary to yourself, yet I do venture to hope that should you know of some member of the government, to whom my services might be acceptable, you would be willing to mention me.'[52] Disraeli promptly appointed him as his secretary, and thereafter Corry grew to be one of the most important people in the lives of both Disraelis. He became a kind of ideal son, affectionate, competent and respectful. 'So I am off, wishing you from my heart a tranquil night', runs one letter from him, written at the end of a busy day at the House of Commons in 1867.[53] He and Mary Anne became fond of each other, and Disraeli had complete confidence in him. He was quick to learn the kind of secretary Disraeli needed him to be, acting promptly on every instruction and request. In 1866 Disraeli entrusted him with the task of preparing his selected speeches for publication, and as Derby grew more infirm it was Corry's efficient protectiveness that made it possible for Disraeli to act as both Chancellor and Prime Minister. 'The relations between a minister and his secretary are, or at least should be, among the finest that can subsist between two individuals', Disraeli wrote in *Endymion*, the novel he published in 1880. 'Except the married state, there is none in which so great a degree of confidence is involved, in which more forbearance ought to be exercised, or more sympathy ought to exist. There is usually in the relation an identity of interest, and that of the highest kind; and the perpetual difficulties, the alternations of triumph and defeat, develop devotion.'[54]

It was Corry who was at Mary Anne's side in June 1866 when Grosvenor Gate was surrounded by rioters. The defeat of Russell's Reform Bill provoked public anger, and a massed meeting in Hyde Park to call for Reform descended into chaos as protesters broke down railings and rallied in Park Lane. Charlotte de Rothschild reported that several windows at Grosvenor Gate were broken, but Mary Anne insisted that the protesters had no malign intent towards her or her house. Indeed, she wrote in a letter designed to reassure Disraeli, 'I am happy to assure you no one takes the slightest notice of this house.'[55] Another note insisted that the demonstrators were 'perfectly orderly', although she could not control her anxiety completely. 'I shall be anxious to see you safe the streets are made dangerous.'[56] For his part Corry was impressed by Mary Anne's calmness. 'The soldiers have moved away to the M. Arch', he wrote to his chief at the end of the second day of demonstrations. 'Mrs Disraeli wishes me to add that the people in general seem to be thoroughly enjoying themselves: and I really believe she sympathises with them.'[57]

Despite the demonstrations Disraeli remained unconvinced of the need for political reform, and it was Derby who insisted the government must confront the issue. But shortly after deciding to introduce a Conservative Reform Bill in the House of Commons, Derby was once again struck by illness. Disraeli was therefore charged with shepherding Reform through Parliament, a task requiring unparalleled energy as competing factions, parties and political demands were reconciled in one Bill. The Reform Act of 1867 was a compromise act, in many respects as far removed from the legislation Disraeli envisaged as it was from the measures the Liberals demanded. Nevertheless it effectively enfranchised all male householders and its passing has historically been seen as Disraeli's greatest parliamentary triumph. It made him a hero to his party and confirmed his position as Derby's successor. At the end of the April night on which the Bill was passed, Disraeli was cheered by his own MPs, Tory gentlemen who had always looked on him with hostility and suspicion. He was swept out of the debating chamber towards the Carlton Club by young supporters who wanted to shake his hand and celebrate over dinner. But he slipped away, returning instead to Grosvenor Gate, where Mary Anne was waiting for him. 'I had got him a raised pie from Fortnum and Mason's, and a bottle of champagne', she told Thomas Kebbel. 'He ate half the pie and drank all the champagne, and then he said, "Why, my dear, you are more like a mistress than a wife."' 'I could see', Kebbel wrote, 'that she took it as a very high compliment indeed.'[58]

~

Thereafter their position was unquestioned. One of Mary Anne's acquaintances wrote to her recalling the peroration of Disraeli's disastrous maiden speech: 'The time will come when you <u>shall</u> hear me.' 'That time has indeed come', commented the correspondent. 'They have done his bidding you must be supremely happy.'[59] In October 1867 they paid a triumphal visit to Edinburgh, where Disraeli was due to speak at a great Conservative banquet. It was his first visit to Scotland since the 1820s, and Mary Anne had never before been north of the border. At the banquet Disraeli toasted Mary Anne's health, declaring, 'I do owe to that lady all, I think, I have ever accomplished, because she has supported me by her counsels and consoled me by the sweetness of her disposition.' Both of them were cheered to the rafters, and when at the end of the evening they were alone, they could not contain their glee. 'We were so delighted with our reception', Disraeli told the essayist John Skelton, 'that after we got back we actually danced a jig (or was it a hornpipe?) in our bedroom.'[60]

Disraeli's devotion to his wife was now a matter of public note, even in an uxorious age. 'It is certainly a very remarkable alliance', Skelton wrote. 'That her heart, however, is as kind as her taste is queer, everybody admits; and she has splendid pluck and illimitable faith in Dizzy.' Did Disraeli feel true chivalry for her? Skelton wondered. Or gratitude? Or something more? 'When visiting at the big houses, where the big ladies fight a little shy of her, he won't stand any nonsense. "Love me, love my Mary-Anne." People will laugh no doubt when he is not looking; but to my mind there is something distinctly fine in this jealous and watchful regard.'[61] At the Hughenden harvest home of 1867, Disraeli again toasted Mary Anne, declaring, '"without offence to anyone", that Mrs Disraeli was the best wife in England',[62] and the consistency of his efforts to protect her from distress is evident in two letters from the second half of the 1860s. To his brother Ralph he wrote that he could not consent to make baby Coningsby his heir until he had spoken to Mary Anne, 'wh: cannot be done hurriedly',[63] suggesting that he feared she would be hurt by formal recognition of a child not her own, and in October 1866 he sent an uncompromising reply through Corry to a man who claimed to be the illegitimate son of Mary Anne's brother John. Mary Anne had not only bought John's commissions, he told Corry, she had also paid his debts. 'I think she had done eno.' 'I don't mention this to her', he continued, 'as I wd. only revive sorrows.'[64]

⁓

In the middle of November 1867 Mary Anne fell ill. One newspaper attributed her condition to a cold caught on the journey back from Edinburgh, but Disraeli's biographers have assumed that her illness stemmed from the onset of uterine cancer. No one recorded her symptoms, but from the severity of her condition and the rapidity with which she deteriorated, it seems likely that she contracted an infection, although it is also possible that she suffered a uterine haemorrhage that left her dangerously weakened. For several days she hovered between life and death in dreadful pain. On 19 November it seemed as if a crisis was imminent. Parliament opened for an autumn session that day, but Disraeli remained absent. In the House of Commons Gladstone spoke of his sympathy. Every day the London papers carried bulletins on her health, gleaned from the information posted on placards outside Grosvenor

Gate. The Queen wrote to ask for news, as did the King of the Belgians and the Prince of Wales. Offers of help poured in from Mary Anne's circle, grand ladies anxious to share in the task of nursing her. An old servant wrote on similar lines, begging to be allowed to look after her former mistress. 'I love her more & more & have found none like her.'[65] Mary Anne's former companion Eliza Gregory wrote Disraeli a guilt-ridden note for having attempted to subject her to blackmail. 'Ask her to forgive me & to believe that my heart was faithful . . . I was easily led by dangerous designing influence of some she had around her.'[66] Not content with expressing his sympathy in a public forum, Gladstone wrote of his sincere esteem for Mary Anne, with whom he maintained a cordial relationship even in the midst of rancorous exchanges with Disraeli. 'I have always been grateful for and have sincerely appreciated Mrs Disraeli's regard, and during the recent crisis I was naturally mindful of it; but, even if I had not the honour and pleasure of knowing her, it would have been impossible not to sympathise with you when the fortitude necessary to bear the duties and trials of your station was subjected to a new burden of character so crushing.'[67]

The crisis passed and Mary Anne recovered. 'This morning, all seemed dark, & he was told to hope no more', Disraeli told the Queen, the protocol of the third-person address contrasting with the intimacy of his account. 'But within three hours of this, there was a change, & everything became hopeful: a state of complete composure but accompanied by increased strength.'[68] 'We are happy to announce a slight improvement in the condition of Mrs Disraeli', proclaimed *The Times*. 'On inquiring at the residence of the Chancellor of the Exchequer at Grosvenor-gate yesterday afternoon, we were informed that she had passed a better night.'[69] As Mary Anne remained confined to her room, gradually recovering some strength, Disraeli was brought low by an attack of lumbago, which left him unable to leave the house or even mount the stairs to see her. Deprived of each other's company, they wrote notes instead from their respective sickbeds. 'I am so grieved my dearest that you are suffering so much, and that I cannot be with you', ran one from Mary Anne. And then, simply, 'I have loved your letter my darling.'[70] 'We have been separated four days – & under the same roof! How very strange!' Disraeli mused. But he was consoled by her presence in the house. 'Grosvenor Gate has become a hospital, but a hospital with you is worth a palace with anybody else.' And even in their unusual predicament she could still surprise and delight him. 'Being on my back, pardon the pencil. You have sent me the most amusing, & charming, letter I ever had – it beats Horace Walpole & Md. de Sevigné.'[71]

~

'Notes from Dear Dizzy during our illness when we could not leave our rooms', wrote Mary Anne on the packet of pencilled letters she added to her archive of papers. 'At the end of the month both quite well.' In her case it was a hopeful overstatement. She was seventy-five in 1867 and her illness left her permanently weakened. Although she marked her recovery in characteristic fashion by sacking the lady's maid who had neglected her on her sickbed and promoting the housemaid who had cared for her tenderly, her days of planting from dawn till dusk at Hughenden were over. So too was her hard-won, contingent reign among the London hostesses. Yet her illness crystallised two things. The first was that she was loved by the public in spite of her absurdities. Kings and queens wrote to enquire of her but so did old servants and strangers and the readers of newspapers. The second was that she was loved by her husband. A romance that had begun as a fantasy became, in its third act, authentic and true. 'Dizzy married me for my money', she told the friends who came to while away the hours with an old lady resplendent in a red and gold drawing room. 'But if he had the chance again, he would marry me for love.' For his part Disraeli came to realise that the love affairs of the old were just as unexpected and romantic as the amorous adventures of the young. 'Threescore and ten, at the present day, is the period of romantic passions' he wrote in 1870. 'As for our enamoured sexagenarians, they avenge the theories of our cold-hearted youth.'[72]

Part Three

Once Upon a Time
(1868–1873)

CHAPTER NINE

Happy Ending

VIRGINIA EDGER

The means of Virginia Edger's parents were modest; her sister worked as a lady's companion and as a governess. Her husband was a soldier and with him she travelled to the frontiers of the Empire. In Hong Kong her children were born and her husband was promoted to an officer rank. In the small world of the colony Virginia became a lady, dancing at balls and mixing with the wives of diplomats. But when her husband died, she and her children had to return home. In England she was not a lady but nor was she a member of her sister's tribe. She rented a house in Shepherd's Bush, saving every spare penny to educate her children. Her sister had been a governess; her daughters had one. They also had music lessons, and as they grew up she borrowed silk dresses for them and sent them to the great houses of London to teach the children of the rich to sing, a suitably genteel way of earning a wage. One of her daughters married a doctor, a man with a respectable profession. Yet within a month of her wedding that daughter became, in the polite language of the day, 'delicate', in need of the care of her mother as much as her medically trained spouse. Music lessons and an education, it transpired, counted for little when one's body threatened to buckle under the pressure of pregnancy.

~

Virginia Edger's story is not one of penury or desperation. There are no strange disappearances here: no runaway grooms, no loose living, no prospective husbands walking out of windows. Instead there is an intelligent woman, a believer in the power of education to remould and remake, determined to equip her children for life among the higher orders. There is also a woman who but for an accident of history would be invisible and who speaks for the legions of silent women marooned by marriage between the social strata of Victorian Britain. What she speaks of is an emptiness, a loneliness that chills all the dimensions of a life. There are few friends in her story. The companions of her girlhood are left behind when she marries and the world of her marriage is, in her long widowhood, a foreign country. That we can hear her at all is the result of her birth. Her sister was Mary Anne's erstwhile companion Eliza Gregory, and Virginia called Mary Anne her 'kindest friend . . . on earth'.[1] Some sixty-five letters from her survive in Mary Anne's papers. Sometimes the letters are irritating, asking for visits Mary Anne cannot pay or favours political protocol will not permit her to grant. Sometimes Virginia's gratitude for Mary Anne's attention grates and letters go unanswered, triggering further distressed epistles. But the correspondence is sustained over a quarter of a century as Mary Anne sends Virginia dresses and food, finds positions for her son and secures her daughters small Rothschilds to teach. There are periods of alienation but always the relationship is recovered and repaired and towards each other Mary Anne and Virginia display loyalty that is absolute. Both are after all remade by marriage, a powerful bond in a world where everyone has her place.

'It reminds me so much of your Husband when I first knew him on his return from the East', wrote Philip Rose of an engraving of Disraeli presented to Mary Anne at the beginning of 1868.[2] The engraving dated from the period of Young England and the mid 1840s; now Disraeli was Prime Minister in waiting. At the end of January he travelled to see the Queen at Osborne to discuss preparations for a handover, and a month later Derby sent in his resignation. To be compelled by ill-health to retire at sixty-eight was a blow for Derby, but he could no longer ignore the doctors who warned that his health would never recover if he remained in office. For Disraeli, Derby's misfortune meant that the greatest political prize could be his. It was particularly pleasing that the Queen's messenger to Grosvenor Gate was her secretary General Grey, the man who had beaten Disraeli in High Wycombe at his first election contest in 1833. On 27 February Mary Anne recorded Disraeli's return to Osborne in her account book, 'to kiss hands as <u>Prime Minister</u>'.³ 'I arrived here yesterday at seven o'ck, & had an audience about half an hour afterwards', he told her the next day. 'The Queen came into Her closet with a very radiant face, holding out her hand, saying "you must kiss hands" wh: I did immediately, & very heartily, falling on my knee. Then she sate down, wh: she never used too, & only does to her first Minister & talked over affairs for half an hour (I standing) & so that I had scarcely time to dress for dinner.' He was particularly pleased that Monty Corry was invited to sleep at Osborne and dine with the household, a rare honour for a private secretary. 'Lucky fellow.'⁴

Disraeli famously described his political trajectory as a climb 'to the top of the greasy pole',⁵ but Mary Anne could not contain her joy with metaphor. 'My very dearest friends, you asked me who was to be Prime Minister', she wrote to Charlotte and Lionel. 'Answer – Your devoted Dizzy.'⁶ Letters of congratulation arrived from all walks of the Disraelis' lives. There were telegrams from the Paris Rothschilds; Charlotte wrote that her felicitations came from the heart. The vicar of Hughenden called Disraeli's promotion 'the most splendid success which has been achieved in modern times'⁷ and Robert Dawson wrote that he was certain Disraeli would use his position for the good of the public. 'I know you have ever been most proud of him', he continued, 'but this realization of the first place in the national councils must indeed satisfy every wish and anticipation that you may have formed for him.'⁸

The Times shared the sense of Mary Anne's correspondents that even though Disraeli's accession was not triggered by a political crisis, it was nevertheless an occasion in the life of the nation. The new Prime Minister had 'fairly won' his place, insisted the paper. *The Times* thought it notable that Disraeli had achieved distinction 'in spite of every disadvantage of birth, of education, and of position, and in spite, above all, of the great and, at one time, apparently unmitigated distrust of the party now accepting him as their leader'. Yet the paper detected a logic to his ascent. 'The Conservatives have never harshly judged the effervescence of youthful independence. Mr Disraeli's first public acts have more justly inspired distrust among his followers because they indicated an artistic quickness and sensibility especially removed from the Conservative type. But the Chancellor of the Exchequer has served the Conservative Party for more than twenty years. He slowly reconstructed its Parliamentary organization, and has thrice brought it into power. By the public he has always been regarded as the ruling spirit of the Cabinet, and it has been evident to all men that the Reform Bill of last Session was only carried by his courage, his readiness, and his unfailing temper in the House of Commons. The time has arrived for the servant to become the master.'[9]

Mary Anne had been the wife of an MP for most of the half-century since 1820 but had never before attended a debate at the House of Commons. Folk legend had it that she had sworn never to do so until she could see Disraeli in command as Prime Minister, and a week after his return from Osborne she took her place in the Ladies' Gallery of the House for the first time. The Speaker wrote to mark the occasion. 'You saw Mr Disraeli perform a delicate operation, with, as I thought, great success' ran his letter. 'Such is the House of Commons, it has long had claims on your good will, and with it you are now united by new ties of sympathy.'[10] Disraeli left the Cabinet virtually unchanged, losing only one Derby loyalist and replacing himself with a new Chancellor of the Exchequer. *The Times* was impressed at the speed with which he formed his administration and allowed Parliament to resume its activities. 'We may perhaps, congratulate ourselves that in this instance the interruption has occurred before the business of the Session had fairly begun', pronounced the leader column for 27 February. 'Once the Ministry is reconstituted there will be no further excuse for delay or avoidance of the great subjects awaiting discussion.'[11] The 'great subjects' included Church appointments and the Irish Question, and Disraeli's programme of legislation was ambitious. The electoral registers had to be redrawn following the passing of the Reform Act, and he determined to reshape Whitehall by establishing separate departments of state for health and education. Disraeli was never an ideologue, and throughout his career his political position was shaped as much by circumstance and practical considerations as by a particular creed. But he was sixty-four in 1868 and had waited in Derby's shadow for years. Now that power was at last his, he was in no mood for further delays.

~

Mary Anne too was triumphal that spring. Undeterred by her recent illness, she decided to hold a party to celebrate on a scale quite unlike that of her previous receptions. Grosvenor Gate was not big enough and 10 Downing Street she dismissed on the grounds that it was 'dingy and decaying'.[12] So Disraeli arranged to borrow the new Foreign Office, designed by George Gilbert Scott and not yet released from the hands of the builders. The *Morning Post* reported that the news that Mary Anne had invited the Prince and Princess of Wales to her party had sparked panic in the desultory Board of Works, prompting at the Foreign Office the rare sounds 'of active labour . . . day and night'. At Downing Street a team of secretaries led by Corry helped marshal guest lists, caterers, table plans, florists, orchestras and the police, who were worried about a crush of carriages. On the day of the party the Commissioner of the Metropolitan Police issued posters detailing the 'Regulations for carriages with company going to Mrs Disraeli's reception', which were plastered along Whitehall to deter errant coachmen. There were strict rules for 'Setting Down', 'Taking Up' and waiting, and drivers were warned that 'carriages are to be stopped by the Police at any Point to prevent Obstructions'.[13] Keeping control of the guest list required comparable levels of discipline as friends and acquaintances wrote pleading for invitations for passing relatives and guests. James Disraeli even attempted to secure a viewing place in the upper reaches of the Foreign Office for his mistress-cum-housekeeper Mrs Bassett, but whether or not his application was successful is not recorded.

The newspapers, enamoured by the combination of royalty, Dizzy, new buildings and lavish entertainment, indulged in highly coloured descriptions of the evening. *The Morning Post* offered its readers the opportunity to experience the party as if they were guests, tracking its account along the route taken by the royal visitors up the grand staircase where Mary Anne and Disraeli were waiting to greet them, into the first reception room and then on into supper. The *Morning Herald*'s correspondent became practically delirious as he evoked 'the brilliant light of gas and wax tapers; the *recherché* dresses of ladies, and numerous uniforms, of both scarlet and blue – military, naval, and civil – relieving the sombre attire which does duty for evening dress; the gorgeous, and yet tasteful and artistic, decorations of the corridors, the grand staircase, and the reception rooms', all of which 'combined to form a picture which, owing to its infinite variety, could be painted neither by pencil nor pen, and which formed nevertheless a harmonious whole, worthy of the host and occasion'. The eventual arrival of the Prince and Princess of Wales sent the *Herald*'s correspondent into further rhetorical extravagances as he described the royal couple, he with Mary Anne on his arm and she accompanied by Disraeli, circulating among the 'noble guests'. 'The supper table boasted a gorgeous array of plate, but it was laid out with the most perfect taste; and beautiful flowers shed their perfume over the table, which fairly blazed with the light of wax candles and with the sheen of diamonds.' The seal of success was set on the evening by a crush in the corridors over which even the Metropolitan Police Commissioner had no power. But, the *Herald* reassured anxious readers, 'in time this was conquered, not without rending of trains and squeezing of elbows into backs, but on the whole with perfect good humour'.[14]

Many of the newspapers commented that the Foreign Office reception marked Mary Anne's return to the world after severe illness. There was talk as the evening's success became apparent of holding more parties at the Foreign Office, but Mary Anne vetoed the suggestion and gave the order for her 'halls of dazzling light' to be dismantled.[15] But even with no more grand parties, 1868 appeared to be her year. In April she was invited to join Disraeli at Windsor to dine and sleep, an invitation only rarely extended to the consort of the Prime Minister. The Queen recorded their presence in her diary. 'She, very amusing & extraordinary, but really touching in her devotion to him.'[16] And in August there was further pageantry when Lord Napier visited Hughenden with his wife. In April 1868 Napier led an expedition to rescue a group of British diplomats held hostage in the Ethiopian Highlands and returned to Britain a national icon, the 'Hero of Magdala'. His arrival in High Wycombe prompted the town to mass in celebration and the Napiers' carriage was cheered as it made its way out through the streets. At the entrance to the Disraelis' grounds, farm workers erected a triumphal arch complete with the words 'Welcome to Hughenden' picked out in moss and berries, and the Disraelis gave a grand dinner during which the local brass band played rousing anthems including a waltz written for the occasion, appropriately entitled 'The Hughenden'.

~

The Disraelis knew that 1868 was their moment: long hoped for, long worked for and achieved despite the ambivalence with which they had always been viewed. But their determination to celebrate could not mask the fragility of their triumph. Mary Anne's return to health was laboured and provisional. There was no entertaining at Grosvenor Gate in January and the doctor was still calling regularly in February. The decision to hold their reception at the Foreign Office rather than Grosvenor Gate was motivated partly by questions of scale and grandeur but also by the need to spare Mary Anne the strain of entertaining several hundred guests in her own home. The newspapers commented on her recovery from illness but not on her continued frailty: in private her guests were less discreet. Bishop Wilberforce noted in his diary that Disraeli appeared 'low' at the party, while Mary Anne looked 'very ill and haggard'.[17] In a 1904 portrait of Disraeli the biographer Walter Sichel related the account of another party guest who had seen Disraeli help Mary Anne down the grand staircase of the Foreign Office with painful care, planting her feet safely before attempting the next step. Sichel also recalled Mary Anne lamenting to a friend that their glory had come too late. 'You don't know my Dizzy, what great plans he has long matured for the good and greatness of England. But they have made him wait and drudge so long – and now time is against him.'[18] Meanwhile Disraeli fretted about Mary Anne's appetite and made Corry responsible for ensuring that there was always a messenger waiting at Grosvenor Gate to summon him should a crisis arise. He wrote to her throughout the day for no reason other than to make her happy. 'This is only an excuse for sending you my love', read a note dating from the end of March. And in May: 'I send you this, that you may have some appetite for the agreeable dinner wh: awaits you.'[19] That such epistles raised her spirits is evident from a rare surviving reply, also dating from May. 'How good & kind of you, my dearest. Your note has made me feel so much gratitude & so much happier.'[20] She was invited everywhere and her circle were kind, arranging for her to be escorted to her carriage when she paid visits without Disraeli and complimenting her on her good looks and renewed vitality. It mattered to Mary Anne that the world should not know of her pain or debility and should instead think her restored and as youthful as ever. That she was not restored was apparent to all who saw her, but her friends connived in the fiction.

Disraeli's government was in a minority in the House of Commons and, once stripped of Derby's authority, its weakness was evident. His ability to retain office depended entirely on the will of an opposition with the numbers to defeat his measures and force his resignation at a time of their own choosing. The passing of the 1867 Reform Act meant that a general election could not be fought until the new electoral registers were ready, but even with this protection Disraeli's position was perilous. In March his plan to create new departments of state was pushed to one side by Irish issues, which then dominated his Premiership. A surge in violence brought the question of Ireland to the fore in 1868; Conservatives and Liberals alike viewed Ireland as a religious problem. Disraeli wanted to increase the endowment of both the Catholic and Protestant Churches in the country, but Gladstone argued for the necessity of dissolving its Anglican Establishment completely. Disraeli's Cabinet was split on how best to respond to Gladstone, and the government struggled to arrive at a unified position. Disraeli himself was against disestablishment, which he thought would increase public fears about a Catholic resurgence in England and lessen the status of the Protestant Churches in Scotland and Wales. He threatened to dissolve Parliament and call an election over the issue, fighting for a final time on the old electoral registers and placing the Liberals at a disadvantage. Gladstone was made furious by this sleight of hand but agreed he would not attempt to inflict a parliamentary defeat on the government (thereby triggering its fall) until the new registers were ready and a legitimate general election might be called.

There were moments of success, many of them the result of fortuitous circumstances. Napier's exploits in Magdala gave the government an easy foreign-policy victory that boosted morale and played on the sentiments of a patriotic country. A number of important Church appointments became vacant during 1868, including the archbishopric of Canterbury, and it also fell to Disraeli to appoint a new governor general for Canada and viceroy for India. Dorothy Nevill wrote to Mary Anne of her delight at how 'everything succumbs to him – Garters – Bishops – Judges all die – in order that he may have places to give away. I should be quite frightened to be in any thing whilst he is in power.'[21] But while recommending candidates for such offices was the responsibility of the Prime Minister, the Queen was not obliged to accept his recommendation and the Liberals were not obliged to support him. Even here Disraeli had to compromise, finding candidates who were sufficiently politically neutral to mitigate a Liberal threat to exercise their right to recall appointees after the general election.

~

Yet despite it all he was the Prime Minister, and by July he knew his position to be safe at least until the end of the year. In September he travelled north by railway to undertake one of the annual duties of his office, attending the Queen at Balmoral. It was official business on which Mary Anne could not join him, even had she been well enough to do so. As a result we have a series of letters written over a three-week period, the first extended marital correspondence since January 1849. We also have their first telegram, sent by him from Perth: 'All well, will write by the post.'[22] Mary Anne dispatched Disraeli northwards with lavish provisions for the train, including a partridge for breakfast, chicken and tongue for dinner and plenty of good wine. Corry accompanied his chief as far as Perth before returning to London to reassure Mary Anne that the carriage in which Disraeli would undertake the final leg of his journey was a good one with 'comfortable chairs'.[23] While the train waited at Carlisle, news spread that Disraeli was on board and a patriotic crowd of Conservative supporters surrounded his window. 'I bowed to them & went on reading', but, he confessed, 'was glad when the train moved'.

Disraeli's anxiety about leaving Mary Anne is evident in his careful instructions to her about how to use the Queen's messenger to send a letter direct to Balmoral every day, and in his plea that she should see her friends and maintain a lively social life. That way, he wrote, she would 'be able to tell me a great deal', but his desire for news and to make her feel useful was underlined by a determination not to allow her to remain at home alone during his absence. 'I was greatly distressed at our separation', he wrote, '& when I woke this morning, did not know where I was. Nothing but the gravity of public life sustains me under a real trial, wh: no one can understand except those, who live on the terms of entire affection & companionship like ourselves – &, I believe, they are very few.'[24]

Mary Anne's sentiments were similar. 'You are the love & delight of my life, but I feel so sad at the thought of being separated from you for so long a time.'[25] She worried that the final stages of his journey would be dark and dull and the news that his train had been delayed by two hours courtesy of a crashed goods train distressed her greatly. 'It takes away my breath when I think of your escape from a dreadful accident.' She herself had an adventure after Disraeli's departure involving the theft of her bag from her carriage by a thief with a hook and a deft touch, but it was the imaginary dangers dodged by her Dizzy that preoccupied her. She agreed to visit her friends but would not consent to accept invitations to stay at their country houses. 'I could not bear to be so much out of the way of your letters & the news of any & I could not be happy.'[26] And even while she passed family evenings with the Rothschilds, her heart was at Balmoral. 'I have eat very well', she promised, 'but as usual a strange disgust takes away my appetite and I missed you so dreadfully coming home.' She consoled herself by thinking of things to send him and counting the minutes until his return. At least by 20 September 'four days are now shortened of your absence'.[27]

Disraeli arrived at Balmoral on 13 September to find the household at dinner. Pleading exhaustion and the dirt of travel, he escaped to his room. 'I cd. only in the shadow catch glimpses of a romantic country', he wrote of his drive. 'During the whole night it has been blowing a gale of wind, with gusty showers, but this morning I see that I look upon a very brilliant flower garden, encircled with green & graceful hills mainly wooded, & further in the distance more mountainous heights.' Balmoral, like Osborne, offered the Queen privacy and a home she could make her own. She and Albert had bought the estate in 1848 and made extensive alterations to the house and parkland. After Albert's death it provided a refuge from the public demands to which Victoria was no longer willing to accede. Her pride in the house and estate was evident throughout Disraeli's visit, and he described its customs and habits for Mary Anne with an outsider's interest. He was rather pleased to receive a message from the Queen's secretary Lord Bridport on his first morning informing him that 'I need not wear frock coats, "wh:, as a country gentleman, I know in the country, you must abominate."'[28]

The Queen was accompanied at Balmoral by her grown-up children and children-in-law, and Disraeli spent one morning dandling a royal grandchild on his knee. He was entertained by the efforts of Victoria's son-in-law Prince Christian to appear like his brother-in-law the Duke of Edinburgh in garb acceptable to the Queen. 'He wears the Tartan & dined in it', he reported to Mary Anne. 'But it was for the first time; & the Duke told me he was an hour getting it on, & only succeeded in getting it all right by the aid of his wife & his affectionate brother in law.' He went to the church with the ladies-in-waiting, toured the estate in the company of Lord Bridport and noted that the Duke of Edinburgh's prowess as a stalker did not match his skills as a valet. 'He hit one stag wh: fell, but in a minute or so, got up again, & galloped off.'[29] When the Queen sent for him he had the chance to peek at her quarters and to witness her pride in her garden. 'Nothing can be more exquisite than the view from her window – an expanse of green & shaven lawn . . . singularly striking in a land of mountains: but H.M. told me, that it was all artificial, & that they had levelled a rugged & undulating soil.' It was, he told Mary Anne in an aside calculated to please her, 'our garden at Hughenden on a grand scale'.[30]

'Yesterday', he wrote on 23 September, 'we went on one of those expeditions you read of in the Queens book. Two carriages posting & changing horses.' The expedition was to the Castle of Braemar and was organised by Victoria for Disraeli's entertainment. 'The party was very merry: all the courtiers had a holiday. Lady Churchill said, that when she asked the Queen, thro' the Princess Louise, whether she was wanted this morning, the Queen replied "No: all the ladies are to go, to make it amusing to Mr Disraeli."'[31] 'I hope the ladies were what the Queen wished them to be – "amusing"', replied Mary Anne. 'I am glad you are going on expeditions, as the more you are in the open air the better, but take care to have your thickest great coat with you, as the Even'gs even here are rather cold.'[32] There were more expeditions thereafter, to the Prince of Wales's house and to adjoining estates. 'The Queen', Disraeli noted, 'is looked upon quite as a minor proprietor among the tremendous territorial "swells" of these parts.'[33]

The Balmoral visit marked the point at which Disraeli's courtly romance with Victoria took flight. Throughout 1868 he wooed her in letters and was ornately deferential in his attitude to everything from her widowed status to her writerly prowess. 'The present Man will do well', she wrote shortly after his appointment, 'and will be particularly loyal and anxious to please me in every way.'[34] Disraeli himself is said to have acknowledged that he laid royal flattery on 'with a trowel', but he understood that the Queen was a lonely figure who would respond well to devotion. And his admiration for her, although extravagantly expressed, appears to have been genuine. Over the course of 1868 he began to exchange gifts with the monarch, who, like Mrs Brydges Willyams before her, sent him flowers for his dressing table and dispatch box. 'Mr Disraeli is passionately fond of flowers', wrote Mary Anne in acknowledgement of a royal bouquet before adding (almost certainly at Disraeli's instigation) that 'their lustre and perfume were enhanced by the condescending hand which had showed upon him all the treasures of spring'.[35] He sent the Queen his novels and received in return her *Journal of Our Life in the Highlands*. 'Did he really say, "We authors, Ma'am?"' asks Robert Blake in his magisterial biography of Disraeli. 'The story has never been authenticated, but it deserves to be true.'[36]

Mary Anne played her part in the romancing of the sovereign. During Disraeli's absence she sent funny photographs of Gladstone to Balmoral with instructions that they were to be given to the Queen: the result, Lord Bridport reported, was a monarch 'in convulsions of laughter' who 'said many kind things about Mrs Disraeli'.[37] Victoria reciprocated by sending Mary Anne a shawl, and also announced that she wanted Disraeli to be photographed by her personal photographer. News of this triggered a flurry of instructions from Grosvenor Gate. 'Remember to wear dark trousers when you are photographed at Balmoral, & to be standing, as that takes in your figure & put your hair about any how.' And then again in the same letter, in case the message was not sufficiently clear, 'Remember to rub your hair about any how.'[38]

To attend the Queen at Balmoral was not merely a matter of photographs and expeditions with the ladies. Every day the Queen's messenger brought red boxes of papers and it was as much as Disraeli could do to carve out time in the day to work through them. The Queen had her own papers and kept Disraeli supplied with questions and instructions, at one point sending him six additional boxes a day. During his stay news came of an insurrection in Spain and he was made to feel the inconvenience of a prolonged Highland retreat. In London he would compensate for late evenings and midnight sittings by sleeping late into the morning, rarely emerging from Grosvenor Gate before midday. At Balmoral he was compelled to follow interminable royal dinners by getting up at seven in order to squeeze four working hours into the day before the royal messenger left for London at twelve. The strange food and the long hours made him ill, and being ill at Balmoral was most unpleasant. The Queen suggested medicines and Mary Anne had sent him north with her preferred patent cures, but even so he suffered. 'Lucci's remedies did very well & spared me from diarrhoea', he wrote on 26 September, 'wh: would have been most distressing here – but the moment I leave them off, & there is some inconvenience in continuing them, I am liable to be attacked again, as I have been this morning terribly and the attacks leave me weak and depressed'. Luckily 'the attack never continues in the day, but then I am in a miserable state in these morning hours, when I have to do the main work, & the work is very heavy'.[39] Towards the end of his visit he was forced to keep to his room during the day and looked forward to his release with eager anticipation. 'The joy at our soon meeting again is inexpressible', he told Mary Anne on 28 September. 'Princess Christian said yesterday, that they were all very sorry I was going, but she knew who was glad, and that was Mrs Disraeli.'[40]

The last letter in the Balmoral sequence is from Mary Anne, and it reveals how much, in her frail state, Disraeli's absence affected her. 'I am so grieved you are not well', it starts. 'Perhaps perfect repose will be the best remedy.' And then, 'I shall be anxiously expecting you on Thursday – Will it be very late? My appetite is very good at ½ past twelve but not at dinner. When I have the joy of seeing you, I shall be more composed & oh so much happier.' She had written, she reported, 'a long letter yesterday – but I am so quiet I have nothing to say – and I am so anxious about you – & again very happy at the thought of our meeting – The Messenger waits – Your own devoted M.'[41]

～

In her diary entry for 21 September 1868 Victoria recorded that Disraeli was optimistic about the chances of securing victory in the general election scheduled for November. Others in his party were less sanguine. The election on the new registers handed Gladstone and the Liberals a victory so comprehensive that Disraeli decided to resign immediately without meeting Parliament, setting a precedent in British politics whereby elections, rather than parliamentary votes, triggered changes of government. On 23 November he saw the Queen, who found him 'very low, & looking ill. He spoke of the defeat as very disappointing & having come as quite a surprise!' Disraeli also asked her 'whether I wished he should continue to lead the Opposition & try to keep the Party together or whether he should look out "for other & younger hands!"' To this he received a determined answer. 'I explained that I thought he would be of the greatest use.'[42]

There was talk as Disraeli retired of bestowing upon him a peerage, an honour to which as an outgoing Prime Minister he was entitled. But despite his pleas of old age he was not prepared to relinquish leadership of the Conservatives in the House of Commons, increasingly the sovereign parliamentary body. Instead he asked Victoria to confer a peerage on Mary Anne in her own right. That Victoria was concerned by this request is evident from her correspondence with General Grey, who felt, like his royal employer, that 'it would not be a kindness to Mrs Disraeli to subject her to what would be made the subject of endless ridicule'.[43] Yet both Grey and Victoria recognised the difficulty of refusing. In her diary the Queen glossed over the episode, writing merely that at her final audience with Disraeli 'I told him, that in recognition of his services, I desired to bestow a Peerage on Mrs Disraeli, which I knew was what he would prefer & that I was writing to Mr Gladstone on the subject. He was deeply grateful, saying it would be such a surprise for his wife, & that she would hardly believe it.'[44] In the letter Victoria wrote to Disraeli on the matter, a letter designed to be seen by Mary Anne, she gave no indication of her doubts. 'The Queen can indeed truly sympathise with his devotion to Mrs Disraeli, who in her turn is so deeply attached to him', she wrote. 'She hopes they may yet enjoy many years of happiness together.'[45] So in the end it was Disraeli's loyalty to Mary Anne that won her a peerage and him the heart of his Queen. Victoria knew what it was to prize one's spouse above public approval and she was moved by the romance of Disraeli's gesture. On 24 November 1868 Mary Anne ceased to be Mrs Disraeli and became instead Viscountess Beaconsfield.

Disraeli's reaction to Mary Anne's elevation colours his letters of the period, letters of pride and delight. Mary Anne's response can be read in her things. Within a week she was sending letters on paper embossed with the 'B' of Beaconsfield and a viscountess's coronet; at Hughenden cushions were hurriedly re-covered with embroidered Bs. A coat of arms had to be designed, in which process she took an active interest; and for ever after she signed her letters to Disraeli 'your devoted Beaconsfield'. Her friends wrote in congratulation, many of them deducing correctly that the honour would please her because of the way it illustrated the Queen's regard for Disraeli. 'My dear ——— What?' pondered Lady Brownlow. 'Mrs Disraeli as usual, or Ldy Beaconsfield?' Would the new honour bring some feeling of regret? she wondered. 'A regret caused by parting with that name so long endeared by associations of affection, & the pride of seeing it rising, & at last risen by talent to the highest eminence.'[46] Dolly Whitmore Jones's daughter wrote from Chastleton; the wife of a former Hughenden vicar sent congratulations from her husband's new vicarage in Norfolk. At Christ Church in Oxford the undergraduate Lord Rosebery, Mary Anne's companion at Raby Castle in 1865, waited very properly to write until the title had been formally announced. Of Disraeli he wrote that he could not 'help believing that none of his triumphs have given him so much pleasure as this: and I am sure he must feel that he never bestowed an honour with such good reason'.[47]

Victoria's fear that Mary Anne would be ridiculed was unfounded. The newspapers approved of the gesture, and even *Punch*, so long a tormentor of Disraeli, published an acrostic in praise of Lady Beaconsfield. The *Imperial Review* was spurred by the occasion of Mary Anne's elevation to a prolonged disquisition on the role of the politician's wife and on the ways Mary Anne had refused its traditional parameters. 'She has believed too thoroughly in his ability and deserts to care to push them by the common influence used by the wives of smaller men.' The *Review* thought the country owed Mary Anne a debt of gratitude for allowing her husband to be honoured while remaining in the House of Commons. 'Mr Disraeli is precisely where he should be. So at last is Viscountess Beaconsfield.'[48] The *Morning Post* wrote of its sincere satisfaction at the news that Disraeli, 'while choosing to remain a Commoner . . . accepts the proffered Coronet to place it on the brow of a wife to whose qualities he has borne public testimony, and to whose affectionate aid he has acknowledged himself indebted for much of his success in life'. It was particularly appropriate, the *Post* thought, its coverage couched in the language of the Disraelis' old fantasies, 'that from the Fountain of Honour – which itself has deeply known and appreciated the value of wedded affection – there should derive dignities and decorations for the Lady whom her Knight chooses to exalt'.[49]

It was all a far cry from the farm in Brampford Speke and the Portsmouth lodgings of Mary Anne's itinerant childhood. It was a far cry too from her life in 1820s London, when she was reliant on relations for company. But at the moment that she was elevated to the ranks of the aristocracy, she acknowledged her past in an action only sparingly recorded in her papers. To mark the occasion of her rise to the peerage, she bestowed a pension on Virginia Edger, the woman who, like her, was remade by marriage. It was done without fuss and with no public comment and it transformed the lives of Virginia and her children. Virginia reserved part of the money to give her son and daughters an extra year of education; the rest bought them security. 'Please allow me to congratulate you on my kind Benefactress being made a Peeress', she wrote to Disraeli. 'If she were made a Queen, it is only what she deserves. – To me, she has ever been, the greatest, & best Lady in all the world, & I wish her, & yourself, every happiness which can be sent to you.'[50] To Mary Anne herself her message was simple. 'You are very dear to us all and I am certain that my children's children, will be taught to love you & honour your memory.'[51]

~

So 1868 offered several happy endings. Disraeli became Prime Minister, and even though he was ejected from office he had secured the loyalty of his country and his Queen. Mary Anne became a peeress, recovered some measure of health and was showered with affection from friends and strangers alike. Virginia Edger had her pension and her daughters a little more education. But years do not end when the drama dictates they should. In December, as Mary Anne and Disraeli were recovering from the excitement of the previous months, James Disraeli fell ill and died. He left a legacy of £4,000 to Mrs Bassett, by whom he had two illegitimate daughters. James had made Disraeli his executor, and so in the final weeks of 1868 he and Philip Rose were faced with the task of disentangling James's affairs and making provision for Mrs Bassett. Rose worried about the propriety of keeping James's house at Cromwell Place open with Mrs Bassett resident; Disraeli about the delicate task of working out what in the house formed part of his brother's estate and what was the property of his mistress. Mary Anne was sent to Cromwell Place to establish the truth of the matter and James was buried at Hughenden. James's death prompted a further spat with Ralph, with whom Mary Anne and Disraeli now had little contact. Ralph wrote that he would come to Hughenden for the funeral even though to be present there was most distasteful to him, and he could not mask his anger at being excluded from James's will. Quoting from *Lord George Bentinck*, he flung a final accusation of disloyalty at his only surviving sibling. 'Certainly my Brothers have not been to me "Brothers not only in name but in spirit" as is written in a certain Political Biography.'[52]

There is a sad coda to James's story. Many years after his death, his daughter Annie wrote a letter to Disraeli pleading for help. Mrs Bassett had died shortly after marrying a farmer and all James's money had gone to her new husband, leaving Annie and her sister penniless. 'Things have turned out very differently from what my father ever wished, I am certain', she wrote. 'For I know how he loved me and no one can tell what my love was for him. Many a time I have wished him back again.'[53] There is nothing in the Disraeli archive to indicate that Annie's plea was even acknowledged, far less received with sympathy. Like so many women before and after her, at the point of her crisis she disappears from history.

Two weeks after Mary Anne turned seventy-six, the Conservative *John Bull* belatedly marked her birthday. *John Bull*'s dates were out by a week but its loyalty was uncompromising. 'On the octave of the birth-day of the First Rose of England, to whom we apologise for our discourtesy in not wishing her many returns of her birth-day last Saturday, owing to the absorbing interest of the elections, we greet Viscountess BEACONSFIELD, of Beaconsfield.' 'Never', continued the article, 'has HER MAJESTY done a more popular act – rarely so graceful a one – as in making MRS DISRAELI a Peeress in her own right.' 'It is a trite remark that great men have very often commonplace wives, but the history of modern English statesmen would seem to disprove it.' Patriotism shaped Mary Anne's path from 'Rose' to the 'First Rose of England' as the country claimed its Prime Minister and his consort as theirs to be cherished and championed. No one who had heard

Disraeli talk, wrote *John Bull*, could doubt that 'amidst the unceasing harrass of a statesman's life, specially of one who has risen by his own exertions and has had to encounter untiring jealousy, MRS DISRAELI has been the judicious adviser, the ministering angel, of the statesmen whose merits an admiring posterity, if not envious contemporaries, will appreciate.'[54]

CHAPTER TEN

Afterwards

MR AND MRS HALL

The husband was 21 wife 42 when they married – he had fifteen thousand a year her fortune 3000, – she very plain & not accomplished he tall agreeable & handsome & violently in love with her – they are first cousins – she took him to his father when borne – she is now 67 & he 42 & one of the happiest couples in the world – he being quite devoted to her they have no children.[1]

If this were a fiction, here is where the story might end, resting on the image of a childless couple, she older than he and less accomplished, happy in spite, or because, of it all. By the end of 1868 both Disraeli and Mary Anne have left their youthful selves far behind. The bullied Jewish schoolboy has become Prime Minister; the sailor's daughter is a viscountess – 'in her own right', her tombstone will tell us. But in real life endings are sadder and slower than they are in make-believe. They are also more interesting.

The story of Mr and Mrs Hall comes from Mary Anne's archive, where it appears on a single sheet of loose leaf. There is nothing in her account to indicate when she heard it or wrote it down, or if she ever retold it. Of the particular circumstances of the Halls' marriage she says little and on the fabric of their existence she is silent. Mary Anne was throughout her life a collector of stories, swapping snippets of the lives of others with her most intimate correspondents, clipping tales of human drama from the newspapers. Among her papers are reports of adultery hearings, frauds perpetrated by servants, women living into extreme old age, and family feuds, and her annotations suggest that such narratives touched her. But we cannot know whether she made her note on the Halls in sorrow or in joy, whether it was inspired by Disraeli's love or a period of mutual alienation. It is tempting to assume that she accorded it importance because it told her something of her own life. Yet all we can be sure of is that it spoke to her and that through her it might also speak to us of her and her world.

~

'Mr Disraeli has provided a new sensation for a jaded public', announced the *Saturday Review* on 9 April 1870. 'The English mind was startled when a retired novelist became *Prime Minister*. It has been not less surprised at the announcement that a retired Prime Minister is about again to become a novelist.'[2] In the autumn of 1869 Disraeli began a new novel, his first for over twenty years. Mary Anne and Corry were the only people to know he was writing again, and even after the news broke they were among the only people to know the new novel's subject: the power of the Catholic Church in England. Disraeli took inspiration for *Lothair* from his struggles with the Irish Church in 1868 and from the sensational conversion to Catholicism of the Marquis of Bute in the same year. Its hero is a young man of immense wealth and the novel tells the story of the struggles of Anglicanism, Catholicism and the Italian liberation movement to win his allegiance and his money. Each faction is personified by a woman of beauty and intelligence, and the eventual triumph of the Anglican Church over Lothair's soul is represented by his marriage to the heroine, Corisande. The novel replicates the features of Disraeli's earlier fiction, padded as it is with scenes of fabulous wealth, thinly disguised caricatures of prominent figures and a creaky plot made subservient to political ideology. Today it is notable chiefly for the storm of interest it generated. In the weeks before its publication the newspapers were thick with discussion about its likely subject. 'Seldom has a literary announcement been welcomed by so general a flutter of excitement, or excited speculation so various',[3] read *The Times*. The *Standard* continued the theme, dwelling on Disraeli's continued capacity to surprise. 'There have been men of rich and varied genius before this among the leaders of party; but which of them was equal to such a feat as "Lothair," after more than thirty years of hard and incessant Parliamentary work – of such work as was needed to advance the landless, and unaristocratic youth, Benjamin Disraeli, to the chief place in the councils of England.'[4]

Lothair's appearance prompted new suspicion within his party about Disraeli's commitment to the Conservative cause. There were mutterings that it proved the former Prime Minister to be a political dilettante, and the reviews gave a mixed verdict on its quality. But no one could deny it was the publishing event of the year. The first edition sold out within two days, and one newspaper reported the sale of 52,000 copies in the United States in the six weeks following publication. A street in Wandsworth was renamed 'Lothair', as was a ship in harbour at Portsmouth; several racehorses were named Corisande after its heroine. A London perfumier created a 'Lothair' scent and sent two presentation bottles to Mary Anne in a black casket with silver clasps and a key. The Prince of Wales requested a copy of the novel and friends wrote in congratulation. In her letter John Manners's wife Janetta referred to *Lothair* as Mary Anne's 'adopted son'. 'I have poured over two reviews of him, and feel how desperately I should have fallen in love with such a person.'[5] One New York publishing firm attempted to have the whole novel telegraphed from London to New York over a forty-eight-hour period in order to steal a march on its rivals. The Associated Cable Company put a stop to the plan on the grounds, the *Observer* reported, that 'the transmission of the contents of a three volume novel might interfere with regular business'. 'We cannot help regretting', the paper continued, 'that Mr Disraeli has been debarred from the honour of being the first author whose work was sent complete through the 3,000 miles of Atlantic cable.'[6]

Lothair is not one of Disraeli's best works, but it is a novel of experience and is particularly entertaining in its invective against those who crossed him during his tenure at 10 Downing Street. Shortly after completing it he began another novel, inspired by the period of his own political apprenticeship. Again he and Mary Anne told no one that he was writing but a few friends guessed the truth. 'We half suspect', Charlotte de Rothschild wrote to her son in September 1871, 'that Dizzy is also composing a romance.' 'This is, of course, a secret.'[7]

Lothair was a financial success for both Disraeli and his publishers, who, inspired by its reception, decided to reissue his earlier novels. Longman's *Collected Edition of the Novels and Tales of Benjamin Disraeli* appeared in September 1870 and was well received by the press. Read together the novels had their fair share of 'affectation, hyperbole, paradox, and sham-sentiment', thought the *Daily News*, which nevertheless found them irresistible. 'Like the author himself they have made their own way, and conquered their own place. Like him they have compelled even opponents to listen; and English literature could no more afford to lose Disraeli's novels than the House of Commons could afford to lose Disraeli.'[8] Disraeli wrote a preface to the *Collected Edition* in which he sketched in his autobiography and the circumstances that had given rise to the various stages of his novelistic career. Of *Henrietta Temple* and *Venetia* he wrote that they were not political works but instead commemorated 'feelings more enduring than public passions', and of the lack of interest that greeted *Contarini Fleming* he expressed the hope that younger writers inclined to despair might 'learn also from my example not to be precipitate in [their] resolves'. Only with *Vivian Grey* did he concede embarrassment. 'Books written by boys, which pretend to give a picture of manners and to deal in knowledge of human nature, must be affected. They can be, at the best, but the results of imagination acting on knowledge not acquired by experience.'[9]

~

In Parliament in the sessions following his resignation Disraeli cut an uncharacteristically quiet figure. Restive backbenchers blamed him for their ejection from government, and the leadership of the House of Lords was thrown into confusion by the death in October 1869 of Lord Derby. The general election had handed Gladstone's Liberals a commanding majority and Disraeli knew there was little prospect of unseating them through crafty political manoeuvring. Not until the beginning of 1872 did he reassert his control over the members of his party, who, despite his withdrawal, could find no one more able to lead them. He knew his personal popularity in the country to be high and by February 1872 was freely prophesying he would be Prime Minister again. But in the years between 1869 and 1871 he appears to have taken pleasure in a retreat to novel-writing and Mary Anne's drawing room. 1869 stands out as a contented year for them both, during which they held a series of dinner parties, enjoyed the company of one another and their friends and appeared in society together, something the pressures of office had during the previous year made impossible. Their round of country house visits passed off easily and they resumed their habit of spending Sunday evenings together at the Rothschilds, dining alone with the family.

At about this time the classical scholar Richard Claverhouse Jebb saw them at a service of thanksgiving at St Paul's. 'One of the figures which I was amused in observing was Mr Disraeli's', he wrote. 'He was clad in a garment which, I believe, he greatly affects – a long white coat, designed, possibly, to assist the curious eye in its search for him. He was paying his wife, Lady Beaconsfield, a degree of attention so unusual in public, and so very unusual in church, as to suggest to the cynical observer that it could scarcely always be maintained in the same perfection under the accomplished gentleman's roof.' Here the editor of the periodical in which this account appeared interjected: 'Dizzy's devotion to his wife was perfectly genuine – Ed.' 'Truly in this land of precedence a statesman profits by being fashionable', Jebb continued. 'Fashionable for his novels, or his eccentricity, or his impudence . . . For every opera-glass which was bent on Gladstone to-day at St Paul's, I am sure that a dozen were turned on Dizzy.'[10]

When he was at the House of Commons Disraeli sent Mary Anne notes; if something of interest happened and he was unable to write, Corry or John Manners would do so on his behalf. 'The Irish Ch. Bill is settled', reads one message from him from July 1869. 'It may be known soon after this reaches you, but it will be prudent not to send the news to anyone.' Mary Anne relied on these dispatches. 'I have seen no one to day – I long to know, how you spoke.'[11] Her concern was as much for Disraeli's health as the measure of his success, as Corry understood. 'He is just down, after speaking for 1 hour and 35 minutes – a most powerful and effective speech, excellently well delivered, intently listened to and heartily applauded', he wrote in February 1870. 'As Mr Gladstone is up to reply, I have had no opportunity of seeing him, but all is well, I am sure, as he spoke to the end with the ire and energy of complete health.'[12] Corry himself was by this point central to the lives of both the Disraelis. In his letters to Disraeli he always sends 'love' to Lady Beaconsfield, and an undated letter from Hughenden underlines his importance as a member of their family and a third host. 'Lady B says you must not engage yourself anywhere at present as the chances are that people will be coming here a good deal the next fortnight & you are wanted.'[13]

To many observers Mary Anne appeared as active as ever. There were no grand parties at Grosvenor Gate, but dinners took place there each month, and in the autumns Hughenden was filled with visitors. She accompanied Disraeli to Windsor in November 1869 and her conversation could still shock. 'She delighted Fortesque by telling him that she had heard him very much praised', Disraeli reported to Corry. 'He pressed her very much when & where – She replied "It was in bed."'[14] In 1871 she became fascinated by the Tichborne Trial (which revolved around the mysterious reappearance of a missing heir and accusations that he was an imposter), exchanging notes with her husband about its progress and visiting the court to witness its dramas in person. With Disraeli she attended the wedding of one of the Queen's daughters, and throughout 1871 she accompanied him on visits to various parts of the country.

In September 1871 Charlotte de Rothschild recorded the details of a visit to Hughenden for the benefit of her son. She was met at High Wycombe by Mary Anne 'in youthful muslins, profusely decorated with blue and yellow ribbons'. 'The Viscountess overwhelmed me with kisses and congratulations', she continued, 'and ere very long we found ourselves at Hughenden, where Mr Disraeli, wearing a suit of pearl grey, a soft hat, a new set of teeth and a new collection of curls, had done all in his power to keep the double headed monster – if I may so express myself – time, with the vicissitudes of the world, and personal old age at bay.' It was a perfect late summer's day and Hughenden appeared mellow and beautiful. 'Without any effort or exaggeration I could praise & admire all I saw. – Both husband & wife seemed delighted with their home.' 'The illustrious man', Charlotte thought, 'ought always to be seen at Hughenden, where he is neither politically severe & spiteful as becomes a great party leader, nor grandly mysterious.' The Disraelis were full of the village flower show, the harvest home and the forthcoming visit of the Bishop of Oxford. 'I do not know whether I was hungry, but the luncheon appeared to be superexcellent & the fruit delicious.' After lunch Charlotte and Mary Anne retired to gossip about the engagement of one of Disraeli's 'most enthusiastic admirers . . . [a] spinster of mature age'. Charlotte's account supports the impression given elsewhere in the Disraelis' papers that the period between 1869 and 1872 was their Indian summer, when, freed from the burdens of office, they took renewed pleasure in each other, their houses and the company of their friends. The other story of these years appears only in archival glimmers. Letters from friends dating from the August of 1870 make tactful references to Mary Anne's suffering, a hand other than hers records lists of visitors in her account book, and it is Disraeli, not Mary Anne, who gives warning in 1871 to a disobliging butcher.

~

Disraeli's determination to assert his control over his party in 1872 took him and Mary Anne in April to Manchester for a massed Conservative meeting. The visit was designed to demonstrate his popularity and the existence of Conservative support in the industrial north. Inexorably British politics was moving towards a system in which electoral rather than parliamentary politics shaped governments, and Disraeli knew that regional party organisations needed to be strengthened if he was to return to power. At the meeting nearly 200 local associations presented addresses in front of a 20,000-strong crowd. The cheers that greeted the Disraelis were so prolonged that both the National Anthem and 'Rule, Britannia!' were drowned out. As the association representatives filed past to shake Disraeli's hand, Mary Anne rose too to add her congratulations, an action commended by many of the newspapers. Disraeli closed the meeting with a short speech of thanks in which he celebrated the loyalty of the Manchester Conservatives as 'the precursor of a triumphant future'.[15] During their journey home on 6 April, crowds of supporters lined the station platforms at Manchester, Stockport, Macclesfield and Stoke, determined to catch a glimpse of the former Prime Minister and his Viscountess.

The Manchester visit represented Mary Anne's final act of electioneering. On their return she appears to have suffered a uterine haemorrhage, which some of her friends subsequently believed she kept secret even from Disraeli. At the end of April Disraeli wrote of his unwillingness to leave her alone at Grosvenor Gate and in May of his regret that the doctor had given her permission to go to Court. 'I don't think he allows enough for her extreme weakness', he told Corry. 'Howr. I shall be with her today, last night she was alone and, I think, fearful.' The visit was not a success. 'She was suffering as she went, & was taken so unwell there, that we had to retreat precipitately.' 'Nothing encouraging at home', he wrote on 14 May. 'To see her every day weaker & weaker is heartrending – I have had, like all of us, some sorrows of this kind – but in every case, the fatal illness has been apparently sudden, & comparatively short . . . to witness this gradual death of one, who has shared so long, & so completely, my life, entirely unmans me.'[16]

Mary Anne was determined not to give in. 'For herself she still makes an effort to enter society', Disraeli confided to Corry. 'It is impossible the effort can be maintained.'[17] He took her to Hughenden, hoping that a break from London would mark the end of her social commitments, and there Mary Anne appeared at peace even though the journey taxed her strength. She was pushed through the walks and groves in a bath chair and took pleasure in the song of a nightingale. 'She thinks "whistling" a capital term for bird noises.'[18] They returned to London, where their marriage settlement was revised and updated in preparation for Disraeli's life alone. In July Mary Anne attended a dinner party but was forced to retire midway through the evening, and in August she and Disraeli paid a quiet morning call on Virginia Edger but otherwise went out no more. Friends wrote to him of her heroism in the face of pain, and to her exhorting her to eat. The Prince of Wales sent game in the hope it would reawaken her appetite and the Rothschilds' cook kept Grosvenor Gate supplied with a stream of delicacies calculated to tempt her. 'You must try & think that every thing you take goes to make you strong & well again', wrote the Countess of Loudoun from Scotland. 'That is really the kindest thing you can do for the husband you love so well.' The Countess recommended drinking a glass of wine before eating, 'then the things wont seem so nasty'.[19] But cancer had spread to Mary Anne's stomach and it was impossible for her to follow these well-meant instructions. In notes to Disraeli dating from July she reassured him that her appetite was good, a sustaining fiction for both of them. 'I miss you sadly, & feel so grateful for your constant tender love & kindness. I certainly feel better this Eveng & have eat a very nice dinner.' And then again: 'The Eveng is got so cold I have sent a light great coat for you – I feel rather hungry, just going to dinner.'[20] His last dated note to her was written in July from the House of Commons:

My dearest darling, I have nothing to tell you, except that I love you, which, I fear, you will think rather dull. Mr Butt, in my opinion, was not equal to the occasion, tho' his speech lasted more than two hours. His voice is husky; he has no fascinating flow; & his papers were always out of order; so that he hummed & hawed to gain time, while he was finding his place.

Natty was very affectionate about you, & wanted me to come home & dine with him; quite alone; but I told him, that you were the only person now, whom I could dine with; & only relinquished you tonight for my country.

My country, I fear, will be very late; but I hope to find you in a sweet sleep.

Your own, D.[21]

~

Repeating the May journey to Hughenden was more than Mary Anne's strength could bear, and they were forced to remain in London over the summer. But rather than stay inside, they drove all over the city, travelling, Mary Anne thought, over 200 miles in short excursions in August and September. They went to Highbury and Westbourne and Hampstead and Lambeth; Putney and Pimlico, Kilburn and Barnes. They were staggered by the reach of London, which had grown like no other city in the world over the course of the half-century throughout which Mary Anne had lived there. 'We never went into our quarter of the town', Disraeli wrote in notes of that summer, possibly intended as a draft of a letter to the Queen. 'What miles of villas! & all sorts of architecture! What beautiful churches! What gorgeous palaces of Geneva!' One day they came across a French castle in Camden; in the kingdom of 'Cockaigne' in the east they found a city quite unlike that in which they lived. It was, Disraeli remarked, 'our first summer in London'.[22] Friends wrote of their sorrow at the news that they were prevented from reaching Hughenden and letters arrived at Grosvenor Gate every day asking for news. From Raby Castle the Duchess of Cleveland sought to keep Disraeli's spirits up by reminding him of 'one privilege you have which is not granted to all. No two people surely can look back upon a life of such loving & perfect companionship.' She recalled her son Lord Rosebery asking Mary Anne from where she derived her youthful energy and his supposition that it was the result of sheer force of character. 'No', was the reply. 'It is not that. It is that my life has been such a happy one – I have had so much affection, & no troubles no contradictions: – that is what has kept me so young & well.'[23]

'Yes, we have been here the whole summer', Disraeli wrote to Dorothy
Nevill on 26 September. 'It tells our sad tale, but I rejoice to tell you also
that absolutely this morning we are going to Hughenden. There has been
of late a decided improvement in my wife's health, and she now fancies that
change of air will greatly benefit her. I am sorry we are to make the experi-
ment in the fall of the leaf in a sylvan country, but we could go nowhere
else.'[24] Mary Anne noted their departure in her account book in her own
hand, and once she was in the country she rallied. Her pain receded and
she was able to eat a little more. The Rothschilds visited for the day and
there was even talk of Disraeli going to Glasgow in December. But on 13
October Disraeli wrote urgently to Corry, asking him to visit. 'All is
changed . . . Things here very bad.'[25] Then there was another rally; Corry
left, and on 13 November Disraeli was able to write that although her appe-
tite was again non-existent, Mary Anne was free of pain and enjoying life.
To distract her he organised a small house party consisting of their old friends
John and Janetta Manners and two younger men, William Harcourt and
Lord Ronald Gower, both of whom could be relied upon to pay their hostess
courtly attention. Gower wrote an account of his visit and was the last person
apart from Corry to leave a record of the Disraelis together at Hughenden.
He was greeted by Disraeli alone, who looked 'quite boyish' in a double-
breasted tailless jacket and who was anxious for news and gossip from London.
'We had little or none, the last scandal of a certain runaway couple not
being new to him. "To think," he said, "of her running away with an elderly
roué who was one of the most notorious dandies even when I was a boy!"'

Gower met Mary Anne in the library before dinner and thought her 'sadly
altered in looks since London – death written on her face – but, as usual,
gorgeously dressed'. He sat next to her at dinner and so had the opportunity
of observing his host. 'Mr Disraeli was evidently very anxious about her, and
although occasionally flashing out into conversation, with all his curious
play of arms and shrugging of the shoulders, he was evidently much depressed
at her state. His attention to her was quite touching and "Mary Ann," as
he sometimes called her, was constantly appealed to.'

To Gower's young eye the interiors of Hughenden looked gaudy and
shabby. There was an empty space over the fireplace in the drawing room
crying out for a painting, and when Gower asked Disraeli why nothing hung

there he was told the space was intended for Mary Anne. 'But she has never sat for her portrait, except to Ross for a miniature; but some day I shall have that copied life-size, and placed in that frame.' The next day Mary Anne did not appear until luncheon and Disraeli did the honours of the house alone, showing his guests around the walks and gardens. When she did emerge from her room she talked ceaselessly about her horses and the peacocks adorning the gardens. That evening, Gower recalled, 'Mr Disraeli spoke to me very despondingly about his wife's state of health. "She suffers," he groaned, "so dreadfully at times. We have been married thirty-three years, and she has never given me a dull moment."' Gower was struck by the strain etched on Disraeli's usually impassive face, still present the next day after a bad night for Mary Anne. 'He, however, seemed much the most distressed of the two, for she was wonderfully brisk and lively, and had her breakfast brought into the library, where we were sitting.' It was a pattern Disraeli had witnessed throughout 1872, where Mary Anne attempted to outface her pain in the company of others, hiding all manifestations of her illness with iron pride. It was raining when the visitors left, and this, Gower wrote, 'seemed to add to the melancholy feeling one had that we should probably never again see poor old Lady Beaconsfield, who, with many oddities as to dress and manners, is certainly a most devoted wife and companion. Both our host and hostess came to the front door to see us drive away to the station.'[26]

On 5 December Mary Anne contracted pneumonia. Corry rushed back to Hughenden and for ten days he kept a vigil with Disraeli. He told Philip Rose that she was 'very changed in looks and very weak, but voice and manners like herself'.[27] She refused to go to bed and so spent her last days in an armchair in her bedroom, in a state of exhaustion and delirium. Disraeli could not leave her, summoning Corry instead by note. 'She says she must see you. Calm, but the delusions stronger than ever – She will not let me go out to fetch you – Come – D.'[28] The newspapers printed daily bulletins and letters and telegrams poured in, prominent among them messages from the Queen asking for news. It was Corry who answered the demands of friends, royalty and press men while Disraeli remained upstairs, oblivious to everything except Mary Anne. She died on 15 December 1872.

Four days later she was buried in the vault adjoining the east wall of Hughenden church, next to James Disraeli and Mrs Brydges Willyams. Shops shut as far away as Ely as a mark of respect and many prominent men asked permission to attend her funeral. All were denied. The only mourners were Disraeli, Corry, Philip Rose, Mary Anne's doctor, and a small group of representatives from the Hughenden staff and tenantry. 'Almost all the paraphernalia of mourning – hearse, mourning carriages, plumes, scarves, and flowing hatbands – were absent from a ceremony which differed little from a humble village funeral, and was touching in its simplicity', reported *The Times*. The path from the house to the church was saturated by days of rain but the journalists watching the scene thought the sight of the funeral procession wending its way down to the church 'on one of the wettest and murkiest days of the year' added to the solemnity of the occasion.[29] They also remarked that Disraeli had aged visibly since his last appearance in London. With no Mary Anne to dye his hair he had gone grey and his figure was stooped. After the service the procession moved outside to the vault, where Disraeli stood bareheaded in the rain, watching the burial. *The Times* was restrained in its description of Disraeli's grief; the reports printed in various regional newspapers less so. The villagers had covered Mary Anne's coffin with flowers, and as Disraeli stopped to look at the tributes he was seen by one reporter to lean sideways on his pew rail where 'it was perceptible by his attempts, as it were, to choke his grief in repressed sobs, that he was suffering the most intense anguish and sorrow'.[30]

Telegrams and letters started to arrive on the day Mary Anne died, the first brought directly by royal messenger. The Queen dwelt on Mary Anne's devotion to Disraeli, reminding him too of her own long widowhood. The Prince and Princess of Wales telegraphed their sympathy and then wrote, and the Queen's lady-in-waiting Jane Ely enclosed her own letter in the royal package. The new Lord Derby told Corry he could not bring himself to write directly to Disraeli, so intolerable was his loss, but Robert Dawson wrote at length on Mary Anne's great qualities. 'It is now more than 45 years since I first knew and loved her, she has always been to me the kindest of friends and I never failed to consult her when in any difficulty, or whenever I required the assistance of a sound and safe judgment.'[31] Gladstone's

letter reminded Disraeli that they had been married in the same year, and
Lord Rosebery, who had fallen for Mary Anne as an adolescent, wrote that
she had simply been always 'the kindest and best of friends'.[32] On the day
before the funeral John Manners told Corry that he had no heart for busi-
ness since all his thoughts were at Hughenden. 'God help him through
tomorrow.'[33] And Charlotte de Rothschild, Mary Anne's most loyal friend,
said that words failed her as she attempted to express her sympathy. Instead
she recalled Mary Anne and 'the rare qualities that adorned a most admi-
rable wife'. 'Cheerful in health & brave in sickness she never knew the
meaning of egotism much less the reality of it. – The affection of her
generous heart never narrowed never changed; it surrounded you at every
moment of the day and in the great political world it followed you with
eager enthusiasm; and if your triumphs as an orator, a statesman and a
minister of the crown were the pride & the joy of dear Lady Beaconsfield's
existence, your gentle & unvarying kindness was the treasure she valued
most truly.' It seemed presumptuous, Charlotte wrote, to speak of her own
loss while Disraeli's was so insupportable, yet 'while you are mourning I
too am painfully aware that the most indulgent of friends will never smile
again upon me & mine'.[34]

Many of those who sent sympathy followed Charlotte's example and
focused on the striking happiness of the Disraelis' marriage. A stranger wrote
that Disraeli must derive consolation from 'the reflection that of all happy
lives Lady Beaconsfield's has been the one which a nation holds up for
admiration & example'; a friend that he 'had the blessing of a union so
perfect as to have become famous in a land where happy unions are common'.
A 'fellow widower' described how he 'always read with delight your delicate
& chivalrous mention of the great worth Lady Beaconsfield was to you both
in private life & especially amid your overwhelming duties as the leading
Conservative Statesmen of our great Country'. 'The union', he continued,
'seemed to be happily unique.'[35] Old friends wrote, but so did political enemies.
There were also anonymous letters, and odd ones from those who felt their
pain was greater than his.

There was even a missive from Rosina Bulwer Lytton, who had long ago
sworn herself the Disraelis' enemy. Rosina's letter opened conventionally
enough with apologies for intruding on Disraeli's suffering. 'I am perhaps the

only person now living, who has the inalienable right of "long ago" to do so.' When she thought of Mary Anne, she wrote, she could feel and remember only one thing: 'how kind to me as a girl, and long after'. 'Since I heard of her dangerous state, oh! how fervently I have prayed night and day for her; for she "had her good things in this world," and was as crucially tried, by happiness, success, pleasure and wealth; as I have been by brutal persecution, bitter injustice, hate, and exceptional ingratitude, and sordid poverty.' Mary Anne's abandonment of her she would try to forget, remembering instead only what was good in her. 'What great things you both did for each other, not in the sense the world estimates them of an exchange of temporal advantages; but the sincere, devoted, and self abnegating love she had for you . . . [and] the generous unstinted gratitude, with which you repaid her.' She knew that but for Mary Anne's wealth Disraeli would never have married her but was sure he would have behaved well had she lost the thing that made her eligible. As the letter progressed, it became more difficult for Rosina to hide her animus. 'She always had great hero worship, more especially for political celebrities, which made her the best help meet in the world for you.' She regretted that Disraeli had been seduced by 'the Sodom called Society' and the 'slippery arena of Politics' but wrote that she knew the cause was his association with Bulwer Lytton, 'no body's friend, not even his own'. In her peroration she did her best to rise above reproach, writing that in spite of Disraeli's faults, 'I do from my heart feel for your bereavement.' 'God who had given you so much, give you more by now comforting you.'[36]

In its news report, *The Times* thought that it was not just Mary Anne's particular qualities and the happiness of her marriage that made her death a national event. 'Something more seems due to the memory of a mutual devotion which has not merely been the private stay of a statesman's life, but in no slight measure the ornament of his public character.' *The Times* held Mary Anne responsible for Disraeli's career and remarked on the strangeness of this. Thirty-five years ago, it noted, 'society would have been as little likely to single out the widow of Mr Wyndham Lewis as destined to play an important part in life as the politicians of the day would have been inclined to see in Mr Disraeli the future leader of the Tory party'. The Disraelis' private history, concluded the report, 'will be remembered as a beautiful episode in political life'.[37]

The elision between public and private was also remarked upon in Mary Anne's obituaries. The longest of these first appeared in *The Times* and then was much reprinted elsewhere. It depicted Mary Anne as an ideal woman standing unobtrusively in the shadow of her husband, and it framed her story with Disraeli's career. Mary Anne's antecedents were burnished into smartness, *The Times* claiming that her fortune derived from the estates of her uncle Sir James Viney rather than from the Lewises. And although it acknowledged that Disraeli married for money, it also claimed that no marriage had ever proved more of a love match than his. 'It was a pretty sight, that of the remorseless Parliamentary gladiator, who neither gave quarter nor asked it . . . it was a pretty sight to see him in the soft sunshine of domestic life.' And while it was an unavoidable truth that Mary Anne talked too fast and too freely, *The Times* noted that she was never indiscreet about the things that mattered to Disraeli. Taken alone it thought Mary Anne unimportant. 'It was not in her to make his *salons* a centre of society, to gather within the range of his influence eminent Englishmen and influential foreigners, or to sway by the reputation of brilliant *réunions* the easy opinions of liberal-minded politicians . . . But perhaps her husband will lose the more that society will lose the less.' In its final reckoning *The Times* thought Mary Anne a heroic figure: unselfish, brave and absorbed in the fortunes of others. And for Disraeli himself it had only sympathy. 'Yet to a veteran in public life there must be comfort in the thought that the public you have served is feeling with you; that England, irrespective of party, deplores even the timely termination of an essentially English union.'[38]

In death Mary Anne was fictionalised, by both her obituary writers and the many strangers who wrote of her to Disraeli. The things about her that were problematic – her background and her refusal to make her conversation or person conform – were smoothed away as she was finally reinvented, in Disraeli's phrase, as a perfect wife, the wife the established order wanted her to be. In the 1840s periodicals had mocked the suggestion that she could ever fit this role. Now she became emblematic of an English ideal, a myth born when she fell seriously ill in 1867 and given its first public expression as the press responded to her peerage in 1869. Coventry Patmore's Angel in the House hovers over Mary Anne's story, revealing for the most part the way she refused the expectations of her sex. Yet in her final years she was increasingly figured as that angel: self-effacing, absorbed in her husband, concerned only with making a happy home. After her death she became her completely. Any sense that she had an emotional existence of her own or that the happiness attributed to her might be more complicated than appeared was subsumed into a vision of Victorian womanhood. In 1872 the first signs of a new epoch made it convenient to celebrate Mary Anne as the epitome of wifeliness. Women's colleges opened in Cambridge in 1869 and 1871, and in 1870 Parliament passed the Married Women's Property Act, which acknowledged for the first time that a married woman could have a legal existence independent of her husband. The Angel in the House probably never really existed, but she was a powerful cultural construct and in the early 1870s she was threatened as never before. And so in her final transformation Mary Anne became that angel: a symbol of a woman she had never been, and a heroine for a dying age.

At Hughenden in his first weeks alone, Disraeli's sorrow was absolute. He told the Prince of Wales that he was unprepared for the loss, 'wh: seems to me overwhelming'.[39] And to Dorothy Nevill he wrote that life seemed empty. 'I cannot in any degree subdue the anguish of my heart. I leave this now, my only home, on Monday next for the scene of my old labours. I have made an attempt to disentangle myself from them, but have failed. I feel quite incapable of the duties, but my friends will be indulgent to a broken spirit, and my successor will in time appear.'[40] Corry stayed with him over Christmas, answering letters, making plans and arranging for removal from Grosvenor Gate. The house had only ever been Mary Anne's for her lifetime, and now the Lewises demanded it back with indecent haste.

At the end of December Disraeli and Corry left Hughenden to oversee the dismantling of the London home that had been Disraeli's for thirty-four years. Friends rushed to offer hospitality, and for a short time Disraeli stayed with the Rothschilds in their house at Gunnersbury before taking rooms at a hotel. It was all, he told Ralph Disraeli in January, 'an awful change'.[41] For the rest of his life he wrote his letters on black-edged mourning paper, and it was years before he acquired a permanent London home of his own.

Disraeli was sixty-eight when Mary Anne died and worn down by her final months. When he wrote to Dorothy Nevill, he believed his political career to be over. Yet his greatest moments were still to come. He remained the leader of his party and in 1873 rejoined the political fray. In 1874 he became Prime Minister again, this time on the basis of a general election victory. In his second term his government enacted significant social reforms centred on improving housing and public health, protecting women and children from exploitation in factories, and establishing the position of the emergent trades union movement. He involved Britain in the tangle of issues and conflicts that became known as the 'Eastern Question' and his government sent soldiers to fight against Afghans and Zulus. After he was made Lord Beaconsfield in 1876, 'Beaconsfieldism' became synonymous for his opponents with imperial aggression and colonial expansion. He made the Queen Empress of India and returned in triumph from the Congress of Berlin. 'The old Jew, that is the Man', said Bismarck as he surveyed the Europe he and Disraeli had made.

Disraeli returned to *Endymion*, the novel begun in 1870. It told the story of his political coming-of-age and earned him a £10,000 advance, then the largest sum ever paid for a three-volume work. Commenting on the qualities of Disraeli and Gladstone, the *Pall Mall Gazette* found *Endymion* agreeably symptomatic of its author. 'It is quite characteristic of the two chiefs of the great political parties that one of them should have hastened to employ his leisure after his fall from power in thunders against the Vatican . . . and that the other in the same circumstances should have betaken himself to the writing of a novel of society.'[42]

His passions became once more all-consuming. He fell in love again, and the object of his affections, Lady Bradford, took on the role of most valued correspondent, receiving many brilliant letters over the course of the 1870s. He contemplated marrying Lady Bradford's sister in order to be nearer to his beloved, but his putative bride would not oblige. His courtly wooing of the Queen became the stuff of legend as he refashioned himself as the conduit between the monarch and her people. His relationship with Ralph remained scratchy although he did make his nephew, the strategically named Coningsby, his heir. At his side throughout was Corry, to whom he was 'My Loved Chief' and who fulfilled many of the functions of a spouse during the second Premiership. Corry became Disraeli's proxy, meeting the Queen on his behalf and standing in for him as age and infirmity made it increasingly difficult to fulfil the demands of power. When the Conservatives were turned out of office in the general election of 1880, Disraeli asked the Queen to make Corry a peer, and so the secretary became Lord Rowton and the history of Mary Anne's elevation repeated itself.

A year later, on 19 April 1881, Corry was with Disraeli when he died of bronchitis, aged seventy-six. Princes attended his funeral and there was talk of a grand ceremony in Westminster Abbey, but in his will Disraeli left clear instructions to the contrary. 'I desire and direct that I may be buried in the same Vault in the Churchyard of Hughenden in which the remains of my late dear Wife Mary Anne Disraeli created in her own right Viscountess Beaconsfield were placed and that my Funeral may be conducted with the same simplicity as hers was.' His wishes were obeyed and he too was buried at Hughenden in the churchyard vault. Afterwards the Queen travelled to Hughenden to visit his grave and took tea in the drawing room, mourning her lost Prime Minister.

After the parliamentary session of 1873 was over, Disraeli returned to Hughenden alone. 'I have been here nearly two months', he told Charlotte de Rothschild in September. 'I have neither seen, nor spoken to, a human being. It is a dreary life, but I find society drearier. I have never been out of my own grounds, & can realise something of the feeling of a prisoner of state of high consideration; the fellow in the iron masque & that sort of thing. One has parks & gardens, & libraries & pictures, & tolerable food, but the human face & voice divine are wanting, & without being miserable it is impossible not to be melancholy.'[43] A formidable task awaited him that summer, to sort through Mary Anne's papers. For a while he avoided it, but by the beginning of August he was ready to begin, allotting two to three hours a day to the process. As he delved into the boxes, he discovered something astonishing. 'She does not appear to have destroyed a single scrap I ever wrote to her, before or after marriage', he told Corry, '& never to have cut my hair, wh she did every two or three weeks for 33 years, without garnering the harvest.'[44] Initially it was a heartbreaking process. 'She had died for me a 100 times.'[45] But as he moved from Mary

Anne's personal correspondence to the wider reaches of her collection, he was struck by an even more extraordinary realisation. She had not just kept letters from him but also every letter he had received of which she was aware. 'All that we have seen, or I have told you, of the correspondence, is nothing to what has since transpired. I am amazed! I should think at least 5000 letters in addition to all I had examined – & apparently, more important & interesting than any.' 'Nothing', he wrote, 'seems to have escaped her.' He found a hundred letters each from Bulwer and Stanley, enough from George Smythe to fill three volumes, the whole of his correspondence with Lady Londonderry. In another box were letters from European men of state he had known: Metternich, Thiers and Brougham. In September he came across the last letter from Count D'Orsay, 'written in pencil, just before his death, on hearing I was C of E and leader of the H of C'. And there next to it was the last letter too from Lady Blessington, 'a most interesting one'.[46]

～

Thus, as autumn came, Disraeli found himself surrounded by papers that revealed the story of his life. There were missives from the vanished world of his youth, where he acted the dandy with Bulwer and D'Orsay and took refuge from debt and disease in Lady Blessington's drawing room, writing tales of Shelley and Byron. There were others that evoked a period when he stood far outside circles of power, building links with European politicians to compensate for his lack of influence at home. And then there were those that told of how a relationship that began as provisional and inauthentic was transformed, over the course of three decades, into something rich and strange. Disraeli never wrote an autobiography, but in *Endymion* he drew on the memories awakened by Mary Anne's papers to fashion a narrative based on his own life. 'I did not marry for love', acknowledges the novel's heroine. 'Though love came, and I brought happiness to one who made me happy.'[47] Tolstoy famously suggested that happy families are all alike, and happiness is not a phenomenon of which poets usually sing. But in the story related in the papers Mary Anne collected, there is a hero and a heroine, and elements of fairy tale, and poetry to be found in the everyday romance of ordinary and extraordinary lives. This, finally, was what struck the anonymous author of Mary Anne's *Times* obituary as, in contemplating her history, he permitted himself a moment of reflection. 'We are glad to believe', he wrote of her marriage, 'that the romance of real life often begins at the point where it invariably ends in fiction.'

List of Illustrations

Select Bibliography

<u>Manuscript Sources</u>
Abinger Papers. The Bodleian Libraries, University of Oxford
Battersea Papers. British Library
Hughenden Deposit (Disraeli Papers). The Bodleian Libraries, University of
   Oxford (National Trust)
John Murray Archive. National Library of Scotland
Letters of Charlotte de Rothschild. The Rothschild Archive
MS Eng 840. Houghton Library, Harvard University
Private Collection
Rosebery Papers. National Library of Scotland

<u>Printed Primary Sources</u>
Beaconsfield Quarterly
The Examiner
Fraser's Magazine for Town and Country
Hansard
Household Words
The Indicator
The Literary Gazette
Manchester Times
The Morning Chronicle
The Morning Herald
The Morning Post
Trewman's Exeter Flying Post or Plymouth and Cornish Advertiser
The Times

Internet Resources
Dictionary of National Biography
Queen Victoria Journals

Primary Reading
Anon, 'A Recollection of Disraeli', *New Century Review* (September 1899), 203–5
Battersea, Constance, *Reminiscences* (London: Macmillan and Co., 1922)
Benson, A. C., and Viscount Esher, eds, *The Letters of Queen Victoria: A Selection from her Majesty's Correspondence between the years 1837 and 1861*, 3 vols (London, 1907)
Bryce, James, *Studies in Contemporary Biography* (London: Macmillan and Co., 1903)
Bulwer Lytton, Rosina, *Very Successful*, 3 vols (London: Whittaker and Co., 1856)
Bulwer Lytton, Rosina, *Unpublished Letters of Lady Bulwer Lytton to A. E. Chalon, R.A.*, ed. S. M. Ellis (Eveleigh Nash, 1914)
Bulwer Lytton, Rosina, *The Collected Letters of Rosina Bulwer Lytton*, ed. Marie Mulvey Roberts, 3 vols (London: Pickering and Chatto, 2008)
Bury, Charlotte, *The Separation*, 3 vols (London: Henry Colburn and Richard Bentley, 1830)
Byron, George Gordon, *Byron's Letters and Journals*, ed. Leslie Marchand, 12 vols (London: John Murray, 1973–94)
Carlyle, Thomas, *On Heroes, Hero-Worship, and the Heroic in History*, ed. Michael K. Goldberg, Joel J. Brattin and Mark Engel (Berkeley: University of California Press, 1993; first published 1841)
Clairmont, Claire, *The Clairmont Correspondence*, ed. Marion Kingston Stocking (Baltimore: Johns Hopkins University Press, 1995)
Crewe-Milnes, Robert, *Lord Rosebery*, 2 vols (London: John Murray, 1931)
Dickens, Charles, *Bleak House* (Harmondsworth: Penguin, 1996; first published 1853)
Dickens, Charles, *Little Dorrit* (Oxford: Oxford University Press, 2012; first published 1857)
Disraeli, Benjamin and Sarah, *A Year at Hartlebury; or, The Election* (Toronto: University of Toronto Press, 1983; first published 1834)
Disraeli, Benjamin, *Coningsby; or, The New Generation*, ed. Thomas Braun (Harmondsworth: Penguin, 1983; first published 1844)
Disraeli, Benjamin, *Sybil; or, The Two Nations*, ed. Sheila M. Smith (Oxford: Oxford University Press, 1981; first published 1845)

Disraeli, Benjamin, *Tancred; or, The New Crusade* (London and New York: The Bodley Head, 1905; first published 1847)

Disraeli, Benjamin, *Lord George Bentinck: A Political Biography* (London: Colburn and Co., 1852)

Disraeli, Benjamin, *Lothair* (London: Longmans, 1881; first published 1870)

Disraeli, Benjamin, *Endymion* (Doylestown, Penn.: Wildside Press, n.d; first published 1880)

Disraeli, Benjamin, *The Revolutionary Epick and Other Poems*, ed. W. Davenport Adams (London: Hurst and Blackett, 1904)

Disraeli, Benjamin, *Collected Edition of the Novels and Tales*, 10 vols (London: Longman, Green and Co., 1870–1)

Disraeli, Benjamin, *Letters*, ed. J. A. W. Gunn (I–II), Donald M. Schurman (I–II), John Matthews (I–V), M. G. Wiebe (I–IX), J. B. Conacher (III–V), Mary S. Millar (III–IX), Ann P. Robson (VI–VIII), Ellen L. Hawman (VIII–IX), Michel Pharand (IX) and Sandra den Otter (IX), 9 vols (Toronto: University of Toronto Press, 1982 — in progress)

Disraeli, Benjamin, *Early Novels*, ed. Daniel R. Schwarz, 7 vols (London: Pickering and Chatto, 2004)

D'Israeli, Isaac, *Curiosities of Literature. A New Edition, Edited, With Memoir and Notes, by his Son, The Earl of Beaconsfield*, 3 vols (London: G. Routledge and Co., 1858; this edition first published 1849)

Everard, H., *History of Thos Farrington's Regiment, Subsequently Designated The 29th (Worcestershire) Foot, 1694 to 1891* (Worcester: Littlebury and Company, The Worcester Press, 1891)

Fraser, William, *Disraeli and his Day* (London: Kegan Paul, 1891)

Gower, Ronald, *My Reminiscences* (London: Kegan Paul, 1885)

Gregory, William, *Autobiography* (London: John Murray, 1894)

Guest, Charlotte, *Lady Charlotte Guest: Extracts from her Journal*, ed. The Earl of Bessborough, 2 vols (London: John Murray, 1950–2)

Hare, Augustus, *The Story of My Life*, 6 vols (London: George Allan, 1900)

Kebbel, Thomas, *Lord Beaconsfield and Other Tory Memories* (London: Cassell and Company, 1907)

Lake, Henry, *Personal Reminiscences of the Right Honourable Benjamin Disraeli, Earl of Beaconsfield, K.G.* (London: Cassell & Company, 1891)

Lang, Andrew, and Richard Doyle, *A Tale of Fairyland: The Princess Nobody* (Toronto: Dover Publications, 2000; first published 1884)

Lucy, Henry, 'Sixty Years in the Wilderness', *Cornhill Magazine* (January 1912), 20–75

Madden, R. R., *The Literary Life and Correspondence of the Countess of Blessington*, 3 vols (London: T. C. Newby, 1855)

Nevill, Ralph, ed., *The Life and Letters of Lady Dorothy Nevill* (London: Methuen and Co., 1919)

Saxe-Coburg, Albert, *Letters of the Prince Consort, 1831–1861*, ed. Kurt Jagow, trans. E. T. S. Dugdale (London: John Murray, 1938)

Shelley, Mary Wollstonecraft, *The Letters of Mary Wollstonecraft Shelley*, ed. Betty T. Bennett, 3 vols (Baltimore: Johns Hopkins University Press, 1988)

Shelley, Mary Wollstonecraft, *Journals, 1814–1844*, ed. Paula R. Feldman and Diana Scott-Kilvert, 2 vols (Oxford: Clarendon Press, 1987)

Sheppard, Elizabeth, *Charles Auchester* (London: Hurst and Blackett, 1853)

Sheppard, Elizabeth, *Counterparts; or, The Cross of Love* (London: Smith, Elder and Co., 1854)

Skelton, John, *The Table-Talk of Shirley: Reminiscences of and Letters from Froude, Thackeray, Disraeli, Browning, Rossetti, Kingsley, Baynes, Huxley, Tyndall and Others* (Edinburgh: William Blackwood and Sons, 1895)

Spencer-Stanhope, Elizabeth, *The Letter-Bag of Lady Elizabeth Spencer-Stanhope*, ed. A. M. W. Stirling, 2 vols (London: John Lane, n.d.)

Thackeray, William, *The Rose and the Ring* (New York: Harper and Brothers, 1855)

Willis, Nathaniel Parker, *Pencillings by the Way* (New York: C. Scribner, 1852)

Wilson, Harriette, *Memoirs* (London: Peter Davis, 1929; first published 1825)

Secondary Reading

Ablow, Rachel, *The Marriage of Minds: Reading Sympathy in the Victorian Marriage Plot* (Stanford: Stanford University Press, 2007)

Aldous, Richard, *The Lion and the Unicorn: Gladstone vs Disraeli* (London: Hutchinson, 2006)

Blake, Robert, *Disraeli* (London: Eyre and Spottiswoode, 1966)

Blakey, Vermeule, 'Gossip and Literary Narrative', *Philosophy and Literature* 30, No. 1 (April 2006), 102–17

Bradford, Sarah, *Disraeli* (London: Weidenfeld & Nicolson, 1982)

Select Bibliography

Brown, Roger L., *The Lewises of Greenmeadow* (Tongwynlais: The Tair Eglwys Press, 1984)

Copeland, Edward, *The Silver Fork Novel: Fashionable Fiction in the Age of Reform* (Cambridge: Cambridge University Press, 2012)

Cronin, Richard, *Romantic Victorians: English Literature, 1824–1840* (Basingstoke: Palgrave, 2002)

Faber, Richard, *Young England* (London: Faber, 1987)

Falk, Bernard, *The Berkeleys of Berkeley Square and Some of their Kinsfolk* (London: Hutchinson and Co., 1944)

Flanders, Judith, *The Victorian House: Domestic Life from Childbirth to Deathbed* (London: Harper Perennial, 2004)

Gallagher, Catherine, *Nobody's Story: The Vanishing Acts of Women Writers in the Marketplace, 1670–1920* (Berkeley, University of California Press, 1995)

Gordon, Jan B., *Gossip and Subversion in Nineteenth-Century British Fiction: Echo's Economies* (Basingstoke: Macmillan, 1996)

Guest, John and Angela V., *Lady Charlotte: A Biography of the Nineteenth Century* (London: Weidenfeld & Nicolson, 1989)

Hardwick, Mollie, *Mrs Dizzy* (New York: St Martin's Press, 1972)

Hawkins, Angus, *Parliament, Party and the Art of Politics in Britain, 1855–59* (London: Macmillan, 1987)

Hawkins, Angus, *The Forgotten Prime Minister: The 14th Earl of Derby*, 2 vols (Oxford: Oxford University Press, 2007–8)

Hilton, Boyd, *A Mad, Bad and Dangerous People? England 1783–1846* (Oxford: Oxford University Press, 2006)

Holmes, Richard, *Redcoats: The British Soldier in the Age of Horse and Musket* (London: HarperCollins, 2001)

Hoppen, Theodore, *The Mid-Victorian Generation, 1846–1886* (Oxford: Oxford University Press, 1998)

Jalland, Pat, *Women, Marriage and Politics, 1860–1914* (Oxford: Oxford University Press, 1988)

Kuhn, William, *The Politics of Pleasure: A Portrait of Benjamin Disraeli* (London: Simon & Schuster, 2006)

Leslie, Doris, *The Perfect Wife* (London: Hodder & Stoughton, 1960)

Marcus, Sharon, *Between Women: Friendship, Desire and Marriage in Victorian England* (Princeton: Princeton University Press, 2007)

Select Bibliography

Mitchell, Leslie, *Bulwer Lytton: The Rise and Fall of a Victorian Man of Letters* (London: Hambledon and London, 2003)

Monypenny, William Flavelle, and George Earle Buckle, *The Life of Benjamin Disraeli*, 6 vols (London: John Murray, 1910–20)

O'Kell, Robert, *Disraeli: The Romance of Politics* (Toronto: University of Toronto Press, 2013)

Owen, John A., *The History of the Dowlais Ironworks, 1759–1970* (Newport: The Starling Publishers, 1973; repr. 1975)

Ragussis, Michael, *Figures of Conversion: 'The Jewish Question' and English National Identity* (Durham: Duke University Press, 1995)

Ramsden, John, *An Appetite for Power: A History of the Conservative Party since 1830* (London: HarperCollins, 1998)

Ridley, Jane, *The Young Disraeli* (London: Sinclair-Stevenson, 1995)

Schor, Hilary, *Dickens and the Daughter of the House* (Cambridge: Cambridge University Press, 1999)

Schwarz, Daniel, *Disraeli's Fiction* (London: Macmillan, 1979)

Seymour, Miranda, *Mary Shelley* (London: John Murray, 2000)

Sichel, Walter, *Disraeli: A Study of Personality and Ideas* (New York: Fung and Wagnalls, 1904)

Styles, Catherine, *Disraeli's Daughter* (Wellington, NZ: Steele Roberts, 2013)

Sykes, James, 'The Strange Story of Viscountess Beaconsfield', *The Gentleman's Magazine* (August 1902), 124–141

Sykes, James, *Mary Anne Disraeli* (London: Ernest Benn Limited, 1928)

Urquhart, Diane, *The Ladies of Londonderry: Women and Political Patronage* (London: I. B. Tauris, 2007)

Vicinus, Martha, ed., *Suffer and be Still: Women in the Victorian Age* (Bloomington: Indiana University Press, 1972)

Vicinus, Martha, ed., *A Widening Sphere: Changing Roles of Victorian Women* (Bloomington: Indiana University Press, 1977)

Weintraub, Stanley, *Disraeli: A Biography* (London: Hamish Hamilton, 1993)

Weintraub, Stanley, *Charlotte and Lionel: A Rothschild Love Story* (London: Simon & Schuster, 2003)

Wilson, Ben, *The Making of Victorian Values: Decency and Dissent in Britain, 1789–1837* (New York: Penguin Press, 2007)

Notes

CHAPTER ONE: STORYTELLING

1. 'To Mrs Wyndham Lewis with the "Book of Beauty".' Dep Hughenden 203, fols 1–2.
2. John Evans to Eleanor Viney, n.d. Dep Hughenden 175, fols 115–16.
3. John Evans to Eleanor Viney, 16/01/1786. Dep Hughenden 175, fols 2–3.
4. John Evans to Eleanor Viney, August 1786. Dep Hughenden 175, fols 20–1.
5. John Evans to Eleanor Viney, 24/12/1786. Dep Hughenden 175, fols 50–1.
6. John Evans to Eleanor Viney, 31/01/1787. Dep Hughenden 175, fols 58–9.
7. John Evans to Eleanor Viney, 08/02/1787. Dep Hughenden 175, fols 60–1.
8. John Evans to Eleanor Viney, n.d. Dep Hughenden 175, fols 115–16.
9. MAD to Eleanor Viney, n.d. Dep Hughenden 169/1, fol 1.
10. Surgeons' mates were not even required to pass a medical examination until 1798. See Holmes, *Redcoat*, pp. 95–6, for an account of the place of the surgeon's mate in the army's medical structure in the 1790s: 'A physician-general and surgeon-general – both civilians with private practices in addition to their military duties – had existed since the time of Charles I, and an inspector-general of hospitals had been established in 1758. In 1794 an army medical board, on which these worthies sat, was set up, largely at the instigation of the Duke of York, in an effort to give more coherent direction to the medical services. Beneath them came the inspectors and deputy inspectors of hospitals, the physicians, surgeons and their mates who served in the hospitals, and the administrative officers who ran them. Each regiment had its surgeons and two mates, later termed assistant surgeons. In the eighteenth century they were essentially the colonel's employees, who purchased their positions, received an allowance collected by captains from their company funds, and were given a grant from which they were expected to purchase all their medical necessities . . . In 1796 surgeons were given captain's status when quarters were allocated, their assistants became

commissioned officers, ranking as lieutenants, and both were to be regularly paid and provided with medicines (though not their medical equipment) by the government. In 1798 it was ordered that physicians must hold a medical qualification, while assistant surgeons were required to pass a medical examination before being appointed. However, regulations accorded them "no claims whatever to military command".'

11. Eleanor Viney to John Evans, 04/11/1814. Dep Hughenden 172/1, fol 1.

12. Eleanor Viney to John Evans, 04/11/1814. Dep Hughenden 172/1, fol 1.

13. James Sykes, in his 1928 biography of Mary Anne (the first full-length account of her life), collated all the sources of this rumour, and gave this account of them: 'Again, the statement has appeared, in various forms, that in her early days Lady Beaconsfield was a milliner, either on her own account or as an apprentice or assistant. When one of these statements appeared in the Press in 1902, Sir Edward Russell, of Liverpool, wrote a letter in which he said he had been told indirectly, on the authority of Sir Stafford Northcote (first Lord Iddesleigh), that once when Lady Beaconsfield was staying with Sir Stafford at Pynes, near Exeter, she privately asked her host to take her for a drive, and on reaching a certain point in Exeter she said to him: "That is the shop where I was a milliner." Another writer said that in 1881, when gathering material for a biography of Lord Beaconsfield, an old lady who had been a companion to Lady Beaconsfield in her younger days, told him that before her first marriage she kept a milliner's shop in Bath or Exeter. Yet another writer said that a former postmistress of Chepstow, whose family had been long connected with the place, informed him that Mary Anne Evans's father left her very poorly provided for, and she took a situation in a milliner's shop at Chepstow, which the postmistress indicated.' Sykes, who was the first biographer to attempt to disentangle truth and fiction in Mary Anne's story, went on to quote others of Mary Anne's contemporaries denying the milliner story, and noted that these competing accounts gave 'support to a conclusion one is tempted to draw from other facts and inferences – that Mary Anne herself was responsible for some of the romantic fiction which came to be associated with her early days' (Sykes, *Mary Anne Disraeli*, pp. 17–18, 18–19).

14. Mrs Duncan Stewart reported the anecdote to Augustus Hare, who recorded it in *The Story of My Life*, V, 344.

15. Dorothea Whitmore Jones to MAD, 08/12/1860. Dep Hughenden 190/2, fols 152–3, and Mary Whitmore Jones to MAD, 03/02/1862. Dep Hughenden 190/2, fols 156–7.

16. Richard Yate to Thomas Yate, 19/12/1812. Dep Hughenden 168/2, Item 1.

17. *Trewman's Exeter Flying Post or Plymouth and Cornish Advertiser*, 31/12/1812, Issue 2469.
18. John Evans to MAD, n.d., 1815. Dep Hughenden 170/1, fols 92–3.
19. Henry Harrison to MAD, n.d., 10/01. Dep Hughenden 194/3, fols 45–6.
20. Dep Hughenden 170/2, fols 17–21, fol 25.
21. John Evans to MAD, n.d., 1815. Dep Hughenden 170/1, fols 92–3.
22. Wyndham Lewis to MAD, 15/11/1815. Dep Hughenden 170/2, fols 5–6.
23. Wyndham Lewis to MAD, 14/11/1815. Dep Hughenden 170/2, fols 7–8.
24. Wyndham Lewis to MAD, n.d. Dep Hughenden 170/2, fols 26–7.
25. Benjamin Disraeli, Preface to D'Israeli, *Curiosities of Literature*, viii.
26. Isaac D'Israeli to John Murray, 21/12/1804. Murray Archive, National Library of Scotland, MS 42162.
27. Isaac D'Israeli to John Murray, 01/01/1805. Murray Archive, National Library of Scotland, MS 42162.
28. George Gordon, Lord Byron to John Murray, 24/11/1818. Byron, *Letters and Journals*, VI, 83–4.
29. Ridley, *Young Disraeli*, p. 18.
30. For a contemporary discussion of this see Leigh Hunt on 'Distressed Seamen' in *The Examiner*, 524 (11/01/1818) 17, 525 (18/01/1818) 33 and 526 (25/01/1818) 49.

CHAPTER TWO: TALL TALES

1. MAD to John Evans, n.d. Dep Hughenden 170/1, fols 10–11.
2. Dep Hughenden, 203/1, fol 166, 203/2, fol 180.
3. MAD to John Evans, 25/11/1836. Dep Hughenden 169/4, fols 75–6.
4. MAD to John Evans, 07/11/1828. Dep Hughenden 169/3, fols 83–4.
5. MAD to John Evans, 19/04/1835. Dep Hughenden 169/4, fols 57–8.
6. Wyndham Lewis to MAD, 29/01/1817, 12/03/1818, 16/03/1818, 24/04/1818. Dep Hughenden 170/2, fols 34–5, 54–5, 56–7, 60–1.
7. MAD Commonplace Book. Dep Hughenden 203, fols 67–8.
8. MAD to John Evans, 09/03/1820. Dep Hughenden 169/2, fol 1.
9. Bury, *Separation*, I, 37.
10. MAD to John Evans, n.d. Dep Hughenden 170/1, fols 4–5.
11. See Mitchell, *Bulwer Lytton*, p. 25.
12. MAD to John Evans, 29/01/1829. Dep Hughenden 169/3, fols 95–6.
13. MAD to John Evans, n.d. Dep Hughenden 170/1, fols 22–4.
14. MAD to John Evans, 03/10/1822. Dep Hughenden 169/2, fols 34–5.
15. MAD to John Evans, n.d. Dep Hughenden 170/1, fols 68–9.
16. MAD to John Evans, n.d. Dep Hughenden 170/1, fols 50–1.

17. Thomas Yate to John Evans, 08/09/1827. Dep Hughenden 169/3, fols 46–9.
18. MAD to John Evans, 10/02/1825. Dep Hughenden 169/2, fols 60–1.
19. MAD to John Evans, 06/03/1826. Dep Hughenden 169/3, fols 4–5.
20. BD to John Murray, ?August 1820. *Letters of Benjamin Disraeli*, ed. J. A. W. Gunn et al., I, 4. Hereafter referred to as *BD Letters*.
21. BD, 'A True Story', *The Indicator*, XV (12/07/1820), 319–20.
22. See Ridley, *Young Disraeli*, p. 22.
23. BD to John Murray, June 1824. *BD Letters*, I, 9.
24. BD to Sarah Disraeli, 29/07/1824. *BD Letters*, I, 10.
25. BD to Sarah Disraeli, 19/08/1824. *BD Letters*, I, 17.
26. Disraeli, 'General Preface' in *Collected Edition*, I, vii–viii.
27. *The Literary Gazette*, 22/04/1826.
28. *The Literary Magnet*, 1826, pp. 1–8. Quoted in Ridley, *Young Disraeli*, pp. 49–50.
29. MAD to John Evans, 15/12/1825. Dep Hughenden 169/2, fols 76–7.
30. MAD to John Evans, 26/05/1826. Dep Hughenden 169/3, fols 7–8.
31. MAD to John Evans, 30/05/1827. Dep Hughenden 169/3, fols 34–5.
32. See Wilson, *Memoirs*, pp. 177–8.
33. Lord Worcester to MAD, n.d. Dep Hughenden 193/1, fols 10–11.
34. MAD to Lord Worcester, n.d. Dep Hughenden 193/1, fols 25–6.
35. *Morning Chronicle*, 23 February, n.d. Dep Hughenden 203/2, fols 158–9.
36. Anon to MAD, n.d. Dep Hughenden 195/3, fols 92–3.
37. MAD to John Evans, 08/09/1827. Dep Hughenden 169/3, fols 46–9.
38. See Hilton, *Mad, Bad and Dangerous People?*, p. 375.
39. MAD to John Evans, n.d. Dep Hughenden 169/3, fols 38–41.
40. MAD to John Evans, 30/05/1829. Dep Hughenden 169/3, fols 107–8.
41. MAD to John Evans, 17/12/1829. Dep Hughenden 169/3, fols 112–13.
42. MAD to John Evans, 11/03/1830. Dep Hughenden 169/4, fols 5–6.
43. MAD to John Evans, 08/01/1828. Dep Hughenden 169/3, fols 62–3.
44. MAD to John Evans, 12/03/1829. Dep Hughenden 169/3, fols 99–100.
45. Edward Lytton Bulwer to BD, 10/04/1830. Dep Hughenden 104/1, fols 11–13.
46. Eleanor Yate to John Evans, 21/07/1830. Dep Hughenden 172/3, fols 64–5.

CHAPTER THREE: TITTLE-TATTLE

1. MAD to John Evans, 20/12/1833. Dep Hughenden 169/4, fols 36–7.
2. MAD to John Evans, 21/08/1822. Dep Hughenden 169/2, fols 29–31.
3. BD to Ralph Disraeli, ?17/09/1830. *BD Letters*, I, 163. For ease of reading, editorial indications of deleted letters and obscured passages have been omitted from this transcription.

4. BD to Isaac D'Israeli, 20/07/1831. *BD Letters*, I, 197.
5. BD to Sarah Disraeli, 20/07/1831. *BD Letters*, I, 201.
6. Sarah Disraeli to BD, 02/02/1834. Dep Hughenden 7/2, fols 11–13.
7. BD, *Contarini Fleming* in Disraeli, *Early Novels*, III, 294.
8. BD to Sarah Disraeli, 19/06/1834. *BD Letters*, I, 414.
9. Willis, *Pencillings*, pp. 491–3.
10. Disraeli and Sarah's authorship of *A Year at Hartlebury* was established by the editors of the *Letters of Benjamin Disraeli* and their fellow researchers at the Disraeli Project at Queen's University, Toronto, in 1982. See *BD Letters*, I, xxii, 374 and passim.
11. Disraeli, *A Year at Hartlebury*, p. 138.
12. Disraeli, *A Year at Hartlebury*, p. 141.
13. MAD to John Evans, 31/12/1832. Dep Hughenden 169/4, fols 32–3.
14. MAD to John Evans, 27/07/1833. Dep Hughenden 169/4, fols 34–5.
15. BD to Sarah Disraeli, 02/04/1832. *BD Letters*, I, 257.
16. Sarah Disraeli to BD, 05/04/1832. Dep Hughenden 7/2, fol 23.
17. BD to MA, ?06/04/1832. *BD Letters*, I, 259.
18. BD to Sarah Disraeli, 02/03/1833. *BD Letters*, I, 330.
19. BD to Sarah Disraeli, 25/04/1833, 03/06/1833, 22/05/1833. *BD Letters*, I, 352, I, 360, I, 357.
20. BD to Sarah Disraeli, 10/08/1833. *BD Letters*, I, 372.
21. MAD to John Evans, 01/11/1834. Dep Hughenden 169/4, fols 47–8.
22. Quoted in Blake, *Disraeli*, p. 125.
23. MAD to John Evans, 20/12/1834. Dep Hughenden 169/4, fols 49–50.
24. Westerman May, 'Lewisiana; or, Hypocrisy Unmasked'. Dep Hughenden 185–2, fols 9–26.
25. MAD to John Evans, 27/04/1836. Dep Hughenden 169/4, fols 65–6.
26. Rosina Bulwer Lytton to MAD. n.d. Bulwer Lytton, *Collected Letters*, III, 213.
27. MAD Commonplace Book. Dep Hughenden 203/1, fols 39–40.
28. Rosina Bulwer Lytton to Sir Francis Doyle, 03/04/1857. Bulwer Lytton, *Collected Letters*, II, 272.
29. See Kuhn, *Politics of Pleasure*, pp. 152–5.
30. See BD to Edward Bulwer Lytton, 08/06/?1858. *BD Letters*, VII, 201.
31. George Gordon, Lord Byron to John Murray, 12/08/1819. Byron, *Letters and Journals*, VI, 207.
32. MAD to John Evans, 22/04/1834. Dep Hughenden 172/4, fols 25–6.
33. MAD to John Evans, 30/01/1837. Dep Hughenden 169/4, fols 81–2.
34. Quoted in Guest and John, *Lady Charlotte*, p. 82.

35. Anon to MAD, 20/06/1825 and n.d. Dep Hughenden 195/3, fols 1–4 and 84–6.
36. MAD to John Evans, 20/12/1833. Dep Hughenden 169/4, fols 36–7.
37. MAD to John Evans, 06/06/1836. Dep Hughenden 169/4, fols 67–8.
38. MS Abinger e. 227, fol 3r.
39. George Beauclerk to Mary Shelley. MS Abinger c. 48, fols 116–17.
40. Charles Beauclerk to MAD, n.d. Dep Hughenden 188/1, fols 147–8.
41. For George Beauclerk's undated letters to MAD see Dep Hughenden 188/1, fols 151–60.
42. Rosina Bulwer Lytton to Rebecca Ryves, 14/04/1853. Bulwer Lytton, *Collected Letters*, II, 49.
43. Bulwer Lytton, *Very Successful*, II, 150.
44. George Beauclerk to Mary Shelley. MS Abinger c. 48, fols 116–17.
45. BD to Lady Blessington, 02/09/1834. *BD Letters*, I, 428.
46. Sarah Disraeli to BD, 04/06/1833. Dep Hughenden 7/1, fols 145–6.
47. Henrietta Sykes to BD, 1833. Dep Hughenden 13/1, fols 56–7.
48. Henrietta Sykes to BD, 04/12/1833. Dep Hughenden 13/1, fols 68–9.
49. BD, 'Mutilated Diary'. *BD Letters*, I, 445, Appendix III.
50. BD to Edward Bulwer Lytton, 22/12/1836. *BD Letters*, II, 202.
51. BD, *Henrietta Temple*, in Disraeli, *Early Novels*, V, 86–7.
52. BD, *Henrietta Temple*, in Disraeli, *Early Novels*, V, 100.
53. Claire Clairmont to Lord Byron, 27/04/1818. Clairmont, *Correspondence*, I, 115.
54. Sarah Disraeli to BD, 20/12/1836. Dep Hughenden 7/3, fols 35–6.
55. Isaac Disraeli to BD, 21/02/1836. Dep Hughenden 8/1, 133–4.
56. See Sarah Disraeli to BD, n.d. Dep Hughenden 7/3, fols 41–2.
57. MAD to John Evans, 04/11/1836. Dep Hughenden 169/4, fols 73–4.
58. MAD to John Evans, 14/01/1837. Dep Hughenden 169/4, fols 79–80.

CHAPTER FOUR: FAIRY STORY

1. Sarah Disraeli to BD, 25/02/1833. Dep Hughenden 7/1, fols 92–3.
2. BD to Sarah Disraeli, 23/01/1837. *BD Letters*, II, 215.
3. BD to Lady Blessington, 21/03/1837. *BD Letters*, II, 245.
4. Disraeli, *Early Novels*, VI, 315.
5. Disraeli, *Early Novels*, VI, 378.
6. BD to Lady Caroline Maxse, 31/12/1837. *BD Letters*, II, 334–5.
7. BD to Mr Collins, 05/03/1837. *BD Letters*, II, 241.
8. BD to William Pyne, 23/03/1837. *BD Letters*, II, 246.
9. MAD to John Evans, 29/07/1837. Dep Hughenden 169/4, fols 89–90.

10. BD to Sarah Disraeli, 04/07/1837. *BD Letters*, II, 277.
11. MAD to John Evans, 29/07/1837.
12. *Maidstone and Kent County Standard*, 23/04/1881. Dep Hughenden 236, fol 17.
13. Henry Lott to BD, n.d. 1880. Dep Hughenden 234/3, fols 132–3.
14. MAD to John Evans, 29/07/1837. Dep Hughenden, 169/4, fols 89–90.
15. BD to Sarah Disraeli, 16/11/1837. *BD Letters*, II, 313–14.
16. BD to Lady Caroline Maxse, 07/12/1837. *BD Letters*, II, 325.
17. MAD to John Evans, 08/09/1837. Dep Hughenden 169/4, fols 91–2.
18. John Evans to MAD, 13/12/1837. Dep Hughenden 170/1, fol 104.
19. Wyndham Lewis to MAD, 13/08/1837. Dep Hughenden 171/2, fols 55–6.
20. Wyndham Lewis to MAD, 01/01/1838. Dep Hughenden 171/2, fols 67–8.
21. Mary Shelley to George Beauclerk, ?19/03/1838. Shelley, *Letters*, II, 297.
22. *Maidstone Journal*, 17/04/1838. Dep Hughenden 185/3.
23. MAD to BD, ?14/05/1838. Dep Hughenden 4/1, fols 6–9.
24. BD to Sarah Disraeli, 14/03/1838. *BD Letters*, III, 35.
25. BD to MAD, 22/04/1838. *BD Letters*, III, 50–1.
26. Rosina Bulwer Lytton to MAD, 05/04/1838. Bulwer Lytton, *Collected Letters*, I, 219.
27. Rosina Bulwer Lytton to MAD, 12/07/1838. Bulwer Lytton, *Collected Letters*, I, 225–6.
28. MAD to Rosina Bulwer Lytton, 15/07/1838. Dep Hughenden 190/3, fols 179–80.
29. Rosina Bulwer Lytton to MAD, 18/07/1838. Bulwer Lytton, *Collected Letters*, I, 227–8.
30. Rosina Bulwer Lytton to MAD, n.d. Bulwer Lytton, *Collected Letters*, III, 218.
31. Rosina Bulwer Lytton to Lydia Becker, c. 05/04/1873. Bulwer Lytton, *Collected Letters*, III, 154–7.
32. MAD to Rosina Bulwer Lytton, 15/07/1838. Dep Hughenden 190/3, fols 179–80.
33. MAD to BD, ?14/05/1838. Dep Hughenden 4/1, fols 6–9.
34. Augustus Berkeley to MAD, 16/04/n.d. Dep Hughenden 188/2, fols 4–5.
35. Augustus Berkeley to MAD, n.d., 1838. Dep Hughenden 188/2, fols 31–2.
36. BD to MAD, 20/05/1838. *BD Letters*, III, 58.
37. BD to the editor of the *Morning Post*, 05/06/1838. *BD Letters*, III, 61.
38. BD to MAD, 25/06/1838. *BD Letters*, III, 62.
39. George Beauclerk to MAD, n.d. Dep Hughenden 188/1, fol 163.
40. MAD Commonplace Book. Dep Hughenden 204/1, item 4.
41. BD to MAD, 25/06/1838. *BD Letters*, III, 68–9.

42. BD to MAD, 19/?o7/1838. *BD Letters*, III, 76.
43. Battersea, *Reminiscences*, p. 229.
44. BD to MAD, 20/08/1838. *BD Letters*, III, 86.
45. BD to MA, 23/08/1838. *BD Letters*, III, 86.
46. See *BD Letters*, III, 88–9.
47. BD to MAD, n.d. *BD Letters*, III, 88.
48. BD to William Pyne, 30/09/1838. *BD Letters*, III, 87.
49. BD to MAD, ?6/10/1838. *BD Letters*, III, 90.
50. BD to MAD, 16/10/1838. *BD Letters*, III, 95.
51. MAD to BD, 17/10/1838. Dep Hughenden 4/1, fols 19–22.
52. BD to MAD, 18/10/1838. *BD Letters*, III, 96.
53. MAD to BD, 19/10/1838. Dep Hughenden 4/1, fols 26–7.
54. BD to MAD, 19/10/1838. *BD Letters*, III, 97.
55. MAD to BD, 23/10/1838. Dep Hughenden 4/1, fols 30–3.
56. MAD to BD, 26/10/1838. Dep Hughenden 4/1, fols 35–6.
57. BD to MAD, 28/10/1838. *BD Letters*, III, 100.
58. MAD Commonplace Book, 203/2, fols 117–18.
59. BD to MAD, 23/11/1838. *BD Letters*, III, 110.
60. MAD to BD, 25/11/1838. Dep Hughenden 4/1, fols 45–6.
61. MAD to BD, ?27/11/1838. Dep Hughenden 4/1, fols 47–8.
62. MAD to BD, 01/12/1838. Dep Hughenden 4/1, fols 50–3.
63. BD to Maria D'Israeli, 01/12/1838. *BD Letters*, III, 115.
64. MAD to BD, 04/12/1838. Dep Hughenden 4/1, fols 54–5.
65. BD to MAD, 06/12/1838. *BD Letters*, III, 117.
66. MAD to BD, 27/12/1838. Dep Hughenden 4/1, fols 62–4.
67. Eliza Gregory to MAD, n.d., Dep Hughenden 194/2, fols 205–7.
68. Charles Williams to Arethusa Milner Gibson, 14/11/1849. Dep Hughenden 189/3, fols 179–80.
69. BD to MAD, 22/12/1838. *BD Letters*, III, 119.
70. BD to MAD, 23/12/1838. *BD Letters*, III, 120.
71. MAD to BD, 23/12/1838. Dep Hughenden 4/1 fols 58–61.
72. BD to MAD, 26/12/1838. *BD Letters*, III, 121.
73. BD to MAD, 29/12/1838. *BD Letters*, III, 122–3.
74. BD to Lady Blessington, 29/12/1838. *BD Letters*, III, 123.
75. MAD to BD, 30/12/1838. Dep Hughenden 4/1, fols 70–3.
76. BD to MAD, 30/12/1838. *BD Letters*, III, 124.
77. MAD to BD, 23/01/1839. Dep Hughenden 4/1, fols 93–6.
78. BD to MAD, 31/01/1839. *BD Letters*, III, 132.
79. Alfred D'Orsay to BD, n.d. Dep Hughenden 125/1, fols 145–6.

80. BD to MAD, ?7/02/1839. *BD Letters*, III, 137.
81. *The Satirist*, 10/03/1839, quoted in *BD Letters*, III, 138.
82. BD to MAD, 07/02/1839. *BD Letters*, III, 138–40.
83. BD to MAD, 07/02/1839. *BD Letters*, III, 140–1.
84. MAD to BD, ?07/02/1839. Dep Hughenden 4/1, fols 105–6.
85. BD to MAD, ?08/02/1839. *BD Letters*, III, 141.
86. MAD to BD, ?08/02/1839. Dep Hughenden 4/1, fol 107.
87. BD to MAD, ?08/02/1839. *BD Letters*, III, 141.
88. BD to Sarah Disraeli, 28/02/1839. *BD Letters*, III, 150.
89. John Evans's final day with his regiment is described in Everard, *History of Thos Farrington's Regiment*, pp. 418–19.
90. BD to Sarah Disraeli, ?28/06/1839. *BD Letters*, III, 183.
91. BD to MAD, 05/07/1839. *BD Letters*, III, 186.
92. MAD to BD, 07/07/1839. Dep Hughenden 4/1, fols 123–5.
93. BD to MAD, 11/07/1839. *BD Letters*, III, 194.
94. Disraeli Marriage Settlement. Dep Hughenden 311/1.
95. BD to William Pyne, ?28/08/1839. *BD Letters*, III, 216–17.
96. BD to MAD, 27/08/?1839. *BD Letters*, III, 216.
97. Mary Dawson to MAD, 28/08/1839. Dep Hughenden 189/1, fols 58–9.
98. BD to Maria D'Israeli, 30/08/1839. *BD Letters*, III, 217.
99. MAD to Isaac D'Israeli, 06/09/1839. Dep Hughenden 187/2, fols 17–19.
100. MAD Account Book. Dep Hughenden 317.
101. Sarah Disraeli to BD, 29/08/1839. Dep Hughenden 7/3, fols 82–4.

CHAPTER FIVE: ON HEROES AND HERO-WORSHIP

1. Sarah Disraeli to MAD, 24/10/1855. Dep Hughenden 186/3, fols 295–8. See also Sarah Disraeli to MAD 17/10/1855. Dep Hughenden 186/3, fols 292–4 and *The Times*, 13/10/1855, 10.
2. BD to Sarah Disraeli, 19/09/1839. *BD Letters*, III, 222.
3. BD to Sarah Disraeli, 02/10/1839. *BD Letters*, III, 223.
4. BD to Sarah Disraeli, 22/11/1839. *BD Letters*, III, 229.
5. BD to Sarah Disraeli, ?09/12/1839. *BD Letters*, III, 237.
6. BD to Sarah Disraeli, ?04/12/1839. *BD Letters*, III, 234.
7. MAD Commonplace Book. Dep Hughenden 204/1.
8. Dep Hughenden 4/2, fols 186–7.
9. BD to Sarah Disraeli, 10/02/1840. *BD Letters*, III, 258.
10. BD to Sarah Disraeli, 19/02/1840. *BD Letters*, III, 262.
11. Prince Albert to Prince William zu Löwenstein-Wertheim-Freudenberg, May 1840. Saxe-Coburg, *Letters*, p. 69.

12. BD to Sarah Disraeli, ?15/01/1840. *BD Letters*, III, 248.
13. BD to Sarah Disraeli, 12/02/1840. *BD Letters*, III, 258–9.
14. Lady Blessington to MAD, 01/02/1840. Dep Hughenden 200/1, fols 141–4.
15. MAD Account Book. Dep Hughenden 317.
16. BD to Sarah Disraeli, 08/10/1840. *BD Letters*, III, 299.
17. BD to Sarah Disraeli, 28/05/1840. *BD Letters*, III, 269. The *Morning Post*'s description of Mary Anne's outfit is quoted in *BD Letters*, III, 269, n.2.
18. BD Autobiographical Notes. Dep Hughenden 26/2, fols 48–50.
19. Quoted in *BD Letters*, III, 276, n.1.
20. Miles Stapleton to MAD, n.d. Dep Hughenden 193/1, fols 90–1.
21. BD to MAD, 28/08/1840. *BD Letters*, III, 293–4.
22. BD to Sarah Disraeli, 15/02/1840. *BD Letters*, III, 261.
23. BD to Sarah Disraeli, ?30/05/1840. *BD Letters*, III, 270.
24. BD to William Pyne, 01/11/1840. *BD Letters*, III, 304.
25. BD to William Pyne, 11/03/1841. *BD Letters*, III, 323.
26. BD to Sarah Disraeli, 29/?03/1841. *BD Letters*, III, 328.
27. BD to MAD, 12/06/1841. *BD Letters*, III, 340.
28. Election Address, 18/06/1841. *BD Letters*, III, 341.
29. Quoted in Sykes, 'Strange Story', p. 139.
30. *BD Letters*, III, 343.
31. Election Address, 25/06/1841. *BD Letters*, III, 345.
32. BD to Sarah Disraeli, 07/07/1841. *BD Letters*, III, 348.
33. BD to Maria D'Israeli, 30/06/1841. *BD Letters*, III, 346.
34. *The Shropshire Conservative*, 03/07/1841. Dep Hughenden 28/4, fol 68.
35. Caroline Maxse to MAD, 23/06/1841. Dep Hughenden 190/4, fols 185–6, n.2.
36. BD to Sarah Disraeli, 31/?08/1841. *BD Letters*, III, 355.
37. MAD to Robert Peel, 04/09/1841. *BD Letters*, III, 356.
38. BD to Robert Peel, 05/09/1841. *BD Letters*, III, 356.
39. BD to Robert Peel, 08/09/1841. *BD Letters*, III, 358.
40. BD to Sarah Disraeli, 06/09/1841. *BD Letters*, III, 357.
41. BD to Sarah Disraeli, 14/09/1841. *BD Letters*, III, 358–9.
42. BD to MAD, 11/11/1841. *BD Letters*, III, 361.
43. MAD to Eleanor Yate, 17/11/1841. Dep Hughenden 169/1, fols 13–14.
44. MAD to Eleanor Yate, 14/11/1841. Dep Hughenden 169/1, fols 11–12.
45. MAD to Eleanor Yate, 07/12/1841. Dep Hughenden 169/1, fols 15–16.
46. MAD to BD, 21/02/1842 and 25/02/1842. Dep Hughenden 4/1, fols 139 and 145–7.

47. BD to MAD, 21/02/1842. *BD Letters*, IV, 11.
48. MAD to BD, 23/02/1842. Dep Hughenden 4/1, fols 143–4.
49. MAD to BD, 22/02/1841. Dep Hughenden 4/1, fols 141–2.
50. BD to MAD, 25/02/1842. *BD Letters*, IV, 17.
51. BD to MAD, 25/02/1842. *BD Letters*, IV, 18.
52. BD to William Pyne, 19/05/1842. *BD Letters*, IV, 45.
53. BD to Isaac D'Israeli, 13/08/1842. *BD Letters*, IV, 54.
54. BD to MAD, 28/08/1842. *BD Letters*, IV, 55.
55. Disraeli, *Coningsby*, p. 280.
56. Carlyle, *On Heroes*, pp. 97, 180.
57. BD to Sarah Disraeli, 21/03/1843. *BD Letters*, IV, 85.
58. BD to Sarah Disraeli, 12/05/1843. *BD Letters*, IV, 95.
59. BD Autobiographical Notes. Dep Hughenden 26/2, fols 23–5.
60. Disraeli, *Coningsby*, p. 103.
61. Disraeli, *Coningsby*, p. 262.
62. Disraeli, *Coningsby*, p. 139.
63. Dep Hughenden 30/2, fol 2, 30/1, fol 9, 30/1, fol 36.
64. Disraeli, *Coningsby*, p. 52.
65. Disraeli, *Coningsby*, p. 495.
66. MAD to William Scrope, 24/11/1843. Dep Hughenden 203/2, fols 1–2.
67. BD to MAD, undated notes. *BD Letters*, IV, 114.
68. BD to Count D'Orsay, 21/12/1841. *BD Letters*, III, 364.
69. *Literary Gazette*, 18/05/1844. Dep Hughenden 226, Item 25.
70. *Morning Chronicle*, 13/05/1844. Dep Hughenden 226, Item 29.
71. BD to MAD, 28/08/1844. *BD Letters*, IV, 141.
72. BD to MAD, 27/08/1844. *BD Letters*, IV, 139.
73. Spencer-Stanhope, *Letter Bag*, II, pp. 195–7.
74. MAD to Sarah Disraeli, 19/01/1845. Dep Hughenden 187/1, fols 224–7.
75. BD to Sarah Disraeli, 20/01/1845. *BD Letters*, IV, 154.
76. Disraeli, *Sybil*, pp. 65–6.
77. *Douglas Jerrold's Shilling Magazine*, June 1845, VI. Dep Hughenden 227, Item 2.
78. *Fraser's Magazine for Town and Country*, January–June 1845, XXXI, 728.
79. BD to Sarah Disraeli, 19/07/1845. *BD Letters*, IV, 178.
80. See *BD Letters*, IV, 177, n.1.
81. BD to James Crossley, 17/07/1845. *BD Letters*, IV, 177.
82. BD to MAD, 28/08/1845. *BD Letters*, IV, 186.
83. BD to Sarah Disraeli, 05/09/1845. *BD Letters*, IV, 189.
84. BD to Sarah Disraeli, 08/09/1845. *BD Letters*, IV, 191.

85. BD to Sarah Disraeli, 06/09/1845. *BD Letters*, IV, 190.
86. Charlotte de Rothschild to Louisa de Rothschild, 06/09/1845. The Rothschild Archive, 000/297.
87. MAD Account Book. Dep Hughenden 314/1.
88. Ridley, *Young Disraeli*, p. 313.
89. Sarah Disraeli to BD and MAD, 26/09/1845. Dep Hughenden 7/3, fols 110–11.

CHAPTER SIX: HOUSEHOLD WORDS

1. BD to Sarah Disraeli, 05/10/1845. *BD Letters*, IV, 193.
2. MAD to Sarah Disraeli, 10/11/1845. Dep Hughenden 187/1, fols 230–1.
3. BD to MAD, 11/11/1845. *BD Letters*, IV, 198.
4. Disraeli, *Tancred*, pp. 137–8.
5. MAD to Sarah Disraeli, 16/12/1845. Dep Hughenden 187/1, fols 232–3.
6. BD to Sarah Disraeli, 11/01/1846. *BD Letters*, IV, 212.
7. Hansard, 3rd Series, 86, 675–6.
8. BD to MAD, 29/06/1846. *BD Letters*, IV, 236.
9. BD to MAD, 07/08/1846. *BD Letters*, IV, 243.
10. BD to Sarah Disraeli, 10/08/1846. *BD Letters*, IV, 248.
11. MAD to BD, 04/08/1846. Dep Hughenden 4/2, fols 16–17.
12. MAD to BD, 06/08/1846. Dep Hughenden 4/2, fols 20–22.
13. BD to MAD, 28/08/1846. *BD Letters*, IV, 250–1.
14. BD to MAD, 11/11/1846. *BD Letters*, IV, 262.
15. MAD Account Book. Dep Hughenden 310/1.
16. Louisa de Rothschild Diary. Battersea Papers, British Library. Add 47950–47952.
17. Sarah Disraeli to MAD, 21/03/1847. Dep Hughenden 186/2, fols 7–9.
18. BD to John Manners, 29/01/1848. *BD Letters*, V, 4.
19. Robert Peel Dawson to MAD, 15/01/1848. Dep Hughenden 189/1, fols 111–12.
20. Sarah Disraeli to MAD, Feb 1848. Dep Hughenden 186/2, fols 134–5.
21. BD to MAD, 06/09/1848. *BD Letters*, V, 81.
22. MAD Account Book. Dep Hughenden 314/1.
23. MAD Account Book. Dep Hughenden 314/1.
24. BD to Lord Henry Bentinck, 23/09/1848. *BD Letters*, V, 86.
25. BD to MAD, 18/10/1848. *BD Letters*, V, 95.
26. BD to Lady Blessington, 31/12/1848. *BD Letters*, V, 122.
27. BD to John Pigott, ?17/04/1849. *BD Letters*, V, 170.
28. BD, Preface to *Curiosities of Literature*, p. xxxiii.
29. BD to Prince Metternich, 31/01/1849. *BD Letters*, V, 131.

30. BD to MAD, 31/01/1849. *BD Letters*, V, 141.
31. BD to Sarah Disraeli, 22/02/1849. *BD Letters*, V, 145.
32. BD to MAD, 25/01/1849. *BD Letters*, V, 137.
33. MAD to BD, 06/01/1849. Dep Hughenden 4/2, fols 42–4.
34. BD to MAD, 24/01/1849. *BD Letters*, V, 136.
35. BD to MAD, 25/01/1849. *BD Letters*, V, 137.
36. Louisa de Rothschild Diary. Battersea Papers, British Library. Add 47950–47952.
37. BD to Lady Londonderry, 12/03/1849. *BD Letters*, V, 152–3.
38. BD to Lord John Manners, 18/03/1849. *BD Letters*, V, 158–9.
39. BD to Sarah Disraeli, 18/07/1849. *BD Letters*, V, 197.
40. BD to Philip Rose, 18/07/1849. *BD Letters*, V, 198.
41. In 2013 Kate's granddaughter published a short book about her grandmother in which Disraeli's possible paternity is fully discussed. See Styles, *Disraeli's Daughter*, and Weintraub, *Disraeli*.
42. BD to Sarah Disraeli, 04/08/1849. *BD Letters*, V, 200.
43. BD to Sarah Disraeli, 19/08/1849. *BD Letters*, V, 205.
44. BD to Sarah Disraeli, 25/08/1849. *BD Letters*, V, 210.
45. BD to MAD, 15/10/1849. *BD Letters*, V, 231.
46. BD to Sarah Disraeli, 16/10/1849. *BD Letters*, V, 232.
47. BD to Sarah Disraeli, 04/11/1849. *BD Letters*, V, 248.
48. BD to Philip Rose, 04/11/1849. *BD Letters*, V, 250.
49. Charles Williams to Arethusa Milner Gibson, 14/11/1940. Dep Hughenden 189/3, fols 179–80.
50. BD to MAD, 14/11/1849. *BD Letters*, V, 255.
51. MAD to BD, 15/11/1849. Dep Hughenden 4/2, fols 46–7.
52. BD to Sarah Disraeli, 23/12/1849. *BD Letters*, V, 273.
53. BD to Sarah Disraeli, 29/12/1849. *BD Letters*, V, 278.
54. 'A Preliminary Word', *Household Words*, 30/03/1850.
55. *Henry V*, IV, iii.
56. Lake, *Personal Reminiscences*, p. 49.
57. BD to George Matthew, 28/08/1846. *BD Letters*, IV, 253.
58. BD Autobiographical Notes. Dep Hughenden 26/3, fols 75–7.
59. MAD to BD, 23/01/1850. Dep Hughenden 4/2, fols 49–50.
60. BD Autobiographical Notes. Dep Hughenden 26/2, fols 84–6.
61. BD to MAD, 11/02/1851. *BD Letters*, V, 410.
62. BD to John Manners, 25/03/1851. *BD Letters*, V, 420.
63. BD to Sarah Disraeli, 01/08/1851. *BD Letters*, V, 459.
64. BD to Sarah Disraeli, 05/09/1851. *BD Letters*, V, 466.

65. BD to Sarah Disraeli, 23/08/1851. *BD Letters*, V, 463.
66. BD to Sarah Disraeli, 01/09/1851. *BD Letters*, V, 466.
67. BD to MAD, 11/11/1851. *BD Letters*, V, 489.
68. BD to Sarah Disraeli, 07/11/1851. *BD Letters*, V, 487.
69. BD to Sarah Disraeli, ?17/11/1851. *BD Letters*, V, 489–90.
70. Sarah Disraeli to BD, n.d. [December 1851]. Dep Hughenden 7/4, fols 111–12.

CHAPTER SEVEN: PRINCESS NOBODY
1. Sarah Disraeli to MAD, n.d. [1853]. Dep Hughenden 187/1, fols 126–7.
2. BD Autobiographical Notes. Dep Hughenden 26/ fols 95–105.
3. MAD to BD, 27/02/1852. Dep Hughenden 4/2, fol 54.
4. Dorothea Whitmore Jones to MAD, 25/02/1852. Dep Hughenden 190/2, fols 277–8.
5. Dorothy Nevill to MAD, n.d. [Feb 1852]. Dep Hughenden 191/1, fols 60–1.
6. Louisa de Rothschild Diary. Battersea Papers, British Library. Add 47952.
7. Augustus Berkeley to MAD, 23/03/1852. Dep Hughenden 188/2, fols 19–20.
8. Queen Victoria Journals. RA VIC/MAIN/QVJ (W). 01/04/1852 and 27/02/1854 (Princess Beatrice's copies).
9. Charlotte Guest diary, 04/03/1852. Guest, *Extracts*, II, 295.
10. Dep Hughenden 203/1, fols 117–18.
11. BD to Sarah Disraeli, 17/03/1852. *BD Letters*, VI, 40.
12. BD to Queen Victoria, 23/03/1852. *BD Letters*, VI, 49.
13. Queen Victoria to the King of the Belgians, 30/03/1852. Benson and Esher, *Letters*, II, 386.
14. BD to Sarah Disraeli, 17/03/1852. *BD Letters*, VI, 39–40.
15. BD to Sarah Disraeli, 22/06/1852. *BD Letters*, VI, 83–4.
16. Viscountess Ponsonby to MAD, 24/04/1852. Dep Hughenden 191/2, fols 80–1.
17. BD to Sarah Disraeli, 08/06/1852. *BD Letters*, VI, 76.
18. BD to Sarah Disraeli, 16/06/1852. *BD Letters*, VI, 82.
19. BD to MAD, 06/10/1852. *BD Letters*, VI, 165.
20. Charlotte Guest diary, 23/06/1852. Guest, *Extracts*, II, 298.
21. BD to Henry Lennox, 07/08/1852. *BD Letters*, VI, 102.
22. BD to Henry Lennox, 01/09/1852. *BD Letters*, VI, 134–5.
23. BD to Henry Lennox, 16/09/1852. *BD Letters*, VI, 148.
24. BD to Henry Lennox, 16/08/1852. *BD Letters*, VI, 118.
25. BD to Lord Londonderry, 26/09/1853. *BD Letters*, VI, 260.
26. BD to Lord Stanley, 15/08/1853. *BD Letters*, VI, 117.

27. BD to Queen Victoria, 13/12/1852. *BD Letters*, VI, 197.
28. BD to Queen Victoria, 20/12/1852. *BD Letters*, VI, 200.
29. BD to Lord Stanley, 20/12/1852. *BD Letters*, VI, 201.
30. Sarah Disraeli to MAD, 16/12/1852. Dep Hughenden 186/3, fols 86–7.
31. Louisa de Rothschild Diary. Battersea Papers, British Library. Add 47952.
32. BD to MAD, 12/12/1853. *BD Letters*, VI, 293.
33. BD to Lord Londonderry, 19/10/1853. *BD Letters*, VI, 271.
34. BD to Adolphus Vane, 28/10/1853. *BD Letters*, VI, 278.
35. BD to Lord Londonderry, 30/01/1854. *BD Letters*, VI, 320.
36. BD to Sarah Brydges Willyams, 23/04/1854. *BD Letters*, VI, 337.
37. Copy of MAD to BD, 06/06/1856. Dep Hughenden 24/2, fols 4–5. This copy, in the hand of Disraeli's secretary Lord Rowton, was made in April 1881, shortly after Disraeli's death. The original, Rowton noted, was buried next to his heart in the shared vault at Hughenden.
38. MAD Account Book. Dep Hughenden 314/4.
39. BD to Sarah Brydges Willyams, 26/10/1854. *BD Letters*, VI, 377.
40. MAD Account Book. Dep Hughenden 314/3.
41. Edward Bulwer Lytton to MAD, 04/10/1853. Dep Hughenden 104/1, fols 138–9.
42. Sarah Disraeli to Elizabeth Sheppard, n.d. [May 1854]. Dep Hughenden 192/4, fols 220–1.
43. Elizabeth Sheppard to MAD, 23/07/1854. Dep Hughenden 192/4, fols 222–5.
44. Elizabeth Sheppard to MAD, 01/09/1854. Dep Hughenden 192/4, fols 226–7
45. H. Cheshire to Elizabeth Sheppard, 04/09/1854. Dep Hughenden 192/4, fols 228–9.
46. Philip Rose Memorandum, 1/05/1882. *BD Letters*, VI, 569 (Appendix X).
47. MAD to Sarah Brydges Willyams, 13/02/1855. Private Collection.
48. MAD to Sarah Brydges Willyams, 02/05/1855. Private Collection.
49. MAD to Sarah Brydges Willyams, 14/05/1855. Private Collection.
50. MAD to Sarah Brydges Willyams, 24/04/1856. Private Collection.
51. BD to Sarah Brydges Willyams, 30/08/1856. *BD Letters*, VI, 498.
52. MAD to Sarah Brydges Willyams, 20/08/1856. Private Collection.
53. MAD to Sarah Brydges Willyams, 04/02/1857. Private Collection.
54. BD to James Disraeli, 11/12/1857. *BD Letters*, VI, 510–11.
55. BD Autobiographical Notes. Dep Hughenden 26/2, fols 48–50.
56. Dep Hughenden 187/1, fols 128–32.
57. Sarah Disraeli to MAD 28/02/1853. Dep Hughenden 186/3, fol 124.
58. Sarah Disraeli to MAD, n.d. [1853]. Dep Hughenden 187/1, fols 126–7.
59. Sarah Disraeli to MAD, 07/07/1854. Dep Hughenden 186/3, fols 180–1.

60. Sarah Disraeli to MAD, n.d. [1851]. Dep Hughenden 186/3, fols 7–8.
61. Sarah Disraeli to MAD, ?26/02/1852. Dep Hughenden 186/3, fols 45–7.
62. Lang and Doyle, *Tale of Fairyland*, p. 13.
63. Lang and Doyle, *Tale of Fairyland*, p. 44. Cf. *Twelfth Night*: 'Journeys end in lovers meetings/ every wise man's son doth know.' II, iii, 46.
64. James Disraeli to MAD, 14/08/1856. Dep Hughenden 187/2, fols 98–9.
65. Sarah Disraeli to BD, 13/10/1856. Dep Hughenden 7/4, fols 117–19.
66. Isabella Disraeli to MAD, 29/01/1857. Dep Hughenden 187/2, fols 178–81.
67. Sarah Disraeli to MAD, 20/06/1857. Dep Hughenden 186/4, fols 79–80.
68. Sarah Disraeli to BD, n.d. [1857]. Dep Hughenden 7/4, fols 122–3.
69. BD to Sarah Disraeli, 31/08/1857. *BD Letters*, VII, 63.
70. BD to Henry Padwick, 25/01/1857. *BD Letters*, VII, 10.
71. *Manchester Times*, 19/06/1858.
72. Rosina Bulwer Lytton to Rebecca Ryves, 29/06/1858. Bulwer Lytton, *Collected Letters*, III, 93.
73. *The Morning Chronicle*, 15/07/1858.
74. Rosina Bulwer Lytton to Rebecca Ryves, 09/07/1858. Bulwer Lytton, *Collected Letters*, III, 105.
75. *Manchester Times*, 17/07/1858.
76. Rosina Bulwer Lytton to Rebecca Ryves, 01/07/1858. Bulwer Lytton, *Collected Letters*, III, 94.
77. BD to Edward Bulwer Lytton, 08/06/?1858. *BD Letters*, VII, 201.
78. See Kuhn, *Politics of Pleasure*, pp. 154–5, 262–3.
79. Rosina Bulwer Lytton to Lord Derby, 23/02/1858. Bulwer Lytton, *Collected Letters*, III, 23.
80. BD to Lord Stanley, 23/01/1857. *BD Letters*, VII, 9.
81. BD to MAD, 06/11/1858. *BD Letters*, VII, 272.
82. BD to MAD, 21/10/1858. *BD Letters*, VII, 264.
83. BD to MAD, 21/01/1859. *BD Letters*, VII, 323.
84. BD to Sarah Brydges Willyams, 17/08/1859. *BD Letters*, VII, 412–13.
85. Sir Henry Drummond Wolff, *Rambling Recollections*, II, 132. See Hawkins, *Forgotten Prime Minister*, II, 458. Here I am following Hawkins's surmise that it was Derby to whom Drummond Wolff was referring. Hawkins notes that 'the host's behavior matches Derby's manner on similar occasions and Disraeli, who always resented any disrespect shown to his wife, never again visited Knowsley after October 1859'. This supposition is supported by the 1903 account of James Bryce: 'A story used to be told how, in Disraeli's earlier days, when his political position was still far from assured, he and his wife happened to be guests of the chief of the party, and that chief so

far forgot good table manners as to quiz Mrs Disraeli at the dinner-table. Next morning Disraeli, whose visit was to have lasted for some days longer, announced that he must leave immediately. The host besought him to stay, and made all possible apologies. But Disraeli was inexorable, and carried off his wife forthwith.' Bryce, *Studies*, pp. 33–4.

86. Sykes, 'Strange Story', p. 130.
87. MAD to Sarah Brydges Willyams, 12/09/1959. Private Collection.
88. Sarah Disraeli to MAD, 24/10/1859. Dep Hughenden 186/4, fols 237–8.
89. Sarah Disraeli to MAD, 03/12/1859. Dep Hughenden 186/4, fols 245–6.
90. See *BD Letters*, VII, 439, n.1.
91. BD to Ralph Disraeli, 09/12/1859. *BD Letters*, VII, 435.
92. Ralph Disraeli to BD, 19/12/1859. Dep Hughenden 9/2, fols 176–8.
93. BD to Lady Londonderry, 12/12/1859. *BD Letters*, VII, 437.
94. BD to William Partridge, 30/12/1859. *BD Letters*, VII, 442.
95. Sarah Disraeli to MAD, n.d. [1859]. Dep Hughenden 186/4, fols 247–50.

CHAPTER EIGHT: THE ROSE AND THE RING

1. George Beauclerk to MAD, 03/08/1867. Dep Hughenden 195/3, fols 57–65.
2. Draft of MAD to George Beauclerk, 07/08/1867. Dep Hughenden 203/2, fol 27.
3. BD to Lord Derby, 18/01/1860. *BD Letters*, VIII, 13.
4. MAD to Sarah Brydges Willyams, 06/05/1860. Private Collection.
5. BD to William Miles, 11/06/1860. *BD Letters*, VIII, 39–40.
6. BD to Ralph Disraeli, 05/12/1860. *BD Letters*, VIII, 73.
7. Charlotte de Rothschild to Leopold de Rothschild, 15/11/1866. The Rothschild Archive, 000/84/3.
8. BD to Sarah Brydges Willyams, 19/01/1861. *BD Letters*, VIII, 90.
9. MAD to Sarah Brydges Willyams, 10/07/1861. Private Collection.
10. MAD to Sarah Brydges Willyams, 24/03/1862. Private Collection.
11. MAD to Sarah Brydges Willyams, 12/05/1862. Private Collection.
12. MAD to Sarah Brydges Willyams, 01/04/1863. Private Collection.
13. BD to Lord Palmerston, 26/03/1863. *BD Letters*, VIII, 264.
14. BD to Francis Espinasse, 06/03/1860. *BD Letters*, VIII, 23.
15. BD to Francis Espinasse, 27/03/1860. *BD Letters*, VIII, 27–8.
16. BD to Thomas Kebbel, 25/11/1860. *BD Letters*, VIII, 69.
17. BD to Sarah Brydges Willyams, 04/03/1860. *BD Letters*, VIII, 260.
18. BD Autobiographical Notes. Dep Hughenden 26/3, fols 5–9.
19. Lady Ely to MAD, 20/03/1860. Dep Hughenden 189/2, fols 208–9.
20. BD to Sarah Brydges Willyams, 21/03/1860. *BD Letters*, VIII, 261–2.

21. BD Autobiographical Notes. Dep Hughenden 26/3, fols 5–17.
22. MAD to Sarah Brydges Willyams, 24/03/1862; 03/02/1862; 05/11/1862; 26/02/1862. Private Collection.
23. MAD to Sarah Brydges Willyams, 07/10/1861. Private Collection.
24. BD to Sarah Brydges Willyams, 15/09/1863. *BD Letters*, VIII, 207–8.
25. BD to Sarah Brydges Willyams, 28/09/1863. *BD Letters*, VIII, 303.
26. BD to John Pakington, 08/11/1862. *BD Letters*, VIII, 323.
27. BD to Sarah Brydges Willyams, 20/09/1863. *BD Letters*, VIII, 302.
28. Battersea, *Reminiscences*, pp. 234–5.
29. BD Autobiographical Notes. Dep Hughenden 26/3, fols 38–40.
30. BD Autobiographical Notes. Dep Hughenden 26/3, passim.
31. MAD to Sarah Brydges Willyams, 17/03/1861. Private Collection.
32. BD to Sarah Brydges Willyams, 30/03/1861. *BD Letters*, VIII, 106.
33. Thackeray, *The Rose and the Ring*, p. 129.
34. BD to Sarah Brydges Willyams, 09/12/1862. *BD Letters*, VIII, 233.
35. Charlotte de Rothschild to Leopold de Rothschild, 07/12/1863. The Rothschild Archive, 000/84/1.
36. Charlotte de Rothschild to Leopold de Rothschild, and to Nathaniel and Leopold de Rothschild, 30/11/1863 and 13/11/1863. The Rothschild Archive, 000/84/1.
37. BD to Lord Derby, 21/11/1863. *BD Letters*, VIII, 330.
38. BD to Francis Villiers, 02/10/1861. *BD Letters*, VIII, 143.
39. BD to Sarah Brydges Willyams, 23/02/1863. *BD Letters*, VIII, 258.
40. BD to MAD, n.d. Dep Hughenden 3/1, fols 119–20.
41. Fraser, *Disraeli and his Day*, pp. 283–4.
42. Lucy, 'Sixty Years in the Wilderness', p. 70.
43. William Gregory, *Autobiography*, p. 95.
44. Crewe-Milnes, *Lord Rosebery*, I, 27–9.
45. Rosebery Papers, National Library of Scotland. MS 10187, fol 6.
46. Crewe-Milnes, *Lord Rosebery*, I, 29.
47. Charlotte de Rothschild to Leopold de Rothschild, 1862–67. The Rothschild Archive, 000/84/2–000/84/4.
48. *Morning Post*, 08/06/1865. Dep Hughenden 201/2, fol 68.
49. Charlotte de Rothschild to Leopold de Rothschild, 31/12/1866. The Rothschild Archive, 000/84/3.
50. Charlotte de Rothschild to MAD, 09/12/1866. Dep Hughenden 191/3, fols 334–5.
51. Charlotte de Rothschild to Leopold de Rothschild, 21/07/1867. The Rothschild Archive, 000/84/4.

52. Montagu Corry to BD, 29/06/1866. Dep Hughenden 94/1, fols 1-2.
53. Montagu Corry to BD, 02/12/1867. Dep Hughenden 94/1, fols 116–17.
54. Disraeli, *Endymion*, p. 195.
55. MAD to BD, ?23/06/1866. Dep Hughenden 4/2, fol 71.
56. MAD to BD, ?23/06/188, 24/07/1866. Dep Hughenden 4/2, fols 73–4, 65–7.
57. Montagu Corry to BD, 24/07/1866. Dep Hughenden 94/1, fols 5–6.
58. Kebbel, *Lord Beaconsfield*, p. 40.
59. Frances Shelley to MAD, 17/07/1864. Dep Hughenden 192/4, fols 103–4.
60. Skelton, *The Table-Talk of Shirley*, p. 258.
61. Skelton, *The Table-Talk of Shirley*, pp. 258–9.
62. Sykes, 'Strange Story', pp. 126–7.
63. BD to Ralph Disraeli, 15/04/1867. *BD Letters*, IX, 299.
64. BD to Montagu Corry, 19/10/[1866]. *BD Letters*, IX, 184.
65. Mrs Burke to BD, 19/11/1867. Dep Hughenden 202/1, fols 30–1.
66. Eliza Gregory to BD, 20/11/1867. Dep Hughenden 202/1, fols 36–7.
67. William Gladstone to BD, 21/11/1867. Dep Hughenden 202/1, fols 40–1.
68. BD to Queen Victoria, 19/11/1867. *BD Letters*, IX, 415.
69. *The Times*, 21/11/1867.
70. MAD to BD, 29/11/1867, Nov 1867. Dep Hughenden 4/2, fols 84–5.
71. BD to MAD, 30/11/1867, 29/11/1867. *BD Letters*, IX, 427, 424–5.
72. BD, *Lothair*, pp. 182–3.

CHAPTER NINE: HAPPY ENDING

1. Virginia Edger to BD, 16/12/1872. Dep Hughenden 202/2, fols 93–4.
2. Philip Rose to MAD, 16/01/1868. Dep Hughenden 308/4, fols 76–7.
3. MAD Account Book. Dep Hughenden 314/9.
4. BD to MAD, 28/02/1868. Dep Hughenden 3/2, fols 4–5, 59.
5. Fraser, *Disraeli and his Day*, p. 52.
6. MAD to Charlotte and Lionel de Rothschild, 25/02/1868. The Rothschild Archive, R/Fam/C/2/10.
7. Charles Clubbe to MAD, 26/02/1868. Dep Hughenden 197/1, fols 28–9.
8. Robert Peel Dawson to MAD, 01/03/1868. Dep Hughenden 197/1, fols 22–3.
9. *The Times*, 26/02/1868.
10. John Denison to MAD, 06/03/1868. Dep Hughenden 189/1, fols 159–60.
11. *The Times*, 27/02/1868.
12. Blake, *Disraeli*, p. 487.
13. Dep Hughenden 196/1, fol 187.
14. *Morning Herald*, 26/03/1868.
15. Charles Freemantle to MAD, 26/03/1868. Dep Hughenden 196/1, fol 153.

16. Queen Victoria Journals. RA VIC/MAIN/QVJ (W). 06/04/1868 (Princess Beatrice's copies).
17. Reginald Wilberforce, *Life of the Right Reverend Samuel Wilberforce, D.D.*, III, 242. Quoted in Blake, *Disraeli*, p. 487.
18. Sichel, *Disraeli* pp. 288, 319.
19. BD to MAD, 27/03/1868 and 14/05/1868. Dep Hughenden 3/2, fols 66, 12.
20. MAD to BD, 25/05/1868. Dep Hughenden 4/2, fol 97.
21. Dorothy Nevill to MAD, 18/03/1868. Dep Hughenden 191/1, fols 229–30.
22. BD telegram to MAD, n.d. Dep Hughenden 3/2, fol 26.
23. Quoted in MAD to BD, 17/09/1868. Dep Hughenden 4/2, fols 105–6.
24. BD to MAD, n.d. Sept 1868. Dep Hughenden 3/2, fols 27–8.
25. MAD to BD, 17/09/1868. Dep Hughenden 4/2, fol 104.
26. MAD to BD, 19/09/1868. Dep Hughenden 4/2, fols 109–10.
27. MAD to BD, 20/09/1868. Dep Hughenden 4/2, fols 111–13.
28. BD to MAD, 14/09/1868. Dep Hughenden 3/2, fols 29–32.
29. BD to MAD, 20/09/1868. Dep Hughenden 3/2, fols 33–6.
30. BD to MAD, 21/09/1868. Dep Hughenden 3/2, fols 37–8.
31. BD to MAD, 23/09/1868. Dep Hughenden 3/2, fols 41–4.
32. MAD to BD, 25/09/1868, 23/09/1868. Dep Hughenden 4/2, fols 119–23; 118a–118b.
33. BD to MAD, 24/09/1868. Dep Hughenden 3/2, fols 45–9.
34. Queen Victoria to the Princess Royal, 29/02/1868. Quoted in Blake, *Disraeli*, p. 490.
35. MAD to Princess Christian, n.d. May 1848. Quoted in Monypenny and Buckle, *Life of Benjamin Disraeli*, V, 48.
36. Blake, *Disraeli*, p. 493.
37. BD to MAD, 25/09/1868. Dep Hughenden 3/2, fols 50–1.
38. MAD to BD, 26/09/1868. Dep Hughenden 4/2, fols 125–7.
39. BD to MAD, 26/09/1868. Dep Hughenden 3/2, fols 52–5.
40. BD to MAD, 28/09/1868. Dep Hughenden 3/2, fol 58.
41. MAD to BD, 28/09/1868. Dep Hughenden 4/2, fols 131–2.
42. Queen Victoria Journals. RA VIC/MAIN/QVJ (W). 23/11/1868 (Princess Beatrice's copies).
43. General Grey to Queen Victoria, quoted in Robert, *Disraeli*, p. 515.
44. Queen Victoria Journals. RA VIC/MAIN/QVJ (W). 01/12/1868 (Princess Beatrice's copies).
45. Queen Victoria to BD, 24/11/1868. Quoted in Monypenny and Buckle, *Life of Benjamin Disraeli*, V, 100.
46. Lady Brownlow to MAD, 30/12/1868. Dep Hughenden 197/1, fols 61–2.

47. Lord Rosebery to MAD, 02/12/1868. Dep Hughenden 197/1, fols 61–2.
48. *Imperial Review*, 05/12/1868. Dep Hughenden 201, fol 112.
49. *Morning Post*, 27/11/1868.
50. Virginia Edger to BD, 29/11/1868. Dep Hughenden 189/2, fols 154–5.
51. Virginia Edger to MAD, 12/04/1869. Dep Hughenden 189/2, fols 158–9.
52. Ralph Disraeli to BD, 26/12/1868. Dep Hughenden 9/2, fols 194–5.
53. Annie Bassett to BD, n.d. Dep Hughenden 8/2, fols 92–7.
54. *John Bull*, 28/11/1868. Dep Hughenden 201, fol 110.

CHAPTER TEN: AFTERWARDS

1. Dep Hughenden 203/2, fols 106–7.
2. *Saturday Review*, 09/04/1870. Dep Hughenden 228.
3. *The Times*, 06/05/1870.
4. *Standard*, 03/05/1870. Dep Hughenden 228.
5. Janetta Manners to MAD, July 1870. Dep Hughenden 190/4, fols 95–6.
6. *Observer*, 21/05/1870. Dep Hughenden 228.
7. Charlotte de Rothschild to Leopold de Rothschild, 08/09/1781. The Rothschild Archive, 000/84/4.
8. *Daily News*, 27/10/1870. Dep Hughenden 228.
9. 'General Preface', Disraeli, *Collected Edition*, pp. xviii, xix, xx.
10. 'Tales and Anecdotes of Dizzy', *Beaconsfield Quarterly*. Dep Hughenden 236, item 16.
11. BD to MAD, 22/07/1869 and MAD to BD, n.d. Dep Hughenden 3/2, fol 61 and 4/2, fols 139–40.
12. Monty Corry to MAD, 08/02/?1870. Dep Hughenden 94/2, fols 9–10.
13. BD to Monty Corry, n.d. Dep Hughenden 95/4, fol 182.
14. BD to Monty Corry, 07/05/1872. Dep Hughenden 95/2, fols 233–4.
15. *Glasgow Herald*, 03/04/1872.
16. BD to Monty Corry, 07/05/1871, 09/05/1872, 14/05/1872. Dep Hughenden 95/2, fols 233–4, 235–6, 237–8.
17. BD to Monty Corry, 14/05/1871. Dep Hughenden 95/2, fols 237–8.
18. BD to Corry, 22/05/1872. Dep Hughenden 95/2, fols 243–4.
19. Countess of Loudon to MAD, n.d. 1872. Dep Hughenden 190/3, 53–8.
20. MAD to BD, 26/07/1872 and 12/07/1872. Dep Hughenden 4/2, fols 159–61.
21. BD to MAD, 25/07/1872. Dep Hughenden 3/2, fol 76.
22. BD Memoranda. Dep Hughenden 202, fols 254–61.
23. Duchess of Cleveland to BD, 12/09/1872. Dep Hughenden 202/1/190–1.
24. BD to Dorothy Nevill, 26/09/1872. *Beaconsfield Quarterly*. Dep Hughenden 236, Item 15.

25. BD to Monty Corry, 13/10/1872. Dep Hughenden 95/2, fols 256–7.
26. Gower, *My Reminiscences*, pp. 294–9.
27. Monty Corry to Philip Rose, 08/12/1872. Dep Hughenden 308/4, fols 21–2.
28. BD to Monty Corry, n.d. Dep Hughenden 95/2, fol 267.
29. *The Times*, 20/12/1872.
30. *The Belfast News-Letter*, 20/12/1872.
31. Robert Peel Dawson to BD, 16/12/1872. Dep Hughenden 202/2, fols 97–100.
32. Lord Rosebery to BD, 20/12/1872. Dep Hughenden 202/2, fols 19–20.
33. John Manners to Monty Corry, 18/12/1872. Dep Hughenden 202/2, fols 162–3.
34. Charlotte de Rothschild to BD, 16/12/1872. Dep Hughenden 202/2, fols 65–6.
35. Various correspondents to BD. Dep Hughenden 202/3, fols 89–90; 202/2, fols 190–1; 202/3, fols 99–100; 202/3, fols 133–4.
36. Rosina Bulwer Lytton to BD, 16/12/1872. Dep Hughenden 202/2, fols 101–4.
37. *The Times*, 16/12/1872.
38. *The Times*, 16/12/1872.
39. BD to the Prince of Wales, 22/12/1872. Dep Hughenden 202/2, fols 7–8.
40. BD to Dorothy Nevill, 31/01/1872. *Beaconsfield Quarterly*, 31/01/1872. Dep Hughenden 236.
41. BD to Ralph Disraeli, 20/01/1873. Dep Hughenden 9/1, fols 15–17.
42. *Pall Mall Gazette*, 24/11/1880. Dep Hughenden 228.
43. BD to Charlotte de Rothschild, 14/09/1873. The Rothschild Archive, R Fam C/2/19.
44. BD to Monty Corry, 03/08/1873. Dep Hughenden 95/3, fols 55–6.
45. BD to Monty Corry, 10/08/1873. Dep Hughenden 95/3, fols 57–8.
46. BD to Monty Corry, 14/09/1873. Dep Hughenden 95/3, fols 60–3.
47. Disraeli, *Endymion*, p. 341.

Acknowledgements

My first debt is to Colin Harris and his staff in the Special Collections Reading Room at the Bodleian Library, Oxford; my second is to the editors of Disraeli's letters at the Disraeli Project at Queen's University, Canada. I have drawn on the expertise of these scholars and librarians at every stage, and their work has made mine possible. Elsewhere I have been assisted in archives by the staff of the British Library, the London Library, the National Library of Scotland, The Rothschild Archive, and the Houghton Library at Harvard University. My thanks go to all of them; as well as to the manager of Hughenden and the occupier of Grosvenor Gate for showing me around the Disraelis' houses. For permission to quote from manuscript material I thank the National Trust, the Rothschild Archive, the National Library of Scotland, the British Library; and, as owners of the Abinger Papers and holders of the Hughenden Deposit (Disraeli Papers), the Bodleian Libraries, University of Oxford. For permission to quote from the *Letters of Benjamin Disraeli* I acknowledge the University of Toronto Press. Extracts from Queen Victoria's Journals appear by the permission of Her Majesty Queen Elizabeth II.

From its inception this book has been enabled by academic institutions and the friendship of those within them. The Warden and Fellows of St Antony's College, Oxford awarded me the Alistair Horne Fellowship in 2009–10 and gave me the opportunity to work without interruption on the Disraelis' papers. My particular thanks go to Alistair Horne; and to the Warden, Margaret MacMillan, for making me so welcome. As a Visiting Scholar at Wolfson College, Oxford from 2010–12 I benefited from the rich programme of activities and conversations at the Oxford Centre for Life-Writing, and from the boundless wisdom of the college's President,

Acknowledgements

Hermione Lee. In 2012–13 I was a Fellow at the Radcliffe Institute for Advanced Study at Harvard University. I wrote the first draft of this book at Radcliffe and it has been shaped by my experiences there. To my meticulous Radcliffe Research Partners, Yen Pham and Carrie Tian, goes the credit for the accuracy of the notes and much else besides; to Judith Vichniac and the Fellowship Class of 2012–13 go my thanks for a magical year of Fellow feeling. I have revised my manuscript and completed my work on the Disraelis over the course of my first year as a lecturer in the Department of English and Film at the University of Exeter, and to my colleagues and students there I am grateful for new ideas and much inspiration. For help with particular questions I thank Judy Bogdanor, Hilary Clare, Angus Hawkins, Naomi Hicks, Katherine Ibbett, Mary Millar, Michel Pharand, Jane Ridley and Miranda Seymour. Alexandra Harris, Hermione Lee, Amanda Mackenzie Stuart, Candia McWilliam and Hilary Schor have all read and commented on drafts, and I could not have asked for a more erudite or constructive circle of readers. For their time and expertise I am more grateful than I can say. My agent Clare Alexander has been a pillar of strength, and I have been immensely lucky to work with two wonderful editors, Clara Farmer at Chatto & Windus and Ileene Smith at FSG. My thanks go too to Susannah Otter for all she has done during production. All mistakes remain my own.

Alexandra Harris, Aoife Ní Luanaigh, Michael, Amanda and Marianna Hay and Paul and Vron Santer have helped this book come to fruition in many and various ways, and to all of them I am beyond thankful. To Matthew and Freddy Santer goes the dedication and, with it, my love.

Index

Index

D'Israeli, Benjamin (Benjamin's grandfather) 14–15, 154

D'Israeli, Isaac (Benjamin's father): family background 13; family life 13; literary career 13–14, 69, 149, 154, 201; death of father and baptism of children 14–15; and children's schooling 28; travels in Belgium and Rhineland with Benjamin 29; and Benjamin's nervous collapse 33, 43; leases Bradenham 42; appointment of Tita as servant 47; on daughter's marriage opportunities 67; and Tita-Mrs Kent affair 68–9; and Benjamin's debts 71, 72, 87; Mary Anne meets 74; declining health 82, 111; and Benjamin's marriage to Mary Anne 87, 105, 106; blindness 111; death 149–50; monument at Hughenden 206–7; *Curiosities of Literature* 13, 14, 149, 154; *History of English Literature* 69; *Life and Reign of Charles I* 154

D'Israeli, Maria (Benjamin's mother): family background 13; birth of children 13; family life 14, 42; relations with Benjamin 14, 92, 149; and children's schooling 28; and Benjamin's nervous collapse 43; and Tita-Mrs Kent affair 68–9; and Benjamin's marriage to Mary Anne 105, 106; death 149

Disraeli, Benjamin (*later* 1st Earl of Beaconsfield): family background xi, 12–13; invented family background x, 12, 15, 154–5; birth 12, 13; childhood and schooling 14–15, 27–8; baptism 15–16; early writings 27–9; works as solicitor's clerk 28, 29–30; travels in Belgium and Rhineland with his father and William Meredith 29; speculation in Latin-American mining companies 30, 43; *The Representative* (daily newspaper) venture 30, 32; publication of first novel, *Vivian Grey* 30–33; nervous collapse 33, 42; European travels and recuperation 33, 42, 43, 45, 47; publication of *The Young Duke* 42–3, 47; death of Meredith 45–6; publication of *Contarini Fleming* 47–8; political awakening 48–51, 66;

stands for Parliament at High Wycombe 50–51; first meets Mary Anne 52–3; further attempts to enter Parliament 53–4; spat with Daniel O'Connell 54; and end of Bulwer Lytton marriage 58–9; affair with Henrietta Sykes 64–7, 92, 144; publication of *Henrietta Temple* and *Venetia* 65–7, 69–71, 144; threatened with arrest for debt 71–2; elected as MP for Maidstone 72–5, 84–5; maiden speech in Commons 75, 218; and death of Wyndham Lewis 78–9, 80–81; beginnings of romance with Mary Anne 81–4; legal dispute over election bribery allegations 84–5, 90; consummation of relationship with Mary Anne 85–6; first intimations of marriage plans 86–90; correspondence during Mary Anne's visits to Theberton and Chastleton 92–5; rows, and continued courtship 95–101; and Bedchamber Crisis 99–100; and death of John Evans 102–3; marriage settlement and wedding 103–6; honeymoon 106, 110–111; early months of marriage 111–13, 114–18; first visits Buckingham Palace 113–14; hosts political dinner parties 114–15; in Society 117–18, 130–31, 134–5, 137, 164; first wedding anniversary 118; 1841 election victory at Shrewsbury 121–2; overlooked for Cabinet post 122–4, 132; holiday in France with Mary Anne 124–5; alone at Grosvenor Gate while Mary Anne nurses mother 125; transfers ownership of contents of house in her absence 126–7; visits Paris and meets French king 128, 129–30; and Young England 128–30, 133, 134, 136, 143; writing and publication of *Coningsby* 127, 130–33, 134, 136; campaigning in Shrewsbury 133–4; votes against Peel 136; publication of *Sybil* 136–7; autumn in Europe 138, 141, 143–5; writing of *Tancred* 143–4; confrontation with Peel over Corn Laws repeal 145–6, 167; and Protectionist Tories 146, 153, 155–6, 164–6; visits

Index

Index